Using

PCs

Using

PCs

Shelley O'Hara, et al.

Using PCs

Contents at a Glance

I | Personal Computer Basics

   1   Defining Your PC   7
   2   How Computers Work: Hardware   19
   3   Setting Up Your PC   31

II | Using Your PC

   4   Starting, Stopping, and Using Your PC   39
   5   Starting Programs and Working with Windows   49
   6   Working with Applications   61

III | Disks, Drives, Files, and Folders

   7   Preparing Disks for Use   75
   8   Managing Your Files   83
   9   Making Backup Copies of Your Files   91
  10   Working with Networks   103

IV | Computer Peripherals

  11   Monitors   111
  12   Keyboards   125
  13   Mice and Joysticks   135
  14   Printers   145
  15   Modems and Faxes   155
  16   Speakers and Sounds   165
  17   Scanners   177

V | Connecting to the Internet

  18   What Is the Internet?   189
  19   Establishing an Internet Connection   199
  20   Using Your WWW Browser   209
  21   Sending and Receiving E-Mail   223
  22   Sending and Receiving Files with FTP   233
  23   Other Internet Options   241

VI | Problem Solving

24   Getting Help with Software   253

25   Getting Help with Hardware   263

26   Upgrading Your Software   273

27   Upgrading Your Hardware   283

VII | Reference Information

28   Glossary of Common Terms and Phrases   297

29   Computer Company Listing   325

30   Top Internet Sites   339

31   Suggested Reading   355

Index   361

Table of Contents

Introduction   1

Who Should Read This Book   2

What This Book Covers   2

The *Using* Philosophy   2

Conventions Used in This Book   2

How to Contact Que   3

I | Personal Computer Basics

1 Defining Your PC   7

The Functions of a PC   8

Desktop and Tower Computers   8

Laptop, Notebook, and Palmtop Computers   9

Switches, Buttons, and Lights on the Case   10

Disk Drives—Internal and External   12

    Internal Hard Disk Drive   12

    Floppy Disk Drive   12

    CD-ROM Drive   12

    Tape Drive   13

    Removable Hard Disk Drive   13

    External Disk Drive   13

Monitors   13

Keyboards, Mice, Trackballs, and Joysticks   14

Connectors, Plugs, and Ports   14

Speakers   15

Printers   16

Modems   16

2 How Computers Work: Hardware   19

Examining the Motherboard   20

Defining Microprocessors   21

Types of Microprocessors   22

How Microprocessors Work   22

Defining Random-Access Memory (RAM) 23

Determining How Much RAM You Have 24

Defining Disk Drives 24
> Floppy Disks 25
> Hard Disks 25

Determining How Much Disk Space You Have 25

What Is the Bus and What Does it Do? 26

Understanding Expansion Slots 27

How Many Open Slots Do You Have? 27

Defining the Power Supply 28

How Software and Hardware Work Together 29

3 Setting Up Your PC 31

Unpacking the Computer 32
> Inspecting Your Computer 32
> Taking Inventory 32
> Saving Boxes and Packing Material 32

Positioning the CPU 33

Plugging in the CPU 33

Positioning the Monitor 33

Plugging in the Monitor 33

Positioning Keyboards and Mice 34

Plugging in Keyboards and Mice 35

Positioning the Speakers 35

Connecting the Speakers 35

Positioning the Printer 35

Attaching the Printer 36

Extension Cables 36

Protecting Your Computer from Electrical Damage 36

II | Using Your PC

4 Starting, Stopping, and Using Your PC   39

Powering Up Your System   40

Identifying Icons   41

Using the Start Button   42

Using the Taskbar   43

Using the System Tray   44

Shutting Down Your Computer   45

Resetting Your Computer   45

Troubleshooting Crashes and Shutdowns   46

    One Program Is Locked Up, but Others Seem to
Be Working Fine   46

    Everything Is Frozen—I Can't Even Get to the Start Button   46

    The Computer Will Not Respond to Ctrl+Alt+Delete   47

Troubleshooting Startup   47

    No Power   47

    Error Message: Keyboard locked or System Locked   47

    Error Message: System Disk or Non-System Disk Error   47

    Error Message: Windows 95 Was Not Properly Shut Down   47

    Computer Starts Normally, but Windows Won't Load   47

    Windows Won't Start in Safe Mode, Either   48

    Windows Is Running in Safe Mode. Now What?   48

5 Starting Programs and Working with Windows   49

Starting Programs in Windows   50

    Starting Programs from the Start Menu   50

    Starting Programs from My Computer   51

    Starting Programs from Windows Explorer   51

    Starting a Program by Opening a Document   53

    Starting Programs with Shortcut Icons   53

    Starting a Program with the Run Command   53

Working with Programs   53

    Switching Between Open Programs   54

    Moving and Resizing Open Program Windows   54

    Closing Open Programs   55

    Finding Missing Programs or Files   55

Adding Shortcut Icons to the Desktop   56

Customizing the Start Menu   57
 Adding Programs to the Start Menu   57

Removing Programs from the Start Menu   58
 Rearranging Programs on the Start Menu   58

6   Working with Applications   61

Describing Types of Applications   62
 Word Processors   62
 Spreadsheets   63
 Databases   65
 Graphics and Presentation Programs   65
 Personal Information Managers   66
 Suites or Bundles   66

Selecting Text and Numbers   66

Formatting Text and Numbers   67

Cutting, Copying, and Pasting Data   68

Automatically Updating and Linking Information   69

Saving Your Work   69

Saving Your Work in Different Formats   70

Opening Your Work   71

Printing Your Work   72

III | Disks, Drives, Files, and Folders

7   Preparing Disks for Use   75

What Is a Drive?   76

Using Floppy Disks   76
 Formatting a Floppy Disk   76
 Copying Files to a Floppy Disk   77

Defining Hard Disks   78
 Checking Disk Space   79
 Using ScanDisk to Check a Drive for Errors   79
 Improving Hard Disk Performance by Defragmenting   80

Using CD-ROM Drives   81

Keeping Your Drives in Tip-Top Shape   82

8 Managing Your Files   83

    Files and Folders Defined   84

    Organizing Your Files and Folders   84

    Viewing Your System Contents   84

        Using My Computer   85

        Using Windows Explorer   85

    Creating New Folders   86

    Renaming Files or Folders   87

    Moving Files or Folders   87

    Copying Files or Folders   88

    Deleting Files or Folders   88

    Using the Recycle Bin   89

    Creating Shortcuts to Files or Folders   90

9 Making Backup Copies of Your Files   91

    Protecting Your Files with Backup   92

    Understanding Full and Incremental Backups   92

    Formulating a Backup Strategy   93

    Using Windows Backup   94

        Performing a Full Backup   94

        Performing an Incremental Backup   97

    Restoring Files to Your Hard Drive   97

    Other Backup Methods   100

10 Working with Networks   103

    What Is a Network?   104

    Why Network?   104

    What Does a Network Consist Of?   104

    Peer-to-Peer Network Software   105

    Dedicated Sever Software   105

    Network Interface Cards   106

    Topology: The Arrangement of Network Connections   106

    Cable   107

    Putting the Pieces Together   108

IV | Computer Peripherals

11 Monitors 111

Monitor Sizes 112

VGA and SVGA Monitors 112

Interlaced Monitors 113

VGA and SVGA Video Cards and Resolutions 113

Video Cards and Colors 113

Video Card RAM 114

Video Cards, Video Games, and Full-Motion Video 115

Special Considerations for Notebook Displays 115

Passive Matrix, Dual-Scan, and Active
Matrix Displays 115
Notebook Display Size 115
Notebook Display Resolution 116

Hooking Up Your New Monitor 116

Setting Up a New Monitor in Windows 95 117

Adjusting Your Monitor Settings 119

Changing the Numbers of Colors
Windows Can Display 119

Changing the Size (Resolution) of the Display 120

Changing Wallpaper and Patterns in Windows 121

Cleaning and Protecting Your Monitor 123

Troubleshooting Display Problems 123

The Picture Is All Wavy, Fuzzy, and Won't Work
in Windows 123
The Picture Changes Size Going from DOS to Windows 124
The Picture Keeps Getting Smaller 124
I Can't Resize the Screen on My Notebook 124
Windows or a Program Tells Me I Can't Display
the Right Number of Colors 124
The Monitor Doesn't Come on When I Turn on the PC 124
The Monitor Doesn't Turn off When Windows 95
Shuts Down the Computer 124
Can I Fix or Upgrade the Inside of My Monitor Like
My PC? 124

12 Keyboards 125

Understanding the Keyboard Layout 126

Using Special Characters and Symbols 126

Typing in Another Language 127

Special Keys for Windows 95 129

Special Software for Keyboards 129

Keeping Your Keyboard Clean and Working 130

Avoiding Keyboard-Related Injuries 131

Special Notes on Notebook Keyboards 131

Using a Standard Keyboard with a Notebook 132

Troubleshooting Common Keyboard Problems 132
  Keys Type Odd Symbols or Letters 132
  Print Screen Key Doesn't Work 132
  Arrow Keys Type Numbers Instead of Moving
  the Cursor/Number Keys Move the Cursor 133
  The Keyboard (or PC) Won't Stop Beeping 133
  I Get a Message That Says *Keyboard Error* or *Keyboard Missing*
  When the PC Boots Up and Then Nothing Happens 133

13 Mice and Joysticks 135

Defining Mice 136

Connecting a Mouse 136

Using the Mouse Buttons 137
  The Left Mouse Button 137

Using the IntelliMouse Wheel 138
  The Right Mouse Button 138

Three-Button Mice 139

Adjusting Mouse Properties 139
  Configuring Mouse Double-Click Speed 139
  Configuring Right- or Left-Hand Mouse Preferences 139

Adjusting Pointer Speed 139

Cleaning a Mouse 141

Defining Joysticks 141

Types of Joysticks 141

Connecting a Joystick 141

Calibrating Your Joystick   142

    Calibrating Your Joystick with Software   142

    Calibrating Your Joystick with Hardware   143

14   Printers   145

Printers Defined   146

Laser Printers   147

Inkjet Printers   147

Dot-Matrix Printers   148

Connecting Your Printer to Your PC   149

Understanding Your Printer Controls   150

Installing Your Printer to Work in Windows 95   151

Other Printing Considerations   153

15   Modems and Faxes   155

Understanding Modems   156

Choosing a Modem   157

Selecting a Fax Modem   159

Connecting a Modem   160

Understanding Your Modem Controls   161

Setting Up Your Modem to Work in Windows 95   161

Troubleshooting Your Modem   162

    The External Modem Isn't Working   162

    The Modem Dials, but Doesn't Connect   163

    The Modem Doesn't Get a Dial Tone   163

    Windows or the Communications Software Displays a Message
Saying It Can't Find the Modem   163

16   Speakers and Sound   165

Components for Sound on Your PC   166

    Sound Cards   166

    Speakers   166

Playing Sounds for Windows Events   167

Playing WAV Sound Files on Your PC   168

Getting New Sounds   169

Playing Music on Your PC   169

Adjusting the Speaker Volume and Tone
in Windows 95   170

Listening to Your CDs on Headphones   171

Microphones   172
   Recording Sounds in Windows 95   172
   Adjusting Microphone and Input Levels in Windows 95   173

Troubleshooting Sound Problems in Windows 95   174
   No Sound from the Speakers   174
   No Sound from Speakers When an Audio CD Is Playing   175
   Can't Record with the Microphone   175
   Background Music in Games and Multimedia Doesn't Play   175
   Background Music in Games and Multimedia Sounds More
   Like a Kazoo than a Symphony   175

17 Scanners   177

Defining Scanner Types   178
   Flatbed Scanners   178
   Sheetfed Scanners   178
   Hand Scanners   180
   Color versus Grayscale Scanners   181
   Understanding Resolution and Dots Per Inch   181

System Requirements   181

Connecting a Scanner to Your PC   182
   SCSI Cards and Cables   182
   TWAIN Drivers   182
   Getting Windows 95 to Recognize Your Scanner   183

Scanning a Document   185

OCR Software   186

V | Connecting to the Internet

18 What Is the Internet?   189

What the Internet Isn't   190

What the Internet Is   190

How Hypertext Weaves the World Wide Web   191

Electronic Mail and the Internet   192

Other Information Sources on the Internet   193

Searching for Information on the Internet   196

19 Establishing an Internet Connection   199

Making Sure You Have the Right Hardware   200
Upgrades to Consider   200

Selecting an Internet Service Provider   201

Connecting with an Online Service   202

Dial-Up Connections to the Internet   202
Connecting to Your Service Provider   203
Downloading the Basic Files from Your Service Provider   203
Configuring Your System for TCP/IP   203

20 Using Your WWW Browser   209

Understanding Web Browsers   210

Which Web Browser?   210
Netscape Navigator   211
Microsoft Internet Explorer   211

Exploring the World Wide Web   211

Understanding the Elements of a Web Page   214
Dealing with Frames   214
Completing Forms   215
Playing Embedded Sound or Video   216
Exploring a Virtual World   218
Running Java   219

Searching for Information on the Web   219

Enhancing the Capabilities of Your Web Browser   222

21 Sending and Receiving E-Mail   223

What Is E-Mail?   224

Using E-Mail Addresses   224

Sending E-Mail   226

Receiving E-Mail   228

Attaching Files to Your E-Mail   230

Saving an Attached File You've Received   231

22 Sending and Receiving Files with FTP   233

What Is FTP?   234

Finding Files to Download   234

Downloading a File   235

Uploading a File   236

Using Archie to Locate a File   237

Using Your Web Browser for FTP   238

    Downloading FTP Directories and Files   238

Alternatives to FTP on the Web   240

23 Other Internet Options   241

Exploring Newsgroups   242

    The UseNet Mechanism   242

    Accessing UseNet Newsgroups   242

    What the Newsgroup Titles Mean   244

Using Internet Relay Chat   244

    Accessing Chat Channels   245

Staying Abreast of the Internet's Evolution   247

    Netcaster and Push Technologies   247

    The Potential of the Internet as a Software Server   248

VI | Problem Solving

24 Getting Help with Software   253

Using the Help System   254

Using Software Wizards   256

Troubleshooting Windows 95   257

Avoiding Viruses   259

Getting Online Support   259

Getting Help by Phone   261

25 Getting Help with Hardware   263

Simple Solutions First   264

Getting the Settings Right   264

Avoiding Problems with Device Drivers   266

Dealing with Interrupt Conflicts (IRQ)   266

Wait, Escape, Reboot, and Other Simple Fixes   267

Diagnosing Hardware Problems   267

Using Device Manager to Identify and Fix Problems   268

Self-Service that Prolongs the Life of Your Hardware   269

Using Technical Support   270

Using the Internet as a Troubleshooting Tool   270

26 Upgrading Your Software   273

Adding New Software to Your PC   274

   Before You Install Software   274

   Installing Software from the Control Panel   275

Upgrading to New Software Versions   277

Installing Over Older Software Versions   278

Removing Old Software   279

27 Upgrading Your Hardware   283

Are You Uncomfortable Opening
Your Computer Case?   284

Upgrading Parts Inside Your PC   285

IDE and SCSI Drives   286

Matching Memory   286

ISA, PCI, and Other Expansion Slots   287

Understanding Plug and Play Technology   288

What to Look for in a New PC   289

Where to Buy New PCs and Upgrades   291

Special Tips for Buying a Notebook Computer   292

VII | Reference Information

28 Glossary of Common Terms and Phrases   297

29 Computer Company Listing   325

30 Top Internet Sites   339

Computers and the Internet   339

Other Popular Web Sites   343

31 Suggested Reading   355

The Complete Idiot's Guide to Networking   356

Introduction to Networking, Third Edition   356

Managing Multivendor Networks   356

Platinum Edition Using Windows 95   357

Que's Computer User's Dictionary   357

Special Edition Using NetWare 3.12   357

Special Edition Using NetWare 4.1, Second Edition   358

Upgrading and Repairing Networks   358

Windows 95 Communications Handbook   359

Index   361

Credits

PRESIDENT
Roland Elgey

SENIOR VICE PRESIDENT/PUBLISHING
Don Fowley

PUBLISHER
Joseph B. Wikert

PUBLISHING DIRECTOR
Brad R. Koch

MANAGER OF PUBLISHING OPERATIONS
Linda H. Buehler

GENERAL MANAGER
Joe Muldoon

DIRECTOR OF EDITORIAL SERVICES
Carla Hall

MANAGING EDITOR
Thomas F. Hayes

DIRECTOR OF ACQUISITIONS
Cheryl D. Willoughby

ACQUISITIONS EDITOR
Angela Wethington

PRODUCT DIRECTOR
Emmett Dulaney

PRODUCTION EDITOR
Lisa M. Gebken

EDITOR
Sarah Rudy

PRODUCT MARKETING MANAGER
Kourtnaye Sturgeon

ASSISTANT PRODUCT MARKETING MANAGER
Gretchen Schlesinger

TECHNICAL EDITORS
Rick Brown
Kyle Bryant
Christy Gleeson
Darralyn McCall
Nadeem Muhammed

MEDIA DEVELOPMENT SPECIALIST
David Garratt

ACQUISITIONS COORDINATOR
Michelle Newcomb

SOFTWARE RELATIONS COORDINATOR
Susan D. Gallagher

EDITORIAL ASSISTANT
Jeff Chandler

BOOK DESIGNERS
Ruth Harvey
Kim Scott

COVER DESIGNER
Sandra Schroeder

PRODUCTION TEAM
Bryan Flores
Julie Geeting
Laura A. Knox
Donna Wright

INDEXER
Sandra Henselmeier

Composed in *Century Old Style* and *ITC Franklin Gothic* by Que Corporation.

About the Authors

Shelley O'Hara has written more than 25 computer books and is one of Que's best-selling authors. Shelley is well known for having written most of Que's *Easy* series. She is an independent technical writer and consultant in Indianapolis.

Jennifer Fulton is a best-selling author of more than 50 books covering many areas of computing, including DOS, Windows 3.1, and Windows 95. She is a self-taught veteran of computing: If there's something that can happen to a computer user, it's happened to her. Jennifer brings what's left of her sense of humor along with her vast experiences to her many books, particularly *Big Basics Book of PCs*.

Catherine Kolecki is an instructional designer and technical writer. She owns DocSolutions, a company specializing in technical and training materials. She has a graduate certificate in technical communication from the Illinois Institute of Technology and a master's degree in adult vocational and technical education from the University of Illinois at Urbana-Champaign. She is a former president of the Chicago chapter of the Society for Technical Communication (STC).

Dan Logan is a book publisher and award-winning freelance writer and journalist living in Cambria, California. He currently publishes an online magazine called *The Tri-tip Computer News* (**http://www.thegrid.net/dlogan/**), a Web site for computer users from Lompoc to San on California's central coast. Dan is on the board of directors of the San Luis Obispo-entral Coast Software and Technology Association, and is a member of the SLO Bytes ·s Group and the Publishers Marketing Association.

Michael O'Mara is a writer and consultant. He has been helping others learn how to use computers and software for nearly 10 years, first in a corporate setting, and then as a staff author with The Cobb Group where he wrote innumerable articles about leading computer software programs and served as editor-in-chief of several monthly software journals. Since becoming a freelance author, he has co-authored or contributed to a dozen Que titles. He can be reached at **momara@usa.net**.

Suzanne Weixel is a self-employed writer and editor specializing in the technology industry. Her experience with computers began in 1974, when she learned to play football on the Dartmouth Time Sharing terminal her brother installed in a spare bedroom. For Que, Suzanne has written and revised numerous books, including *Easy PCs*, Third Edition. She also writes about non-computer-related subjects whenever she has the chance. Suzanne graduated from Dartmouth College in 1981 with a degree in art history. She currently lives in Marlborough, Massachusetts with her husband their sons Nathaniel and Evan, and their Samoyed, Cirrus.

Acknowledgments

The authors would like to thank the following players in Que for their help in writing, developing, and organizing the material for this book:

Emmett Dulaney	Lorna Gentry	Brad Koch
Jim Minatel	Lisa D. Wagner	

We'd Like to Hear from You!

Que Corporation has a long-standing reputation for high-quality books and products. To ensure your continued satisfaction, we also understand the importance of customer service and support.

Tech Support

If you need assistance with the information in this book or with a CD/disk accompanying the book, please access Macmillan Computer Publishing's online Knowledge Base at **http://www.superlibrary.com/general/support**. If you do not find the answer to your questions on our Web site, you may contact Macmillan Technical Support by phone at 317-581-3833 or via e-mail at **support@mcp.com**.

Also be sure to visit Que's Web resource center for all the latest information, enhancements, errata, downloads, and more. It's located at **http://www.quecorp.com/**.

Orders, Catalogs, and Customer Service

To order other Que or Macmillan Computer Publishing books, catalogs, or products, please contact our Customer Service Department at 800-858-7674 or fax us at 800-882-8583 (International Fax: 317-228-4400). Or visit our online bookstore at **http://www.mcp.com/**.

Comments and Suggestions

We want you to let us know what you like or dislike most about this book or other Que products. Your comments will help us to continue publishing the best books available on computer topics in today's market.

Brad R. Koch
Product Director
Que Corporation
201 West 103rd Street, 4B
Indianapolis, Indiana 46290 USA
Fax: 317/581-4663
E-mail: **bkoch@iquest.net**

Please be sure to include the book's title and author as well as your name and phone or fax number. We will carefully review your comments and share them with the author. Please note that due to the high volume of mail we receive, we may not be able to reply to every message.

Thank you for choosing Que!

Introduction

Things have changed a great deal since PCs found their way into the business place and the home. In less than 20 years, they have revolutionized the way we work, think, and play. We've grown from text-based applications to a world dependent on graphics, mice, trackballs, and user-friendly everything. No longer do you need to memorize finger-twisting, multiple-key shortcuts to perform simple tasks; today, you use your mouse to click a button or pull down a menu.

That said, the computers and software programs of today are still less than intuitive. While increased computing power has enabled the graphical user interfaces that make some operations easier, the addition of hundreds of extra features means you have more operations to learn. ■

Who Should Read This Book

This book was written for the everyday user. There's enough basic information included to help beginners get started, and enough coverage of other topics to act as a reference for more experienced users. If you consider yourself a power user, however, you're probably better off with a thicker, more comprehensive book, such as Que's *PCs Illustrated* or—for the most advanced users—*Upgrading and Repairing PCs*. Everyone else should be able to find the answers to their questions in this book.

What This Book Covers

This book covers the most common features of Intel-based PCs through such topics as:

- Personal computer basics
- Using your PC effectively and efficiently
- Disks, drives, files, and folders
- Computer peripherals
- Connecting to the Internet
- Troubleshooting
- Other sources of reference information

The instructions in this book apply to all Intel-based PCs, regardless of the operating system they are using. When operating system specifics must be given, Windows 95 version 4.00.950 B is used as the default. If your version of Windows 95 is different, your steps for some tasks will vary. (To check your version of Windows, right-click the My Computer icon, select Properties from the pop-up menu, choose the General tab, and look at the System entry.)

The *Using* Philosophy

Que's *Using* books help you cover the most ground with the least amount of hassle, and in a minimum amount of time. We try to pack as much information as possible between the front and back covers, so that whatever your problem, you're likely to find the solution in this single book.

In addition, this book gets to the point *quickly*. Your time is valuable, so each task in this book is written with economy in mind. There's little fluff in these pages, just essential explanations and step-by-step instructions.

Conventions Used in This Book

This book uses certain conventions in order to guide you through the various tasks. For example, you'll find the following special typefaces used in this book:

Type	Meaning
underline	Shortcut key combinations for menu commands and dialog box options that appear underlined on-screen.
boldface	Information you are asked to type.
`computer type`	Direct quotations of words that appear on-screen or in a figure.
italics	Important or new terms you should be familiar with.

In addition, you will find special elements sprinkled throughout the book. These annotations supply you with additional information not present in the general text.

N O T E Extra information (above and beyond the topic being discussed) we think you'll find helpful and interesting is placed in Notes throughout each chapter.

 Tips are quick pieces of advice, sometimes about shortcuts or tricks, sometimes drawing on the expertise and experience of the author.

CAUTION
We'll put a caution on a page to warn you when a procedure might create a problem, and tell you the circumstances under which that problem is likely to occur.

How to Contact Que

You can find more information about Que Publishing at our Web site; the address is **http://www.quecorp.com**.

Personal Computer Basics

1   Defining Your PC   7

2   How Computers Work: Hardware   19

3   Setting Up Your PC   31

Defining Your PC

Technically, the term "PC" refers to any type of personal computer, regardless of brand or type. An Apple Macintosh, for example, is a personal computer. Over the years, however, the term PC has come to more generically refer to the most popular type of personal computer: the IBM PC and compatibles, such as Compaq, Dell, or Hewlett-Packard. And because IBM-compatible machines are by far the industry leaders, this book focuses only on computers of this type. ■

Understand your PC

Explore an overview of personal computers: what they are and what they do.

Identify the main components

Take a quick look at popular PC styles and the basic parts common to all of them.

What are peripherals?

Anything attached to the main system is a peripheral. This chapter describes the peripherals you're likely to have attached to your system.

The Functions of a PC

PCs can be used to write letters, balance checkbooks, play games, keep track of business records, and even teach children how to read. No matter what task you use it for, it all boils down to six basic functions:

- Storing. Whatever you enter can be saved and stored for later use.
- Retrieving. Anything stored can be retrieved and used again.
- Displaying. The information you're working with "in" the computer appears on a screen or monitor so you can see what you are doing.
- Editing. After you retrieve the information, you can change it, add to it, or erase it.
- Printing. One of the greatest capabilities of a computer is that after you finalize your work, it can be transferred to paper.
- Sending and receiving. With the development of modems and networks, you can communicate with other computer users by sending them documents or messages, regardless of where in the world those users are.

To learn more about using PCs, it's important to understand the basic parts, types, and styles of PCs and what role each part plays in the overall computing process.

Desktop and Tower Computers

The PC consists of several parts and pieces, but the main action takes place inside the system unit—the big box to which all other parts are attached. System unit cases come in two basic styles, desktop and tower, with slight variations available for each type.

A *standard desktop* PC case (see Figure 1.1) is the most common. Longer than it is tall, it sits on top of your desk or workstation.

N O T E Most of the examples in this book are based on a standard desktop PC, because they are the choice of an overwhelming majority of users. ■

Compact desktop cases are somewhat smaller than the standard case, but look very much the same.

A *tower* PC case serves the same purpose as the desktop, but is designed to sit vertically on the floor below the work area, or on the desktop next to the monitor. You may also find a *mini-tower* case, shown in Figure 1.2, which is a smaller, more compact version of the tower case.

Computer experts and technicians tend to prefer tower cases because they usually offer more configuration and upgrade flexibility. Like the difference between a full-size Chevy pickup truck and a subcompact Geo Metro, there's also less chance of scraping your knuckles while working "under the hood."

FIG. 1.1
Desktop-style cases generally sit on the desktop, with the monitor resting on top.

Laptop, Notebook, and Palmtop Computers

In addition to the desktop and tower computer cases, a third alternative is becoming more and more popular: the *laptop* or *notebook* computer. These computers are very convenient because they are designed for portability. The system case, monitor, keyboard, and all internal workings are all in one light, compact case. Plus, although these computers come equipped with AC adapters, they can run on batteries, making it very easy to pick up and go at a moment's notice.

There is very little difference between a laptop and a notebook computer. Notebooks, like the one in Figure 1.3, tend to be smaller, lighter, and as a result, a bit more expensive, so the terms are often used interchangeably. Either way, portable computers typically are more expensive than desktop PCs with equivalent features.

Hand-held, or *palmtop*, computers are gaining popularity. Although they become more sophisticated with each new model, palmtops generally have limited features and capabilities compared to their full-sized counterparts. They are very handy, however, for quick tasks when you're on the road, and many include the capability to synchronize and communicate with your primary computer.

FIG. 1.2
Towers and mini-towers easily stand alone on the floor, which is especially convenient if you want to keep your workspace as uncluttered as possible.

Switches, Buttons, and Lights on the Case

Regardless of the style, nearly all computers have several features in common. Odds are very good that you will find one of each of the following on the front panel of your PC (see Figure 1.4):

- *Power switch.* As you might suspect, this button or switch turns the computer on and off; it can be located on the front, side, or back of the computer.

- *Lock.* Most cases let you physically lock the system for additional security. When the computer is locked, you can turn the power on, but nothing (including the keyboard) works.

FIG. 1.3
Notebook computers are convenient, although you might find the compact keyboard a little hard to get used to.

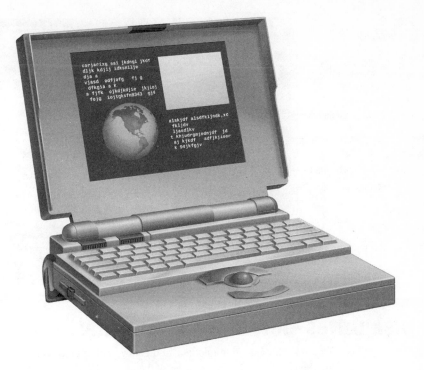

- *Reset button.* If your system crashes and you have to reboot the computer, use the Reset button. This "soft boots" the system without completely cutting the power. You'll learn more about resetting your computer in Chapter 4, "Starting, Stopping, and Using Your PC."

- *Hard drive light.* Indicates activity on the hard drive. If you suspect your system is locked up or has crashed, check this light. If it's lit constantly and not flickering at all, you probably need to reboot.

- *Floppy drive light.* Indicates activity on the floppy drive. Never remove a floppy disk if this light is on—you may lose data or otherwise damage the disk.

- *Turbo button.* Older computers offer a choice between Normal speed and Turbo mode. Although performance is improved in Turbo mode, the difference may be negligible.

- *Turbo light.* Indicates whether Turbo mode is on or off.

NOTE The Turbo option is no longer applicable for Pentium and higher-speed computers. If you have a Turbo button on your late-model PC, it is probably just a dummy switch; if you have a Turbo light, it's most likely always on, regardless of the switch position. ■

FIG. 1.4
A typical front panel
includes a variety of
buttons, switches, and
lights.

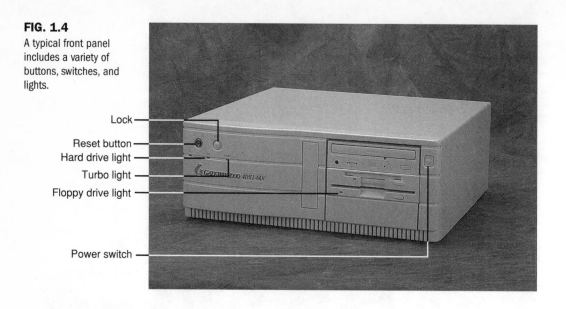

Lock

Reset button
Hard drive light
Turbo light
Floppy drive light

Power switch

Disk Drives—Internal and External

Disk drives store the information, data, and files you create, as well as all the software needed
to operate the computer. There are several flavors of disk drives.

N O T E You'll learn a great deal more about disks and disk drives in Chapter 2, "How Computers
Work," and in Part III, "Disks, Drives, Files, and Folders." ■

Internal Hard Disk Drive

The hard disk drive is almost always located inside your computer, where you can't see or
touch it. As a general rule, the hard disk stores the largest amount of data of the various types
of disks.

Floppy Disk Drive

Floppy disks are the small plastic squares you insert in the front panel of your computer. They
don't hold nearly as much data as a hard disk, but they are handy for carrying files from one
computer to another, or storing important documents in a safe place away from the computer.

CD-ROM Drive

Similar in appearance to music (audio) CDs, CD-ROMs are convenient for large programs,
collections of graphic or multimedia files, and so on. One CD-ROM can hold the data of more
than 500 floppy disks. Many software manufacturers now use CD-ROMs to distribute their

programs; it's much easier to install new software from one CD-ROM instead of 3, 10, or 30 floppies. Unless you have a special device called a recordable CD-ROM drive (CD-R), you can only read and copy files from a CD-ROM—you can't add, edit, or remove anything yourself.

 TIP   Most CD-ROM drives can also play audio CDs, as long as you have a sound card and speakers or headphones to hear the music.

Tape Drive

The primary purpose of a tape drive is to create system backups, which help you get your computer back to normal in the event of a system crash or other disaster.

▶ **See** "Making Backup Copies of Your Files," **p. 91**

Removable Hard Disk Drive

Increasingly popular due to their speed, convenience, and capacity, removable storage devices are now included with some new computers. With a removable hard drive, you will never run out of storage space, because when you fill up one, you can take it out and put in a new one. The most popular types on the market today are known as Zip, Jaz, and SyQuest drives. One Jaz drive cartridge can hold as much as 1G of data—more than twice the capacity of internal hard disk drives installed in many computers.

External Disk Drive

An *external disk drive* is any kind of disk drive that is not installed inside the case of the computer, but instead is attached to the computer via a cable. Any of the drive types mentioned here can be external or internal. They usually don't come with a new computer and have to be purchased separately.

Monitors

Monitors, also called *displays* or *CRTs*, come in a variety of sizes. Like a television, a monitor's screen size is measured diagonally. Your new computer most likely came with a 14- or 15-inch monitor. Less common but also popular are 17- and 21-inch monitors, which offer a bit more "real estate" on the screen. People who use computers for design, graphics work, or desktop publishing often prefer larger monitors, because it's easier to see a full page on the screen at one time.

Most monitors can be set to different display resolutions. The *resolution* defines how crisp and clear the monitor's display is based on the number of *pixels* (short for *picture elements*), or dots, used to create the display signal. Your monitor is probably set to display at 640×480 pixels, but you can increase the resolution to gain a clearer display. See Chapter 11 to learn more about monitors and the video adapter cards that control them.

Keyboards, Mice, Trackballs, and Joysticks

Anything you use to interface with the computer is called an *input device*. Without an input device, you can't do much with your computer. The different kinds of input devices include:

- *Keyboard.* The keyboard is used to type in data and feed information to the system. When you press a key or set of keys on the keyboard, that action sends a signal to the computer's processing unit. That signal can make the character you typed appear on the screen, or it can trigger a response based on a command issued by your input. (See Chapter 12, "Keyboards," for a discussion on the various types of keyboards available.)

- *Mouse.* This device sits on the desk next to your computer and is an integral part of the computer's graphical user interface. You use the mouse to position your cursor, navigate through documents, enter commands, and more. It's the greatest improvement to computers since the PC itself, but if you've never used one before, it may take a little practice. You push the mouse across the desktop, through which a series of electronic signals makes the *mouse pointer* or *cursor* on the screen move in the same direction as the mouse.

- *Trackball.* A trackball is basically an upside-down mouse. Instead of pushing the mouse around on the desk, you roll a small ball around inside the "mouse's belly." Some people prefer trackballs because they take up less room on the desk, and often are more comfortable for persons with carpal tunnel syndrome and other hand and wrist problems. Most notebook and laptop computers come standard with a trackball built right into the computer, just in front of the keyboard, as you saw in Figure 1.3.

- *Joystick.* Typically, a joystick is used in place of the mouse for computer gaming. Most joysticks have a slender handle for steering and a trigger button. If you've spent any time at all in a video arcade, you've no doubt used a joystick.

There are a few other types of input devices available such as a pen-like pointer for precise drawing and various wireless mice; however, these devices have very specialized uses and won't be covered in this book.

Connectors, Plugs, and Ports

Computers come with a variety of plugs and ports for connecting monitors, mice, and other peripheral devices—components not installed inside the system case (see Figure 1.5):

- Serial (COM) ports most often connect external modems, although some computers also use COM ports for connecting the mouse.

- Parallel (LPT) ports are for printers and a few other devices.

- Game ports connect your joystick or similar game-controlling input device.

- SCSI ports are used only for devices that are SCSI-enabled, such as certain scanners, external disk drives, and so on. Your computer may or may not have a SCSI port.

■ Other ports, such as those labeled Monitor, Phone, Speaker, Keyboard, and so on, offer obvious indicators of their use. If you're not sure where something plugs in, check your computer's manual.

Although it may look like a confusing mess, manufacturers make it as easy as possible to hook everything up yourself. For example, a printer cable will only fit in a parallel port, due to the connector's shape and number of pins. It's possible to mismatch a few types of connections, but as long as you pay attention to what you're doing and don't try to force anything that doesn't seem to fit, you'll do just fine.

FIG. 1.5
What goes where?
Fortunately, most
connectors and plugs
are designed so they
only fit one way. Not
completely fool-proof,
but close.

Serial (COM) ports are
used for mice, modems,
and other devices.
Notice this computer
has two different
flavors of COM ports

The joystick goes here
if you're into gaming

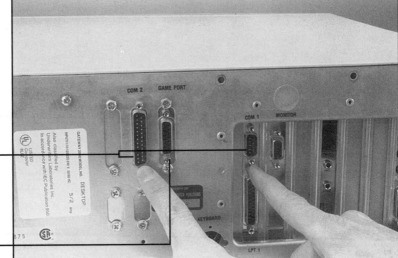

Speakers

If you have a multimedia PC, it includes the capability to play sounds and music. The computer generates or plays sounds as a digital signal, which is translated to audio by the *sound card* inside your computer. The sound card then sends the signal to the speakers which enable you to listen to the sound.

A wide range of speakers are available, varying in output, price, and general quality. The ones that came with your computer are probably a basic model that is just fine for most uses. Just like building a custom home stereo system, however, serious audiophiles may want to upgrade to a more sophisticated sound system for their computer as well. You will learn a great deal more about your computer's sound system in Chapter 16, "Speakers and Sound."

▶ **See** "Components Sound on Your PC," **p. 166**

Printers

A *printer*, of course, is the peripheral device that takes the data inside your computer and translates it to paper. Your system may or may not have included a printer in the package; either way, you'll most certainly need one at some point.

There are three basic types of printers available today:

- *Laser.* Laser printers generate images from the computer using a very fine dust called *toner* (the same process used by most copying machines). Laser printers produce very good quality images and are especially nice for graphics. Although laser printers are much cheaper than they used to be, they still are more expensive than the other types described next—and you'll pay a *real* premium for a color laser printer.

- *Ink or bubble jet.* Inkjet and bubble jet printers work on the same basic technology: Liquid ink is transferred to paper. Ink and bubble jet printers are more affordable than laser printers (even a mid-priced color inkjet printer is cheaper than most laser printers). Their quality is not as good as that of a laser printer, but the difference is insignificant, especially for most everyday printing tasks.

- *Dot-matrix.* Dot-matrix printers used to be the standard. Dot-matrix printers use inked ribbons to transfer data to paper, just like the typewriters of old. Some more sophisticated dot-matrix printers can produce decent-looking graphics, but even the best ones can't match the quality of a good inkjet or laser printer. However, dot-matrix printers still have some advantages: Most are extremely affordable, and they are much better suited to printing documents such as perforated, continuous-feed forms. And as long as they're not trying to do anything fancy, they're very fast.

  Due to the increased popularity of higher quality printers, don't be surprised if they're hard to find. Some retailers have stopped selling dot-matrix printers, but you can always still buy them via mail order, from a smaller computer specialty shop, or at most office supply stores.

Chapter 14 explains printers in more detail, and helps you get your PC's printer configured and ready for use.

▶ **See** "Printers Defined," **p. 146**

Modems

A *modem* is the device that connects your computer to the outside world. Using a regular telephone line, your computer can connect to online services, the Internet, and even other computers.

If your computer came with a modem included, it is most likely an internal one (inside the computer), and all you have to do is attach the phone line to the back of the computer. If you're buying one separately, you might want to consider an external modem so that you don't have to open up the system case and install it yourself. Internal and external modems work identically, so choose whichever you're most comfortable with.

Modems are graded according to the speed at which they can transmit and transfer data over the phone line; this speed is measured in kilobits per second (Kbps). The most common speed you'll find on the shelf today is the 33.6Kbps modem, although 56Kbps is quickly gaining popularity. Obviously, the faster the modem's speed, the more quickly you can send and communicate. If you spend much time on the World Wide Web, you'll quickly appreciate why this is important: A faster modem can save you a significant amount of time downloading graphics, images, and files.

Most modems can also send and receive faxes directly from or to your computer, virtually eliminating the need for a separate fax machine. In Chapter 15, you'll learn more details on modems, how they work, and how to install and set one up.

▶ **See** "Understanding Modems," **p. 156**

CHAPTER 2

How Computers Work: Hardware

The physical components that make up a computer are called *hardware*. Every PC has basically the same hardware; the differences in size and power of that hardware is what makes one PC more expensive or powerful than another.

When you purchased your computer, you probably received a keyboard, system unit, monitor, and mouse. (You may have a few other items, too, such as a printer or a CD-ROM drive.)

This chapter discusses the components that are inside the *system unit*—the big box that sits either on your desktop or on the floor next to your desk. The system unit holds the "guts" of your computer. If you remove the outside cover (see your manual for specific instructions), you should be able to see the main elements of the system unit:

What is the motherboard?

The motherboard is the main controller board inside your computer that everything else attaches to.

Understand microprocessors and their role in your computer system

Learn more about the various types of microprocessors, how they work, and the impact they have on system performance.

What is RAM and how much do you need?

Get the details on RAM memory and how to determine how much you have in your machine—and learn how easy it is to add more.

Understand disks and disk drives

This chapter explores not just hard disk drives, but floppy disks and other types of removable storage devices.

Expansion slots and buses

Learn how to determine what kinds of expansion slots you have available, and what you can use them for.

How it all works together

After you understand how the individual components work, take a quick look at how the parts work together to perform all the many tasks you expect your computer to do.

■ Motherboard

■ Microprocessor

■ Memory (RAM) chips

■ Hard disk and floppy disk drives

■ Expansion cards and slots

■ Power supply

The following sections describe each of these parts in more detail. ■

Examining the Motherboard

The motherboard is a thin, rectangular circuit board that forms the foundation of your computer. It contains many computer chips and connections, and provides your PC its capabilities. Attached to the motherboard (see Figure 2.1) are the following:

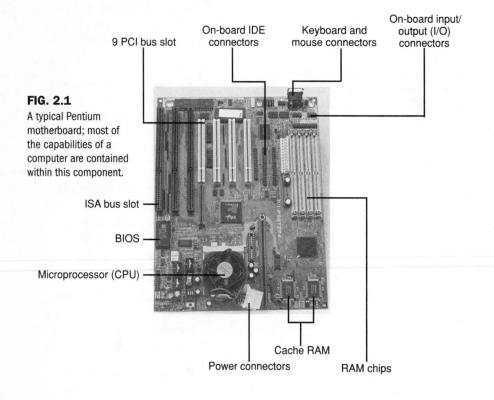

FIG. 2.1
A typical Pentium motherboard; most of the capabilities of a computer are contained within this component.

9 PCI bus slot

On-board IDE connectors

Keyboard and mouse connectors

On-board input/ output (I/O) connectors

ISA bus slot

BIOS

Microprocessor (CPU)

Power connectors

Cache RAM

RAM chips

- *Microprocessor*. This is your computer's "brain," also called the *central processing unit*, or *CPU*.

- *Math coprocessor*. Only a separate element in some PCs, the math coprocessor is a computer chip that gives your processor faster math skills. Your PC can still handle numbers without this chip; the "co" in coprocessor simply means it assists the processor. All Pentium and higher computers have the coprocessor built in, so you won't be able to see it as a separate piece.

- *RAM (random-access memory)*. RAM chips provide the working memory for your software. Rows of RAM chips are inserted on your motherboard. You can easily find and add more of these chips yourself.

- *Cache RAM*. This component is a portion of memory built into the microprocessor. This extremely fast memory stores the most recently accessed data from a disk or file. Because this data is easily accessible within the cache RAM, your computer can work faster.

- *ROM (read-only memory)*. ROM chips control your computer. The most important ROM chip is the *Basic Input/Output System*, or *BIOS* (pronounced *BUY-ose*). The BIOS contains instructions that tell the microprocessor how to deal with input and output. The computer reads the BIOS before it even loads the operating system.

- *Expansion slots*. These are electrical connections into which you insert *expansion cards*, such as an internal modem or a sound card.

Defining Microprocessors

The microprocessor, or CPU, is a single computer chip about the size of a matchbook (see Figure 2.2). Its many legs or pins are inserted into the motherboard. The CPU, which does the bulk of your PC's thinking, is the motor behind your software. The processor can calculate the ongoing checkbook balance in your personal finance software, or it can compare your words in a document against the software's built-in dictionary. Other chips and circuitry support it, but the CPU is the most important determinant of computer speed.

FIG. 2.2

The microprocessor is about the size of a matchbook.

Types of Microprocessors

With the systemcase open, you should be able to tell what type of CPU your system contains by reading the information that's printed on the top of the chip. You'll probably see a combination of numbers and letters that includes the numbers 386, 486, or 586, or the words Pentium or Pentium Pro. The 386 and 486 designations indicate that your system contains a microprocessor compatible with the Intel 80386 or 80486 microprocessors, respectively (or most likely, contains an actual Intel microprocessor). The higher the microprocessor number, the more quickly it can process information, and the more megabytes of RAM it can address.

A Pentium designation indicates your system contains an Intel Pentium processor. The Pentium chip has more than three million transistors and offers more than twice the processing speed of a 468 DX2 microprocessor. The Pentium Pro is even more robust than the Pentium. A designation of 586 indicates that the chip is a non-Intel chip that is compatible with a Pentium processor.

After you locate the chip designator, look in the same spot for an indication of the chip's speed, which is expressed in megahertz. Basically, the speed of the chip defines the number of commands it can perform per second. The higher the number, the faster the CPU (and thus, your computer) can perform. In other words, a 166MHz Pentium performs faster than a 100MHz Pentium. But, a 100MHz 486 might not perform faster than a 90MHz Pentium.

To determine the system's speed, look in the same spot you found the CPU's type designation. Look for 25, 33, 50, 60, 90, 100, 120, 133, 150, 166, or 200. This number indicates the chip's speed.

How Microprocessors Work

The CPU is kind of like a traffic cop. Information is constantly flowing back and forth between the various parts of the PC and the CPU. The CPU stands in the middle, deciding what goes where. One of the CPU's jobs, then, is control of information flow. When you type at the keyboard, the CPU receives every keystroke and redirects it to the right place. When you print a letter, the CPU takes the characters from the screen or the disk and sends them streaming through the cable that connects your PC to your printer.

Every once in a while, the CPU notices that some of the data flowing by is actually a command to perform a mathematical calculation. It stops the traffic for a second and performs the calculation. Then it returns to its traffic-control duties.

The CPU gets its orders from the software program that is loaded into the computer's memory. Some of the information being shuttled around by the CPU takes the form of program commands.

The CPU directs your keystrokes to the computer's electronic memory, or RAM. Your PC's RAM constantly cycles through millions of characters that may need the CPU's attention. In order to process the characters stored in RAM, the CPU must move data to and from RAM at an incredible pace. The faster the CPU, and the more efficiently it moved data to and from RAM, the more processing power in the computer.

Defining Random-Access Memory (RAM)

The *random-access memory*, or *RAM*, is the CPU's memory, or workspace. Software you want to work with is loaded from the hard disk drive into RAM. RAM is a type of short-term memory; when power is turned off, the information is lost. (This is why you must save your work to a floppy or hard disk before you turn off your computer.) RAM speed is measured in nano-seconds, with a smaller number indicating faster performance. Most systems today use RAM speeds between 60–100ns.

Generally, the system's RAM is located on *SIMMs (Single Inline Memory Modules)* that install in sockets on the motherboard. Figure 2.3 shows two types of SIMMs. One uses a 30-pin con-figuration, and the other, larger SIMM uses a 72-pin configuration.

FIG. 2.3
Most memory comes in one of two configura-tions, either 30-pin or 72-pin.

Memory chips come in different shapes and sizes. *DRAM (dynamic random-access memory)* chips are the most common type of computer memory, and they need to be energized hun-dreds of times per second to hold the information.

Another type of RAM chip, usually found in higher-end systems, is called a *DIMM (Dual Inline Memory Module)*. DIMMs effectively pack twice as much memory in one package compared to SIMMs, although DIMMs are slightly longer than SIMMs.

One other type of memory you might have in your system is *EDO (Extended Data Out)* memory. Without launching into a detailed technical explanation, let's just say that EDO memory is more efficient and offers faster performance than non-EDO memory. EDO and non-EDO chips look identical; to find out which one your system uses, you need to look closely at the SIMM chip. In all likelihood, the SIMM will have EDO printed somewhere on it if it is an EDO chip.

Determining How Much RAM You Have

There are a couple of ways to find out how much RAM you have, even without opening the case. The easiest way is to watch the screen right after you turn on the computer's power. As the computer performs its power-up process (see Chapter 4, "Starting, Stopping, and Using Your PC"), it goes through a self-diagnostic procedure that verifies the memory installed in the system. The highest number reached before the screen goes blank and the operating system loads is how many kilobytes of memory you have. For example, it may show 16384 or 8192. Round this number off and divide by 1,000 to determine the measurement, which is usually referred to in megabytes. Thus, the two numbers here would equal 16M and 8M of RAM, respectively.

If you're running Windows 95, there's another easy way to determine your RAM. From the desktop, right-click My Computer and choose Properties. When the System Properties dialog box appears (see Figure 2.4), you'll see the General tab, which includes your Windows 95 version and registration numbers. At the bottom of the list, you'll see your CPU type and amount of RAM.

FIG. 2.4
The System Properties dialog box tells you about your computer, including how much RAM you have.

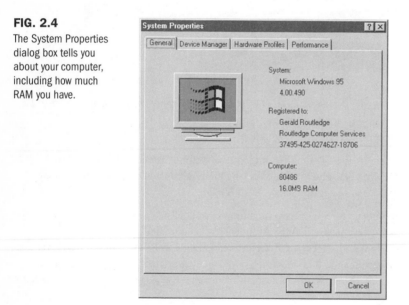

Defining Disk Drives

Because RAM is erased when you turn off the computer, the only safe place for permanent storage of information is on a disk. There are two main types of disk drives: floppy disk drives and hard disk drives. With both, you save your work to what are called *files*. A letter to your brother, for example, may be saved as one file. A list of all the CDs in your music collection may be saved as another file. You can save many files to a disk drive.

Floppy Disks

A floppy disk drive, or simply floppy drive, allows you to store your work on a removable disk. Your PC likely has at least one floppy drive, maybe even two. The floppy drive is the thin, usually horizontal opening in the front of your PC. The floppy drive comes in two sizes, based on the size of this opening:

- *3 1/2-inch.* The 3 1/2-inch disk is a small, plastic square with a spring-loaded metal door or shutter. 3 1/2-inch disks typically come in two capacities: the most common 1.44M (high-density) disk, or 720K (double-density) disk. Some newer machines may also support extra-density floppies, which hold 2.88M—twice the amount of data as a high-density disk. A very, very rare dinosaur is the 360K 3 1/2-inch disk. You'll probably never see one of these, but they do exist.

- *5 1/4-inch.* These disks are very thin, truly floppy disks. Although there are many, many still in use today, 5 1/4-inch floppies are rapidly disappearing; they hold less data than 3 1/2-inch floppies, and they are much more easily damaged.

Hard Disks

Hard disks serve the same purpose as floppy disks, with three key differences: The hard disk is located inside the computer and is not removable; it can store and retrieve your work more than 10 times faster than a floppy; and it stores a great deal more data than a floppy disk. In fact, even the smallest hard disks usually hold as much information as 500 floppy disks. Common hard disk capacities in computers sold today range from 120M to a whopping 4G+ (gigabyte; one G equals 1,000M). The average, however, is usually around 800M to 1.2G.

N O T E   Some hard disks *are* removable. These external drives are generally called *removable storage devices*. Although you may or may not have a removable hard disk connected to your system, you will almost certainly have an internal, non-removable hard drive. ■

Determining How Much Disk Space You Have

Windows 95 makes it easy to tell how much disk space you have in total, how much you've used, and how much you have left. To see the information on a single disk, follow these steps:

1. From the desktop, double-click My Computer. The My Computer window opens.

2. Right-click the disk you want to examine (for this example, choose your main hard drive, probably labeled C:), then choose Properties from the shortcut menu. The disk's Properties dialog box will appear.

3. On the General tab, you'll see a collection of information, including Used Space (how much data you're currently storing), Free Space (how much blank space you have left), and Capacity (how much total disk space exists). You'll also see a nice colorful pie chart that shows you the same information at a glance (see Figure 2.5). Click OK or Cancel when you're finished viewing the information.

FIG. 2.5

Windows 95 shows you at a glance how much space you have left on your hard or floppy disk drive.

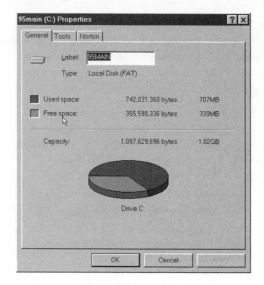

> **TIP** By changing the view of the My Computer window, you can see the information on all of your disks at the same time. From the View menu, choose Details, and the windows will change to a list of all your drives, showing each drive's type, total size, and amount of free space.
>
> You can also check out your drive space by choosing Start, Programs, Accessories, System Tools, DriveSpace. In the Drive Space dialog box that appears, select a drive in the list, then choose Drive, Properties to see its space details.

What Is the Bus and What Does it Do?

Information travels within your PC on thin metal conductors, called the *bus*. Your CPU uses the bus to shuttle information between parts of your PC. The faster the bus, the faster the PC can work.

There are three basic types of buses in a personal computer:

- *Address bus.* Identifies which memory location will be used next.
- *Control bus.* Carries signals from the control unit, making sure the bus traffic flows smoothly.
- *Data bus.* Transfers data to and from the microprocessor and the memory. The data bus includes both internal and external data buses.

You don't have to do anything to or with a bus, but knowing which types you have can be helpful. There are several different bus *architectures* (or designs). The most common terms you will hear are VL (or VESA local), ISA, EISA, and PCI. PCI is the standard architecture for Pentium computers, although ISA and EISA are usually included as well to support older hardware devices you may already own.

Understanding Expansion Slots

The motherboard offers expansion slots where you insert cards or adapters, including expansion cards for adding new components to your PC. Most PCs come with some slots already filled. For example, your monitor attaches to a video card that's plugged into one slot. The remaining slots are for adding sound cards, internal modems, SCSI adapters, and other devices. The appearance of the slots depends on the type of bus the system uses. Most Pentium and Pentium Pro motherboards use a combination ISA/PCI bus slots, which typically contains three or four ISA slots and three or four PCI slots.

Part
I
Ch
2

How Many Open Slots Do You Have?

You might be able to tell how many open slots you have by reading your computer's manual and determining how many extra devices are installed that are not mentioned in the book. But to be safe, it's best to open the case and count them for yourself. This will also help you understand the physical differences between PCI and ISA slots. If you look back at Figure 2.1, you can easily tell a PCI slot (and card) from an ISA slot by two characteristics:

- The PCI slot is shorter than the ISA slot.
- The ISA slot is divided into two sections, one longer than the other.

The PCI slot is in one section, although there's a short piece at one end divided by a small notch. Likewise, the PCI and ISA cards' connectors match the size and shape of their slots (see Figure 2.6).

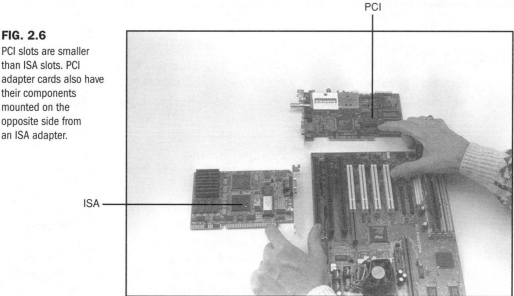

FIG. 2.6
PCI slots are smaller than ISA slots. PCI adapter cards also have their components mounted on the opposite side from an ISA adapter.

PCI

ISA

Logically, you can only install cards that match the slot type. When shopping for new equipment that requires installing a new adapter card, be sure you know which kind(s) of slots you have available and what kind of card you are buying.

Defining the Power Supply

All of your computer's internal components connect to the power supply in one way or another, usually by way of a bundle of wires. These wire bundles end in a plug that is pushed into the component.

Assuming you live in North America, your PC includes a power supply that turns the 110v alternating current (AC) from your electrical outlet into both 5 and 12v direct current (DC). This process generates plenty of heat, which is one reason the power supply has its own cooling fan. This fan also provides cool air for the rest of the computer, which generates heat as the electronic circuits are powered. The cooling fan doesn't draw cool air into the computer; rather, it blows hot air out of the rear of the computer. The result of this decompression is that cooler air is pulled in through the front and then over the components of the motherboard.

Power supplies are rated in watts. Most PCs have 200- to 300-watt power supplies. If you have a lot of extra devices installed and several peripherals attached to your computer, be sure you have an adequate power supply. The power supply's job is not an easy one; it starts the computer's hard disk from a dead stop to 3,600 revolutions per second while providing a safe, stable current to the motherboard. The motherboard can be ruined by simple static electricity, not to mention unstable power. And although it has plenty of built-in power protection, it may not be able to handle some electrical snafus, such as the following:

- *Voltage spikes*. Short-duration surges in the power line. Spikes can be quite short, as brief as a billionth of a second. Although unnoticed by lights and other electrical equipment, your computer can easily be damaged by a spike.

- *Power surges*. A longer version of the spike, these last several milliseconds. Power surges are invisible, but your PC may restart itself or simply shut down.

- *Brownouts*. Also known as a *power sag*, a brownout is when the line voltage falls below that required by your PC and other electrical devices. During a brownout, you will see lights dim, electrical motors slow down, and the display on your computer's monitor may shrink.

- *Blackout*. This involves complete interruption of power for more than a fraction of a second.

Power failures cost U.S. businesses more than $12 billion annually. The two best ways to protect yourself from these maladies are to use a surge protector and an uninterruptible power supply (UPS). *Surge protectors* protect you from simple voltage spikes, which are the most common type of damaging electrical failure. Some surge protectors also include protection for phone lines, which is important if you have a modem attached to your computer. (If the power doesn't get you, the phone line might, especially in an electrical storm.)

CAUTION

Absolutely no computer should ever be used without a surge protector, unless you have money to burn and really enjoy taking chances. The odds are just too great—ask any experienced computer user you know.

For highly important work or for areas that are prone to unreliable power, a UPS is a good idea. A UPS always runs your PC from a battery that is continually recharged by the electrical outlet. If an outage occurs, you'll have plenty of battery power to save your work and turn off the computer until the power is restored.

Part

I

Ch

2

How Software and Hardware Work Together

Now that you understand how the individual components of your computer work, let's put them all together.

As you enter information (*input*) from an input device (like the keyboard), electrical impulses are generated. The microprocessor (*CPU*) translates and temporarily stores these impulses in its electronic memory (*RAM*). The *software*, also stored temporarily in RAM, translates these impulses appropriately according to the task or command you've just entered. This information is then sent by the CPU to your monitor (*output*) so you can see what you're doing. If you're creating a document, for example, it appears on-screen. When you edit the document, you're changing data that's stored in temporary memory.

When you are finished with a document, you save it permanently to a magnetic disk (your hard drive or floppy drive). Whenever you want to work on the document again, you load the document into RAM from the disk. When you want to print (*output*) your document, you send a command to the software, which in turn sends your document as impulses to the CPU. The CPU translates the signal and sends it on to the printer. The printer reads the data in small units and places dots in appropriate places on the paper. ●

CHAPTER 3

Setting Up Your PC

When setting up your PC for the first time, it's important for you to do several things first, before you even start thinking about installing any software. Learn the do's and don'ts in this chapter. ■

Unpack and inspect your computer equipment

Make sure you have everything you need to set up your computer.

Positioning your computer for best use

Discover different ways to arrange your computer equipment to suit the way you work.

Connecting all the cables

Learn how to hook up all those wires and cables and protect your equipment from electrical damage.

Unpacking the Computer

It may seem simple, but sometimes it is difficult to unpack your computer without damaging the computer, packaging material, or yourself. The following steps show the best way to unpack your computer:

1. Cut the tape holding the box closed. Use just the tip of the knife so that you don't scratch anything.
2. Fold all four flaps of the box flat down against the sides of the box.
3. Slowly roll the box upside down so that the open end is facing the floor.
4. Lift the box up and away from the equipment and the packing material.
5. Remove all packing material and return it to the box.

Inspecting Your Computer

Once your computer equipment is out of the box, inspect it for damage. There shouldn't be any dents, broken switches, or cracked parts. You'll have a better chance of getting damaged components replaced if you identify them quickly after your purchase. If you wait, your dealer may be a little more skeptical when you explain that the cracked monitor base was "like that when we bought it."

Taking Inventory

Take a minute to confirm that you have everything you paid for and that the serial numbers on the equipment match both the boxes they arrived in, and the serial numbers on your receipt.

Matching serial numbers on the invoice and equipment are important if you ever need service under warranty. Your receipt proves the date of purchase, and the specific computer (via the serial number) you purchased. If the serial numbers on the receipt don't match those on the computer, you may have difficulty getting your computer serviced under warranty.

If the serial numbers on the box and computer don't match, it is likely that your computer was either returned by another customer and resold to you, or that the dealer had the system out of the box—possibly as a demonstration unit. That's not necessarily bad, but it is something you should know.

Saving Boxes and Packing Material

Computer boxes are bulky and difficult to store, and it may be tempting just to throw them out. However, if you think you'll ever need to move or ship your computer, you should keep all the boxes and packing material. This is especially important if you bought your computer through a mail order company, because shipping the computer back to them may be the only way you'll get warranty service on your computer (if you ever need it).

Positioning the CPU

Where you place the CPU (central processing unit) is largely a personal preference. There are, however, several things to watch out for:

- Place your computer where you can easily access the disk drives, power switches, reset buttons, and CD-ROM drawers.

- Try to keep it from sitting directly in front of a heater vent. Besides preventing the (remote) possibility of raising the operating temperature of your system beyond reliable limits, you're likely to greatly reduce the amount of dust that gets forced into your case.

- Make certain it is solidly placed so that an accidental bump won't send it crashing to the floor.

Plugging in the CPU

All computers require grounded, three-prong outlets for electrical power. Before plugging in your computer for the first time, make certain the power switch is in the off position (your computer may use the symbol I for on, and O for off).

NOTE   If your home doesn't have grounded, three-prong outlets, you'll need to get an adapter with a grounding strap. These adapters can be found at any hardware store. They plug into a standard two-prong outlet, and use a grounding wire that attaches to the screw in the center of your electrical plate cover to provide a ground. ▪

Positioning the Monitor

Like the CPU, setting up the monitor is simple. Here are a few basic tips:

- Position your monitor to reduce the amount of glare from both internal and external lighting.

- Make certain the power and video connector cables can reach their respective sockets (see the section "Extension Cables" later in the chapter if you need extra cable lengths).

- Your monitor should be elevated enough so that you can comfortably view the screen without having to crane your neck up or down.

Plugging in the Monitor

Your monitor's electrical cable may connect either to the wall (again a three-prong, grounded outlet) or to a power connector on the back of the computer.

Part

I

Ch

3

The monitor's video cable is a D-shaped connector that plugs into the matching connector on the back of your computer. Most computers sold in the last five years use VGA or SVGA monitors and video cards. That means they use a D-shaped connector with 15 pins. See Figure 3.1 for illustrations of the various connectors and ports. Once you've identified the video connector on the back of the CPU, carefully align the monitor cable connector and press it into place. For more information on connecting a monitor, see Chapter 11, "Monitors."

FIG. 3.1
Because each connector has a special shape and size, it's usually not hard to determine which device goes into which port.

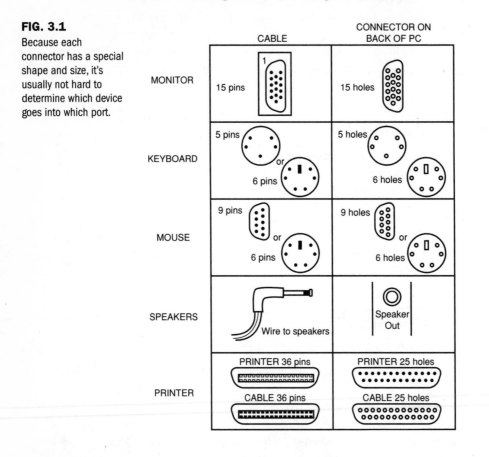

Positioning Keyboards and Mice

You want to position the keyboard and mouse at a height that is comfortable and one that reduces your risk of getting a repetitive stress injury such as carpal tunnel syndrome.

To determine the best height for your keyboard and mouse, follow these steps:

1. Sit comfortably in front of your keyboard.
2. Let your arms hang naturally at your sides and then lift your forearms until they are at a 90-degree angle from your upper arms.

3. Adjust your keyboard height so that your fingers rest lightly on the keyboard.

You may want to purchase a wrist rest so that your wrists are supported at that height as well.

Plugging in Keyboards and Mice

You'll notice a number of ports and plug-ins on the back of your computer. Two of those are for your mouse and keyboard. To plug in your keyboard and mouse, follow these steps:

1. Carefully examine the connector attached to both the keyboard and the mouse.
2. Find their matching connectors on the back of the computer.
3. Carefully align the connectors and press them into place.

Refer to Figure 3.1 for illustrations of the various connectors. For more information on connecting keyboards and mice, see Chapter 12, "Keyboards," and Chapter 13, "Mice and Joysticks."

Part

I

Ch

3

Positioning the Speakers

One of your computers speakers (if they aren't built-in) is likely to have a power switch, as well as volume and tone knobs. You'll want to be able to reach this speaker while sitting.

If your computer sound system has a subwoofer (which you can identify from your check of the packing list and serial numbers), you can place that speaker anywhere. This is because low-frequency sound is nondirectional—your ears can't tell which direction low-frequency sound is coming from.

Other than those two tips, you only need to make certain your speaker's cables can reach the CPU.

Connecting the Speakers

Most PC speakers have separate power and audio cables. The power cords typically have a transformer built-in to the AC power connector. The audio connector looks much like those found on the headphones of Walkmans. That connector connects to the Audio Out port on your sound card. Because these connectors are round and have no pins, all you need to do is find the Audio Out port and plug your speakers in. Refer to Figure 3.1 for illustrations of speaker connectors. For more information, see Chapter 16, "Speakers and Sound."

Positioning the Printer

Your printer can go pretty much anywhere. It is convenient, but not necessary, to have it close enough to reach the various buttons, power switches, and the paper output tray. It should also be positioned so that you have room to add paper when necessary and so that nothing obstructs the paper as it exits the printer.

Attaching the Printer

Most new printers connect to the computer via a parallel cable (refer to Figure 3.1 for illustrations of a parallel cable and connectors). Your printer may have a serial cable and will need to connect to one of the serial ports on your computer. After you've determined which port on the CPU matches the one on your printer cable, align the connector and press it in place. You can then plug the power cable into the wall.

N O T E If your printer connects via a serial connector, Windows will require you to configure your serial port before you can print. You'll have to refer to your printer's documentation for advice on which settings to select. ▧

Extension Cables

Depending on how you set up your computer, you may need extender cables for your monitor, printer, or keyboard. You can get these cables from your computer dealer. Extender cables give you additional flexibility in where you place your monitor, keyboard, or printer. For example, you might decide to place the CPU on its side on the floor, and your monitor and keyboard above on the desk. Typically, the cables from your monitor and keyboard won't be long enough to reach a CPU set up under the desk. Using extension cables allows you to increase the length of your monitor and keyboard cables, thus allowing you to place your system exactly as you want.

Protecting Your Computer from Electrical Damage

Normal AC outlets in your house provide electrical current that surges (increases in voltage) and spikes (brief, high increases), which can damage your computer equipment. To prevent this damage, your computer manufacturer strongly recommends the use of a high-quality surge suppresser. Surge suppressers regulate the flow of electricity to your computer equipment. A decent surge suppresser, with six protected outlets and a main power switch, typically costs more than $30. Don't be fooled by the multi-outlet powerstrip devices that have some small fuse as protection— they aren't worth the money.

One additional benefit of a surge suppresser is that its master power switch can be used to turn all of your equipment on or off at the same time. ●

Using Your PC

4 Starting, Stopping, and Using Your PC 39

5 Starting Programs and Working with Windows 49

6 Working with Applications 61

CHAPTER 4

Starting, Stopping, and Using Your PC

Just like anything electrical, your computer must be turned on before you can use it. It's important to know how to power up the computer and its attachments correctly, what to do when it's ready to go, and how to close up shop when you're finished working. This chapter will run you through all of these steps. You'll also get help on some common problems that might pop up during start up and shutdown.

Powering up

Understand how Windows 95 "pulls itself up by its bootstraps" and gets the computer ready for you to use.

Overview of the Windows 95 desktop

Take a guided tour of the main screen parts and tools and what they're used for.

Why it's important to shut down the system properly

The extra minute or two you take to power down correctly *now* could save you hours of work and a lot of money later.

How to deal with problems during startup and shutdown

Windows is not perfect, and sometimes you'll run into trouble getting in or out. Check this section for solutions to common problems.

Powering Up Your System

Just like anything electrical, your computer must be turned on before you can use it, and it's important to know how to power up the computer and its attachments correctly to avoid possible damage to your system or loss of data.

To start up the computer and get it ready for use:

1. Make sure the surge protector is turned on and plugged in. Check your floppy drive to make sure you didn't leave a disk in it. If you did, remove it before proceeding.

2. Turn on the monitor. During startup, your computer may give you information or ask you questions.

3. Turn on the printer, along with any other attached equipment such as the modem, speakers, or external drive, and give them a few seconds to warm up. As long as the devices are running prior to system boot up, Windows 95 will automatically recognize the equipment and have it ready to go for you. If not, you may have to restart the system when you want to use the device. And in some cases, the system may not start at all without the devices.

TIP

Check the volume level on your speakers to make sure you don't blow yourself away when the system sound starts to play.

4. Turn on the system unit last.

CAUTION

You might be tempted to use the surge protector's power button to turn on all the equipment at one time instead of the individual component's power buttons. *This is not a good idea.* Not only could this lead to problems during startup, it could cause a power surge itself—which certainly defeats the purpose of the surge protector.

After you turn on the system, the computer begins its bootup routine (or startup procedures). It puts itself through a series of short tests to make sure all of its internal chips and boards are working correctly. You will see several messages flash by, usually telling you information about the make, model, and manufacturer, how much memory and CPU speed the computer has, and other details.

Next, the CPU identifies the operating system (watch for the message Starting Windows 95...) and looks to it for further instructions. It reads information from special configuration files on the hard drive, and loads any needed drivers or files based on those instructions. After a few moments, the Windows 95 logo appears on the screen. When the operating system has completed setup and loading, you are presented with the Windows 95 desktop, as seen in Figure 4.1.

FIG. 4.1
The desktop is the central point of operation for Windows 95.

Shortcut icons —

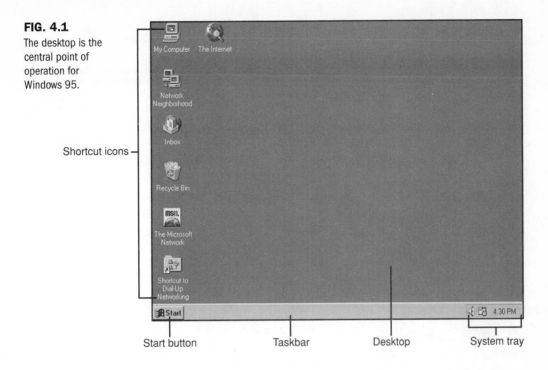

Start button · · · · Taskbar · · · · Desktop · · · · System tray

Part

II

Ch

4

N O T E If your computer is attached to a network, or it's set up for use by more than one person, Windows may ask you for your account name and password before it makes the desktop available. See also the section "Troubleshooting Startup" later in this chapter. ▪

Identifying Icons

In Figure 4.1, you'll notice several small pictures running vertically down the left side of the screen. These pictures are called *icons*; they give you easy shortcut access to the files, programs, and tools buried within your computer. Each type of file (such as a Word for Windows document, an Excel spreadsheet, or the applications themselves) has a different type of icon so that you can easily identify the file's type.

▶ **See** "Creating Shortcuts to Files or Folders," **p. 90**

Because different manufacturers and suppliers provide different software with their computers, your desktop may have a few more or less icons. Table 4.1 shows you what the most common ones represent.

Table 4.1   Standard Windows 95 Desktop Icons

Icon	Name	Description	For More Information, See
	My Computer	Gives you access to all the files and folders on your computer.	Chapter 8, "Managing Your Files"
	The Internet	Shortcut to Internet Explorer, Microsoft's free Web browser.	Chapter 18, "What Is the Internet?"
	Click here for Neighborhood	Network access to other computers on your network.	Chapter 10, "Working with Networks"
	Inbox	The Inbox is where you receive, send, and organize your e-mail and faxes.	Chapter 21, "Sending and Receiving E-Mail"
	Recycle Bin	If you delete files, they are stored here for a period of time— just in case you need to get them back.	Chapter 8, "Managing Your Files"

Using the Start Button

As you might suspect, the Start button is the beginning point for many Windows tasks. When you point the mouse to the Start button and click, the Start menu appears, showing you all the different programs you have on your computer. You also click the Start button to get to tools like Help, and to shut down Windows when your work is complete.

N O T E If you've never used a mouse before, you should go immediately to Chapter 13, "Mice and Joysticks." In that chapter, you learn how a mouse works and why it can save you valuable time. ■

The Start menu is the primary control center for Windows 95 applications and tools. From here, you can open programs and files, access customization tools and settings, and launch utilities that help you keep your PC in good shape.

As Figure 4.2 illustrates, the Start menu is a collection of folders and shortcuts. Most of these items are installed during Windows installation, or when you add new software to your PC.

FIG. 4.2
The Start menu is the control center for Windows 95 applications.

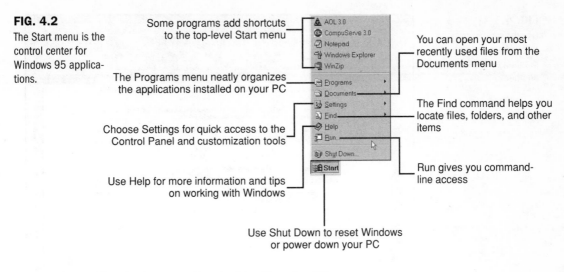

Some programs add shortcuts to the top-level Start menu

The Programs menu neatly organizes the applications installed on your PC

Choose Settings for quick access to the Control Panel and customization tools

Use Help for more information and tips on working with Windows

You can open your most recently used files from the Documents menu

The Find command helps you locate files, folders, and other items

Run gives you command-line access

Use Shut Down to reset Windows or power down your PC

▶ **See** "Starting Programs from the Start Menu," **p. 50**

Using the Taskbar

Along the bottom of your screen, you should see a long gray box (to which the Start button is connected). This is the *Windows taskbar*, and knowing how it works will greatly improve your productivity.

One of the great things about Windows is that you can run several different programs at the same time. You might have Word running to write a memo, the Calculator open to check some figures for the memo as you write, and My Computer open to access files on your hard drive. As you open each program, a new button for that program appears in the task bar. The taskbar helps you keep track of all running applications and allows you quick, point-and-click access to switch between them (see Figure 4.3).

To switch to another open application, click the program's button in the taskbar. The chosen window will come to the front and other open windows will wait patiently in the background until you switch back to them.

T I P To temporarily hide all the open windows on your screen and get back to the desktop, right-click an empty place on the taskbar and choose Minimize All Windows from the shortcut menu that appears.

The taskbar is an integral part of working with Windows 95 and your PC. You'll find additional tricks and tips for using the taskbar in the next chapter.

Part
II

Ch
4

FIG. 4.3
Use the taskbar to switch from one open program or document to another.

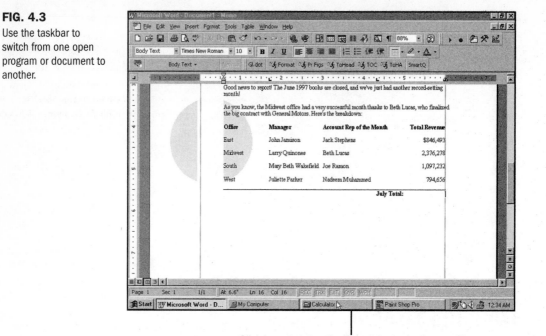

Click here to bring the Calculator to the front and add up the sales figures for your report

Using the System Tray

The *System Tray* is a special area at the right end of the taskbar. You may see several different icons in the Tray—and almost always the system clock. The Tray gives you quick access to certain programs and tools. Depending on your computer setup and installed programs, the Tray may include a volume control for your sound card, easy access to your monitor's display settings, and more. Some Windows applications, such as Corel WordPerfect Suite, add even more items to the Tray.

 T I P To quickly check today's date, point your mouse to the clock in the Tray. After a slight pause, a box (called a *ToolTip*) appears, momentarily showing the date, as shown in Figure 4.4.

FIG. 4.4
Forgotten what day it is? Point to the clock in the System Tray for a quick reminder.

Shutting Down Your Computer

When you're finished working on the computer, be sure to shut down the system properly. Just like you wouldn't turn the power off to your cassette player without stopping the tape first, you shouldn't simply turn the power off to shut down your PC. Windows needs to clean up after itself, close all the files it has open in memory, make sure everything is saved to disk that should be, and stop and cool down its internal moving parts. Simply flipping the power switch can damage important files, eat up room on your hard drive, and cause your system unnecessary problems.

To properly and safely shut down the computer, follow these steps:

1. Save any work you currently have open, such as documents or games. Close any running applications and modem connections. If you have an MS-DOS session window open, close it, too.

2. Click the Start button on the taskbar and choose Shut Down.

3. In the Shut Down Windows dialog box that appears, click the Shut Down the Computer? check box and click OK or press Enter.

Windows performs its shut down routine. When it's complete, you'll see the message It is now safe to turn off your computer. At that point, it's okay to flip off the power switch. (Some computers automatically turn the power off for you, so you don't even have to do that.) See also the section "Troubleshooting Crashes and Shutdowns" later in this chapter for more information.

Part
II

Ch
4

Resetting Your Computer

There are a number of instances when you might need to temporarily shut down your computer and boot it back up again immediately. For example, if you install a new software program, it's usually best to restart the computer before using the new program.

Just like shutting down when you're finished working, don't just flip the switch—not even the Reset button. Instead, there is a safe and easy way to reboot the system that won't cause you problems down the road: *a warm boot*. A warm boot prevents wear and tear on the computer's internal parts. Here's how to perform a warm boot:

1. Click the Start button, then choose Shut Down.

2. In the Shut Down Windows dialog box that appears, choose Restart the Computer? and then click OK or press Enter.

TIP If you only want to restart Windows itself and not go through the entire reboot process, press and hold down the Shift button when you click OK.

Windows will temporarily close up shop and restart the computer for you. If for some reason the computer locks up and won't let you restart from the Shut Down menu, or fails to complete the Restart routine properly, *then* it's okay to use the computer's Reset button.

Troubleshooting Crashes and Shutdowns

Occasionally, you may find that your computer has locked up and won't respond. The following tips should help you get around those problems and get back to work.

One Program Is Locked Up, but Others Seem to Be Working Fine

Because of its multitasking capabilities, Windows is pretty good about controlling applications individually. If a single application is frozen and won't respond, it normally doesn't effect other running applications.

To close a single frozen application, follow these steps:

1. Press Ctrl+Alt+Delete. The Close Program dialog box appears, displaying a list of all open programs.
2. Look for any program with the words [not responding] next to the problem application. When you find it, click it to select it.
3. Click the End Task button. Windows will shut down the frozen program.

N O T E   If Windows does not respond immediately, wait a few seconds. You should see a second dialog box appear with information about the frozen program. Read the message and respond accordingly.

4. Repeat these steps for any other programs that say [not responding]. When all errant programs have been closed, it's a good idea to save your work, close all running applications, and restart the computer as described earlier in this chapter.
5. If there is no frozen application, or if step 3 doesn't unfreeze your system, click the Shut Down button in the Close Program dialog box.

Everything Is Frozen—I Can't Even Get to the Start Button

Sometimes one bad application causes everything else to freeze up, too. (This is especially true if you are running older applications that were not specifically designed for Windows 95.) If this is the case, try these steps:

1. Press Ctrl+Alt+Delete. The Close Program dialog box appears, displaying a list of all open programs. Follow the steps in the previous section to close any errant applications.
2. If this doesn't help, press Ctrl+Alt+Delete again and click Shut Down. Windows will attempt to resolve the problem(s) and shut the system down properly.
3. When you get the message that it's okay to turn off the power, press the Restart button on your computer. (If your computer automatically turns its power off, wait at least 20 seconds before turning it back on.)

The Computer Will Not Respond to Ctrl+Alt+Delete

If you can't get any response at all from your computer—no mouse, no keyboard, no anything—as a last resort, press the Restart button on your computer. You will lose any work that has not been saved, and you may need to run some system maintenance utilities, such as ScanDisk, before you can get back to work. If you're running the OSR2 version of Windows 95, ScanDisk runs automatically when the computer is shut down without the typical shutdown procedures.

Troubleshooting Startup

Your PC may occasionally have trouble powering up, loading the operating system, or getting itself ready for use—especially if the shutdown procedure was not normal. This section offers some advice on common problems you may run into.

No Power

Check to make sure that the surge protector switch is turned on, and that all your cables and cords are snugly connected.

Error Message: *Keyboard locked* or *System Locked*

Some computers have a security lock to prevent it from being used. Insert the key and turn it to the unlocked position, then press any key to continue.

Error Message: *System Disk* or *Non-System Disk Error*

You've probably left a floppy disk in the drive. Remove it, then press any key to continue. Startup should proceed normally. If there's no floppy disk in the drive, you may have a serious problem. Seek help from a qualified professional.

Error Message: *Windows 95 Was Not Properly Shut Down*

You may see this message if you had a system crash or abnormal shutdown. Windows may say it needs to run ScanDisk before starting. If so, press any key to continue and follow the instructions on-screen.

Computer Starts Normally, but Windows Won't Load

If Windows locks up during startup, you need to restart Windows in Safe mode.

1. Press Ctrl+Alt+Delete. (If no response, press the Reset button.) During reboot, watch the on-screen messages. When you see the message Starting Windows 95..., press the F8 key.
2. From the DOS menu that appears, press 3 to select Safe mode, then press Enter. See the next section for help on working in Safe mode.

Windows Won't Start in Safe Mode, Either

If you tried the preceding steps and Windows won't launch in Safe mode, insert your Windows Startup floppy disk and restart the computer again. You may need to get help from a qualified professional to get Windows working again. If all else fails, you may have to reinstall Windows 95.

Windows Is Running in Safe Mode. Now What?

Safe mode is a special Windows troubleshooting that uses a very simple configuration. When running in Safe mode, you may not have access to your network or to some of the devices attached to your computer. You only use Safe mode to solve problems—don't try to run it this way all the time.

If Windows starts you in Safe mode, follow these steps:

1. Often, Windows can correct problems all by itself—just starting once in Safe mode is all it needs. Exit Windows by clicking the Start button and selecting Sh<u>u</u>t down. When the Shut Down Windows dialog box appears, select the <u>R</u>estart the Computer? option.

2. If Windows starts in Safe mode again, check your configuration settings—especially display and device settings. (You may need to get help from a qualified professional.) Correct any settings as needed and repeat step 1.

CHAPTER 5

Starting Programs and Working with Windows

Thanks to tools like the Start menu and the taskbar, Windows 95 makes working in two or more programs even easier. In this chapter, you'll learn how to start up applications and manage them when they're running. You'll also discover and learn how to use some of Windows' other tools when the Start menu just isn't enough. ∎

How to start a program

The Windows 95 Start menu gives you quick access to all your applications. You'll also learn some shortcuts to opening programs and files.

Resize program windows

You can make a window smaller, larger, and even hide it temporarily.

Switch between programs already running

Learn some quick tips for moving back and forth between the programs you have running.

Locate missing programs or documents

If a program isn't on the Start menu, but you know it's been installed, use Window's Find feature to hunt it down.

Customize the Start menu

Windows doesn't always set things up the way you think is best. If you have a better idea, you can rearrange the Start menu to make it work for you.

Starting Programs in Windows

Windows users can employ a number of techniques to find and launch programs, and—thanks to Windows' multitasking capability—users can have several programs open and running at the same time. The most common methods for starting programs in Windows are:

■ By using the Start and Programs menus

■ Through My Computer or Windows Explorer

■ By creating and using a desktop shortcut icon

■ By starting an application from a document

■ By using the Run command

The following sections review each of these techniques and provide information on managing and moving between multiple program windows.

Starting Programs from the Start Menu

The Start menu is the primary control center for Windows 95 applications and tools. From here you can open programs and files, access customization tools and settings, and launch utilities that help you keep your PC in good shape.

▶ **See** "Shutting Down Your Computer," **p. 45**

▶ **See** "Troubleshooting Windows 95," **p. 257**

To start a program from the Start menu, use the following steps. For this example, we'll open *Notepad*, a simple text editor that comes with Windows 95:

1. Click the Start button to produce the Start menu shown in Figure 5.1.

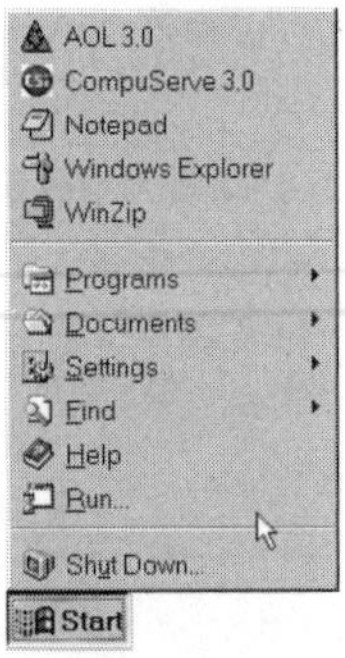

FIG. 5.1

The Start menu is a launching point for Windows 95 applications.

2. Point to Programs; the selection is highlighted and a list of installed programs appears.

3. Point to Accessories (the folder in which the Notepad shortcut resides), as shown in Figure 5.2. The Accessories folder is highlighted and opens, showing available programs and utilities.

FIG. 5.2
Sometimes the program you want is a few layers down in the Programs menu.

4. Click Notepad. Windows 95 closes the Start menu and opens a blank Notepad window, ready for you to begin working.

Notice that the taskbar has added a button indicating that an untitled Notepad document is open.

Starting Programs from My Computer

If the Start menu is not your style, or if you aren't quite sure where a program is, you can use My Computer to open a program as well. Again, we'll use Notepad as our example:

1. From the desktop, right-click My Computer and choose Open from the shortcut menu that appears. A window appears showing all the drives on your computer.

2. Double-click the icon that represents your primary hard drive (usually, the C drive). My Computer opens a new window, displaying the contents of the drive.

3. Double-click the Windows folder. A long list of folders and files appears. You may need to drag the scroll bar to the left to see more files, as shown in Figure 5.3.

4. Find the file called Notepad.exe, and double-click it. Windows opens another blank Notepad session, and adds its button to the taskbar.

Starting Programs from Windows Explorer

Windows Explorer is a file management utility that helps you find and organize all the files and programs on your computer. You'll learn more about using Windows Explorer in Chapter 8, "Managing Your Files." Once you're used to working in Windows Explorer, you may find that sometimes it's easier to launch a program directly from Explorer than to use another method.

Part
II

Ch
5

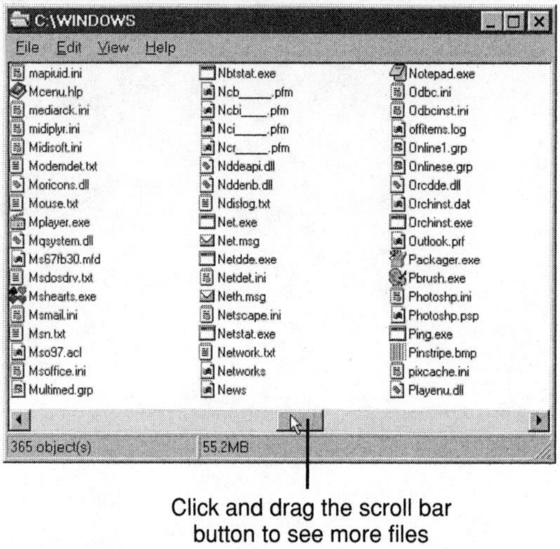

FIG. 5.3

Scroll bars help you see more of the contents if the open window can't display it all.

Click and drag the scroll bar
button to see more files

For this example, we'll open the Windows Calculator. To launch a program from Windows Explorer, follow these steps:

1. Click the Start button and click Programs.
2. Click Windows Explorer. A two-paned window opens, displaying the contents of your primary hard drive (see Figure 5.4).

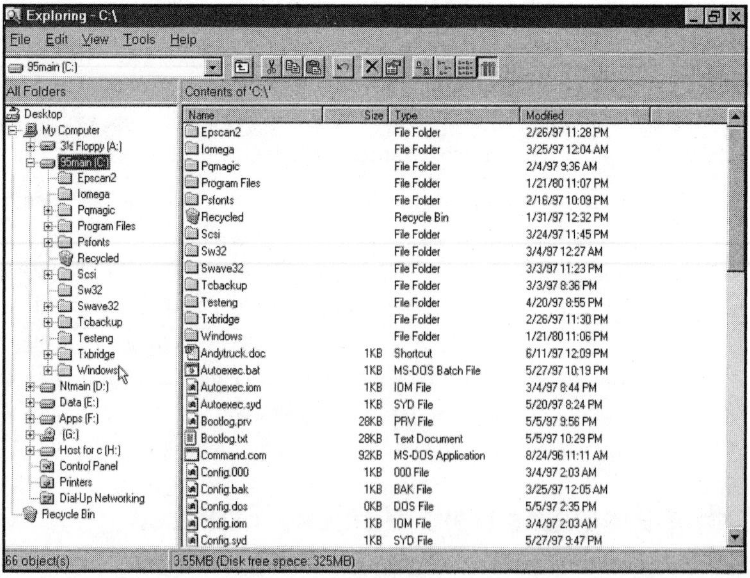

FIG. 5.4

Windows Explorer helps you manage files and folders, giving you access to everything in one handy window.

3. In the left pane, you see all the drives attached to your computer. If your primary hard drive is not selected, double-click it now.

4. The right pane of Windows Explorer shows you all the files and folders on this drive. Look for the folder called Windows and double-click it.

5. Because the Windows folder contains many items, you will probably need to drag the scroll bar on the right side of the screen to find the file you're looking for. Drag down until you see the file called Calc.exe.

6. When you find it, double-click it to open the Windows Calculator. Notice that Windows has added the Calculator to the taskbar.

Starting a Program by Opening a Document

You can also start many programs by opening documents created in those programs. You can use this technique by opening documents in the Documents list, My Computer, or Windows Explorer. To start the program and open the document, use the Documents list from the Start menu, My Computer, or Windows Explorer to locate the document. Double-click the document icon or listed name. The program in which the document was created opens, as does the document.

Starting Programs with Shortcut Icons

If the program you want to open has a shortcut icon on the Windows desktop, you easily can start the program by double-clicking the icon. If the program has no desktop icon, you can create one in Windows using the techniques described in the "Adding Shortcut Icons to the Desktop" section later in this chapter.

Starting a Program with the Run Command

You can use the Run command to start applications that don't automatically appear on the Start menu. To use the Run command:

1. Click the Start button.

2. Click the Run option. The Run dialog box opens.

3. Type the Run command required by your software. If you don't remember the command, check your software documentation for command instructions. Alternatively, click the Browse button in the Run dialog box, then locate the file for the program you want to open; select the file to enter it in the Run dialog box.

4. Click OK.

Working with Programs

Windows multitasking capabilities make it easy to work with several open programs at once, and to size and move windows. The following sections describe the techniques for working with program windows.

Part

II

Ch

5

Switching Between Open Programs

As explained in Chapter 4, "Starting, Stopping, and Using Your PC," the Windows 95 taskbar enables you to easily switch between open programs. The taskbar adds a button for each open program. To switch to another open program, you simply click that program's button in the taskbar (see Figure 5.5).

TIP Another quick way to switch between open windows is to press and hold the Alt key, then press the Tab key repeatedly to highlight the window you want to bring to the front.

FIG. 5.5
Use the taskbar to switch between open windows.

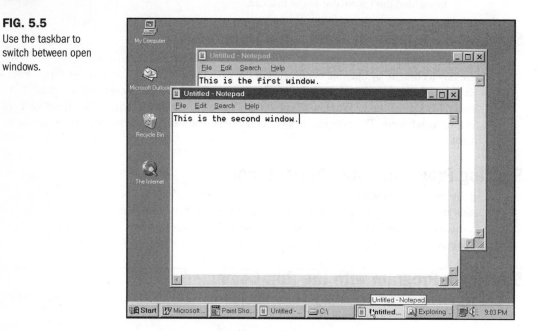

Moving and Resizing Open Program Windows

To make working in Windows more convenient, you can change the size of any open window on the screen—make it smaller, larger, or even temporarily hide it out of the way.

N O T E In the steps for this section, use the Notepad window we opened in an earlier section. To make your screen less cluttered, you may want to close any other open windows following the steps in the "Closing Open Programs" section later in this chapter. ■

There are a variety of methods you can use to move or resize a window:

■ *Move.* To move a window to a different place on the screen, click its title bar and drag it to the desired location.

- *Resize.* If you want to make a window a little bigger or smaller, click and drag the lower-right corner until the window is the desired size.

- *Minimize.* To temporarily hide a window, click the Minimize button. Click the program's taskbar button to unhide the window.

- *Maximize.* To make a window fill the entire screen, click the Maximize button or double-click the window's title bar.

- *Restore.* To return a maximized window to its original size, click Restore or double-click the window's title bar.

TIP To minimize all open windows at once and return to the Windows desktop, right-click a blank area on the taskbar and choose Minimize All Windows.

Closing Open Programs

There are several ways to close open applications, but the easiest way is to use the Close button at the top-right corner of the program's window (see Figure 5.6).

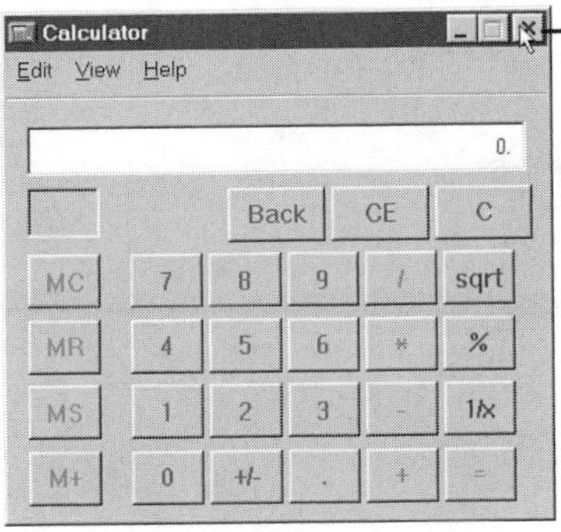

FIG. 5.6
Use the Close button to quit an application when you're finished with it.

Click the X to close the program

Part
II

Ch
5

Another easy way to close an open window is to right-click the program's button on the taskbar, then choose Close from the menu that appears.

Finding Missing Programs or Files

If you've forgotten where you stored a particular program or file, and can't find it on the Start menu or in Windows Explorer, Windows 95's Find feature can help you locate it quickly.

To find a missing file, follow these steps:

1. From the Start menu, click Find, then choose Files or Folders. The Find: All Folders dialog box appears.

2. Type the name of the file you want to find in the Named box (see Figure 5.7). (You can enter the entire file name, or just part of it; Windows will list all file names containing the letters you supply. It does not matter if you use upper- or lowercase letters.)

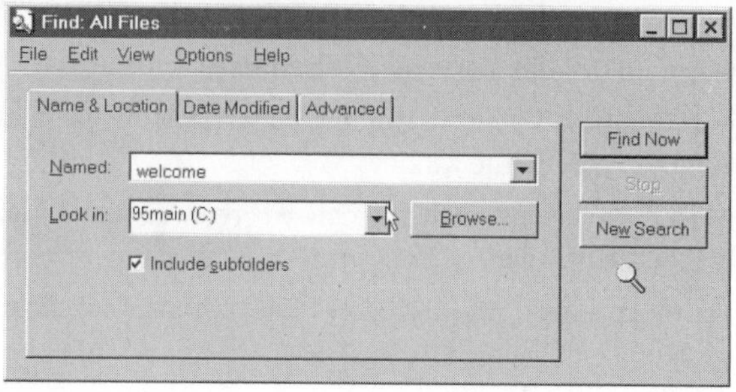

FIG. 5.7
Windows 95's Find feature comes in handy when you don't remember where you saved a file or installed a program.

3. Use the Look In box to tell Windows where you think the file might be located. Click the arrow next to the box to see a list of each drive on your PC. If you want to choose a specific folder on a specific drive, click Browse, then select the appropriate folder.

4. If you want Windows to look in all the subfolders (folders inside other folders) on the chosen drive, click the Include Subfolders option to select it.

5. When you're ready to begin the search, click Find Now. Windows searches the designated areas and provides a list of its findings in the lower portion of the Find dialog box (see Figure 5.8).

6. You can run the found program directly from the list.

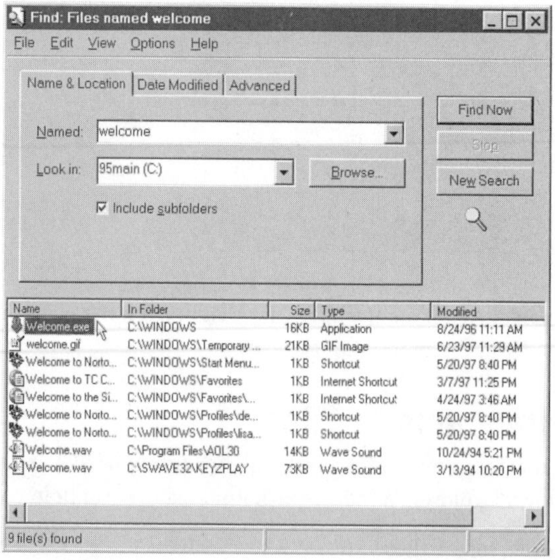

FIG. 5.8
Windows gives you a list of all files that match your specifications. It's up to you to determine exactly which file it is you wanted.

Adding Shortcut Icons to the Desktop

Starting programs from the Windows desktop or the Start menu is the easiest and quickest way to get to work quickly. Windows installation automatically creates some shortcut icons, but you may want to add others. To place a shortcut icon on the Windows desktop:

1. Use My Computer to locate the program for which you want to create a shortcut icon. (In most cases, you can locate the program by clicking the C drive, then clicking the Program Files folder.) If necessary, size the My Computer window so you can see the Windows desktop.

2. Click the program to select it.

3. Open the File menu and select Create Shortcut. Windows places a shortcut icon in the active window.

4. Drag the shortcut icon to the desktop.

To delete a shortcut icon:

1. Right-click the shortcut icon.

2. Select Delete from the pop-up menu.

3. A dialog box asks you to verify that the shortcut is to be deleted. Click Yes.

Customizing the Start Menu

In Windows 95, you can add programs to and remove programs from the Start menu. You also can rearrange the order of programs within the Start menu.

Adding Programs to the Start Menu

Most programs designed for Windows 95 will automatically add themselves to the Start menu during installation. If you have an older program or one that runs in DOS, it may not have a Start menu shortcut.

To add a program to the Start menu, use the following steps:

1. Using Find or Windows Explorer, locate and select (click the name to highlight) the program you want to add.

2. Drag the file to the Start button and release it. Windows adds a shortcut for the program to the main level of the Start menu.

3. To see the shortcut, click the Start button to open the Start menu (see Figure 5.9).

Part
II

Ch
5

FIG. 5.9

Adding files and programs to the Start menu could not be easier.

> **TIP** You can add any kind of file to the Start menu—programs, shortcuts to favorite folders, even frequently used documents. The procedure is identical no matter what type of file you're adding.

Removing Programs from the Start Menu

Programs designed specifically for Windows 95 will remove their Start menu shortcuts when you uninstall the program. If you remove a program that wasn't designed specifically for Windows 95, you can remove the menu item manually. Follow these steps:

1. Right-click the Start button and choose Open from the menu that appears. Windows opens the Start menu in a window that shows you all the installed shortcuts.

2. Find the shortcut you want to remove. (If the program is located in the Programs submenu of the Start menu, you will have to open the Programs subfolder to get to the shortcut.) Select it, and press Delete.

3. If Windows asks you to confirm the deletion, click Yes.

Rearranging Programs on the Start Menu

Microsoft designed Windows 95 to be as user-friendly as possible, and one example of this effort is the ability to customize the Start menu to your liking.

To customize the arrangement of your Start menu, follow these steps:

1. From the Start menu, click Settings, then choose Taskbar. The Taskbar Properties dialog box appears.

2. Click the Start Menu Programs tab at the top of the dialog box (see Figure 5.10).

FIG. 5.10
The Taskbar Properties dialog box offers another way to manage your Start menu shortcuts.

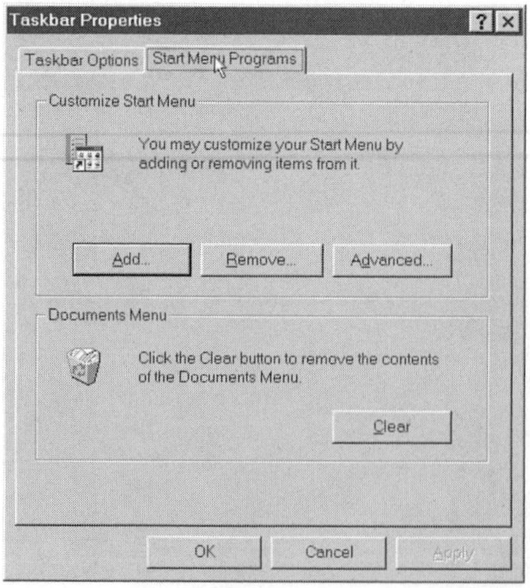

3. Click the Advanced button to open an Explorer window showing all the items in the Start menu and its folders (see Figure 5.11).

FIG. 5.11

You can add, delete, rename, and rearrange Start menu shortcuts just like you would any other files on your computer.

Exploring - C:\WINDOWS\Profiles\desktop\Start Menu			

File Edit View Tools Help

Start Menu

All Folders | Contents of 'C:\WINDOWS\Profiles\desktop\Start Menu'

Start Menu
Programs

Name	Size	Type	Modified
Programs		File Folder	7/6/97 5:51 PM
AOL 3.0	1KB	Shortcut	5/10/97 8:37 AM
CompuServe 3.0	1KB	Shortcut	5/12/97 11:31 PM
Notepad	1KB	Shortcut	5/16/97 9:19 PM
Windows Explorer	1KB	Shortcut	5/13/97 2:33 PM
WinZip	1KB	Shortcut	6/12/97 12:22 AM

6 object(s) | 1.64KB (Disk free space: 293MB)

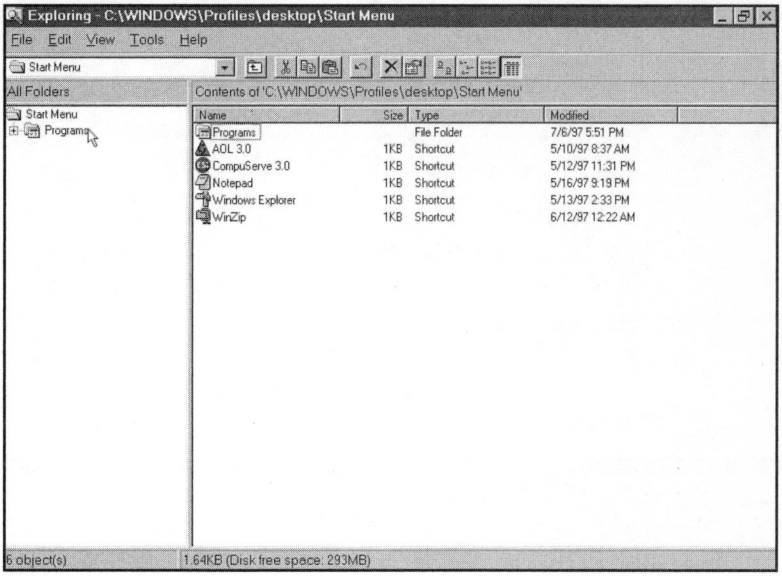

4. From here, you can add or delete shortcuts, rename menu items, layer folders inside one another, and more. Start menu shortcuts are managed just like any other files on your computer. For more details on how to move, rename, or work with shortcut files in Windows Explorer, see Chapter 8, "Managing Your Files."

Part

II

Ch

5

CHAPTER 6

Working with Applications

Most of your time spent using your computer will actually be spent using an application. In this chapter, you first learn about the different types of applications. Then you learn some key skills for working with applications. ■

Work with applications

Get a quick overview of the different types of applications.

Select and format text and numbers

Some skills—like selecting and formatting text—are so fundamental they apply to nearly all applications. This chapter shows you the fundamentals of selecting and formatting text.

Cut, copy, and paste information

The key editing skills—cutting, copying, and pasting—are covered here.

Automatically update and link information

Learn the basics of linking data in this section.

Save, open, and print your work

You can't learn a more important skill than how to manage your files. This chapter shows you how to save your text (even in a different format, if you choose), open files, and print your work.

Describing Types of Applications

To perform a certain type of task using your computer—for example, typing a letter—you need an application or program for that task. When you purchase a new PC, you may receive some applications as part of the purchase. Windows 95 also includes some mini-applications. Though these applications will get you started, you may want to purchase additional applications as you learn to do more and more with your PC.

The basic types of applications are:

- Word processors
- Spreadsheet programs
- Database programs
- Graphics and presentation programs
- Personal information managers
- Suites or bundles

The following sections discuss each of these application types in more detail.

N O T E   You will hear the terms *program*, *application*, or some combination (*application program*) used interchangeably. They all mean the same thing.

Word Processors

The most common type of application is word processing. Microsoft Word and Corel Word-Perfect are two examples of word processing applications. WordPad is a word processing mini-application that comes packaged with Windows 95.

You can use word processing applications to create documents such as letters, memos, reports, manuscripts, and so on.

Word processing programs, however, are more than just a fancy typewriter. They offer many editing and formatting features so that you have a great deal of control over the content and look of your document. Here's a quick list of some of the things you can do with this type of program:

- *Easily edit text.* You can move text from one page to another, even one document to another. You can also copy or delete text with just a few keystrokes.
- *Format text, paragraphs, and pages.* Formatting means changing the appearance of text. You can make text bold, change the font, use a different color, and so on. Most word processing programs also enable you to format paragraphs (indent, add bullets, add a border) and pages (change the margins, add page numbers, insert a header). Later in this chapter you learn how to make some formatting changes.
- *Check accuracy.* Most programs include a spell check program for checking spelling. Some programs also include programs for checking grammar.

Word processing programs differ in what features they offer. If your tasks are basic, WordPad (the simple word processing program included with Windows) may meet your needs. WordPad includes key editing and formatting features.

You need a more complete word processing program if you plan to create a lot of documents and want more control and features. One of the most popular programs, Word for Windows, includes all of the preceding features as well as desktop publishing features for setting up columns, inserting tables, adding graphics, and so on (see Figure 6.1). Word for Windows also includes features for sending faxes, creating Web documents, and much more.

FIG. 6.1
Word for Windows is the most popular word processing program.

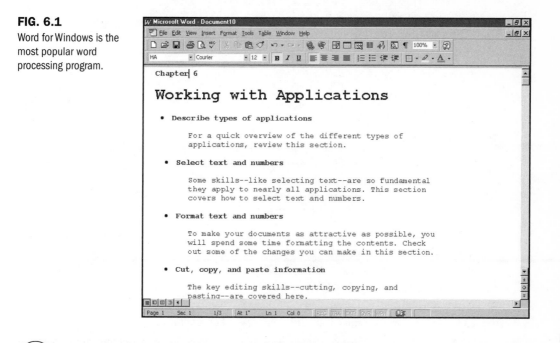

> **TIP**
> If you want the utmost control over the printed document, you may want to use—in addition to a word processing program—a desktop publishing program. These programs provide even more control of the layout of the page. Microsoft Publisher is a fairly simple desktop publishing program. Adobe PageMaker is a more robust package.

Part
II

Ch
6

Spreadsheets

If numbers are your game, then you will most likely work with a spreadsheet application. This type of program enables you to enter and manipulate all kinds of financial information: budgets, sales statistics, income, expenses, and so on. You enter these figures in a *worksheet*, a grid of columns and rows (see Figure 6.2). The intersection of a row and a column is called a *cell*, and you enter text, numbers, or formulas into the cells to create a worksheet.

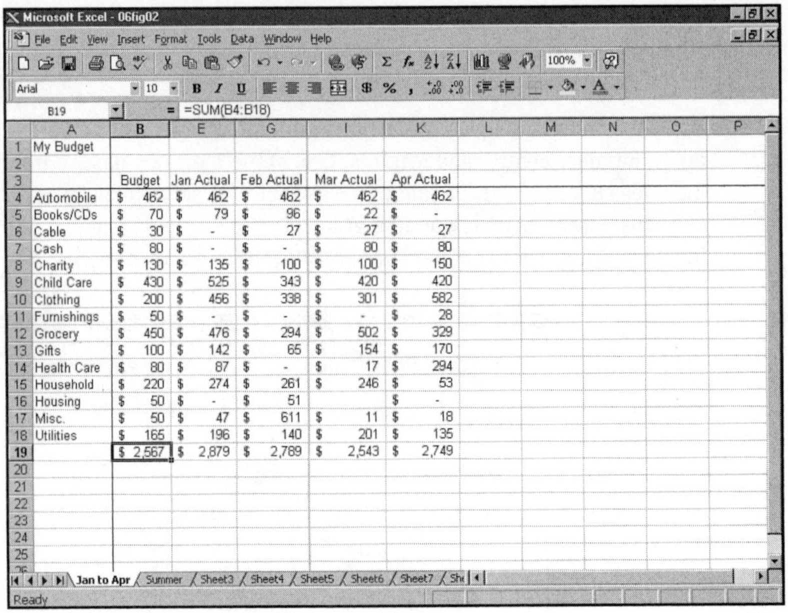

FIG. 6.2
Use a spreadsheet program for any type of numerical data you want to calculate or track.

Microsoft Excel - 06fig02

File Edit View Insert Format Tools Data Window Help

Arial — 10 — B I U | $ % , | B19 = =SUM(B4:B18)

My Budget

	Budget	Jan Actual	Feb Actual	Mar Actual	Apr Actual
Automobile	$ 462	$ 462	$ 462	$ 462	$ 462
Books/CDs	$ 70	$ 79	$ 96	$ 22	$ -
Cable	$ 30	$ -	$ 27	$ 27	$ 27
Cash	$ 80	$ -	$ -	$ 80	$ 80
Charity	$ 130	$ 135	$ 100	$ 100	$ 150
Child Care	$ 430	$ 525	$ 343	$ 420	$ 420
Clothing	$ 200	$ 456	$ 338	$ 301	$ 582
Furnishings	$ 50	$ -	$ -	$ -	$ 28
Grocery	$ 450	$ 476	$ 294	$ 502	$ 329
Gifts	$ 100	$ 142	$ 65	$ 154	$ 170
Health Care	$ 80	$ 87	$ -	$ 17	$ 294
Household	$ 220	$ 274	$ 261	$ 246	$ 53
Housing	$ 50	$ -	$ 51		$ -
Misc.	$ 50	$ 47	$ 611	$ 11	$ 18
Utilities	$ 165	$ 196	$ 140	$ 201	$ 135
	$ 2,567	$ 2,879	$ 2,789	$ 2,543	$ 2,749

Jan to Apr / Summer / Sheet3 / Sheet4 / Sheet5 / Sheet6 / Sheet7 / Sh

Ready

The benefit of a spreadsheet program is that you have so many options for working with the data you enter. You can do any of the following:

- *Perform calculations.* You can total a row of numbers, calculate a percentage, figure the amortization of a loan, and more.
- *Format the data.* You can make changes to how text and numbers appear in the worksheet. You can also adjust the column width, add borders, change the alignment of entries, and more.
- *Chart the data.* You can create different types of charts to visually represent the data.
- *Manage data lists.* Most spreadsheets also include features for managing simple data lists. You can enter, sort, and query simple data lists using the grid structure of a worksheet.

Microsoft Excel for Windows, Lotus 1-2-3, and Quattro Pro are all popular spreadsheet programs.

TIP

In addition to spreadsheet programs, you can also use other types of financial programs. For example, you can purchase a program to keep track of your check register. One of the most popular check management programs is Quicken. You can also find programs for calculating your income tax, managing your small business, handling major accounting tasks, and so on.

Databases

Database programs are useful for tracking and managing any set of data: clients, inventory, orders, events, and so on. Database programs vary from simple list managers to complex programs you can use to manage linked systems of information.

Databases offer a lot of advantages when you are working with large amounts of information. First, you can easily search for and find a particular piece of information. Second, you can sort the data into different orders as needed. For example, sort a client list alphabetically for a phone list. Or, sort by ZIP code for a mailing. Third, you can work with subsets of the data: all clients in Indiana, all clients that ordered more than $10,000 worth of products, and so on.

Some popular database programs include Access, Approach, and Paradox.

Graphics and Presentation Programs

Even if you aren't artistic, you can use your PC and the right software program to create graphics. Depending on your needs (and skill level), you can consider any of the three types of programs in this category:

- *Simple drawing programs.* You can use a simple drawing program, such as Paint, which is included with Windows 95, to create simple illustrations. Figure 6.3 shows a drawing created using Paint.

FIG. 6.3
You can use Paint to create simple drawings.

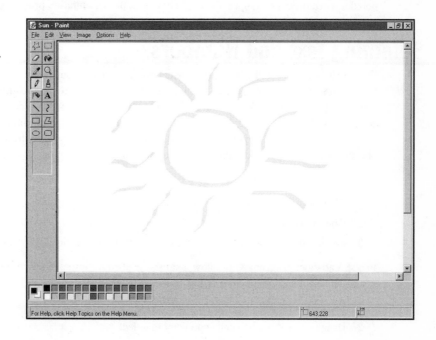

Part
II

Ch
6

■ *Complex drawing programs.* You can also find more sophisticated programs for drawing and working with images. For example, Adobe Illustrator and Adobe Photoshop are two such packages.

■ *Presentation programs.* If you ever have to give a presentation, you may want to use a program designed just for creating presentations. You can use this program to create slides, handouts, and notes. Microsoft PowerPoint, Corel Presentations, and Lotus Freelance Graphics are popular presentation programs.

Personal Information Managers

Most people have several things to keep track of: people, events, appointments, places, and so on. *Personal information managers* (*PIMs*) are just the program for storing names and addresses, keeping track of your schedule, jotting down notes, and so on. You can think of this type of program as your "electronic" day planner.

Suites or Bundles

One of the recent trends of software is to create a package or suite of the most popular programs and sell them together. For example, Microsoft offers several versions of Office, its suite of applications. The standard Office suite includes Word, Excel, PowerPoint, and Outlook; the professional edition adds Access. Corel and Lotus offer similar suites that include their most popular word processing, spreadsheet, database, and presentation programs.

Selecting Text and Numbers

While this book can't tell you how to use each of the applications you have on your PC, it can teach you some key skills used in many programs. Probably the most common skill is selecting something (text, numbers, an object). When you want to work with something, you start by selecting it. If you want to make text bold, you select the text. If you want to chart a set of figures, you select the data to chart. If you want to copy an object you've drawn, you select that object. Selecting is the first step for many editing and formatting tasks.

To select text, follow these steps:

1. Click at the start of the text you want to select.
2. Hold down the mouse button and drag across the text.
3. Release the mouse button. The text appears in reverse video as shown in Figure 6.4.

In a spreadsheet program, you follow a similar procedure for selecting a set of cells, called a *range*. To select a range of cells, follow these steps:

1. Click the first cell you want to select.
2. Drag across the other cells you want to select.
3. Release the mouse button.

To select a graphic image, click it once.

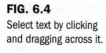

FIG. 6.4
Select text by clicking
and dragging across it.

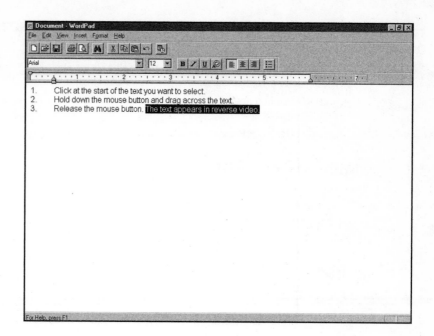

Once the item you want to work with is selected, you can then perform the editing or formatting task.

T I P You can often use mouse and keyboard shortcuts to more quickly select text and other data. Learn these shortcuts—and save time.

Formatting Text and Numbers

To make your document look as nice as possible, you can spend some time formatting—that is, changing the appearance of the contents. Most programs enable you to change the font or font size and make text bold, italic, or underline. You can use menu commands or look for toolbar buttons for the most common formatting features. Depending on the program, you may have many other text formatting options; these are the simplest. Figure 6.5 shows some formatting changes made to a WordPad document. The steps will vary from program to program, but they are basically as follows:

1. Select the text you want to change.

2. Make the formatting change. Most programs include a toolbar with buttons for common formatting changes. Also, try the commands in the Format menu.

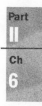

Part
II

Ch
6

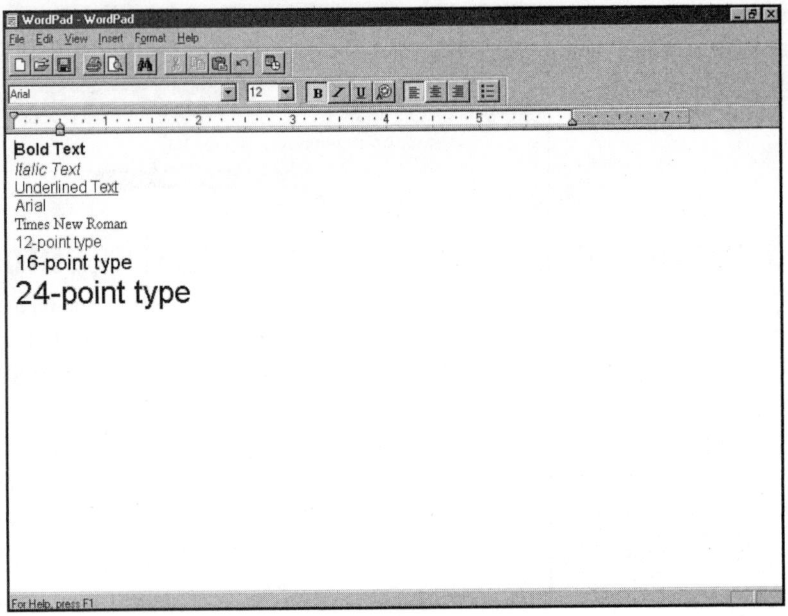

FIG. 6.5

The easiest way to make formatting changes is to use the toolbar buttons.

Cutting, Copying, and Pasting Data

One of the greatest benefits of an electronic document is that the data is not yet committed to paper; therefore, you can easily make editing changes. You can delete text you don't need, move text to a different location, or copy text you want to reuse.

Windows programs use the metaphors of scissors and paste for these editing tasks. You first "cut" the text you want to move or copy and then "paste" the text to its new location. (If you simply want to delete text, you can cut it without pasting.) If your program includes a toolbar, look for buttons for cutting, copying, and pasting. You can also find these commands in the Edit menu of most programs. The process for moving and copying text is similar from program to program.

To move something, follow these steps:

1. Select the item you want to move. To select text or a range in a worksheet, drag across it. To select a graphic object, click it.
2. Click the Cut button or open the Edit menu and select the Cut command.
3. Move the cursor to where you want to paste the text.
4. Click the Paste button or open the Edit menu and select the Paste command.

Copying text is similar to moving, but you will have two copies of the selected text: one in the original spot and one where you paste the copy. Follow these steps:

1. Select the item you want to copy.
2. Click the Copy button or open the Edit menu and select the Copy command.

3. Move the cursor to where you want to place the copy.

4. Click the Paste button or open the _E_dit menu and select the _P_aste command.

 TIP You can copy or move text to another document. To do so, simply move to that document after cutting or copying and then paste the selection into the new document.

Automatically Updating and Linking Information

In some documents, you may want to incorporate more than one type of information. For example, consider a sales report. You may include text, a worksheet of sales figures, and a chart. Pulling together all this information involves copying the various data into one document. But what if one piece of information changes?

With most programs, you can use a special command to paste the data so that it remains linked to the original. When the original data changes, the document that contains the copy is updated. Programs will vary somewhat in the exact commands and options for linking data, but here's the basic procedure for Word for Windows:

1. Select the item you want to copy and link.

2. Click the Copy button or open the _E_dit menu and select the _C_opy command.

3. Move to where you want to place the copy.

4. Open the _E_dit menu and select the Paste _S_pecial command. You see a dialog box that gives you the options for how to paste the data (see Figure 6.6).

5. Select the Paste Link option, select how you want the link pasted, and click OK.

FIG. 6.6
You can use the options in this dialog box to link data.

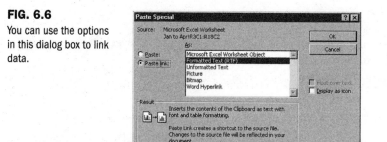

Now, updates you make to your file will automatically be reflected in the linked data.

Saving Your Work

One of the most important things you can learn about using a PC is to save your work. There's nothing more frustrating than spending hours getting every word in a document just perfect and then having some accident happen before you've saved. If the power goes off, if your system crashes, if you turn off the PC without saving, all that work is lost. You should get in the habit of saving your work and saving often.

When you save a document, you do two things. First, you select a location for the file—a folder on your hard disk where the file will be stored. (You learn more about disks and files in Part III.) Second, you enter a name for the file. You may be able to use as many as 255 characters, but you rarely will need such a long file name. Use something descriptive, but don't go overboard.

Again, the procedure for saving a document is very similar from application to application. The following steps use WordPad as an example. In your program, you may find other features and options for saving, but the general process is the same:

1. Open the File menu and select the Save command. The first time you save the document, you are prompted to select a location and file name (see Figure 6.7).

Up One Level button

FIG. 6.7
Enter a file name for the document you are saving.

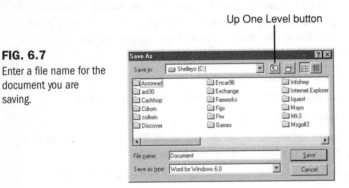

2. Select a drive from the Save In drop-down list.

3. Select a folder from the folders listed. You can use the Up One Level button to move up one folder in the folder structure.

4. Type a file name in the File Name box.

5. Click the Save button.

After you've saved the document once, you don't have to reenter the folder and file name. You can simply select File, Save to save the document to the same folder and with the same name.

 TIP   Look for a Save button in the toolbar as a shortcut for selecting the Save command. Also, to save a document with a new name or in a new location, use the File, Save As command.

Saving Your Work in Different Formats

Not everyone uses the same programs. For example, you may use Word for Windows, but work with someone that uses WordPerfect (another popular word processing program). So that you can share files with other users, most programs enable you to save data in different formats. For example, you can save a Word document as plain text, as formatted text, or as another type of word processing document (WordPerfect, Works, and so on). The type of available formats vary depending on the program and the program type. For example, the formats for saving a database program are different than those for a spreadsheet program.

1. Open the File menu and select the Save As command.
2. Select the drive and folder where you want to store the file.
3. Enter a new file name, if necessary.
4. Display the file type drop-down list and select the format. (The name of this option will vary from program to program.)
5. Click the Save button.

Opening Your Work

The purpose of saving a document is so that you can open it again. You may want to open a document so that you can use it again. Or perhaps you weren't finished and you need to make additional editing or formatting changes. When you want to work on a document you've saved previously, use the Open command.

1. Open the File menu and select the Open command. You see the Open dialog box. Figure 6.8 shows the dialog box used for WordPad. The dialog box will look a little different for other programs.

FIG. 6.8
Use the Open dialog box to open documents you have previously saved.

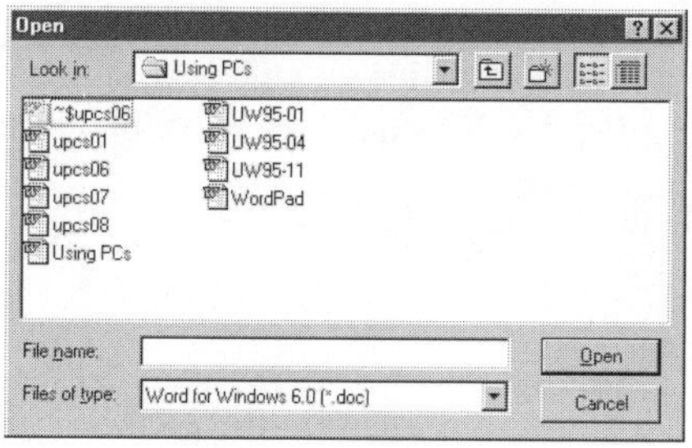

2. If necessary, change to the drive and folder that contain the file. You can use the Look In drop-down list to select a different drive. Use the Up One Level button to move up a level in the folder structure.
3. When you see your file listed, double-click it.

TIP As a shortcut, look for the Open button in the program toolbar.

Part
II

Ch
6

Printing Your Work

Most documents are created with the intent of being printed and possibly distributed. If your printer is connected and set up, you can use the Print command to print. (For more information on printers, see Chapter 14, "Printers.")

1. Open the File menu and select the Print command. Most programs display a Print dialog box where you can select such printing options as what to print and the number of copies to print. Figure 6.9 shows the dialog box for WordPad.

FIG. 6.9

Use this dialog box to select options for printing a document.

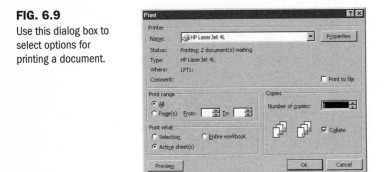

2. Make any changes to the options.

3. Click the OK button.

Many programs include a command for previewing a document before you print it. You can check the preview to see how the document flows on the page and then make any changes before printing. Look for a Print Preview button in the toolbar or a PrintPreview command in the File menu. ●

Disks, Drives, Files, and Folders

7   Preparing Disks for Use   75

8   Managing Your Files   83

9   Making Backup Copies of Your Files   91

10   Working with Networks   103

CHAPTER 7

Preparing Disks for Use

When you use a PC, you need some place to keep your programs and your data files, and that place is your hard disk. How do you get a program onto the hard disk or get a file off of the hard disk? With a floppy drive. This chapter discusses the different types of drives on a PC and explains how to use and take care of them. ▪

Work with disk drives

Understand what a drive is and what types of drives you have on your PC.

Format and use a floppy disk

Learn about floppy disks and floppy disk drives, and how to format a floppy disk. Then, learn how to copy files to and from floppy disks.

Know your hard disk

Understand how your hard disk houses all of your programs and data files.

Check a drive for errors

Drives can develop problems, so it's a good idea to periodically check your drive for problem areas using the tools provided with Windows 95.

Defragment your hard drive

If you think the performance of your drive is not up to snuff, you can optimize the hard drive by defragmenting the files. Learn a definition of defragmenting as well as the steps to defragment your files.

Define a CD-ROM drive

Review this section for help on using a CD-ROM drive.

What Is a Drive?

Computers need a place to store information (files and programs) and that place is on a disk drive. When you save a file, the information is recorded magnetically onto the drive's surface. When you want to use that information again, the disk reads the information from the drive. On most new PCs, you can expect to have the following drive types:

- *Floppy drive.* The floppy drive(s) on your PC works with portable floppy disks. Floppy drive portals look like mail slots on the front of your system unit. To get data onto and off of your hard drive, you can use a floppy disk and drive.

- *Hard drive.* The hard drive inside your system unit is the computer's main "cabinet" for storing data.

- *CD-ROM drive.* Newer PCs usually come with a CD-ROM drive as standard equipment; older computers may not have this type of drive. For information on CD-ROM drives, see the section "Defining CD-ROM Drives" later in this chapter.

TIP If you don't have a CD-ROM drive, adding one is a fairly simple upgrade. You can add this and other types of internal or external drives, as explained in Chapter 27, "Upgrading Your Hardware."

Using Floppy Disks

A floppy disk drive provides the medium for moving information—both program and document files—onto and off of your hard drive.

The original floppy disk was 5 1/4 inches across and was flexible—or *floppy*. Modern disks are smaller (3 1/2 inches) and cased in hard plastic sleeves.

If you have a fairly new PC, you probably have a single, 3 1/2-inch floppy disk drive; in most systems, this is drive A. Older PCs may have a second floppy drive (for 5 1/2-inch disks), named drive B.

To insert a disk into the drive, slide it label up (and with the metal tab forward) into the drive until you hear a click. To eject a disk, press the disk drive button.

TIP As technology advances, newer types of floppy disks are emerging. You can, for example, purchase a Zip drive. This type of disk and drive can store even more information than the standard 3 1/2-inch variety.

▶ **See** "Disk Drives—Internal and External," **p. 12**

Formatting a Floppy Disk

Before you can use a floppy disk, you must prepare it for use, and this process is called *formatting*. Formatting divides the disk up into storage units, where the data will be saved. You can purchase preformatted floppy disks to save time. If you did not purchase a preformatted disk or you want to format an existing disk, you can do so using Windows 95:

CAUTION

Formatting erases all of the information on a disk. If you are formatting an existing disk, be sure the disk does not contain any information that you need.

1. Insert the disk you want to format into the drive.
2. Double-click the My Computer icon on the Windows desktop.
3. Right-click your floppy drive (usually drive A) and select the Format command. You see the Format dialog box (see Figure 7.1).

FIG. 7.1
Use this dialog box to format a floppy disk.

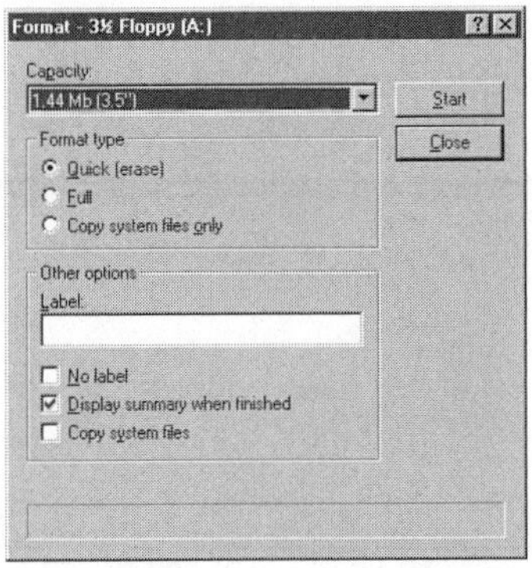

4. If necessary, display the Capacity drop-down list and select the correct capacity for your disk.
5. Select the type of format. Quick formats the disk and erases all of the files; this method does not check the disk for bad sectors. Full erases the files, prepares the disk, and checks for bad sectors. Copy System Files Only adds the system files to the disk so that you can use this disk to start your PC.
6. If you want to label the disk, enter the label into the Label text box.
7. Click the Start button.
8. When you see a message telling you the format is complete, click the OK button.

Copying Files to a Floppy Disk

Floppy disks enable you to store and transport your files and programs. You may want to keep backup copies of important files in a fire-safe location, for example, or carry files between your work and home computers. Whatever the reason, Windows 95 makes it easy to copy files from your hard disk to a floppy disk:

Part
III

Ch
7

> **TIP** It's a good idea to frequently back up all the data files on your PC. You can set up a regular backup routine. For more information on backing up, see Chapter 9, "Making Backup Copies of Your Files."

1. Insert the floppy disk into the drive.

2. Open the drive and folder that contains the files you want to copy. (Chapter 8, "Managing Your Files," covers finding and displaying files in more detail.)

3. Select the file(s) you want to copy by clicking its name. If you are copying a single file, you can skip the next part of this step. To select a list of contiguous files (the names are next to each other in the list), click the first file then press and hold down the Shift key while you click the last file. The first and last files and all files in between are selected. To select non-contiguous files from a list, hold down the Ctrl key and click each file you want to select.

4. Right-click the file(s).

5. From the shortcut menu, select Send To and then select your floppy drive (usually drive A). The files are copied to the floppy drive.

Defining Hard Disks

Most systems have just one hard disk drive, usually labeled drive C. You can always add another hard drive, either another internal drive housed in the system unit or an external drive that is connected to the PC via a cable.

Hard drives are measured in terms of size and speed. *Size*—which translates into storage capacity—is the more important distinction (you'll be surprised how quickly your drive fills up with files and programs). Hard drive size is measured in megabytes (M) or gigabytes (G); more megabytes or gigabytes means more storage capacity. Most new computers have between 1 and 2G of drive space. When you hear someone boasting of their system's "two-gig drive," this is the measurement they're referring to. *Drive speed* determines how fast the drive finds and accesses information. The speed is measured in milliseconds (ms). Anything in the 8–12ms range is a good speed.

The microprocessor and hard drive communicate with each other via a controller, and drives differ in the type of controller they use. The following table shows a quick breakdown of the different controller types.

Name	Description
IDE	Integrated Device Electronics. An older, but decent controller. Mostly now replaced by EIDE.
SCSI	Small Computer Systems Interface. A controller that enables you to chain different devices together.
EIDE	Enhanced Integrated Device Electronics. A newer version of the IDE controller.

Checking Disk Space

When you first purchased your PC, you probably knew the size of the drive, but you may forget the size over time. Windows 95 enables you to quickly review how much drive space you have used and how much is still available. To review this and other hard drive information, follow these steps:

1. Double-click the My Computer icon on the desktop.
2. Right-click the icon for your hard drive.
3. From the submenu that appears, select Properties. You see the Properties dialog box, shown in Figure 7.2. You can see the capacity of the drive, the space used, and the space free.
4. Review the information and then click the OK button.

FIG. 7.2
Review drive information using this dialog box.

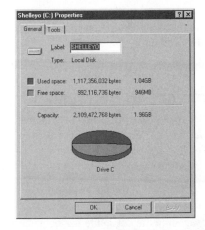

Using ScanDisk to Check a Drive for Errors

Hard drives can develop problems. Sometimes files aren't stored in the appropriate cluster or disk space (see the following section for a complete explanation of clusters). Sometimes file names don't match up with the folders in which they're stored. To check for and fix any errors, you can use ScanDisk, a program included with Windows 95.

1. Double-click the My Computer icon to display the contents of your computer.
2. Right-click the disk you want to check.
3. Select Properties from the shortcut menu that appears.
4. Click the Tools tab. This tab includes programs you can use to manage and optimize your disk drives (see Figure 7.3).
5. Click the Check Now button. Windows displays the ScanDisk dialog box.
6. Click the Start button to start checking the drive. Windows checks your drive. If it finds any errors, it displays a dialog box that explains the error and gives you options for repairing the error, deleting the file, or ignoring the error.

Part
III

Ch

7

FIG. 7.3

The Tools tab provides access to disk management tools like ScanDisk.

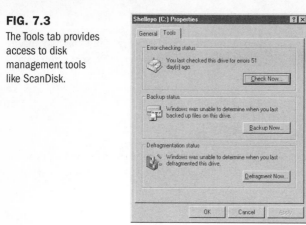

7. Select a correction method for each problem, then click OK. When ScanDisk is complete, you see a summary of its findings.

8. Review this information and then click the Close button.

Improving Hard Disk Performance by Defragmenting

To understand why defragmenting can improve performance, you need to understand a little about how data is stored on your hard drive. Your hard disk is divided into small units called *clusters*. Clusters are further divided into *sectors*. All the clusters on one hard drive are the same size, but the size of clusters may vary from one hard drive to another.

When you save a file, Windows puts as much of the file as possible in the first cluster it finds. If the file won't fit into one cluster, Windows moves to the next available cluster and puts more of the file in it, and continues in this way until the entire file has been stored. The *file allocation table (FAT)* keeps track of which clusters hold the pieces of each file. When you open a file, Windows goes to each of the clusters in turn, gathering the pieces of the stored file until it has gathered and can read the entire file.

On a new drive, the clusters used to store the files are contiguous (next to each other), so you don't have much delay as Windows collects the different pieces of the files. Over time, as you add and delete files, the open clusters become scattered, and when you store a file, its pieces are scattered all over the drive. That is, the disk is *fragmented*, and it takes longer for Windows to gather the pieces and open a file.

To improve the performance, you can straighten up the disk and put the files back in order by defragmenting the disk. Windows 95 includes *Disk Defragmenter*, a defragmentation program that reads the clusters on the drive and then rearranges them so that they are in a better order.

CAUTION

It's a good idea to back up your system before you make a major change such as defragmenting your hard disk. Chapter 9, "Making Backup Copies of Your Files," covers backing up.

1. Double-click the My Computer icon.

2. Right-click the disk you want to check.

3. From the submenu that appears, select Properties.

4. In the drive Properties dialog box, click the Tools tab.

5. Click the Defragment Now button. Defrag analyzes the drive and displays the Disk Defragmenter dialog box. The Disk Defragmenter also makes a recommendation on whether defragmenting is needed (see Figure 7.4).

6. Click the Start button. Windows displays the progress of the defragmentation process on-screen.

T I P To see a detailed map of the changes, click the Show Details button and then click the Legend button. You see a map of the clusters on the system as they are being read and written.

7. When the defragmentation is complete and you are prompted to defragment another drive, click the No button.

FIG. 7.4

You can defragment your hard drive to improve performance.

Using CD-ROM Drives

CD-ROMs (ROM stands for *read-only memory*) became standard equipment on PCs when multimedia became popular. Multimedia programs—which combine text, video, graphics, and sound—contain really large files. Because CD-ROMs can store more than 700M of data, they are the ideal medium for distributing information like programs, encyclopedias, and other large collections of information. As their name indicates, however, CD-ROMs are read-only disks. You can't edit or add data to a CD-ROM using the standard CD-ROM drives.

If you have a newer PC, you most likely have a CD-ROM drive as part of your system. Usually this drive is housed inside the system unit. If you have just one hard drive, your CD-ROM drive is most likely named Drive D.

CD-ROM drives differ in speed. You often see the speed advertised as 8x or 16x. These speed designations may be particular to a given manufacturer's standard, but in general, the higher a CD-ROM drive's speed, the faster it processes information (if you're a gamer, you'll appreciate the faster speeds).

To insert a disc into the drive, you press the Eject button to eject the CD-ROM carriage and then lay the disc inside the drive. Press the eject button again to insert the disc. Some drives have a removable cartridge, or *caddy*. Insert the disc into the caddy, and then insert the cartridge into the drive.

Part
III

Ch

7

> **TIP**   New versions of CD drives are becoming available that enable you to both read and write data to a CD.

Keeping Your Drives in Tip-Top Shape

Your drives store all your programs and files. While you can always reinstall programs, your data files are irreplaceable. Therefore, you should take good care of yourdisks. Keep these tips in mind:

- Keep your floppy disks in a safe place; they can be ruined by extreme temperatures.
- Never jam a disk into the drive. If the disk won't go in, check to be sure there's not a disk in the drive already. Be sure you are inserting the disk with the right side up.
- Hard disks and floppy disks store data magnetically. To avoid damaging your disks and drives, always keep magnets away from them.
- It's a good idea to organize the files and programs on your hard disk to avoid accidentally deleting or copying over valuable information.

You can learn more about setting up folders and managing files in the next chapter, "Managing Your Files," where you also learn to make backups to safeguard your data. ●

Managing Your Files

The end result from using most applications is some type of file—a memo, a sales report, a client list, a presentation, a newsletter, and so on. As you use your PC more and more, these files will multiply. This chapter covers some strategies for maintaining the files on your PC. ■

Define and organize files and folders

Learn about files and folders and how to organize them.

Create new folders

Learn how to create new folders on your system.

Rename and move files or folders

If you don't like the name you've used for a file or folder, or the location where you've stored a file or folder, you can change it.

Copy files or folders

Understand how to make a copy of a file, group of files, or entire folder.

Delete files or folders

Check out this section for housekeeping tips on deleting unwanted files.

Create shortcuts to files and folders

For fast access to your most often used files and folders, learn how to create a shortcut on the desktop.

Files and Folders Defined

Think of your hard disk as one big filing cabinet. Just as you use files and folders to organize information in a filing cabinet, you can use Windows files and folders to organize the information on your hard drive. You can divide your hard drive into folders, then store similar files together in each folder. In fact, a folder can even contain other folders.

Although you can create your own folders, you probably already have various folders in your system. Usually, programs are installed in their own folder, so you probably have a folder for each program on your system. That folder may contain other folders for different parts of the program. Windows 95, for example, has its own folder with many subfolders for different items.

Each time you create a document and save it, you are creating a file. (You can learn about saving a file in Chapter 6, "Working with Applications.") That file is saved with a name in a particular location or folder on your hard drive. Here's a typical file name:

```
C:\My Documents\Using PCs\Chapter 1
```

This file name includes the drive (C), the path name or chain of folders where the file is stored (My Documents\Using PCs), and then finally the name assigned to the file (see Chapter 1).

Organizing Your Files and Folders

Before your drive becomes cluttered with a large number of unorganized files, you should spend some time thinking about how to best organize your hard disk—that is, how to best divide it into folders. Here are some tips to consider when planning your organization strategy:

- *Keep your program and data files separate.* Doing so will make it easier to upgrade the program when a new version comes out, and to back up your data files.
- *Come up with a folder structure for storing your work.* You may want to set up folders for each application, and then create subfolders for each document type. For example, you can have one folder for your Word documents and then subfolders for Memos, Letters, Reports, and so on. Alternatively, you may choose to organize your folders by project, or simply use the My Documents folder and then create subfolders for each type of document.
- *Don't be afraid to change your mind.* If you come up with a plan and it isn't working, remember that it is easy to move and copy files and folders using Windows 95. Make changes as needed.

Viewing Your System Contents

Windows 95 includes two tools for viewing and working with the files on your system: My Computer and Windows Explorer. The two methods provide basically the same features with a few key differences, as explained in the following sections.

through the drives and folders on your system. The con-
ayed in a separate window; this offers what's called a
ontents. To use My Computer, follow these steps:

er icon on your desktop.

ant to open.

want to open.

olders until you find the folder or file you want to work with.
older with several data files.

Close (X) button.

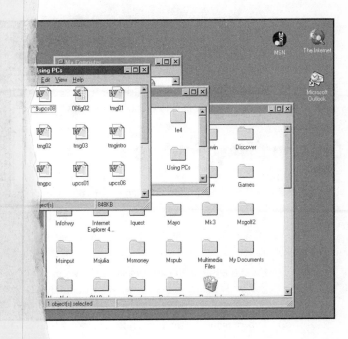

Using Windows Explorer

You can also use Windows Explorer; this program presents your system in a hierarchical structure in a divided window. In this *double-pane* structure, you can see the entire system in the left
pane, and individual folder contents in the right pane. To use Windows Explorer, follow these
steps:

1. Click the Start button.
2. Select Programs and then Windows Explorer. The program is started, and you see the
   contents of your system in a hierarchical view (see Figure 8.2).

FIG. 8.2

Use Windows Explorer for an overall view of all the drives on your system.

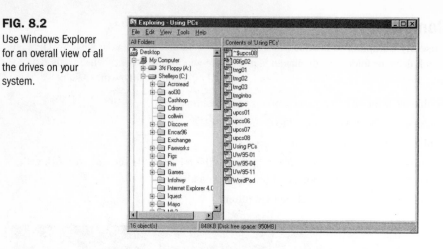

3. To expand a folder (see the subfolders within), click the plus sign next to the folder. To collapse the folder and hide these subfolders, click the minus sign.

4. To view the contents of a drive or folder, click the item in the left pane. The right pane shows the contents of that selected item.

Creating New Folders

As mentioned, to keep your files organized, you should create your own set of folders for your data files; the organization and names for your folders are up to you:

1. To use My Computer, open the drive or folder where you want to place the new folder.

   To use Windows Explorer, select the drive or folder where you want to place the new folder.

2. Open the File menu and select the New command. In the submenu that appears, select Folder. Windows adds a new folder (named New Folder) to the window. The name is highlighted so you can type a more descriptive name.

3. Type a name for the new folder and press Enter.

When naming either folders or files, you can use up to 255 characters, including spaces. You cannot use any of the following characters:

\ ? : * " < > |

N O T E Some DOS and Windows applications display long file names as truncated, eight-character names to fit the old limitation. When a program displays a truncated folder or file name, it adds a tilde (~) to indicate that the name includes more characters. ▪

Renaming Files or Folders

You can easily rename a folder or a file by following these steps:

1. In Windows Explorer or My Computer, display the file or folder you want to rename.
2. Right-click the file or folder and select Rename from the shortcut menu that appears. Windows highlights the current name and displays a box around it.
3. Type the new name and press Enter.

Moving Files or Folders

Occasions will arise when you need to move files and folders. You may decide to use a different organization and want to move a group of files to another folder. Or maybe you inadvertently saved a document in the wrong folder, or perhaps your projects have grown so much you need to reorganize your files and put them in different folders.

The easiest way to move files or folders is to use Windows Explorer. This program works better than My Computer because you can drag and drop the file or folder all in one window.

To move a folder from one location to another, follow these steps:

1. Start Windows Explorer.
2. Click the folder you want to move. You may have to expand the folder list to see the folder you want. You can also scroll down through the list.
3. Hold down the mouse button and drag the folder to the new folder. The selected folder (from step 2) is placed inside this folder.

To move a file or group of files from one folder to another, follow these steps:

1. Start Windows Explorer.
2. Display the files you want to move. Do this by selecting the folder that contains the files in the left pane. The right pane will display the contents of the selected folder.
3. Scroll the left pane until you see the folder to which you want to copy the file(s).
4. Select the file(s) you want to move. To select a single file, click it. To select multiple files next to each other, click the first file and then hold down the Shift key and click the last file. To select multiple files not next to each other, press and hold down the Ctrl key and click each file you want to select. Figure 8.3 shows files selected for moving.
5. Hold down the mouse button and drag the files to the new folder in the left pane of the window.

Selected files

FIG. 8.3
You can drag and drop files from one folder to another using Windows Explorer.

Folder to move to

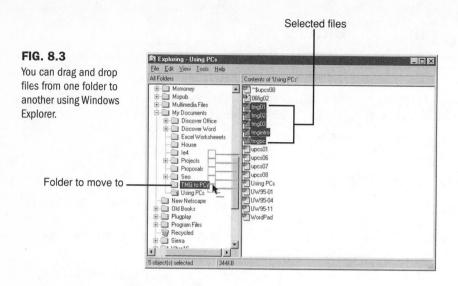

Copying Files or Folders

Copying is similar to moving, but instead of one version of the selected file or folder, you end up with two. The best program to use for copying is Windows Explorer:

1. Start Windows Explorer.
2. To copy a folder, select the folder in either the left or right pane of the Windows Explorer window.
3. To copy files, display the files you want to copy on the right side of the window and then select the ones you want to copy.
4. On the left side, scroll through the window until you can see the drive or folder in which you want to place the copies.
5. Hold down the Ctrl key and drag the selected folder or file(s) to the drive or folder where you want to place the copy.

TIP To copy files to a floppy disk, you also can use the Send To command. See Chapter 7, "Preparing Disks for Use," for more information on using this command.

Deleting Files or Folders

As you use your computer more and more, your files and folders will multiply; eventually, you will have to weed out the old, unneeded stuff. Deleting files or folders you don't need frees up the disk space for new files and folders:

1. Using either My Computer or Windows Explorer select the file(s) or folder(s) you want to delete.

2. Right-click the selected item(s) and then select the Delete command.

3. When prompted to confirm the deletion, click the Yes button.

Deleted files are sent to the Recycle Bin, as explained in the following section.

Using the Recycle Bin

When you delete a file or folder, keep in mind that Windows 95 does not really delete the file or folder, but simply moves it to the Recycle Bin. You can undo the deletion and recover the item from the Recycle Bin if you make a mistake and delete a file you need:

1. On the desktop, double-click the Recycle Bin. You see the contents of this system folder (see Figure 8.4).

2. Select the item(s) you want to undelete.

3. Right-click the selected item(s) and then select the Restore command. The item(s) is returned to its original folder.

FIG. 8.4

You can retrieve deleted items from the Recycle Bin.

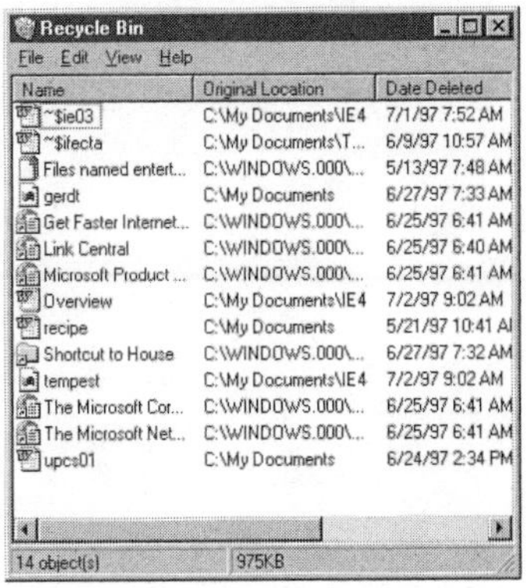

Files in the Recycle Bin also use up disk space. To free up the disk space and truly get rid of the file, you must empty the Recycle Bin:

1. Double-click the Recycle Bin icon.

2. Check out the contents and be sure it does not contain any files or folders you want to keep. Once you empty the Recycle Bin, you can't get the contents back.

3. Open the File menu and select the Empty Recycle Bin command.

4. Confirm the deletion by clicking the Yes button.

Creating Shortcuts to Files or Folders

In your work, you may find there's one folder or file you use all the time. For quick access to a file or folder, you can create a shortcut to it and place the shortcut on the desktop. Double-click a folder shortcut, and you see the contents of that folder. Double-click a file shortcut, and that file is opened:

1. In Windows Explorer or My Computer, select the file or folder for which you want to create a shortcut. Be sure that you can see at least part of the desktop.

2. With the right mouse button, drag the icon from the window to the desktop.

3. From the shortcut menu, select Create Shortcut(s) Here.

TIP The default name used is Shortcut to *xx*, where *xx* is the file or folder name. You can rename the shortcut icon. Right-click the icon, select the Rename command, type a new name, and press Enter.

CHAPTER 9

Making Backup Copies of Your Files

In the Information Age, we spend much of our time and energy gathering and generating information. Computers have become indispensable tools because they can help us gather and generate information, and also because they are so good at saving that information in a way that keeps it accessible.

Unfortunately, the potential for disaster exists. The information in a computer is stored in a form that is readable by the computer, not by humans. If the computer system isn't working properly, the information stored on it becomes inaccessible. It's an unfortunate fact of life that computer drives sometimes fail and files become corrupt. When that happens, the programs that make your computer do the things it does won't work anymore and hard-won data is lost.

If you use a computer for very long, sooner or later you will lose data. However, some common-sense precautions, such as making backup copies of important files, can soften the blow when the inevitable happens and you lose files to a computer problem of some kind. Making backup copies of your important programs and information will ensure that you won't lose your only copy of something vital. If you have a good backup, you'll be able to restore

Protecting your files with backup

Discover the advantages of using a specialized backup utility instead of simply making copies of your files with Explorer.

Backing up your files and folders

Learn the difference between full and incremental backups.

Formulating a backup strategy

Plan now to have the backup files you'll need to recover from disaster.

Using Windows backup

Learn how to use the backup program supplied with Windows 95 to back up your files.

Restoring files to your hard drive

Learn to use your backup files to replace lost or damaged files on your hard drive.

Other backup methods

Consider alternatives to the trusty floppy disk for storing your backup files.

the lost or damaged files and continue working. You may need to redo some work to replace any data you've added in the hours or days since you made the backup, but at least you won't have to start over from scratch, perhaps re-entering months of accumulated data.

So, you can think of backup copies of your files as data insurance. You could create backup files by simply copying files using Windows Explorer or other file management tools. But there's a better way—using specialized programs that are designed to make backing up and restoring files easier and more convenient. ■

Protecting Your Files with Backup

It's an unfortunate fact of life that computer drives sometimes fail and files become corrupt. Making backup copies of your important programs and information will ensure that you won't lose your only copy of something vital. You may need to redo some work to replace any data you've added in the hours or days since you made the backup, but at least you won't have to start over from scratch.

Any technique that creates a spare copy of a file that you can use if something happens to render the main file unusable is a valid backup technique. Many programs automatically create backup files every time you create or save a document file. This affords some protection from mishaps such as over-enthusiastic editing or accidental erasure of the main file. However, because the program-generated backup files are usually saved on the same hard drive as the main file, they offer no protection from a hard drive failure. Some people do a sort of manual backup on every file and document by saving each file twice—once on their hard drive and again on a floppy disk. You can also use Windows Explorer to copy files from your hard drive to another drive to create backup copies.

These types of annual backups can work, but they're tedious and time-consuming. A backup utility is a better alternative for most people because it automates the backup procedures, making the backup process much more convenient. Backup utility programs, such as Microsoft Backup that is supplied with Windows 95, can also compress files for storage efficiency and automatically manage the multiple floppy disks needed for large backups. Furthermore, backup programs can often use tape cartridges, which are cheaper and more convenient than floppy disks for backup.

Understanding Full and Incremental Backups

The safest form of backup is to make copies of all your files—this is called a *full backup*. A full backup requires huge amounts of storage and time, especially if you're backing up all the files on your hard drive. Fortunately, you don't have to do a full backup every time. Instead, you can save time by backing up only the files that have changed since the last full backup. This is called an *incremental backup*.

Incremental backups are possible because the operating system helps you keep track of what files have been backed up with a special marker, called the *archive attribute*, embedded in each file. When you make a backup copy of a file, the backup software sets the archive attribute of the file to indicate that it has been backed up. Any change in the file resets the archive attribute to indicate that it needs to be backed up again. Backup software can scan your hard drive and select files for incremental backup based on the archive attribute status of each file. Backing up only the files that have changed since the last backup is usually much faster than performing a full backup.

If you decide to use incremental backups, you must remember that the incremental backups do not contain all the files you selected for backup. Instead, an incremental backup set contains only the files that have changed since the previous backup. In order to have a complete backup set, you must keep the original full backup, plus all the subsequent incremental backups. All those backup disks or tapes must be carefully labeled. To restore the backup files to your hard drive, you must start by restoring files from the full backup and then adding each of the incremental backups in sequence. If that sounds like a hassle, it is. But you'll rarely need to restore files from your backup sets, and the time you save by using incremental backups more than makes up for the extra time you'll spend restoring those files.

Formulating a Backup Strategy

Good insurance protection for your data requires that you formulate a backup strategy and stick to it. If you do, you'll always have a recent backup on hand in case disaster strikes. Doing a full backup every day is the ideal backup strategy; but it's much too time-consuming for most people, and not really necessary. Some combination of full and incremental backup works best for most computer users.

The classic backup strategy is based on backing up all your files at the end of each working day. It starts with a full backup on Friday evening. Then you add incremental backups (quick and easy) each day Monday through Thursday. When Friday arrives again, you start over with another full backup.

N O T E Some people who aren't heavy computer users can do backups weekly or even monthly instead of daily. The important thing is to make sure your backups are frequent enough that it won't be too difficult to replace or redo what you've done since the last backup. ■

Another good strategy separates system and program files (which seldom change) from data files (which change frequently). You start with a selective, full backup of all your system files. You add incremental backups of the system files on an as-needed basis after any minor system change, and repeat the full backup of system files after major changes such as adding or modifying software. Data files get separate treatment with daily backups starting with a full backup on Friday and incremental backups on the other days of the week. Because you're only backing up data files on a daily basis, your backup chores should go much faster.

T I P The separate program and data backup strategy is easier if you install all your programs on one drive, partition, or folder and keep all your data files in a separate drive, partition, or folder.

Some people omit the system and program files from their backups on the theory that they can always reinstall programs from the program disks. That leaves only your data files that must be backed up. The trouble with this approach is that you could lose all your user preferences and other customization when you reinstall your programs. To protect against that eventuality, you could back up the files that contain user preferences, but that presumes that you can locate and identify all the preference settings—something that is not always obvious or easy (even for experienced users).

Using Windows Backup

Microsoft Backup is supplied with Windows 95 and it's usually included as part of the default installation. (If Backup isn't already installed on your system, you can install it using the Add/Remove Programs applet in the Control Panel. Just open the Add/Remove Programs dialog box, click the Windows Setup tab, and then double-click Disk Tools in the list box. In the next dialog box, make sure there is a check mark beside the Backup icon, then click OK twice and supply the Windows 95 disk when prompted.)

Performing a Full Backup

When you're ready to use Backup to make backup copies of your files, follow these steps:

1. Click the Start button on the taskbar. When the Start menu appears, choose Programs, Accessories, System Tools, Backup. This starts the Backup Wizard, which greets you with the welcome screen shown in Figure 9.1.

FIG. 9.1

The Microsoft Backup utility welcomes you with this screen. If you don't want to see the welcome screen in the future, click the Don't Show This Again check box.

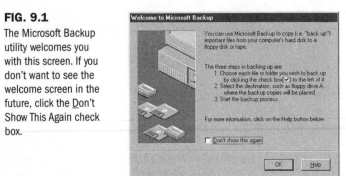

2. Click OK to dismiss the welcome screen; the Microsoft Backup window appears. (If no tape drive is located, or if the tape drive is not working properly, a message screen will appear informing you of either situation.)

3. Click the Backup tab to display the options shown in Figure 9.2. The Backup tab is similar to the two-panel Windows Explorer window. Like Windows Explorer, Backup allows you to select a drive or folder in the left panel and view the contents of that drive or folder in the right panel.

FIG. 9.2

Selecting files and folders to back up is similar to using Windows Explorer.

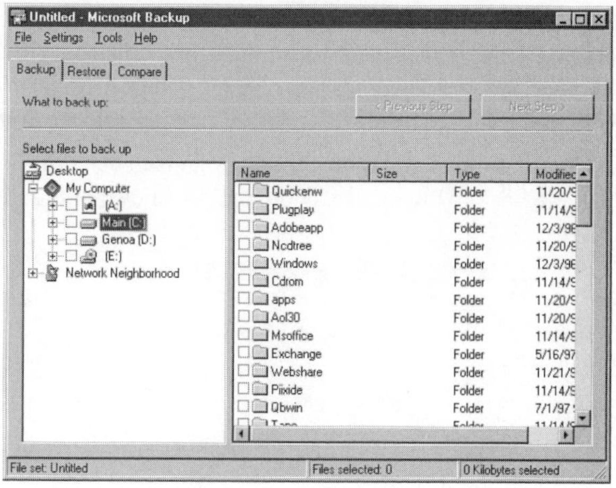

4. Select the files you want to back up by clicking the check box beside the drive, folder, or file icon. A check mark beside a drive, folder, or file icon marks that file (or files) for backup. Checking a collapsed drive automatically checks all folders and files in that drive, and checking a collapsed folder checks all subfolders and files in that folder. Expanding a drive or folder enables you to selectively check folders and files in that drive or folder.

TIP You can quickly mark all your files for a full system backup by placing a check mark beside the collapsed icon for your hard drive in the file tree. If you have more than one hard drive, be sure to select them all.

5. When you have selected all the drives, folders, and files to be backed up, click the Next Step button. The next page of the Backup Wizard appears (see Figure 9.3).

FIG. 9.3

After selecting the files to back up, you need to select the location of the backup copies.

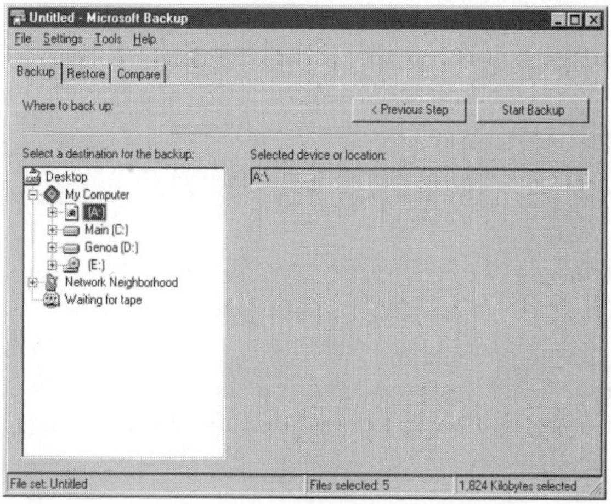

Part III

Ch 9

6. From the list on the left, select the location where you want to store your backup files. Typically, you'll click A: to select your floppy disk drive, but you can select a tape drive (if one is available), another hard drive, or a network drive or folder. Be sure the drive is available and a disk or tape is inserted before you select a drive.

7. Click the Settings menu and then choose Options to open the Settings - Options dialog box. Click the Backup tab to display the options shown in Figure 9.4.

FIG. 9.4

You can choose between full and incremental backup and also adjust other optional settings.

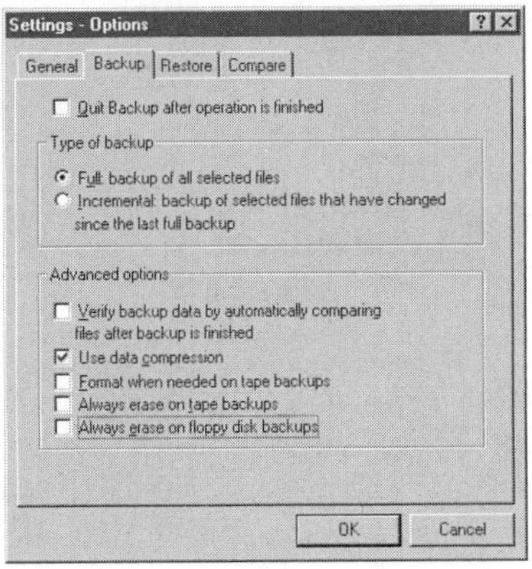

8. In the Type of Backup area, make sure the Full Backup of All Selected Files option is selected. You can also select other backup options as desired. The Use Data Compression option enables Backup to compress your backup files so that they occupy less storage space than the original files. You might also want to check the Verify Backup Data by Automatically Comparing Files After Backup is Finished option. This option instructs Backup to compare the backup copy of each file to the original file to make sure you have an accurate copy and then report any errors. The other options are self-explanatory. After selecting the options, click OK to close the Settings - Options dialog box and record the settings.

TIP If you expect to use these same backup settings (file selection, backup destination, and options) again in the future, you can save the backup set in a file. Simply select the File menu and choose Save As to open the Save As dialog box. Give your set of backup settings a file name and click the Save button to save the file. In the future, you'll be able to repeat this same backup by choosing Open File Set from the File menu, selecting this file, then clicking the Open button. The saved settings will be loaded into Microsoft Backup, ready to use.

9. When all the files are selected and options set, click the Start Backup button. Backup will display the Backup Set Label dialog box as shown in Figure 9.5.

10. Type a name for the set of backup files in the text box and then click OK. When you do, the Backup message box appears (see Figure 9.6) and Backup begins copying your selected files to the specified destination. The Backup message box keeps you informed of the status of the backup operation.

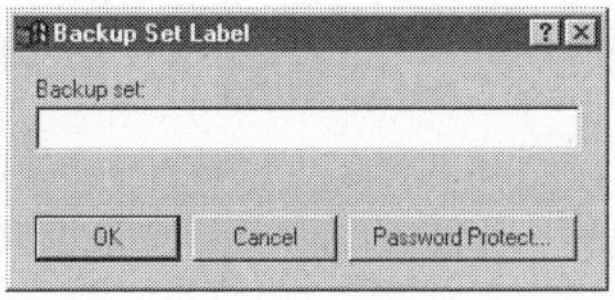

FIG. 9.5
You'll need to give
your backup set a
descriptive name.

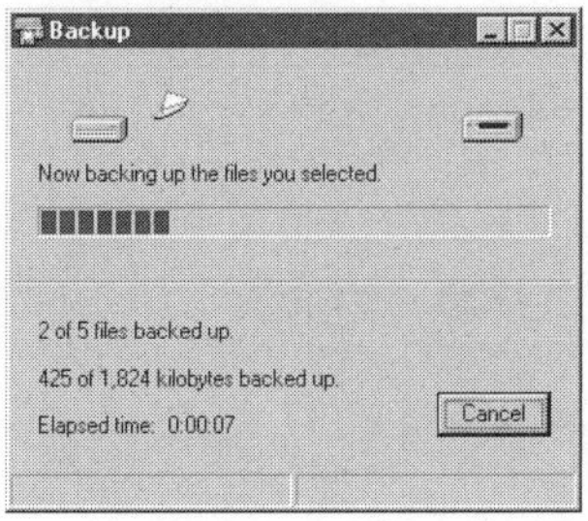

FIG. 9.6
The backup process
takes a while, but
Microsoft Backup keeps
you informed of its
progress.

N O T E If all the backup files won't fit on a single floppy disk (or tape), the program will prompt you to insert another disk when the current disk is full. Do so, then click OK to continue the backup.

11. When Backup finishes copying files, it will display a small Operation Complete message. Click OK to close the message box and then click OK in the Backup status box to close that box as well. This will return you to the Microsoft Backup dialog box. Click the Close (X) button in the title bar to close Backup.

Congratulations, you've made backup copies of the selected files on your hard drive. The backup files will be available to save the day if anything should happen to the original files.

Performing an Incremental Backup

To perform an incremental backup, follow all of the previous steps until you reach step 8. In that step, select the Incremental Backup of Selected Files That Have Changed Since Last Backup option in the Settings - Options dialog box. Proceed with the remaining steps as shown previously to complete the incremental backup.

Restoring Files to Your Hard Drive

The problem that sends you scurrying for your backup disks might be a major disaster such as a hard drive crash, or something as simple as a single file getting inadvertently erased or corrupted. When you need to restore files from your backup set to your hard drive, you can do so by following these steps:

CAUTION
Backup files are stored in a special format. You can't just use Windows Explorer to copy a file from a backup set to your hard drive. You must use the Backup program to restore the files.

1. Click the Start button on the taskbar. When the Start menu appears, select Programs, Accessories, System Tools, Backup. This opens the Microsoft Backup window. (If the welcome screen appears first, click OK to step past it to the main Backup window.)

2. Insert the first disk or tape of the backup set containing the files you want to restore into the appropriate drive.

3. Click the Restore tab to display the options shown in Figure 9.7. Like the Backup tab, the Restore tab is a two-panel window similar to the Windows Explorer window. When you click a drive or location in the left pane, Backup displays a list of the available backup sets on that drive in the right panel.

FIG. 9.7

To restore files to your hard drive, you must first select the backup set containing the needed files.

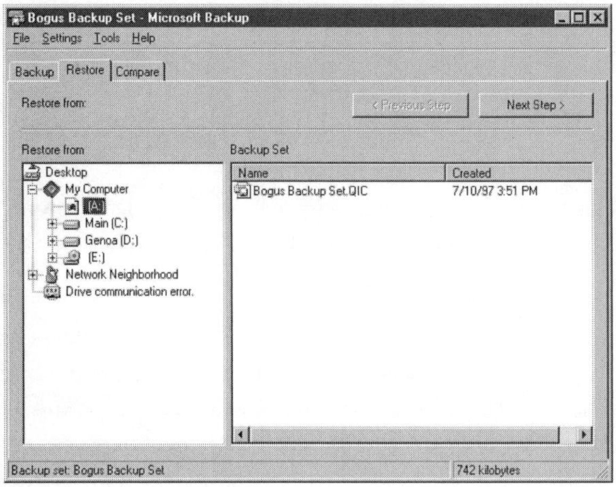

4. Select the drive and then the backup set by clicking them. Click the Next Step button to proceed to the next screen. Backup displays another two-panel file selection window as shown in Figure 9.8.

FIG. 9.8

After you select a backup set, you select the files from that backup set that you want to restore.

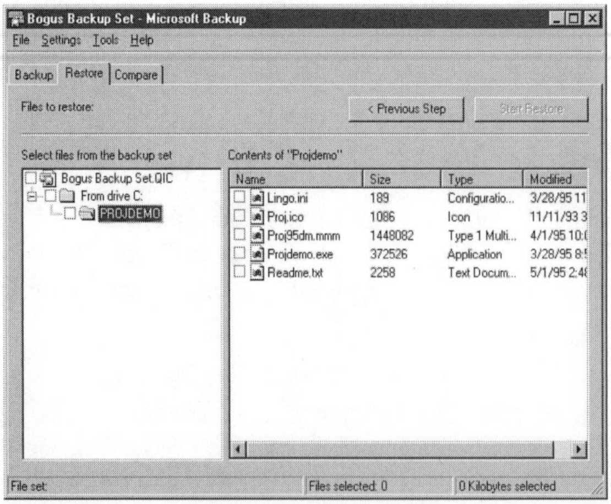

5. Select the files you want to restore by clicking the check boxes beside the backup set, folder, or file icons in either panel. A check mark beside the backup set, folder, or file icon marks that file (or files) to be restored to your hard drive. Checking a collapsed backup set or folder in the left panel automatically checks all subfolders and files in that backup set or folder. Expanding a folder enables you to selectively check subfolders and files in that folder.

6. Select the Settings menu and then choose Options to open the Settings - Options dialog box. Click the Restore tab to display the options shown in Figure 9.9.

FIG. 9.9
Make sure the setting
for overwriting existing
files is set correctly for
the task at hand.

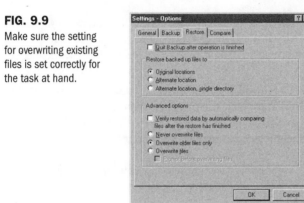

7. Select the location to which you want to restore the backup files. Ordinarily, you'll want to restore the files back to their original locations, but you may need to select an alternate location in some cases. In the Advanced Options area, you can specify whether Backup should automatically compare the backup files and the restored copies to verify that the files were restored correctly. You can also specify how Backup should handle overwriting existing files on your hard drive with files from the backup set. After selecting the options, click OK to close the Settings - Options dialog box and record the settings.

TIP If you are trying to replace a newer, but corrupted, file with an older version from the backup set, be sure to select the Overwrite Files option.

N O T E You can't save restored file selections and settings in a settings file like you can backup settings. ▦

8. When all the files are selected and options set, click the Start Restore button in the Microsoft Backup dialog box. Backup displays the Restore message box (see Figure 9.10), which keeps you informed of the status of the operation as it begins copying your selected files from the backup set to your hard drive.

FIG. 9.10

Backup keeps you informed of its progress as the program restores your files.

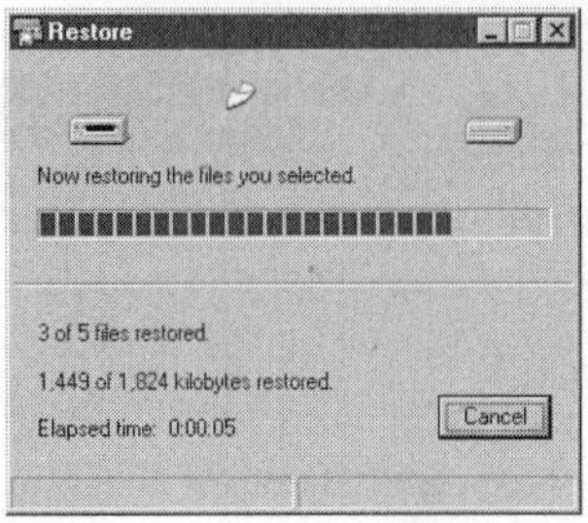

9. If all the backup files aren't contained on a single floppy disk (or tape), Backup will prompt you to insert another disk when it copies all the files from the current disk. Insert the requested disk when prompted to do so, then click OK to close the message box and continue copying files.

10. When Backup finishes copying files, it will display a small Operation Complete message. Click OK to close the Operation Complete message box and then click OK in the Restore status box to close that box as well. This will return you to the Microsoft Backup dialog box. Click the Close (X) button in the title bar to close Backup.

N O T E   If you have incremental backups in addition to a full backup of the files you want to restore, you must repeat this procedure for each of the incremental backup sets in sequence to ensure that the latest versions of all files are restored. ▪

Other Backup Methods

If you're like most people, you'll probably use the Microsoft Backup program that comes with Windows 95 to back up files onto floppy disks. That may be all you'll ever need. However, there are other backup options available. There are several third-party backup programs that can provide options and automation you won't find in the Windows backup utility.

The backup alternative you're most likely to need is a different storage medium. Floppy disks have the advantage of being universally available, but the standard floppy disk holds only 1.44M of data. To back up your entire system, you might need several dozen floppy disks. Large numbers of floppy disks can be expensive, time-consuming to use (you must keep swapping disks as the backup progresses), and difficult to store and manage (just labeling the disks becomes a major chore).

Fortunately, there are several excellent alternatives to floppy disks for backups. Most of the alternative backup media require separate drives as well as purchasing the backup media itself, but the speed, convenience, and cost-efficiency of the higher-capacity storage media can easily offset the extra initial cost for anyone who must frequently back up large quantities of data. Here's an overview of the most common alternate backup media:

▪ *Tape.* One of the most attractive backup media options is cartridge tape. Tapes and tape drives come in a variety of sizes and some of the newer units can store huge quantities (gigabytes) of data on each tape cartridge. It's often possible to back up the entire contents of your hard drive on a single tape. Tape isn't as popular as standard storage because information is recorded and read sequentially, which makes it difficult to access information randomly. However, tape makes an inexpensive and convenient backup medium.

- *Recordable CD-ROM.* Yes, you can record your own CD-ROM disks—provided you have the right equipment and software. The result is a CD just like the ones you use to install games and other software. Each CD can hold up to 650M of data. The drives and blank disks are a little pricey and each CD can be used only once to record data (you can read the data as often as you want). This makes recordable CD-ROM better suited to archiving data for long-term storage than routine backups.

- *Removable Hard Drives.* Undoubtedly, the fastest way to back up your hard drive is to copy the backup files to another hard drive. Most people can't afford redundant hard drives dedicated to backup. However, removable hard drives such as Iomega Jaz drives and SyQuest SyJet drives can be a cost-effective alternative for someone looking for the ultimate in speed and capacity.

- *ZIP Disks and other Removable Media.* You can think of a group of high-density removable media as *super* floppy disks. Products such as Iomega ZIP disks (100M each), SyQuest EZ Flyer disks (230M each), and various brands of magneto-optical disks (120–230M each) are all about the same size as a floppy disk, but they hold a lot more data. Basically, after the drives are installed on your system, you can use them for backups just like you use floppy disks; you just don't need nearly as many disks.

Part

III

Ch

9

CHAPTER 10

Working with Networks

What is a network?

Understand what is meant when referring to a network.

Why network?

Learn what the benefits are to networking.

What does a network consist of?

Understand what components are needed to connect computers together.

It is becoming more and more uncommon these days to find a company of any size that does not employ a computer network of some sort. As a business grows, the need to share information between employees does as well. When a small business only has three people working there, finding out if a customer's package went out on Thursday is as simple as yelling across the room to Jerry and asking if he sent it. With 30 or 300 employees trying to find Jerry to ask him about a separate package, the lines of communication break down. ■

What Is a Network?

A *local area network*, more commonly referred to as a *LAN*, is nothing more than the ability for two or more computers to communicate with each other. The communication between them can be as simple or as complex as you want to make it. While some purists would argue the point, in a very crude form, one computer can be connected to another via an RS232 cable connected to the serial or parallel port of each.

More often, a network consists of multiple computers connected for the purpose of sharing software and peripherals such as printers or CD-ROM drives.

Why Network?

As mentioned, there are two things commonly shared on a network: software and peripherals. The reasons for sharing software are multifold and best illustrated with examples.

Suppose your company is in the business of doing mass mailings. On your computer you have software with which you maintain a huge database of your mailing list. This database holds millions of entries, and conducting a mass mailing to this list requires the services of several people. If there are 26 people accessing this database, and all 26 have a copy of the database on their own computer, then you must update 26 separate copies every time the list changes.

A far better solution is to maintain the database on a single computer and let every user access that common database—through a network. When changes come in, they are made only once, and everyone works from the same information. One database maintained with a single software program represents a huge benefit for working with shared data.

The second reason for networking is to share peripherals. This is purely a cost benefit. If every computer is a stand-alone, then each computer must have a printer connected to it for a user to get output from the PC. Even if you purchase cheap laser printers, the cost adds up—and the output on those printers will be poor.

The solution is to invest the money and buy one good network laser printer for the network. Every user, regardless of how many there are, can send their output to that printer. Every user has access to a good printer, and the business saves several thousand dollars it would have invested in purchasing multiple, lower-quality printers.

What Does a Network Consist Of?

Network workstations require three components. Every computer connected must have a *network interface card*, usually shortened to *NIC*, installed within it. Additionally, it must have the software necessary to interface between the internal operating system (DOS, Windows 3.x, Windows 95, and so on) and the network. The third component is the physical link itself—usually, a common cable connecting the bodies of the computers.

There are two types of networks: *peer-to-peer* and *client-server*. The interface cards and wiring are the same between the two types, and the only difference is in the server. With a peer-to-peer network, the computers that hold databases accessed by all users are also used as workstations by those users. With a client-server layout, the computer containing the shared data is not used as a workstation, but is dedicated to the network.

Peer-to-Peer Network Software

While it is true that using a dedicated server is the preferred way to go, quite often small companies decide not to use that route initially. A peer-to-peer network is a good first step for a company in many aspects:

- With a small number of users, the delay in processing time is minimal.
- The cost of peer-to-peer is considerably cheaper. You save the expense of a computer that will not be used by any keyboard operator.
- A peer-to-peer network can usually be upgraded or converted to a client-server. By using the same cables and cards, the only additional expense of an upgrade (besides the dedicated server) is the software.

Microsoft's Windows 95 and virtually every operating system available today (Windows NT Workstation, OS/2, and so on) includes the ability to create a peer-to-peer network with no additional software. If you are running an older operating system, consider Microsoft's Windows for Workgroups, Novell's Personal NetWare, or Artisoft's LANtastic.

In summary, the advantages of peer-to-peer networking are:

- You can use the PCs you presently have and do not need to purchase more.
- Computers in peer-to-peer networks are traditionally easier to install and maintain.
- The software, itself, is cheaper.

And the disadvantages of peer-to-peer networking are:

- Each computer functioning as a server must have its processor split requests between the user sitting at the terminal and the users requesting data over the network, thus slowing things down for everyone.
- If a user leaves for the day and turns off his machine, no one can access the data stored there, or use the printer attached to that computer.
- Memory (particularly conventional memory) is used up by the server software and the local applications.

Dedicated Sever Software

There are two market leaders in the dedicated server world: Microsoft (with Windows NT Server) and Novell (with NetWare and IntraNetWare). In the world of DOS PCs, Novell NetWare is available in variations of 5 users up to 1,000 users. Version 3.12 is the one most in

Part
III

Ch
10

use today, featuring a host of utilities that have been perfected in the 15 years or so Novell has been releasing NetWare. Its processing is based on the architecture of the 80386 and 80486 chip (32 bit) and it can recognize up to 4G of RAM.

NetWare Version 4.x, still based on 386 and 486 architecture, has yet to see wide acceptance in small offices and is aimed at businesses that have so many users that they must use multiple servers. Rather than requiring a user to log in to a different network each time he changes servers, 4.x maintains his identity across all servers, known as the *enterprise*. The latest release of 4.1—4.11—is called IntraNetWare.

Microsoft's Windows NT Server is a newer entry in the marketplace than NetWare, but is quickly overtaking it as the market leader. Easy to install and administer, the latest version, Windows NT Server 4.0, is a multipurpose operating system optimized to run as a file, print, or application server.

Network Interface Cards

The network interface cards go into the PC (or connect to the back, in the case of laptops) and provide the go-between allowing the PC to connect to the network. The card slides into an expansion slot on the PC and allows the network cable to connect to it. Every single message traversing the network cable is received by the interface card; it is the responsibility of the card to determine if the message it received was intended for the PC, and if so, to send it on to the processor. If the message was not intended for the PC, the card ignores the message and awaits the next.

Interrupts, or *IRQs*, represent unique numbers assigned to each component within a PC. One of the most common problems with NICs is that they have the same interrupt as another hardware component. If this is the case, lockups or unexplained garbled screens can occur. Most NIC manufacturers are aware of this and provide a default address not commonly used by other equipment, as well as an alternative address in case there is a conflict. A driver/diagnostic disk usually comes with the NIC, and you can use this disk to set the IRQ, test the NIC's connection to the network, and install the drivers.

Topology: The Arrangement of Network Connections

There are essentially three topologies used today for creating networks: bus, ring, and star. First we'll talk about the *bus*, also known as a *daisy chain*. With a daisy chain, each NIC is connected to a Tee connector. The cable connected to the right side of the Tee comes from one computer, while the one connected to the left goes to another.

The two computers at the end of the chain have 50 ohm terminators connected to the one side of the Tee, rather than another cable. The terminator is at the end of the cable, because its job is to kill all messages coming to it. As was mentioned earlier, every NIC hears every message sent on the cable and decides whether to respond to it or not. Without a terminator, every message sent would echo back down the cable again and again, causing an exponential growth in messages that each NIC would have to check. Eventually the number of messages, and therefore the amount of traffic on the wire, would become so great that the entire network system would crash due to message collisions.

The second topology is the *ring*. With a ring, of which the most common is IBM's Token Ring, shielded wires connect each workstation in a loop. With a ring, as opposed to a daisy chain, each NIC listens to the network cable and waits until there is no traffic on it before sending its own messages out and awaiting a response.

The third topology is the *star*. The star represents a combination between a ring and a daisy chain. A concentrator, or hub, is centrally located and each computer is connected to it. The hub is then connected to the server. Star topology is mainly used for dedicated servers, and not of great application in peer-to-peer networks.

Each topology and cable type supports its own maximum cable length. Ring topology supports a relatively short cable length. If all computers are in close proximity, then the ring topology is acceptable because the distance between any two computers is minimal. If, however, the computers are spread out, and even in different rooms, then it becomes impossible to stay within the distance restrictions and a daisy chain topology must be used instead (though star topology may work for computers located in separate rooms).

Cable

The type of cabling used in a network is dependent on several things—mainly the topology and the type of network interface cards used. The most common cabling choices are coaxial cable, twisted pair (or telephone wire), shielded twisted pair, and fiber optic. Wireless networks are seeing a surge in notoriety, and they use radio signals in place of cable.

When discussing cable, there are three key phrases used:

- *Attenuation*. This tells how much of the signal is lost over a distance. Unshielded twisted pair has the greatest loss, while fiber-optic cable maintains the majority of its signal. Fiber-optic cable may be the better choice if the cable will be exposed to a great deal of electrical interference.
- *Bandwidth*. This is the number of simultaneous transmissions a cable can carry. The higher the bandwidth, the more capacity, and also the higher the cost.
- *Impedance*. This is the amount of resistance the cable itself gives to the messages it is carrying. The higher the impedance, the more force working against the signal you are trying to send.

The cheapest cable scenario to use is twisted pair. For a bit more, however, you can upgrade to coaxial cable, and it provides an excellent backbone on which to build a network. Fiber-optic cabling, not surprisingly, is the most expensive way to go.

Putting the Pieces Together

A network consists of computers with network interface cards installed, a cable connecting them all together, and software. These three components work together to form a total picture. The type of cards used is dependent on the type of cable and software, while the cable and software is dependent on the cards. ●

Computer Peripherals

11   Monitors   111

12   Keyboards   125

13   Mice and Joysticks   135

14   Printers   145

15   Modems and Faxes   155

16   Speakers and Sounds   165

17   Scanners   177

CHAPTER 11

Monitors

Your monitor is plugged into a video card (also called a *video adapter* or *graphics adapter*) in your computer. In most PCs, the video card fits into an expansion slot on the motherboard. (A few PCs have the video card built into the motherboard, but the end result is the same.)

Your monitor is connected by a cable to the video card. (We'll look more closely at that connection in the later section "Hooking Up Your New Monitor.") The video card receives instructions from the processor and sends them to the monitor. Any information you see on-screen makes use of the video card as a messenger to the monitor. The monitor doesn't do any processing itself. The monitor only displays the information that the video card tells it to. ■

How the monitor and video card work

Learn the essentials of what each part of the display system does and how they work together.

Monitor types and terminology

Understand monitor types and the terms used to describe their specifications.

Video card types and terminology

Learn video card terms like resolution, colors, RAM, and speed for video games.

How to get your monitor ready for use

From plugging in the cables to making some simple software adjustments, getting ready to use your monitor is easy if you know what to do.

Adjusting the controls for your monitor in Windows

Learn the key Windows 95 and monitor controls, and how to adjust them for peak display.

Monitor Sizes

The two most common monitor sizes are 15-inch and 17-inch. If you have an older, hand-me-down PC or a very inexpensive starter PC, you may have a smaller 14-inch monitor. 21-inch monitors are also available but mostly used by graphics professionals.

 TIP In the U.S., monitors are measured diagonally from one corner of the tube to the other, but part of the tube is hidden by the case so the actual viewing area is reduced. Lately, most stores have begun to also list the "viewable" size.

VGA and SVGA Monitors

The two most common acronyms you will see on current monitors are VGA or SVGA. Both of these terms generally refer to how many dots (or pixels) in each direction the monitor can display. VGA is 640×480 (width by height) and SVGA is 800×600. This measurement is called the monitor's *resolution*, and more is better! Most new monitors are capable of displaying at least SVGA quality. In fact, 1,024×768 is somewhat of a minimum to look for.

Almost any VGA or SGVA monitor made in the last few years is capable of displaying any of these resolutions. However, it's actually the video card that determines what resolution your monitor displays at any time. The monitor is capable of switching from one resolution to another on command from the video card.

You'll want to consider the size of your monitor when deciding which resolution to use. While these monitors can display many possible resolutions, higher resolutions may be too small to read on small monitors, and low resolutions will look huge and clunky on large monitors. Table 11.1 recommends some good resolutions for common monitor sizes.

Table 11.1   Recommended Resolutions for Common Monitor Sizes

Monitor Size	Recommended Resolutions
14-inch	640×480
	800×600
15-inch	800×600
	1,024×768
17-inch	1,024×768
	1,280×1,024

N O T E EGA, CGA, and MDA are older, greatly outdated monitor types that do not work with Windows 95. ▣

Interlaced Monitors

The picture that you see on the monitor at any time is constantly being *refreshed* (redisplayed) on the screen. Most monitors are capable of refreshing every pixel on the screen about 60 times per second. However, some monitors take a slight shortcut and refresh only every other line of pixels each time. So, the monitor still may refresh 60 times a second, but each line of pixels is refreshed only 30 times a second—a process called *interlacing*.

Interlaced monitors are always less expensive than non-interlaced monitors with similar features, but interlaced monitors flicker more than non-interlaced monitors. If you work under fluorescent lights or spend long periods of time in front of the screen, you should consider going with a non-interlaced monitor.

VGA and SVGA Video Cards and Resolutions

Like monitors, video card capabilities are measured in terms of resolutions. The two most common sets of resolutions are given special acronyms: VGA and SVGA. VGA resolution is 640×480. SVGA is 800×600 and is usually also used to refer to any resolution higher than this. (However, you may sometimes see XGA used when referring to super-high resolutions like 1,024×768 and higher.)

Any new PC will come with an SVGA card. Some older PCs will still have a VGA card. While it's not the most recent, a VGA card will do just fine as long as you don't want to play intense video games or have several windows visible on-screen at the same time.

Your video card and monitor work together as a pair. The highest resolution you will be able to use is limited to the highest that either can use. So, a video card that can display up to 1,600×1,200 resolution with a monitor that can only display 1,024×768 will be limited to 1,024×768 as a pair.

Part
IV

Ch
11

Video Cards and Colors

Another measure of video card performance is how many colors it can display at once. While you might think that a video card should be able to display "all" of the colors, it's not quite that simple.

Video displays use three different basic colors—red, green, and blue (called *RGB color*)—to display all of the possible colors. Each pixel on-screen actually has a red, blue, and green component. By varying the brightness of each of these colors for each pixel, the video card mixes the three basic colors to come up with all of the hues it displays.

But because a video card is digital, each of these colors has to be broken down into digital increments. This is where video color gets a little confusing, so follow a little math.

Color capabilities are coded with two sets of terms. In some settings, you'll see these described by the number of colors displayed, in others by the number of "bits" used to display the colors. Table 11.2 puts these two measures together.

Table 11.2   Terms for Color Capabilities

Bit Depth	Math	Colors Displayed	Other Name
4	$2^4=16$	16 color	
8	$2^8=256$	256 color	
16	$2^{16}=65{,}536$	65K	Hi-color
24	$2^{24}=16{,}777{,}216$	16 million	True-color

So, how does this relate to the digital increments? 256 colors means that the card can have 256 sets of increments across the three colors. A video card can actually display any of the total possible 16 million colors. What is really limited at any time is the number of colors it can remember and display at once. The more colors your programs need to display at once, the more memory your card will need. This is the topic of the next section.

Video Card RAM

RAM in your computer stores the information and programs that you are working with. RAM on the video card stores information about each screen pixel—what color it is, and how bright it is.

The more pixels you are displaying on-screen at once (higher resolution), the more RAM it takes on the video card to track the colors for all of the pixels. And the more colors you are displaying, the more RAM it takes to track the color for each pixel.

An 800×600 display has about 50 percent more pixels than a 640×480, and a 1,024×768 has about 160 percent more. So, to display the same number of colors in these higher resolutions will take about 50 percent and 160 percent more video RAM, respectively.

Table 11.3 shows maximum numbers of colors that can display at various resolutions with different amounts of RAM. The numbers shown are "general-rule-of-thumb" numbers, and will vary from card to card.

Table 11.3   Maximum Number of Colors Displayed at Different Resolutions

RAM	Resolution	Maximum Colors
1M	640×480	16 million
	800×600	65,000
	1,024×768	256
2M	640×480	16 million
	800×600	16 million
	1,024×768	65,000

RAM	Resolution	Maximum Colors
4M	640×480	16 million
	800×600	16 million
	1,024×768	16 million

Video Cards, Video Games, and Full-Motion Video

For general everyday computing needs like using a word processor, spreadsheet, or presentation program, video card speed is not a big issue. But for playing action-oriented video games or full-motion videos, the speed of the video card is important. The faster the video card, the less "jerky" the action will seem as you fly through space in your favorite flight simulator game, or the fewer frames of a movie the card will miss.

For video cards, there are a couple of key benchmarks. ZiffDavis Benchmarks has a bench-marking group that measures video cards in terms of *graphics winmarks*. This is essentially a measure of how fast the card is in Windows and is important for Windows games. Similarly, they have a DOS graphics rating for DOS games.

Another measure of graphics speed is *polygons per second*. This measures how many shapes per second the card can draw.

With any video benchmark, faster is better and higher scores are always faster.

Part
IV

Ch
11

Special Considerations for Notebook Displays

Notebook displays have a few unique factors and features that don't apply to desktop monitors. In general, these features relate to the type of display technology used in notebook construction.

Passive Matrix, Dual-Scan, and Active Matrix Displays

The first term you may encounter in regard to notebook displays is *passive matrix*. Most bargain-priced notebooks use this type of display technology. The display can be dim and hard to see if you aren't looking at it in the right light from the right angle. An improved version of this is called dual-scan; dual-scan screen notebooks are sometimes sold under the descriptions DSTN or CSTN.

Another type of notebook computer screen technology is *active matrix*. Active matrix screens—sometimes listed as TFT in system descriptions—are used in top-of-the-line notebooks. Though more expensive, active matrix displays are brighter and crisper.

Notebook Display Size

The other key difference in notebook displays is size. As explained earlier, viewable area on a desktop monitor is usually smaller than the monitor's stated size. But, a 12.1-inch notebook monitor measures 12.1 real inches diagonally. So, you can get away with a smaller display on a notebook because you don't lose any unviewable area. 12.1 inches is becoming a good entry point. 13-inch displays are starting to come on a lot of laptops, but right now they are probably not worth the big price premium.

Notebook Display Resolution

In general, notebook displays are limited to 640×480 resolution for a 10–11-inch display. Most 12-inch displays can run at 800×600, and some of the new 13-inch displays run at up to 1,024×768.

Hooking Up Your New Monitor

When you are ready to hook up your monitor, carefully unpack it and save all of the packing and boxes. If you ever need to move or have it serviced, you'll want the box and packing to transport it. Look in the box to see if there are any disks or CDs. If there are, read the labels; they may be software that you need to use the monitor. Or, they may just be freebies like games or giveaway bonus software.

The monitor should have two cables. One should be a familiar power cord with a standard three-prong plug. The other is the cable you will use to connect the monitor to the video card. This cable should have an end that looks like Figure 11.1.

FIG. 11.1
This is the end of a standard monitor cable that you will connect to your video card. Most of these have thumbscrews to attach them to the video card.

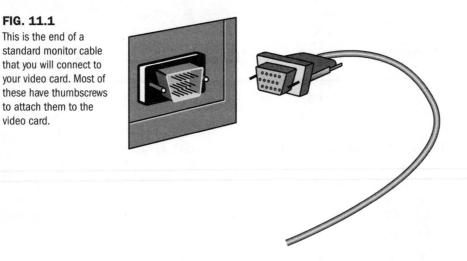

To connect the monitor:

1. Shut down the PC and turn off the power to the PC and monitor, then disconnect the monitor and PC from the electrical outlet.

2. Look at the back of the PC and find where the monitor cable is attached. Carefully loosen the thumbscrews of the old monitor cable and detach it from the card. Be sure not to disturb other wires and make sure you see where you disconnected it from.

3. Move the old monitor out of the way and move the new monitor into its place.

4. Connect the new monitor cable to the video card connector that you detached the old monitor from. Don't force the connection. The connector is longer on one side than the other so you may need to turn it over to line it up.

5. Once you feel the connector slide into place, tighten the thumbscrews. Some people like to leave these loose. I prefer not to have my monitor cable fall off while I'm working.

6. Plug the monitor into the power outlet and then turn on the PC and monitor.

If the picture looks odd, you may need to adjust it. We'll look at adjusting the monitor settings in the next couple of sections.

Setting Up a New Monitor in Windows 95

To get the most out of your monitor in Windows 95, you'll want to tell Windows what type of monitor you have. To do this:

1. Click the right mouse button on any blank area of the desktop and choose Properties from the pop-up menu.

   Or, click the Start menu, choose Settings, then choose Control Panel and double-click the Display icon in the Control Panel folder.

2. In the Display Properties dialog box, click the Settings tab, then click the Change Display Type button to open that dialog box (see Figure 11.2).

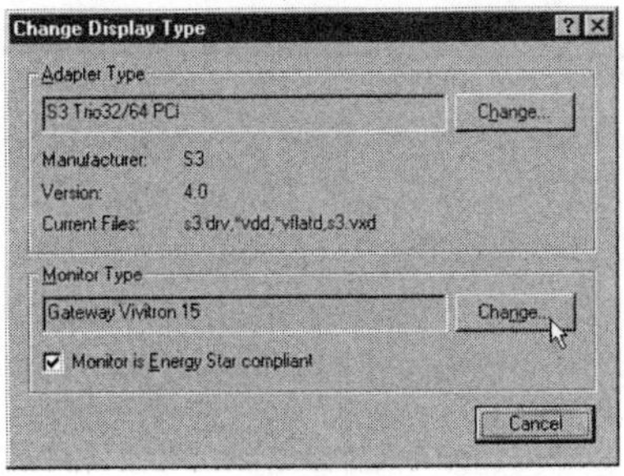

Part

IV

Ch

11

FIG. 11.2

This dialog box shows your computer's current monitor type. Click the Change button to set up a different type.

3. Click the Change button to open the Select Device dialog box, which should look similar to the one shown in Figure 11.3. In the middle of the dialog box is the area where we choose the monitor type.

4. Scroll through the Manufacturer list in the dialog box and select the brand of monitor you have. Then, in the Models list (to the right) select the model. Click OK.

N O T E   If your monitor came with a disk with driver software for Windows 95, insert the disk and click the Have Disk button. Click the Browse button in the Install from Disk dialog box to select the drive with the installation disk, then click OK. This will then give you a list of possible monitors to choose from in the Select Device dialog box in step 4. ▨

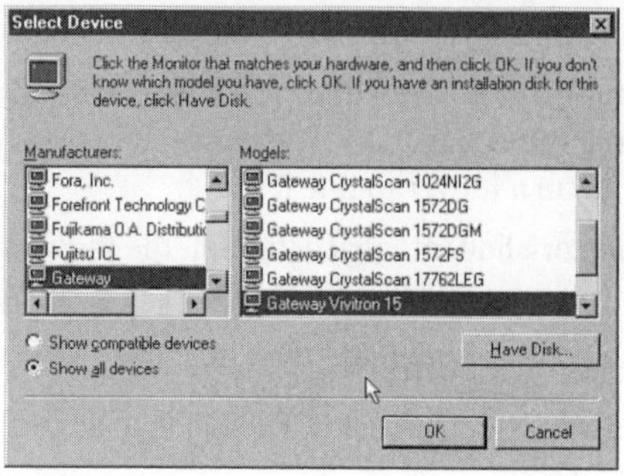

FIG. 11.3

This is a list of all of the brands and models of monitors that Windows supports.

5. Windows now enters your selection in the Change Display Type dialog box. Click Close in that dialog box, then click OK in the Display Properties dialog box and you are ready to go.

> **CAUTION**
>
> Choosing the wrong monitor display type during the preceding procedure can damage your monitor. If your brand and model aren't listed, call the maker's technical support number to find out what setting you should use.

N O T E Some cool graphics cards come with their own utilities for changing the monitor settings. In fact, they may even add extra features in Windows 95's own Display Properties dialog box, like the one shown in Figure 11.4.

Each of these cards is different, and if you want to make the most of the extras they provide, read the manual or help that came with it. If your display properties dialog box has some extras in it like this, some of the tasks in this chapter may work a little differently with your computer. ▧

FIG. 11.4

This Matrox Mystique video card added extra tabs and controls for adjusting the color on-screen, getting inform- ation about the display system, and more.

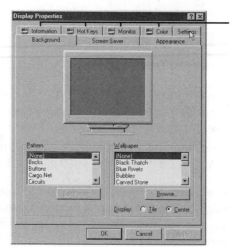

Extra tabs added by video card

Adjusting Your Monitor Settings

On the front of your monitor, there are usually several controls that affect the appearance of your monitor display. These controls may be small dials or buttons. Here are some typical controls that you will find and what they do:

- *Brightness.* This controls the overall brightness of the picture on-screen. Use this when the picture is either too bright or too dark.

- *Contrast.* This changes the contrast between the light and dark areas displayed on-screen. Adjust this if your picture looks washed out, gray all over, or if the whites hurt your eyes.

- *Horizontal and vertical sizing.* If the picture on-screen doesn't reach close enough to the top and bottom or the sides, use these controls to resize it.

N O T E On most monitors, there will be a small black border area around the picture when it is correctly sized. Adjusting the picture too large to try to get rid of this border will distort and curve the edges of what's on-screen. ■

- *Centering.* If your picture isn't centered on-screen, use the centering controls to adjust it. You may need to work with the centering and sizing alternately to get it centered and sized.

- *Deguass.* This is almost always a button. Monitors generate large magnetic fields; over time these fields can build up and distort the picture. Other magnetic items (like un-shielded speakers) can also generate fields that distort the picture. If this happens, press the Deguass button. You will usually hear a pop, and the picture will disappear and resize. When it comes back, it should look better. If not, you may want to see the troubleshooting section at the end of the chapter.

Most monitors' controls have "centers" that put these settings at their middle grounds or factory presets. On dial controls, you may feel a small click as you turn the control to the center point. On button controls, there will usually be an indicator on-screen that shows the center.

Part

IV

Ch

11

T I P Notebook computer users will usually find the monitor brightness and contrast controls as function keys on the keyboard. Notebooks don't have the ability to adjust the display size or recenter it, and there is no need to degauss them. See your notebook manual if you need details on using those.

Changing the Numbers of Colors Windows Can Display

How many colors do you want to be able to see on-screen? That answer depends a lot on what you use your PC for and what kind of video card you have. If all you use your PC for is word processing or spreadsheets, the standard display options of showing 16 or 256 colors at once should work for you.

But, if you like to look at pictures or video or play photo-realistic games, you may find that the colors look all wrong on-screen with the default settings. To change the number of colors Windows 95 can display at once, follow these steps:

1. Click the right mouse button on any empty space on the desktop and choose Properties from the pop-up menu.

2. Click the Settings tab in the Display Properties dialog box.

3. Click the Color Palette drop-down list and choose from one of the options as shown in Figure 11.5. The options available here will depend on your video card and desktop display size. Windows won't display options that are over the limit for your card.

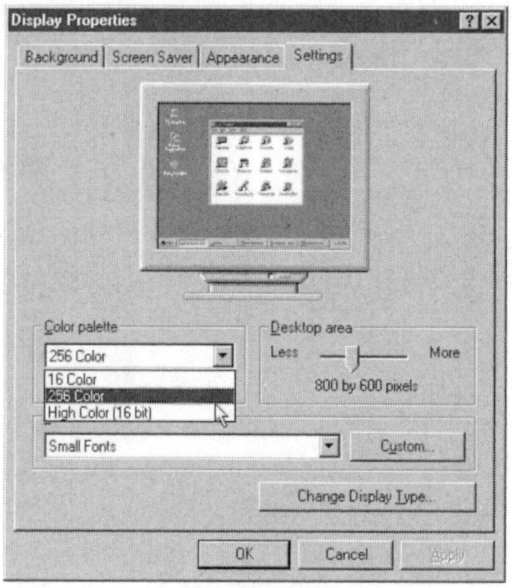

FIG. 11.5

Choose from a minimum of 16 colors at once to a maximum of 16 million.

4. Click OK once you have made your selection.

5. In order for this change to take effect, Windows must restart. Click Yes to allow Windows to restart.

Changing the Size (Resolution) of the Display

You can increase the size of the desktop display area to be able to fit more visible open windows on-screen at once, or see a bigger area of the windows you have open. However, because you monitor doesn't actually change size when you change the resolution of the display area (that would take a small miracle), making the display area "bigger" makes each item on-screen look smaller. Look at the typical 800×600 desktop in Figure 11.6.

To change the display area size, follow these steps:

1. Click the right mouse button on any empty space on the desktop and choose Properties from the pop-up menu.

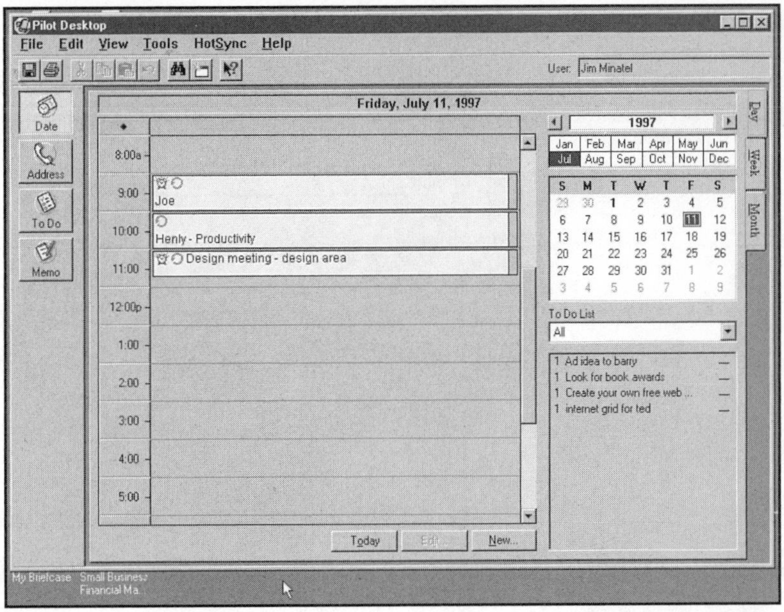

FIG. 11.6

This shows an application open on a typical 800×600 desktop, which is a good size for a 15-inch monitor.

2. Drag the slider for the Desktop Area to a higher or lower setting. If the slider is all the way to the right edge of the control area, then you can't make the display area larger. Likewise, when it is all the way to the left, it is as small as it will get.

3. Click OK to resize. Windows will inform you that this setting may cause problems. Click OK to continue.

4. If all goes well, the picture will "hiccup" a little and return to normal. If it looks normal, click OK to keep the new setting.

   If things didn't go well and the display doesn't look right, click Cancel and Windows will return you to the previous settings. If the display is so messed up that you can't see it to cancel it, Windows will return to the old settings after 15 seconds if you do nothing.

Figure 11.7 shows the results of changing the desktop display area to 1,024×768. This shows two additional applications open without having to resize the original application. Notice how there is more area on-screen but everything looks smaller.

Changing Wallpaper and Patterns in Windows

Wallpaper and patterns are just decoration on top of Windows. While they don't really relate to the monitor, you do see them on the monitor. So if you want to change them, follow these steps:

1. Click the right mouse button on any empty space on the desktop and choose Properties from the pop-up menu.

2. Click the Background tab of the Display Properties dialog box.

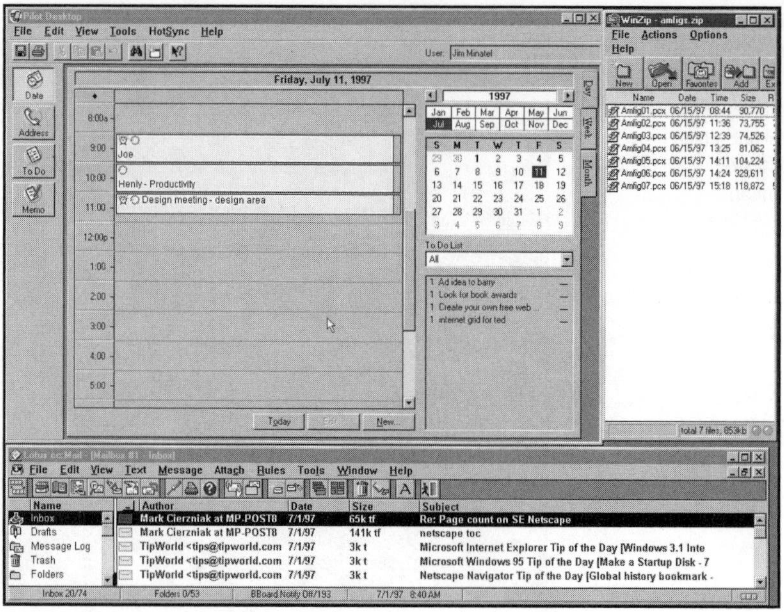

FIG. 11.7

You'll need a larger monitor, probably a 17-inch model to provide enough screen area to see this high resolution well.

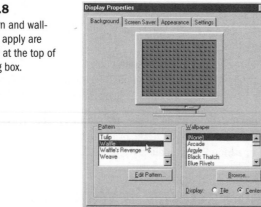

3. In the Pattern list, select a pattern. This pattern will be applied to your desktop. A preview of any changes you make here is shown in the drawing of the monitor in the top of this dialog box as shown in Figure 11.8.

FIG. 11.8

The pattern and wallpaper you apply are previewed at the top of this dialog box.

4. To apply one of the existing wallpapers, select it in the Wallpaper list. You will probably want to select the Tile option to fill the desktop with the wallpaper as most of these are very small.

5. If you have a picture that you would like to use as wallpaper, click the Browse button to find the right file and click OK after you have selected it. Usually, pictures are larger and look best with the Center option selected.

TIP Windows can only use pictures in the Windows Bitmap format for wallpaper. If you are downloading picture files from the Internet, most of these are in GIF or JPEG format. You'll need to use a graphics program like Microsoft Photo Editor (that comes with Office 97) or a shareware program like PaintShop Pro to save these as bitmaps that can be used as wallpaper.

6. Click OK when you have made your changes to close the dialog box.

Cleaning and Protecting Your Monitor

Monitors, like most computer parts, are susceptible to damage and decay from dirt, dust, and misuse. A few simple guidelines will help extend the life of your monitor.

First, try to keep the exterior clean and free of dust. You can use any lint-free rag to dust the case and screen. For a small investment of a couple dollars, you can get monitor cleaning "wipes" that will do a better job keeping dust off of the screen. You can use a common, non-abrasive household cleaner if you want but it's not necessary. If you do, use it sparingly, be sure the monitor is off, and spray it on the rag, not the monitor. If you use the monitor in a really dusty area, you will want to get a cover for it and keep it covered when not in use.

Second, if you have speakers attached to your PC, be sure they are shielded to prevent electrical static from passing between your PC and speakers. If they aren't, move them away from the monitor. If you are shopping for computer speakers, be sure to buy shielded ones. Almost all speakers designed for PCs are shielded, but you will find some cheaper models that aren't. Likewise, speakers that you bought outside the computer department at the local electronics store to use with your Walkman may not be shielded.

Finally, your monitor throws off a lot of heat. It has a lot of openings on the top and maybe the sides and back to let it cool. Don't stack papers, books, or other junk on top of the monitor or around the sides. In addition to causing the monitor to overheat, these could be a fire hazard, or your cheap, plastic toy you used as a monitor hood ornament could melt and ruin the guts of the monitor.

Troubleshooting Display Problems

The following sections present some common monitor and display problems and offer some potential solutions.

The Picture Is All Wavy, Fuzzy, and Won't Work in Windows

This usually means that the video card or monitor settings are wrong. Shut down the computer and restart it in Safe mode; then check to be sure your display settings match the brand and model of monitor and card that you have. If this doesn't work, try setting the display settings to the generic VGA or SVGA display card and monitor types. Contact the video card vendor's technical support to see if they have a more recent set of drivers.

The Picture Changes Size Going from DOS to Windows

This is fairly normal and is only a problem if the change is so dramatic that either DOS or Windows screens are too small or large to use. If this is the case, check your display settings to be sure the correct monitor is selected.

The Picture Keeps Getting Smaller

Bad news: The picture tube in the monitor is going bad. If it's under warranty, send it back for repair. Otherwise, it's probably a better investment (and no more expensive) to shop for a new monitor.

I Can't Resize the Screen on My Notebook

Notebook screens are a fixed size. They can't be resized like a monitor. Some will allow you to resize the desktop resolution, and if you do, you may have to pan to see the whole desktop on-screen at once.

Windows or a Program Tells Me I Can't Display the Right Number of Colors

Your screen resolution may be too high to display more colors with your video card. Try selecting a lower screen resolution in the Display Properties dialog box.

The Monitor Doesn't Come on When I Turn on the PC

Look for a separate on/off switch on the monitor itself and turn it on there.

The Monitor Doesn't Turn off When Windows 95 Shuts Down the Computer

Look for a separate on/off switch on the monitor itself and turn it off there.

Can I Fix or Upgrade the Inside of My Monitor Like My PC?

No! The inside of your monitor is a dangerous electrical place even when unplugged. Leave servicing the monitor to a professional. ●

CHAPTER 12

Keyboards

The keyboard is one of the simplest parts of the computer to understand. This chapter goes beyond the keyboard basics, however, to show you how to do tasks such as inserting special characters or typing in another language. This chapter also looks at how to take care of your keyboard and how to take care of yourself when using it.

The standard keyboard layout

Learn the layout and use of the main parts of a keyboard.

Inserting special characters and symbols

See how to type characters that don't appear on the keyboard itself.

Windows 95 enhancements

See how some new keyboards save you time with special Windows 95 keys.

Taking care of your keyboard

Learn a few simple guidelines to keep your keyboard working for years.

Avoiding keyboard injuries

Repetitive stress is painful and serious. See how to lower your risk of injury from the keyboard.

Notebook keyboards are different

Find out what corners have to be cut on notebook keyboards to make them fit and still work.

Understanding the Keyboard Layout

The basic function of almost every keyboard is compatible with what is called a *standard 101-key keyboard*. The standard keyboard is divided into four main groups of keys:

- *The typewriter or alphanumeric keys.* These are all of the standard letters, numbers, Tab, Shift, and the spacebar arranged in the usual QWERTY order. The Return key is replaced by an Enter key, and some special computer keys (Alt and Ctrl) are added at the bottom.

- *The function keys.* These are usually labeled F1 through F12, and have different functions in each program you use (some programs may not have any features that use them).

- *The cursor keys.* These are the arrows and other keys that move the cursor or insertion point on the screen. In addition to the up, down, left, right keys, some keyboards add diagonal keys. This block of keys also includes Insert, Delete, Home, End, Page Up, and Page Down keys.

- *The numeric keypad.* This has two functions. When the Num Lock light is on, this functions as a 10-key calculator. When the Num Lock light is off, this functions as another set of cursor movement keys.

Most keyboards carry a variety of additional keys, including Esc (Escape), Print Screen, Scroll Lock, and Pause. The uses of these specialty keys varies from system to system. In most systems:

- Esc can be used to undo commands or actions and in keyboard combinations.

- Print Screen can be used to copy the current screen contents to the Clipboard, from which you can then Paste the contents into a document for printing (see the Print Screen entry in "Troubleshooting Common Keyboard Problems" later in this chapter).

- Scroll Lock changes the action of the directional arrow cursors.

Check your user manual to find the details of the specialty keys on your system's keyboard.

Using Special Characters and Symbols

Many documents include characters that don't appear on the keyboard. These special characters include letters from the Greek alphabet, scientific values, symbols for foreign currency, and copyright and registration symbols. Some applications have shortcuts for entering these special characters; Windows 95 provides its own set of special characters in its Character Map accessory. To use the character map, follow these steps:

1. Check to see what font you are using in the document to which you want to add the characters.

2. Click the Windows 95 Start button and choose Programs, Accessories, Character Map.

3. In the Character Map application font list, select the name of the font you're using in your document.

4. Find the character(s) you want to insert in the program document and double-click them. This enters the characters in the Characters to Copy box shown in Figure 12.1.

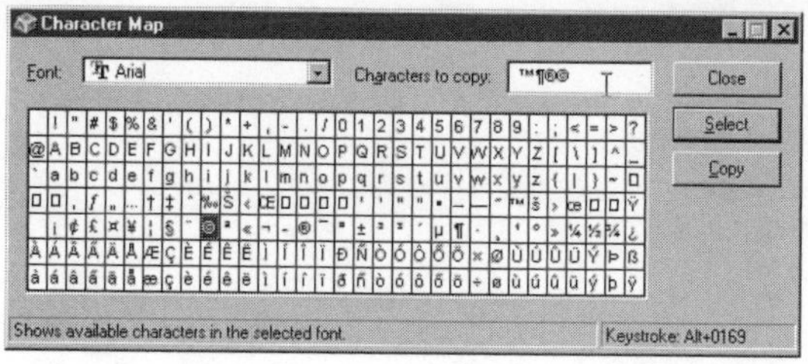

FIG. 12.1
You can select several characters for insertion in your document—all at the same time! The characters that you double-click are shown in the Characters to Copy box.

5. When you have the characters you want to use, click the Copy button.

6. Return to the program that you want to use these in and click the mouse where you want to insert them.

7. Open the Edit menu in that program and choose Paste. This pastes a copy of those characters in the document. You can then cut and copy the individual characters into their appropriate locations in your document.

Typing in Another Language

When you installed Windows, it came with a default language for the keyboard. If you bought your PC or your copy of Windows 95 in the U.S., that language is English (United States). If you need to type in another language, Windows allows you to select another language for the keyboard. To do this, follow these steps:

1. Click the Start menu; choose Settings, Control Panel.

2. Double-click the Keyboard icon in the Control Panel to open the Keyboard Properties dialog box.

N O T E Only the CD-ROM version of Windows 95 includes multi-language support. If you installed from floppy disks, you'll need to download and install the multiple language support from Microsoft's Web site at **http://www.microsoft.com/windows/software/cdextras.htm** to add another language.

▶ **See** "Exploring the World Wide Web," **p. 211**

3. Click the Language tab so you see the dialog box as shown in Figure 12.2.

4. Click the Add button to open the Add Language dialog box, shown in Figure 12.3.

5. Select the new language from the drop-down list and click OK.

Part
IV

Ch
12

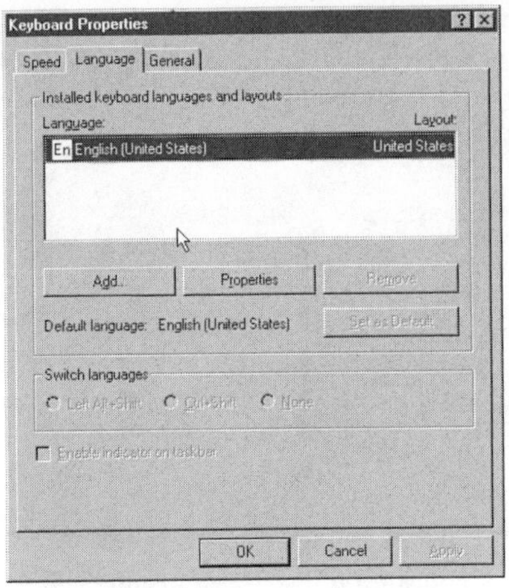

FIG. 12.2

This dialog box shows what languages are installed and which one is the default.

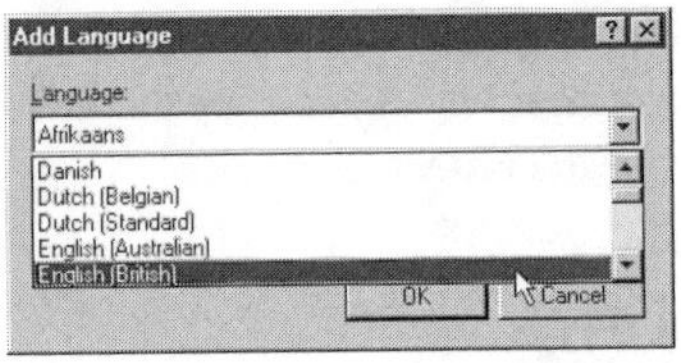

FIG. 12.3

Select the language from this list. Some languages (like English) have several varieties.

6. The language is now added. By default, Windows 95 will still use the original language. The dialog box indicates that if you want to switch between languages, you press the Left Alt key and Shift at the same time. By default, Windows will also show you an indicator of which language is being used in the taskbar as shown in Figure 12.4. When you are done adding languages, click OK.

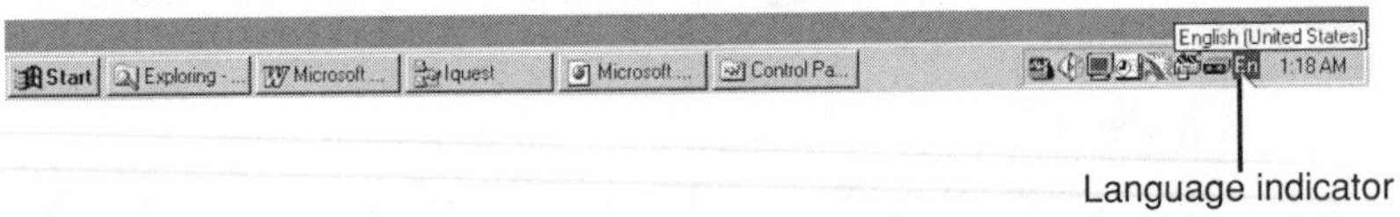

FIG. 12.4

Hold the mouse pointer over the indicator to see a ToolTip pop up with the full name of the language. Click the indicator to produce a menu with which you can switch between languages.

Language indicator

You can now type in Windows in the new language. But, even with multiple language support, you need to keep in mind a few limitations when selecting a new language for your system:

■ Some languages employ characters not used in English. The font that you use also has to have all of the available characters for that language.

- Your keyboard still has the U.S. English layout and keys. The foreign language feature is designed with the assumption that users are familiar with the keyboard for the language they've chosen, and the characters are matched to that placement on your current keyboard. If you're unfamiliar with the keyboard for the language you've chosen, you'll just have to type each key and find out which keys type what characters.

- Finally, not every world language is available. If the language you're seeking doesn't appear in the list, check with Microsoft Technical Support to see if they know a Windows 95-compatible source for the language.

Special Keys for Windows 95

Some keyboards have special keys that perform special tasks in Windows 95. The idea of these keyboards is to give you access to some common mouse functions on the keyboard so that you don't have to take your hands off of the keyboard to perform them. These Windows 95 keyboards usually have three special function keys bringing the total number of keys to 104. These are:

- The Windows logo keys (there are usually two of these, one each just to the outside of the Alt keys), both marked by the Windows logo

- The Menu key (usually located between the Windows logo key and the Ctrl key on the right side of the spacebar), marked by a stylized drop-down menu and an arrow pointer

The Windows logo key (referred to as WINDOWS in the following table) performs these actions:

Key Combination	Action
WINDOWS	Opens the Start menu.
WINDOWS+R	Opens the Run dialog box.
WINDOWS+M	Minimizes all windows.
Shift+WINDOWS+M	Undoes Minimize All.
WINDOWS+F1	Opens Help.
WINDOWS+E	Opens Windows Explorer.
WINDOWS+F	Opens the Find: All Files dialog box.
Ctrl+WINDOWS+F	Opens the Find Computer dialog box.
WINDOWS+Tab	Cycles through current taskbar buttons.
WINDOWS+Break	Opens System Properties dialog box.

Part
IV

Ch
12

The menu key has one simple application. Select any object and press the menu key and the same pop-up menu that appears when you right-click the mouse on that object appears.

Special Software for Keyboards

Several computer and keyboard makers have special programmable keyboards that you can make perform special tasks. For example, you can record a long set of keystrokes, and then play it back with just a few simple keystrokes (like speed dial on your phone).

If you have a programmable keyboard, you should also have received some keyboard control software and a manual explaining how to use the software. To master the use of a programmable keyboard, you'll need to read the instructions carefully. Even if you don't want to use it, it's a good idea to at least know how to take the keyboard out of "program" mode and put it back into "normal typing" mode, for those times when you accidentally trigger the program mode.

Keeping Your Keyboard Clean and Working

Never spill liquids on your keyboard. Coffee, soda, and other beverage spills can ruin your keyboard. Liquid spills on the keyboard have even been known to cause electrical damage to the PC itself. With that in mind, though you may not stop drinking coffee around your computer, you should at least get a spill-proof mug or keep the coffee on the other side of the desk.

Another enemy of keyboards is static electricity. Static electricity can have the same damaging effect on your keyboard as does liquid. If your keyboard doesn't respond properly after a strong static charge, you may just need to turn off the PC and turn it back on to reset the keyboard. In some cases, however, the static discharge can zap the keyboard and even parts of the PC. If you shuffle your feet across carpet or your PC is in a room with dry air, avoid touching the PC or the keyboard until you have touched something metal to discharge any static. If you don't have a metal desk or bookcase in your work area, consider buying an antistatic mat and keeping it where you can touch it before touching the PC.

Dust, dirt, food crumbs, and hair are other enemies of keyboards. Try to avoid eating over the keyboard and if your computer is in a dirty, dusty area, keep the keyboard covered when not in use.

Some dirt and dust is unavoidable. To keep the keyboard working well, you should occasionally clean it. Any time you clean the keyboard, turn off the PC first; then try any or all of these three techniques for cleaning the keyboard:

- Turn it upside down and shake it. This should shake loose some of the crumbs and dirt that collect between the keys.

- Get a can of compressed air (available for a few dollars at most PC or electronics stores) and use it to blow the dirt and dust from between the keys. Be sure to read the directions on the can before using it. If you hold the can wrong or use it incorrectly, you may blow cold liquid into the keyboard instead of air. Generally, you need to hold the can upright and tip the keyboard up at an angle so the debris will fall out when it is blown loose.

- If the keys themselves are dirty or sticky, wet a cleaning rag with some rubbing alcohol or a little bit of any non-abrasive household cleaner (something like Windex or Formula 409 is fine) and use it to clean the keys. Don't spray or pour any cleaner directly on the keyboard, and don't get the rag dripping wet.

Avoiding Keyboard-Related Injuries

Carpal tunnel syndrome, tendonitis, and other repetitive stress injuries have become serious health problems for many computer users. If you will use your computer a lot, you should know how to avoid these injuries and what the symptoms are.

First, if you feel any pain after typing or using the PC for extended periods, consult a physician immediately. Symptoms can include:

- Pain in the wrists
- Numbness or tingling of fingers

To avoid this type of injury, you need to use the proper posture and position of the body while typing. Always sit with your back straight. Your shoulders should be relaxed, and your upper arms should hang almost straight down.

At this point, adjust your chair and desk so that your forearms are parallel to the floor and your hands are just above the keyboard. Don't rest your wrists on the desk or the keyboard.

While typing, your knuckles, wrists, and forearms should form a straight line. While a lot of people have started using wrist pads to rest their wrists on while typing, you should know that these generally don't keep your hands and arms aligned correctly.

If you type for hours on end, you should stop and take a break for just a few seconds every few minutes. This is even more important for touch typists whose actions are probably more repetitive than those who "hunt and peck."

Beyond these issues, you may want to consider investing in a special ergonomic keyboard. The Microsoft Natural keyboard and several others like it are specially designed to reduce the risk of this type of injury. These keyboards are generally split down the middle and angled to allow your arms and wrists to rest in the proper alignment. If you think you want to try one of these keyboards, find a store with one set up in a display where you can sit down and try the keyboard. Many computer professionals who work constantly at their PCs won't use anything but one of these special keyboards.

Special Notes on Notebook Keyboards

Notebook keyboards have special configurations designed to fit all the keys into a smaller-than-standard keyboard. For those accustomed to a standard-sized keyboard, a notebook's keyboard can take some getting used to. The keys themselves are usually smaller and spaced closer together. Further, notebook keyboards almost always have fewer keys.

Notebooks rarely have a built-in numeric keypad, and they don't have duplicate Alt and Ctrl keys (as do standard keyboards). Notebook keyboards do have special function keys which you use in combination with other keys to replicate the function of a numeric keypad, or to control color, contrast, or brightness. These keys usually have another set of labels printed on them in a color other than the alphabet color on the keys. Your notebook's manual or online help feature will explain the use of these and any other special function keys.

Using a Standard Keyboard with a Notebook

Most notebooks have a plug that allows you to plug in an external keyboard. If you have a notebook and you would really prefer to use a standard keyboard, check to see that you have a keyboard with the right size connector to fit your notebook. With the notebook off, plug in the keyboard and turn on the notebook. Most notebooks will automatically detect the external keyboard and know to use it and not the built-in keyboard.

> **CAUTION**
> Don't plug in or unplug the external keyboard while the notebook power is on.

If you plan to use the notebook a lot with the external keyboard, you may want to invest in a port replicator or docking station. The notebook snaps into place in one of these and the keyboard remains attached to the replicator or docking station. This saves you the trouble of plugging the keyboard into the notebook each time you want to use it. This is even more handy if you also use an external mouse and monitor with the notebook.

Troubleshooting Common Keyboard Problems

The following tips may help you diagnose (and perhaps resolve) some of the most common keyboard problems.

Keys Type Odd Symbols or Letters

To solve this dilemma, do any of the following:

- See the section "Using Special Characters and Symbols" earlier in this chapter, and be sure that the language selected in Windows 95 is English (United States) or whatever language you want the keyboard to be typing in.
- Check the font selection in your application to be sure that you haven't selected a symbol font like WingDings or Symbol. Try selecting Times or Arial and see if the problem is fixed.
- If the problem happens only occasionally and only with a few keys, the keyboard itself may be bad. Borrow a keyboard from a friend or buy a cheap spare at the store. Plug it in and see if it works. If you get the same problem, your problem may be in the PC itself, not the keyboard, and the PC will require professional service.

Print Screen Key Doesn't Work

In Windows 95, the Print Screen key doesn't print to the printer. What it does do is copy the screen to the Clipboard. To print a screen, press the Print Screen key to copy what you want to print. Next, click the Start menu and choose Programs, Accessories, Paint. In Paint, click the Edit menu and choose Paste. You now have a Paint picture of your screen. Click the File menu and choose Print. You can save the Paint picture if you want to save the picture of your screen.

Arrow Keys Type Numbers Instead of Moving the Cursor/Number Keys Move the Cursor

Look for the light that indicates the Num Lock on your keyboard. When this is lit, the numeric keyboard is in number mode and is used like a 10-key calculator. When the light is off, the numeric keypad is used for the arrow key movements indicated on the keys.

The Keyboard (or PC) Won't Stop Beeping

There's a key stuck somewhere. If there is an application running, look to see if the same letter or number is filling the screen. The key may be jammed, broken, or so dirty underneath that the contact is jammed shut. Try cleaning the keyboard and restarting the PC.

I Get a Message That Says *Keyboard error* or *Keyboard missing* When the PC Boots Up and Then Nothing Happens

Try any of the following:

- Check first to be sure that the keyboard is plugged in correctly.
- Your keyboard and mouse may have similar plugs and connectors. Check for an icon on the computer case or a description in the computer manual showing which plug is the correct one for the keyboard, and be sure it is in the right plug.
- Turn off all power to the PC, waiting a few minutes, and restarting it.
- Borrow a keyboard from a friend or buy a cheap spare at the store. Plug it in and see if it works. If you get the same error, your problem is in the PC itself— not the keyboard— and the PC will require professional service.

NOTE Keyboards are cheap and generally not worth the trouble to fix. If something does go wrong with the keyboard and it is still under warranty, call customer service and get it replaced. If it isn't under warranty, just buy a new one. A plain no-frills keyboard costs anywhere from $10 to $30 and lasts several years under normal wear.

Part
IV

Ch
12

CHAPTER 13

Mice and Joysticks

A mouse is the primary input device for modern computers that feature operating systems with a graphical user interface, such as Windows 3.11 or Windows 95. While keyboards obviously excel at entering text, numbers, and symbols, your mouse is the tool you'll use to tell your computer what to do with all the data you've entered.

Joysticks are almost exclusively used with game software and help the user more effectively control the actions of computer-simulated airplanes or arcade-style games.

Defining a mouse

Learn what a mouse is and how it works.

Connecting a mouse

Find out how to connect different kinds of mice.

Using mouse buttons

Discover exactly what is meant by click, double-click, click and drag, and so on.

Adjusting and cleaning a mouse

Learn to adjust your mouse to match your personal preferences while keeping it clean and working well.

Defining, connecting, and adjusting joysticks

Learn what a joystick is, how to connect one to your computer, and how to calibrate your joystick for optimum performance.

Defining Mice

All modern PC operating systems (Windows 3.11, Windows 95, and the Macintosh) rely on an on-screen pointer to select and execute commands. A mouse is simply an input device built to help the user control this on-screen pointer in as natural and efficient a manner as possible.

The pointer on the screen mimics the movements of your mouse. As you move your mouse, a ball encased in the bottom of your mouse rolls on the desk and in turn sends signals to the computer as to which direction to move the pointer on the screen. Move the mouse side to side, or up and down, and the on-screen pointer moves in a similar manner.

Once you have the mouse positioned to select the command or data you want to act on, you use the mouse buttons to execute the command (see Figure 13.1).

FIG. 13.1
The mouse controls the on-screen pointer and lets you select program icons, manipulate property sheets, and access data.

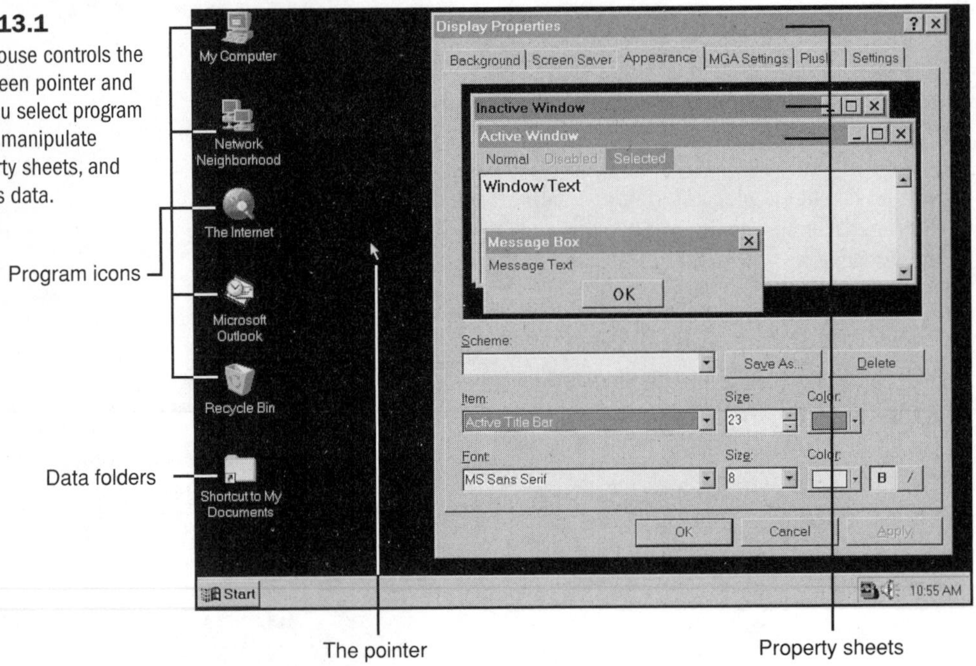

Program icons

Data folders

The pointer

Property sheets

Connecting a Mouse

Your mouse connects to your PC either through a dedicated mouse port or a standard 9-pin serial port. Once you're familiar with what the mouse connectors look like you can go ahead and connect your mouse using the following steps:

1. Save any open documents, and then close all active applications.

2. Identify which type of mouse connector you have and its corresponding connector on the back of your computer.

3. Carefully position the connector so that it matches the connector on the back of your PC, and gently press it into place.

4. In most cases, you'll have to restart your computer in order for the operating system to recognize your mouse.

N O T E For computers running Windows 3.11, the process is a little more involved and requires installing MS-DOS mouse drivers (mouse.com and mouse.sys in most cases). If you have Windows 3.11, you'll need to refer to the manual that came with your mouse for complete installation instructions. ▩

Using the Mouse Buttons

Most mice have two buttons. In Windows 95, the left button selects text and data, executes commands, and manipulates data, while the right mouse button accesses context menus.

Pressing a mouse button and then releasing it is known as *clicking your mouse*. You can click both left and right mouse buttons. Pressing the button and releasing it twice in quick succession is called *double-clicking*.

The Left Mouse Button

It seems simple, but there are a lot of things you can do by combining various types of mouse clicks with mouse movements. Table 13.1 gives you some examples.

Table 13.1 Left Mouse Button Operations

Task	Mouse Button
Select items	Press and hold down the left mouse button. Move the mouse to select desired text, numbers, or objects. Release mouse button. The selected text is highlighted.
Move selected items (also called *click and drag*)	Position mouse over highlighted text. Press and hold left mouse button down. While holding down left mouse button, move mouse (and the selected items) to their new location and release mouse button.
Access a menu or command	Position pointer over menu or property box button; press and release left mouse button quickly.
Start a program	Quickly press and release the left mouse button twice (double-click).

Part
IV

Ch
13

N O T E Windows 95 lets you customize what each of the buttons does through the Mouse
Properties dialog box. This can be a help if you have a three-button mouse. See the section
"Adjusting Mouse Properties" later in the chapter for examples. ▇

The Right Mouse Button

The right mouse button is generally reserved for special uses. In Windows 95, the right mouse
button accesses a context menu that lists the available options for the item you've just clicked
(see Figure 13.2).

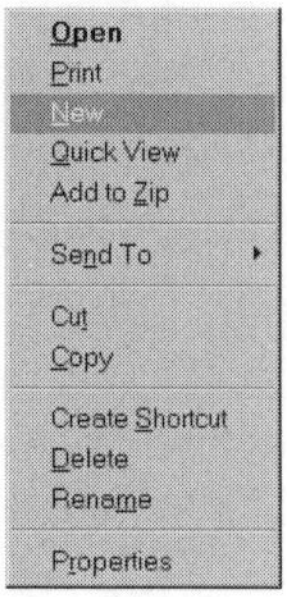

FIG. 13.2
Right-clicking a file gets
you a menu of options.

The right mouse button does different things, depending on which type of item you click. See
Table 13.2 for some examples.

Table 13.2 Right Mouse Button Operations

Action	Menu Options
Right-clicking a file	This pulls up a menu that asks you if you want to open, print, delete, or send the file somewhere.
Right-clicking a program	Presents you with a menu that lets you open, create a shortcut, or access that program's property sheet.
Click and drag a file (press and hold the mouse key while moving it)	Presents you with a menu that lets you choose to move or copy the file to its new location.

Using the IntelliMouse Wheel

Microsoft's newest mouse features a small wheel in between the two mouse buttons. The
wheel directly controls an application's scroll bar (see Chapter 6, "Working with Applications")
letting you move up and down in a document without having to move the pointer off to the
right of the screen. You can also use the IntelliMouse to pan in documents by clicking the
wheel and moving the mouse in the direction you'd like to pan. When you're ready to stop
panning, click the wheel again.

Three-Button Mice

Some mice have three buttons. Usually the mouse comes with software that lets you customize what that third button does. Windows 95 also supports many of the more popular three-button mice and may have built-in support for that third button. If you have a three-button mouse, see the following section for tips on how to use the third button.

Adjusting Mouse Properties

Windows 95 allows you to customize your mouse to best suit your style. You can adjust the speed at which the mouse moves the pointer across the screen, the amount of time allowed between the clicks of a double-click, and how the pointer appears on the screen. Left-handed computer users can configure the mouse to work best with the left hand.

These adjustments are made through the Mouse Properties dialog box. The Mouse Properties program is in Windows 95's Control Panel. You can get to it by clicking Start, Settings, Control Panel. You should then see the Mouse icon. Double-click the Mouse icon to start the Mouse Properties program.

Configuring Mouse Double-Click Speed

To configure mouse speed when double-clicking:

1. Click Start, Settings, Control Panel and then double-click the Mouse icon.
2. Click the Buttons tab.
3. To adjust the amount of time needed between double-clicks, slide the bar in the bottom half of the Buttons tab of the Mouse Properties dialog box either left or right. (Hold the left mouse button down while moving the mouse, then release after you've moved the slider.)
4. You can test your setting by double-clicking the jack-in-the-box—if he pops up, you've clicked fast enough (see Figure 13.3).

Configuring Right- or Left-Hand Mouse Preferences

To change your mouse for right or left-handers:

1. Click Start, Settings, Control Panel and then double-click the Mouse icon.
2. To switch between right- and left-handed mouse configurations, click either the Right-handed or Left-handed option buttons in the top of the Buttons tab of the Mouse Properties dialog box (see Figure 13.3).

Adjusting Pointer Speed

You can control how fast the pointer moves on the screen in relation to your mouse movements on your desk. You can have the pointer move completely from one side of the screen to the other with only the slightest mouse movement, or you can slow the pointer down for greater control.

Part

IV

Ch

13

FIG. 13.3

Select the Buttons tab of the Mouse Properties dialog box to configure your mouse for right or left-handed button actions.

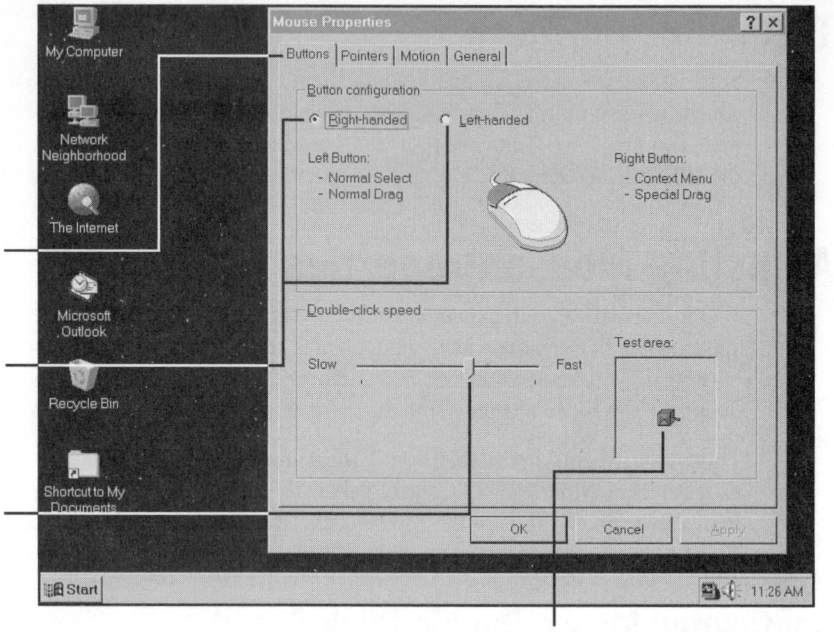

The Buttons tab —

Click here to switch between right- and left-handed mouse configurations —

Slide this bar to set the amount of time allowed between the clicks of a double-click —

Double-click here to test the double-click speed setting

The pointer speed is set in the same Mouse Properties dialog box as mentioned earlier:

1. Click Start, Settings, Control Panel, then double-click the Mouse icon.
2. Once the dialog box is open, click the Motion tab (see Figure 13.4).

FIG. 13.4

You can choose to show pointer trails in the Mouse Properties dialog box with the Motion tab selected.

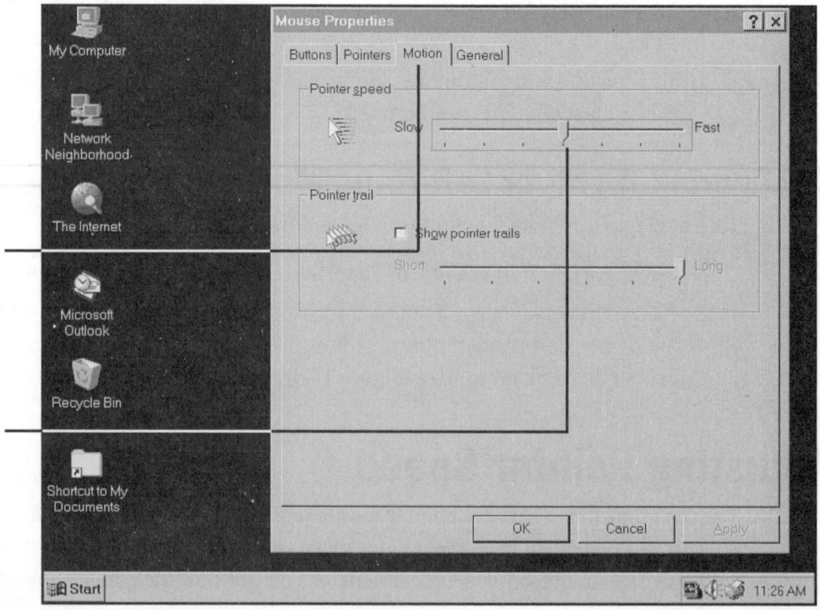

The Motion tab —

Slide this bar to set the relative speed of the pointer to your mouse movements —

Cleaning a Mouse

If your pointer starts moving erratically, or your mouse isn't moving smoothly, it's probably time to clean your mouse. This is a simple process:

1. Carefully remove the mouse ball. On the bottom of your mouse there will be a cover plate that usually just twists off. If you have trouble getting the cover off, refer to your mouse manual.

2. Once the ball is out, roll it between your fingers to remove any dirt.

3. Inspect the inside of the mouse and carefully remove any dirt you find in there, especially any dirt that has collected on the little rollers that come in contact with the mouse ball.

4. Reassemble your mouse and give it try.

A thorough cleaning usually does the trick. If no amount of cleaning helps, you may be in need of a new mouse.

Defining Joysticks

Joysticks are basically sticks attached to a base unit that measures the distance the stick is moved left, right, up, down, or diagonally. Electronic sensors in the base unit translate those motions into motions that are understood by the computer and software.

Joysticks are almost exclusively used with game software; they are not designed to replace a mouse.

Types of Joysticks

Joysticks come in various shapes and sizes. Some are built to mimic the flight controls of an airplane, complete with buttons to fire guns and missiles. Others aren't sticks at all, but may be steering wheels designed to help the user more effectively play driving simulation games. In general, computer input devices used to help users play computer games are called joysticks.

Connecting a Joystick

Joysticks all connect with a 15-pin D-shaped connector. See Figure 13.5 for an example of a joystick connector.

Connecting a joystick is simple. To connect yours, follow these steps:

1. Save any open documents, and then close all active applications.

2. Identify the joystick connector on the back of your computer.

3. Carefully position the connector so that it matches the connector on the back of your PC, and gently press it into place.

4. In most cases, you'll have to restart your computer in order for the operating system to recognize your joystick.

FIG. 13.5
The 15-pin D-Shell is a typical joystick connector.

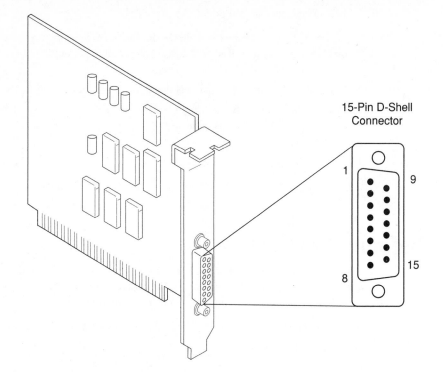

15-Pin D-Shell
Connector

If the computer doesn't initially see your joystick, you'll need to run Windows 95's Add Hardware Wizard. You can access the Add Hardware Wizard by clicking Start, Settings, Control Panel. The Add Hardware Wizard will be one of the icons in the Control Panel folder.

Calibrating Your Joystick

Calibrating your joystick lets you "center" your joystick so that when released it returns to a neutral position. It also makes certain that movements from side to side, or front to back result in smooth and predictable movement on the screen.

There are two ways to calibrate your joystick. One is through the Joystick Properties dialog box, and the other is through calibration sliders on the joystick itself.

Calibrating Your Joystick with Software

To calibrate your joystick through the Joystick Properties dialog click Start, Settings, Control Panel and double-click the Joystick icon. There, you'll see sliders that let you set the default X and Y axis positions of the joystick. You calibrate your mouse by adjusting these sliders.

Calibrating Your Joystick with Hardware

You can also calibrate most joysticks via slider bars, or wheels, that are on the joystick itself. Inspect your joystick to see if it has built-in calibration adjusters. ●

CHAPTER 14

Printers

Printing files and documents can be as simple as clicking an application's Print button. The hard part is deciding which printer is right for you. This chapter defines printers, and explains the differences between the most common printers available. In addition, you learn how to connect a printer to your computer, and how to make sure it will work with Windows 95. ▪

Understand the different types of printers that are available

What does a printer do, and which printer should you buy? Learn about the types of printers you can use.

Connect a printer to your system

How do you add a new printer to your computer system? Learn how to install new printers here.

Make sure your printer will work with Windows 95

Use a wizard to set up your printer to work with Windows 95.

Go ahead and print a document

Printing is as easy as clicking a toolbar button. But if something goes wrong, you can use these troubleshooting tips to locate the problem, or you can use Print Manager to check the printer status.

Printers Defined

A *printer* is the computer component that lets you create copies of the information stored in your computer on paper. The printed material is often called *hard copy*, to differentiate it from the data stored on a disk, or held in the computer's memory.

There are three basic types of printers available for use with personal computers:

- *Laser printers*. These combine a magnetic roller with powdered ink called toner to transfer high-quality characters or images onto a page.
- *Inkjet printers*. These have small nozzles that actually spray fast-drying ink onto the page to form characters or images.
- *Dot-matrix printers*. These use a print head to strike an inked ribbon against paper, like a typewriter, creating characters out of a series of dots.

The type of printer you choose depends on your budget and the type of output you need. For example, if all you need to print are grocery lists, you may be happy with a dot-matrix printer. In general, dot-matrix printers are noisier, slower, and produce a poorer-quality image than do laser or inkjet printers, but they are also less expensive. If you need to print newsletters, brochures, or illustrated reports, you will probably want a high-quality laser printer.

In general, there are three main factors to consider when purchasing a printer:

- *Cost*. Printers are available ranging in price from a few hundred dollars to a few thousand dollars, but the purchase price is just the beginning. Paper, ink, toner, printer ribbons, and the other *consumables* are required to keep the printer running, and they all cost money.
- *Resolution*. Resolution is measured by how many dots per inch (dpi) the printer can print. The more dots per inch, the higher the resolution of the printed image. The higher the printer's resolution, the better is its quality.
- *Speed*. Printer speed is rated by how many characters printers output in a second (cps) or how many pages printers output in a minute (ppm). The higher the number, the faster the printer.

Although the primary considerations involved in selecting a printer are usually cost, speed, and resolution, there are other issues that come into play as well. Available fonts, the ability to print in color, and the amount of maintenance involved may weight your decision:

- *Noise*. Impact printers such as dot-matrix printers are noisier than non-impact printers such as laser or inkjet printers. If you have a small or crowded office, noise can be an important factor.
- *Software support*. PCs communicate with printers using software programs called printer drivers, and some printers come with built-in printer languages, such as PostScript. Be sure that the software programs you use support the printer driver and printer language for the printer you purchase.

- *Fonts*. A font is the style of letters that your printer puts on the paper. They are important if you want control over the appearance of text on the printed page. Most printers come with built-in fonts called internal or resident fonts. Some dot-matrix printers may only have a few resident fonts, while some laser printers may have dozens. In addition, laser and inkjet printers can use soft fonts that come with your software applications.

- *Color*. Color spices up most printed documents, but it can significantly increase the cost of printing. Not only do color printers cost more, but the ink, toner, or ribbon cartridges cost more as well. Although the cost of laser color printers is coming down, color inkjet printers still offer the best combination of cost effectiveness and print quality.

- *Maintenance*. The amount of time you spend cleaning a printer, refilling a paper tray, or changing a toner cartridge may vary greatly from printer to printer.

Laser Printers

Laser printers are similar to copy machines—they use laser beams to burn special toner onto the page to create a permanent impression (see Figure 14.1). They create high-quality output at a relatively fast speed, without making too much noise. The downside is the price; most black-and-white laser printers cost $500 or more, and each toner cartridge (which lasts about 3,000 pages) can cost an additional $50.

When considering a laser printer, here are some things to keep in mind:

- Laser printers offer resolutions ranging upwards from 300 dpi–600 dpi is common, and very high-quality printers can output at resolutions as high as 3,386 dpi!

- Laser printers are available in speeds of 4, 8, or 12 ppm. However, keep in mind that these are the top speeds. The actual speed will depend on whether you are printing plain text, or complex characters and images.

- The amount of desk space a printer uses is called the *footprint*. If you don't have much room, you'll want a small footprint printer.

- Some printers can hold only 50 sheets of paper, while others can hold 250 sheets. Some have more than one paper holder, which increases capacity, and makes it possible to switch between different sizes of paper. That means you don't have to reload when you want to print legal size pages or envelopes.

Inkjet Printers

Inkjet printers spray a fine, quick-drying ink through small nozzles to produce characters and images on paper. Although the results are not quite as sharp as those of laser printers, inkjet printers provide very good quality output at a lower cost.

FIG. 14.1
Laser printers cost more than other printers, but they may be worth the price because they are fast, quiet, and produce high-quality text and graphics.

When considering an inkjet printer, here are some things to keep in mind:

- Inkjet printers are quiet.
- Inkjet printers, which start at about $200, are less expensive than laser printers, yet produce output almost as well.
- Inkjet printers are slower than laser printers, but faster than dot-matrix printers.
- Replacement ink cartridges are expensive, costing about $45 each.
- Many inkjet printers can use color ink cartridges.

Dot-Matrix Printers

Dot-matrix printers are the cheapest printers available (see Figure 14.2). They create text and images on the page by hammering several small pins against an inked ribbon. The more pins used, the better the image—9-pin and 24-pin are common options. The 24-pin printers produce a better quality output, but are somewhat slower than the 9-pin printers.

Print quality for dot-matrix printers is often described in terms of mode: draft mode (low resolution), near-letter-quality mode (medium resolution), or letter-quality mode (high resolution). The speed depends on the mode, with draft mode being the fastest.

When considering a dot-matrix printer, here are some things to keep in mind:

- Dot-matrix printers are the cheapest. Prices start at about $100; the ribbon cartridges last a long time and cost about $15 apiece.
- The sound made by the pins banging away can be quite loud; 24-pin printers are louder than 9-pin printers.

- Most dot-matrix printers can use different types of paper, including continuous feed as well as cut-sheet paper. In addition, they can be used to print on multipart forms. Some let you switch back and forth between the different types without reloading.

- Narrow carriage dot-matrix printers can accommodate standard letter size paper, while wide carriage dot-matrix printers can handle 11×17-inch pages. Wide carriage printers cost generally about $100 more than narrow carriage printers.

FIG. 14.2
A dot-matrix printer is noisy but cheap to operate.

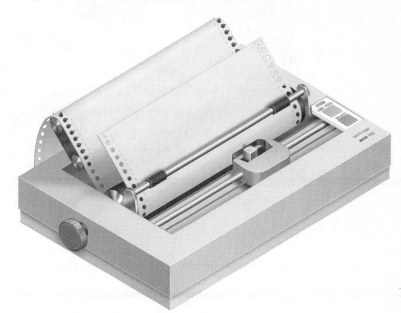

Connecting Your Printer to Your PC

Most printers have two cables: one is a power cord, and the other is the printer cable. Connecting a printer involves attaching the printer cable to the correct port on your computer's system unit, then plugging the power cord into an electrical outlet.

To attach a printer cable to the system unit, follow these steps:

1. Locate the printer cable. The easiest way is to find the one that isn't a power cord. It is probably heavy, gray, about six feet long, and it ends in a D-shaped connector with 25 pins.

> **N O T E** For laser and inkjet printers, the printer cable is probably permanently attached to the printer. For dot-matrix printers, you will have to manually attach one end of the cable to the printer (see Figure 14.3). Locate the end that *is not* the D-shaped 25-pin connector and attach it to the port on the printer. Secure it using two clips that snap into place. ■

2. Locate the parallel port on the system unit. The parallel port also has 25 sockets, arranged in the same configuration as the 25 pins on the cable connector.

Part
IV

Ch
14

FIG. 14.3
On a dot-matrix printer, you will have to connect one end of the cable to the printer and the other end to the system unit.

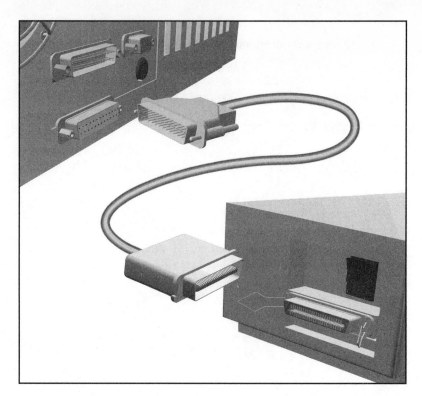

3. Plug the connector on the cable into the port on the system unit.

4. Secure the connector by tightening the screws on either side.

Understanding Your Printer Controls

Although most commands that affect your printer come from your PC and your PC applications, most printers also have a set of controls. For example, you may be able to select the mode of operation as well as which paper tray to use for a particular print job. Status lights on the front of the printer let you know which controls are active.

If you look at the front of your printer, these are some of the controls you are likely to find:

▪ *Online* or *ready light*. A printer must be online in order to work, which means it must be active and ready to accept data from the computer.

N O T E   Although some printers automatically come online when you print a file, most have an on/off switch. If none of the status lights on your computer are lit, locate the on/off switch and turn the printer on. ▪

▪ *Mode indicator*. Dot-matrix printers are likely to have different modes such as draft mode, near-letter-quality mode, and letter-quality mode.

■ *Error indicator.* If there is a problem with printing such as no paper, or a paper jam, the error light will be lit.

Be sure to read the documentation that comes with your printer for complete instructions on using the printer controls.

Installing Your Printer to Work in Windows 95

Windows 95 uses the Add Printer Wizard to assist you in installing a printer. If your printer is not already installed, run the wizard to add the printer.

N O T E These instructions are for installing a local printer, one that is attached directly to your computer. If you have a networked printer, ask your network administrator for information about installing it for use with your computer. ■

1. Double-click My Computer and then double-click the Printers folder icon. Double-click the Add Printer icon to start the Add Printer Wizard. Choose Next.

2. On the second screen of the wizard, select the Local Printer option button to install a printer directly attached to your computer. Then click Next again.

3. Select the printer's manufacturer in the Manufacturers list box (see Figure 14.4). Select the specific printer in the Printers list box and then choose Next.

N O T E If your printer is not on the list, either choose the Generic manufacturer and Generic/Text Only printer, or click the Have Disk button and follow instructions to install a vendor-supplied driver. ■

4. Choose the printer port, typically LPT1, and then click the Configure Port button. Check the Spool MS-DOS Print Jobs and the Check Port State Before Printing check boxes. Choose OK and then choose Next.

5. In the Printer Name text box, type a name for the printer or keep the name that is displayed. Select the Yes option button if you want Windows-based programs to use this printer as the default printer. (If a different printer is the default printer, choose No.) Choose Next.

6. Select Yes if you want to print a test page, and then choose Finish. The test page prints (if you selected Yes). The wizard copies the printer drivers to your system, prompting for the Windows 95 disks or CD if needed.

After you install a printer in Windows, you can make changes to the configuration to customize it for different printing requirements. You make these changes in the printer's Properties dialog box:

1. Click the Start menu, select Settings, Printers, and then select the printer icon for the printer you want to configure.

2. Right-click the printer icon and then select Properties to open the Properties dialog box (see Figure 14.5).

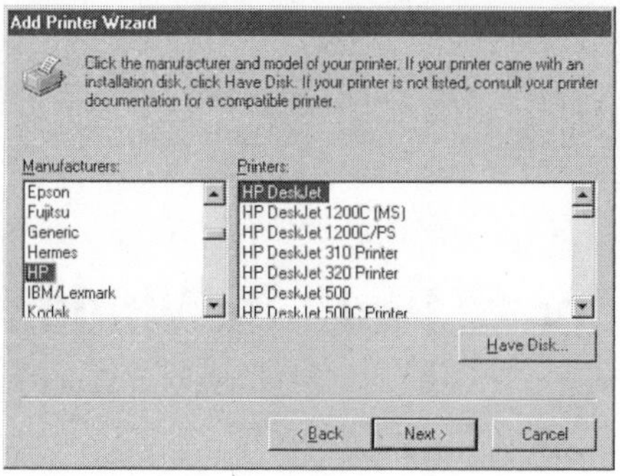

FIG. 14.4

Windows 95 makes it easy to install a new printer by using the Add Printer Wizard. Just pick the right make and model from the list.

3. The Properties dialog box contains several tabs. Select each tab to view the settings. Click the Help button (the question mark in the upper-right corner) and then click a feature to read details about that property. Properties vary according to each printer's capabilities.

4. Change settings as desired, and then choose OK to save the new settings. Choose Cancel to get out of the dialog box without making any changes.

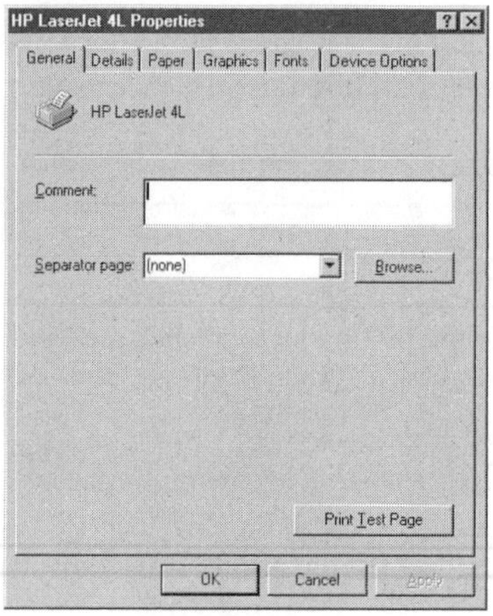

FIG. 14.5

Use the Properties dialog box to configure the specific details of your printer to work with Windows 95.

If you no longer need a printer that is installed in Windows 95, you can delete it from the Printers folder window:

1. Double-click My Computer and then double-click the Printers folder icon.

2. Select the printer you want to delete. Open the File menu and select Delete.

3. Windows asks if you are sure that you want to delete the printer. Choose Yes. The printer icon is deleted.

4. Windows then asks if it can remove files that were used only for this printer. Choose Yes. (If you plan to reattach this printer in the future, choose No.)

Other Printing Considerations

Printing a document is similar in most Windows applications. You can open the application's File menu and select Print to open the Print dialog box. In the dialog box, you can select options such as which pages you want to print and how many copies to print. To quickly print the current document without setting options, click the Print button on the toolbar.

A printer icon on the taskbar near the clock indicates that printing is in progress. A quick way to check the status of print jobs is to point to the printer icon on the taskbar.

After you issue the print command, the Print Manager takes control of the *print job* (see Figure 14.6). You can use the commands in Print Manager to check the status of a print job, to cancel a print job, or to pause a print job.

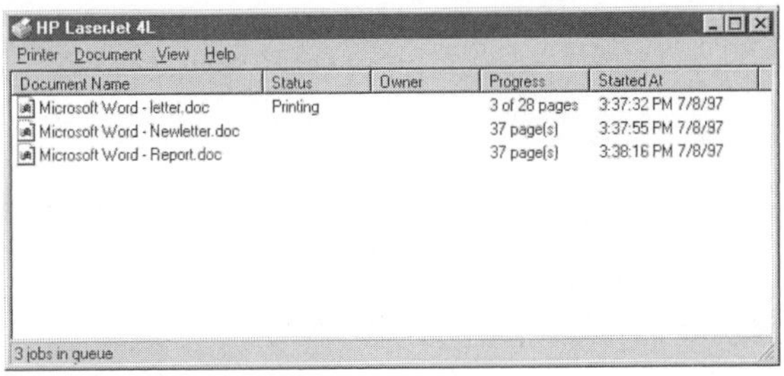

FIG. 14.6
Print Manager keeps track of documents waiting to be printed.

There are several ways to open Print Manager:

- If a print job is in progress, double-click the printer icon in the taskbar.
- Click the Start button and select Settings, Printers. Then double-click the printer icon for the printer you want to manage.
- Double-click the My Computer icon and then double-click the Printers folder icon. Double-click the printer icon for the printer you want to manage.

If your printer is not working, here are a few things to check:

- Is the printer turned on?
- Is the printer online?
- Are the cables between the printer and the computer attached correctly and securely?
- Is the printer power cord plugged in?
- Is there paper in the printer?
- Has the printer been paused in the Print Manager?

Part IV

Ch 14

T I P To check if a printer has been paused, open the Print Manager, then open the Printer menu. If there is a check mark next to the Pause Printing command, the printer has been paused. To restart it, select the Pause Printing command.

CHAPTER 15

Modems and Faxes

Modems let you link your computer to the outside world. Connected properly, you can use a modem to send data and files to anyone else with a modem and a computer. You can also access information and download it for use on your PC.

This chapter explains what a modem is, and how to set one up for use with your PC. In addition, you learn about using a modem as a fax machine and how to troubleshoot modem problems.

Understand how a modem works

It's not magic that moves the data from here to there through the telephone cables. Find out how modems work and which modem is right for you.

Connect a modem to your system

Learn how to install a modem inside or outside of your computer.

Make sure your modem works with Windows 95

Use a wizard to detect and set up your modem so it works with Windows 95.

Learn to catch problems before they catch you

When a modem doesn't work, there could be problems with the hardware, software, or the communication settings. Find out what you can do to solve these problems and get back online.

Understanding Modems

A *modem* is a hardware device that lets two computers exchange information over telephone lines (see Figure 15.1). Using a modem, you can connect directly to another computer that is also equipped with a modem, to an online service provider such as America Online, or to the Internet and World Wide Web. When you're connected, you can send and receive files or communicate in *real time*—which means you communicate with little or no delay, as if you were face-to-face with the person at the other computer.

These days, a modem is a vital part of a PC; without one, you'll miss out on a wide range of opportunities. Here's a small sampling of things you can do with a modem:

- Exchange data directly with other computer users.
- Access an online service or the Internet to gather information or to distribute information about anything, anywhere.
- Exchange electronic mail.
- Play interactive online games.
- Make hotel or airline reservations.
- Check stock prices.

FIG. 15.1

Modems let you communicate over standard telephone lines with other computer users. You can transfer data, exchange electronic files, and even carry on a typed conversation in real time.

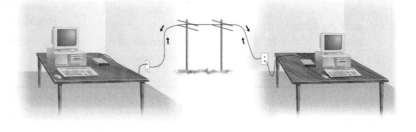

The word *modem* is actually an abbreviation of the terms *modulator-demodulator*, which describe how a modem works.

Here are the basic steps involved in transferring data using modems:

1. Software in your computer activates the modem, which listens on the phone line for a dial tone, then dials a specified number.
2. The receiving modem on the other end answers the call and sends out a signal which the sending modem recognizes, establishing a connection.
3. The modem sending information converts the computer's digital signals into analog signals that can be sent over the phone lines (this is called *modulating*).

4. The receiving modem translates the incoming data back into digital signals that its computer can understand (this is called *demodulating*).

5. When the online session is over, the computers issue a command telling the modems to hang up.

In order to make a connection using a modem, you need the following:

- *Access to a telephone line.* Modems have two jacks where you plug in standard telephone cables. You use one jack to connect the modem to the telephone line, and the other jack to connect the modem to a phone.

- *Data communications software.* You need software to control the modem. Data communications software issues commands such as telling your computer when to dial and when to hang up. It also lets you set communications parameters such as the data transfer rate. The software must be compatible with both the modem and your PC. (Windows 95 comes with a basic data communications software called HyperTerminal.)

- *Software drivers.* You must have the necessary drivers for the modem to work with your operating system. Windows 95 comes with drivers for most modems.

For more information about using a modem to access the Internet and the World Wide Web, see the chapters in Part V, "Connecting to the Internet."

Choosing a Modem

Choosing a modem is not as difficult as choosing some other computer components because there is less variety. There are two basic types of modems:

- *Internal.* These are hardware boards you plug into an expansion slot in your PC's system unit (see Figure 15.2). Internal modems are convenient because they don't take up desk space, and they use the computer's power supply so they are on whenever the computer is on.

- *External.* These are connected to the PC by plugging a cable into a port on the system unit (see Figure 15.3). External modems also have their own power cords. You must turn on the modem when you want to make a connection. One benefit of an external modem is that you can move it to another computer if necessary.

N O T E You can attach a telephone to either kind of modem so when you are not using the modem, you can use the phone to make regular calls. ▮

Aside from choosing an internal or external modem, the other main factors to consider are:

- *Communications speed.* A modem's speed, called the *baud rate*, is measured in bits per second (bps). Currently, speeds range from 300 bps to 56Kbps, but to satisfy the need for speed, manufacturers are developing faster modems all the time.

FIG. 15.2

An internal modem plugs into an expansion slot inside your PC. The phone jacks are accessed through a port on the back of the system unit.

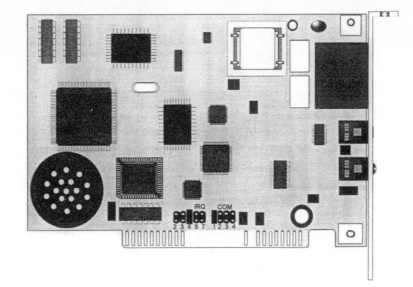

FIG. 15.3

An external modem has controls and status lights on the front that you can use to monitor transmissions.

■ *Cost.* The faster the modem, the higher the cost—although faster transmission times may save you money on your phone bills. Also, external modems generally cost about $30 to $50 more than internal modems. For example, a 56Kbps internal modem will probably cost between $150 and $200. A 56Kbps external modem would range from $180 to $240.

N O T E If you only use your modem to send and receive e-mail messages, you may be able to get
by with a modem as slow as 14.4Kbps. If you use your modem to transmit and download
files, or if you like to surf the World Wide Web—which uses a lot of graphics images—you should
purchase the fastest modem available. ■

■ *Communications software.* Most communications software programs have features for storing telephone numbers as well as for automatic dialing and answering. Even more important, you use the communications program to set *communications parameters*, which are the rules the modem uses to make the call and transmit the data. You want to choose a modem that supports the communications parameters you plan to use.

N O T E The communications parameters set for the sending modem must match the communications parameters set for the receiving modem. ■

Modems also operate under communications parameters. Modem communications parameters include:

■ *Transmission speed.* As mentioned earlier, speed can range from 300 bps and up.

■ *Transfer protocol.* This helps to make sure the data the modem transfers is error-free. Common transfer protocols include XMODEM, YMODEM, and ZMODEM. The Internet uses FTP (File Transport Protocol), and some online services have their own transfer protocols. For example, CompuServe uses CompuServe B.

■ *Data format.* This is usually text for unformatted text files, and binary for graphics or formatted text files.

■ *Compression standard.* This allows modems to compress data before transmitting it, effectively increasing transmission speeds. Common compression standards include MNP 5 and CCITT V.42bis.

Selecting a Fax Modem

One final consideration when purchasing a modem is whether or not you want fax capabilities. Because most modems currently available include fax capabilities, it's not much of a decision. Fax modems generally don't cost any more than standard modems, so in addition to using the modem to communicate with other computers, you can use it to communicate with facsimile machines.

With a fax modem, you can:

- Transmit standard computer files to a receiving fax machine.
- Receive fax transmissions and store them as computer files.

NOTE If you already have a stand-alone fax machine, you do not have to use the fax options on the modem. The device will work fine as a plain modem.

To use the fax capabilities, you need to have specific fax software or data communications software that includes fax support.

Connecting a Modem

Connecting a modem involves attaching the modem device to your PC and to the telephone line. The modem should come with the necessary equipment, including a standard RJ-11 telephone cord. The steps you take depend on whether you have an internal modem or an external modem.

If you have an internal modem, you must install it by removing the cover of the system unit and plugging the modem card into a vacant expansion slot. Unless you are extremely confident about working inside your computer, you should have the modem installed by a professional computer technician.

If you have an external modem, however, you can easily connect it yourself. To connect an external modem to your PC, follow these steps:

1. Locate the serial cable that came with the modem. It should have a 25-pin male connector at one end and a 25-hole female connector at the other end.
2. Plug the female connector into an open 25-pin serial port on the PC's system unit, and plug the male connector into the modem device.
3. Secure the connectors using the screws on either side.
4. Locate the power cord for the modem device and plug it into an electrical wall socket, power strip, or uninterruptible power supply.

After the modem is connected to your PC, you must connect it to the phone line. This procedure is the same for both external and internal devices.

To connect a modem to the phone line, follow these steps:

1. Locate the two phone jacks on the modem, labeled Phone and Line. They will be on the outside of an external modem, or on the back of the system unit if you have an internal modem. They look just like the phone jacks on your telephone.
2. Plug one end of a standard RJ-11 telephone cord (it should come with the modem) into the Line jack, and the other end into the wall jack for your telephone.
3. Plug one end of another RJ-11 telephone cord into the Phone jack, and the other end into your telephone.

> **TIP** If you have a phone line dedicated for use with your computer, you do not need to connect the modem to the telephone. You only need to connect to a phone if you want to be able to use the phone for regular calls when the modem is not in use.

Understanding Your Modem Controls

An internal modem is integrated into your PC; you will interact with it using your data communications software. If you have an external modem, however, you can control and monitor certain functions on the device itself. For example, status lights on the front of the modem let you know whether the modem is on, and whether it is in *send mode,* ready to dial and transmit data, or *receive mode,* ready to answer and download data (refer to Figure 15.3).

If you look at the front of your external modem, these are some of the controls you are likely to find:

- *Power On light.* An external modem must be turned on in order to work. When you press the on/off switch, the power light will come on.
- *Speed indicator.* Most modems can operate at different speeds; this light tells you which speed is currently in use.
- *Mode indicator.* If you have your modem set to answer an incoming call, the Answer mode indicator will be lit. If it is set to dial, the Dial mode indicator will be lit.
- *Error indicator.* If there is a problem with the transmission, the Error light will be on.

Be sure to read the documentation that comes with your modem for complete instructions on understanding the modem controls and status lights.

Setting Up Your Modem to Work in Windows 95

Windows 95 uses the Install New Modem Wizard to help you identify and set up newly installed modems. Before starting the wizard, it helps to know the manufacturer and model of the modem. Also, if you have an external modem, make sure it is turned on.

To use the Install New Modem Wizard, follow these steps:

1. Double-click My Computer and then double-click the Control Panel folder icon. Alternatively, click the Start button, then open the Settings menu and click Control Panel.
2. Double-click the Modems icon in the Control Panel folder to open the Modems Properties dialog box. Click the Add button to start the Install New Modem Wizard, then choose Next.
3. Windows 95 immediately tries to detect and identify the modem. When it does, it displays the Verify Modem screen of the wizard, displaying the name or type of modem that it finds. It also identifies the communications port where the modem is connected (see Figure 15.4). If the information is correct, choose Next, then choose Finish.

4. If Windows 95 cannot detect the modem, the wizard displays a screen where you can select the modem information yourself. (You can display the same screen by clicking the Change button if the information on the Verify Modem screen of the wizard is incorrect.) Select the modem's manufacturer in the Manufacturers list box. Select the specific modem in the Models list box, then choose OK.

N O T E   If your modem is not on the list, choose the Standard Modem Types manufacturer and select the model according to speed. Or, click the Have Disk button and follow the instructions to install a vendor-supplied driver. ▨

5. Choose Next, then choose Finish. Windows 95 installs the necessary drivers for the modem, then closes the wizard. Choose Close to close the Modems Properties dialog box.

FIG. 15.4

On the Verify Modem page of Windows 95's Install New Modem Wizard, you see the port and modem type Windows has detected. Click Change to select a different modem.

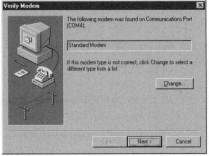

N O T E   If Windows 95 detects the new device when you first turn on your PC, it will prompt you to run the Add New Hardware Wizard to detect it and set it up. Go ahead and use the Add New Hardware Wizard; it performs the same function as the Install New Modem Wizard, but will detect and set up other types of hardware devices as well. ▨

Troubleshooting Your Modem

When a modem doesn't work, there could be problems with the hardware, the communications software, or the software settings. Here are a few tips for locating the problem and fixing it.

The External Modem Isn't Working

If your external modem is not working, here are a few things to check:

▨ Make sure the modem is turned on.

▨ Make sure the cables between the modem and the computer attached correctly and securely.

- Make sure the modem power cord is plugged in.
- Make sure the modem is set to the correct mode. Use Answer mode if you are trying to receive a transmission, or Dial mode if you are trying to initiate a transmission.

The Modem Dials, but Doesn't Connect

If your modem dials, but doesn't connect, here are a few things to check:

- Make sure both the sending and receiving modems are set to the same communications parameters.
- Make sure the modem is dialing the correct number. If another modem doesn't pick up on the other end, the call can't go through.
- Make sure there isn't interference on the telephone line. Modems are more sensitive to static and other interference on a line. Someone picking up an extension phone, crossed wires, even thunderstorms in the area can cause enough disturbance to cancel a call. Make sure the line is clear, or try a different phone number.

The Modem Doesn't Get a Dial Tone

If your modem doesn't get a dial tone, here are some things to check:

- Make sure the RJ-11 telephone cords are connected correctly. You may have the Phone jack connected to the telephone line, and the Line jack connected to the telephone.
- Make sure the telephone is working.
- Make sure your communications software is correctly installed.

Windows or the Communications Software Displays a Message Saying It Can't Find the Modem

If Windows or your communications software displays a message telling you that it can't find your modem, here are some things to check:

- If you have an external modem, make sure it's plugged in, that the cable is attached securely to the port on the system unit, and that the device is turned on.
- Make sure the correct driver is installed. If necessary, run the Install New Modem Wizard again.
- Make sure the COM port setting is correct. If the modem is set up with COM1, but Windows 95 thinks it's in COM4, Windows won't be able to find it. Check the COM port setting on the Properties page of the Modems Properties dialog box, and make sure it is the same as the COM port setting in your communications software.
- The interrupt request (IRQ) setting may be conflicting with another device. This is a relatively technical problem, and you should have a qualified technician look into it.

- Check for an IRQ conflict. To do so, from the Start menu, choose Settings, Control Panel. Click the System icon, then click the Performance tab of the System Properties dialog box. The status area of this tab will report an IRQ conflict if one exists. You're not advised to try to fix this conflict, but the information will help you accurately report the problem to a technician.

- The modem may be damaged. Have a technician check it out.

CHAPTER 16

Speakers and Sound

Sound is one of the favorite options on today's PCs. In fact, sound is a standard feature of most new PCs.

Everyone has their own uses for sound. You may just want to play a few music CDs with your CD-ROM drive while you are working, or you may use multimedia applications for presentations or educational programs. You may just like the sound of your jet engines roaring as you punch the throttle in a flight simulator. This chapter explains the basics of sound in Windows and shows you how to get the most sound out of your PC. ■

Learn how PC sound systems work

Find out what your PC's sound card, speakers, and micro-phone do.

Understand what types of sound files your PC plays

Learn how your PC plays WAV files and music on audio CDs.

Record your own sounds

Learn how to record sounds with a microphone or from a CD in the CD-ROM drive. See how to adjust the volume for playback and recording.

Troubleshoot common problems

Getting sound to work right with Windows isn't always easy. See some common problems and where to look for solutions.

Components for Sound on Your PC

To produce sound on your PC, you need a sound card and speakers. The *sound card* is an expansion card that plugs into one of the slots on your motherboard. This card processes all of the instructions that have to do with sound, and then sends the sounds to the speakers to be played. The speakers plug into the sound card and usually have a power plug as well.

TIP Many motherboard manufacturers include sound chip(s) on the motherboard itself. If you have a new PC, check the specifications of its make and model to see if it uses this technology.

Sound Cards

Sound cards plug into an expansion slot in your PC. The card has a set of connectors that are exposed on the back of the PC; you can plug a microphone and speakers into the connectors. Some cards include an optional connector for a *line input*, which is used to connect another input source such as the output from a tape player or portable CD player. Other optional connectors can include a joystick connector and a MIDI connector (for connecting a MIDI keyboard). The card may include a volume control, which controls the volume of the speakers and/or headphones. Figure 16.1 shows the connectors of a typical sound card.

FIG. 16.1
The connectors on the Sound Blaster card are typical of those on most sound cards.

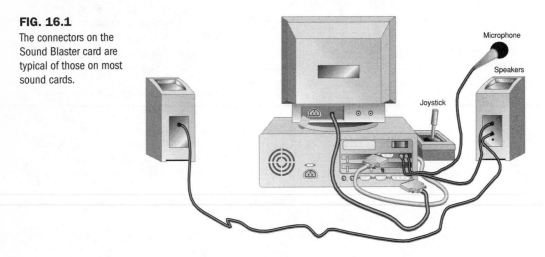

Speakers

The built-in speakers in most PC cases are used just for making system sounds, such as warning beeps and action indicators. To play more sophisticated sounds on your PC, you need a set of external speakers. Usually speakers come in pairs, and there is a plug that connects them to your sound card. Arrange the speakers with one on the left and one on the right of your desk or work area to get a stereo effect.

Optionally, some speakers come with a *subwoofer*. This improves the bass (low notes) sound. If you have a subwoofer with your speakers, it should go on the floor under your desk.

> **CAUTION**
>
> Be sure your speakers are shielded. Otherwise, if they get too close to the monitor, they will distort the display. Even with shielded speakers, take care not to get floppy disks too close to them as the magnets in the speakers can damage data on the disks.

Playing Sounds for Windows Events

By default, Windows 95 plays a sound when it starts and when it closes. You can change the sounds that are played for these events, and you can assign sounds to be played for other events. To do this, follow these steps:

1. Click the Start menu, choose Settings, and then choose Control Panel.
2. Double-click the Sounds icon in the Control Panel. This opens the Sounds Properties dialog box shown in Figure 16.2.
3. To assign a sound to an event, scroll the list at the top of the dialog box to find the event.

FIG. 16.2
You can choose and preview sounds in this dialog box.

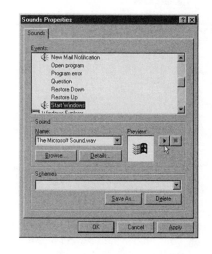

N O T E Some programs add additional events that you can assign sounds to. These will appear at the bottom of the list.

4. Click the Name box and choose a sound from the list. If you don't see a sound you want to use, click the Browse button and find any sound file in the WAV format.

5. To test the sound (to be sure it is the right one), click the Play button next to the Preview box.

6. Assign as many sounds as you want to different events, then click OK when you are finished.

Playing WAV Sound Files on Your PC

You're not limited to the built-in event sounds that came with your operating system; you can play other types of sound files as well. WAV files are the most common type of PC sound file. Windows has a built-in player, called Sound Recorder, for playing WAV files. To play a WAV file, use Explorer or My Computer to find the file you want to play, and double-click it to start it. Sound Recorder starts, and the WAV file begins playing immediately (see Figure 16.3). When the file is finished playing, Sound Recorder closes automatically.

FIG. 16.3
The Sound Recorder opens, plays the sound file, and closes unless you stop playback.

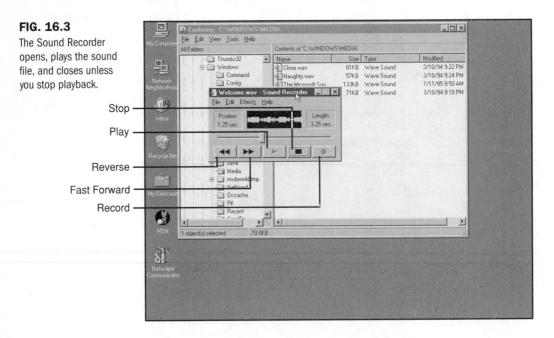

If you want to stop the playback, rewind it, and play it again, click the Stop button before it finishes playing. Once you click stop, you can play and rewind it as much as you want and the player won't close when the sound is finished playing.

You'll see how to use this same application to record your own sounds later in the section "Recording Sounds in Windows 95."

Getting New Sounds

If you are really into sounds and want more on your PC, there are several ways to get more sound files. The Windows CD-ROM installation includes many additional sound schemes, which you can add by using the Add/Remove Programs option in the Control Panel.

You can also buy any of a number of CD-ROMs that contain whole collections of additional sounds in the WAV format. And, you can find thousands of sound clips on the Internet.

Part
IV
Ch
16

 ON THE WEB

Use your Web browser to go to the following site for a good starting list of sites with WAV sounds:

http://www.yahoo.com/Computers_and_Internet/Multimedia/Sound/Archives/WAV/

▶ **See** "Exploring the World Wide Web," **p. 211**

Playing Music on Your PC

With a CD-ROM, sound card, and speakers, you can use your $2,000 PC like a $100 CD player. The sound probably won't be as good as your home stereo, but it is more convenient than setting up a stereo with your PC.

To use your computer to play audio CDs, put a CD into the CD-ROM drive. If your computer has AutoPlay features (as do all Windows 95 systems), it will automatically detect the CD and start the Windows CD player.

N O T E If you installed Windows from floppy disks, you won't have the Windows CD player installed.
If you installed Windows from a CD but didn't install the CD player, you need to use the Add/Remove Programs option in the Control Panel to add the CD Player. ■

When the CD Player starts, the controls display will be similar to that shown in Figure 16.4. These controls should look familiar, like the controls on a CD player in your home or car.

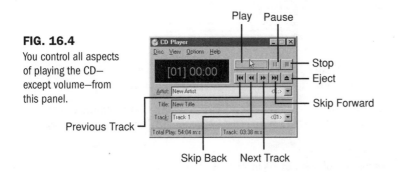

FIG. 16.4
You control all aspects of playing the CD—except volume—from this panel.

Adjusting the Speaker Volume and Tone in Windows 95

There are three ways to adjust the volume to your speakers. First, you can just adjust the volume control on the speakers themselves. See the instruction manual that accompanied your speakers to find the specific location of and adjustment instructions for the volume controls on your speakers.

Within Windows, you can also adjust the speaker volume by clicking the speaker icon in the taskbar to bring up the volume control shown in Figure 16.5. Drag the slider up or down to adjust the volume, or click the Mute box to turn the speakers off all together. This Mute option is what you want to use if you are listening to a CD on headphones and don't want it to play on the speakers.

FIG. 16.5
Slide the control up to increase the volume. Click Mute to turn off the sound through the speakers.

If you want more control over the speaker output, click the speaker icon in the taskbar with the right mouse button and select Volume Controls from the menu. This opens the Volume Control dialog box shown in Figure 16.6.

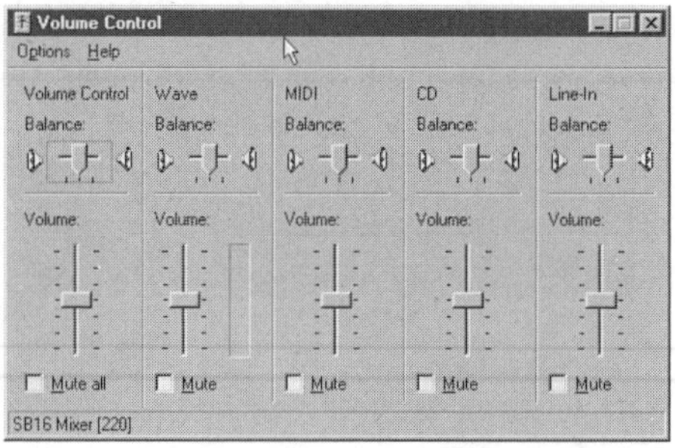

FIG. 16.6
This is the master control for playback volume.

The control at the far left is the master volume control. It controls the overall volume going to the speakers. Above it, you can adjust the balance to the left and right speakers.

Because the sound in your PC can come from several different sources, the Volume Control dialog box also provides controls for adjusting the relative volume of each of those sources. These sources are:

- *Wave.* Used to control the volume of files in the WAV format.
- *MIDI.* Used to control the volume of synthetic MIDI sounds, often used in games.

■ *CD*. This is a separate control for the audio CD's volume or volume of audio CD sounds in games.

■ *Line In*. If you have another external audio device plugged into the line in jack on your sound card, this controls its volume.

From the Volume Control dialog box, you can also control the bass and treble settings for your speakers. This adjustment is made for all sound, though, and doesn't differentiate between different sound sources. To adjust bass and treble settings, follow these steps:

1. Select the Options menu in the Volume Control dialog box and select the Advanced Controls item in the menu.

2. This adds an Advanced button to the Volume Control dialog box. Click it.

3. This opens the dialog box shown in Figure 16.7. Adjust the Bass and Treble settings using the sliders, then click OK.

FIG. 16.7
Bass and Treble settings are adjusted by opening the Advanced Volume Control options.

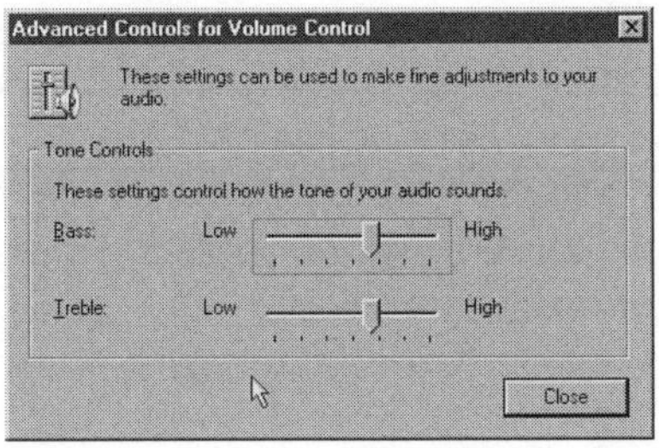

Listening to Your CDs on Headphones

Most CD-ROM drives have a headphone built-in jack and a volume control on the drive itself. To listen to a CD on the headphones instead of playing it over the speakers, follow these steps:

1. Put a CD into the CD-ROM drive.

2. Plug in the headphones.

3. Click the speaker icon in the taskbar and select the Mute check box to mute the speakers (otherwise, sound will issue from both the PC's speakers and the headphones).

4. Click the Play button in Windows' CD Player application to start the CD.

5. Adjust the volume using the control on the CD-ROM drive, and put on the headphones.

If your CD player doesn't have a volume control dial on it, you can use Windows to control the volume to the headphones. Follow these steps:

1. Click the speaker icon in the Windows taskbar; a Volume control box with slider pops up.

2. Click with the left mouse button on the slider, and drag the slider up to raise the sound level, or down to lower the sound level (see Figure 16.8).

3. Click anywhere outside the control box to close it.

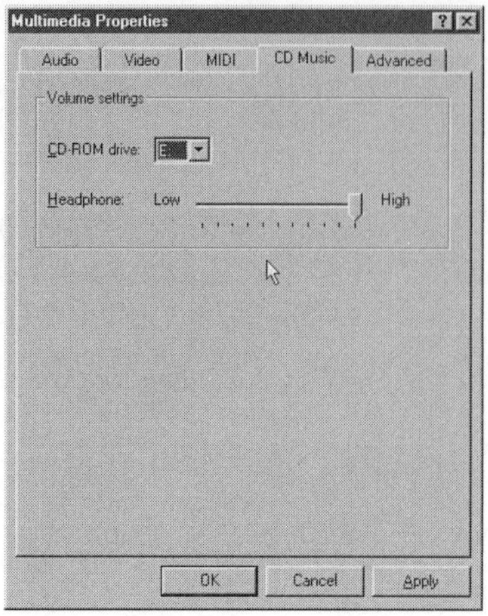

FIG. 16.8
If your CD drive doesn't
have a volume control,
use the Headphone
slider here to control the
headphone volume.

> **T I P** You can also plug a set of headphones into the Speaker jack on the sound card and listen to all of
> your sounds from CDs, games, and Windows on headphones instead of speakers. If you do that, all
> of the Windows speaker volume controls discussed in this chapter will control the volume for the
> headphones. In that case, be sure not to mute the speaker volume, or you won't hear anything on the
> headphones.

Microphones

Your computer may have come with a microphone. The microphone plugs into the sound card
and is used to record your voice or other sounds. Another new use of a microphone is to make
telephone-like conference calls over the Internet. Like any conference call, when you speak
into the mic, the person you call hears you on his speakers.

Recording Sounds in Windows 95

The most common way to record a sound in Windows is by using a microphone. To do this, be
sure the microphone is plugged into the microphone input jack on your sound card. If your mic
has an on/off switch, be sure it is on. Then follow these steps:

1. Click the Start menu, and choose Programs, Accessories, Multimedia, Sound Recorder.

2. This opens the Sound Recorder shown in Figure 16.9. Click the Record button and begin
   speaking, singing, or making noise into the mic. When you are finished, click the Stop
   button. You can click Record again to record more at the end of the file.

3. When you are finished recording, select the File menu and choose Save. Find a directory
   to save the file in, then give it a name and click Save.

4. To hear how the recorded sound sounds, click the Play button.

FIG. 16.9

The recording meter shows the volume of your sound as your record.

Recording meter

You can also easily record a sound clip from a CD. To do this, follow these steps:

1. Click the Start menu, and choose Programs, Accessories, Multimedia, Sound Recorder to start the Sound Recorder.

2. Insert an audio CD into the CD to start the CD Player as discussed in the section "Playing Music on Your PC" earlier in this chapter.

3. Find the right song and the right point in the CD that you want to record. Then click Pause in the CD Player.

4. Click the Record button in the Audio Recorder.

5. Click Pause again in the CD Player to start the playback. You should see the sound meter showing the recording in the Audio Recorder as shown in Figure 16.10.

FIG. 16.10

The Sound Recorder and CD player are both running here recording sound from the CD.

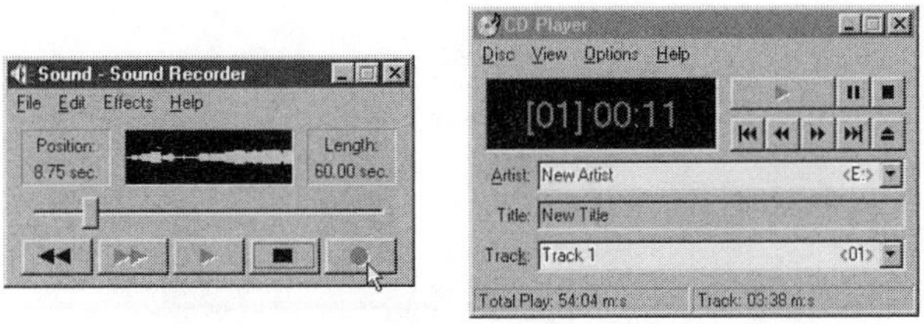

6. When you're finished, click Stop in both the recorder and the player and save the file in the recorder.

N O T E Recording sounds from CDs on your PC is a legal gray area. If you are just using a few clips for your own enjoyment on your PC, you won't get arrested or fined. But sharing these clips with others by trying to sell or distribute them, or by putting them on a Web site is a definite copyright infringement. ▓

Adjusting Microphone and Input Levels in Windows 95

To control the level of incoming sounds from the microphone and other devices for recording, follow these steps:

1. Click the speaker icon in the taskbar with the right mouse button and select Volume Controls from the menu.

2. Select the Options menu in the Volume Control dialog box and choose Properties from the menu.

3. This opens a Properties dialog box shown in Figure 16.11. Be sure the Microphone option is selected at the bottom of the dialog box.

FIG. 16.11

This is where you choose which set of volume controls you will see the sliders for.

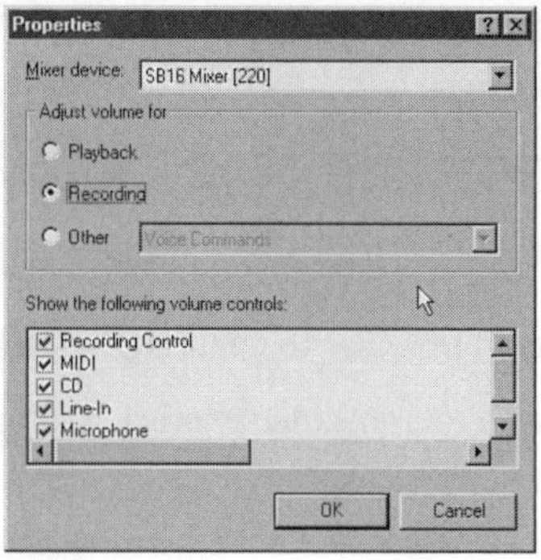

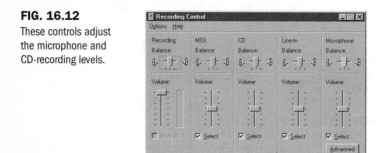

4. Select the Recording option in the Adjust Volume For section and click OK.

5. Now the controls that you see in Figure 16.12 are for devices you can record from. Adjust the volumes for any of these. Close the Recording Control dialog box when you are finished.

FIG. 16.12

These controls adjust the microphone and CD-recording levels.

> **TIP** If you leave the Recording Control open while you are recording, you can continue to adjust the controls as needed while you record.

Troubleshooting Sound Problems in Windows 95

Sound problems are common in Windows 95 and here are some common problems and solutions.

No Sound from the Speakers

Check to be sure that the speakers are plugged into the correct speaker output jack on the sound card and that the speakers are plugged into the power source or have live batteries.

If there are volume controls and an on/off switch on the speakers, be sure the controls are turned up and the speakers are turned on.

Does the sound card have a volume control dial where the speakers plug into it? If so, are these volume controls turned up?

Check the volume control shown in Figure 16.5 to be sure that the Windows volume to the speakers isn't turned down too low and that the speakers aren't muted.

Check the volume controls as shown in Figure 16.6 to be sure the volume isn't turned down or off there.

No Sound from Speakers When an Audio CD Is Playing

Check the volume controls as shown in Figure 16.6 to be sure the CD volume isn't turned down or off.

There is a cable inside your PC that connects the CD-ROM audio to the sound card. If your PC wasn't assembled professionally or you added the CD-ROM or sound card yourself, check to be sure that this cable is there and connected properly.

Can't Record with the Microphone

Check to be sure that the microphone is connected to the mic input jack on the sound card. It should not be connected to line in.

If there is an on/off switch on the mic, check that it is in the On position.

Check the recording level controls in Figure 16.12 to be sure your microphone recording level is on.

Background Music in Games and Multimedia Doesn't Play

If all of your other sounds play okay, the problem may be with your MIDI volume. MIDI is a type of synthesized (rather than recorded) music used in a lot of games and multimedia. Check the settings in Figure 16.6 to be sure the MIDI volume isn't down or off. Raise the volume for that if needed.

Many games and multimedia programs also use CD audio mixed in with the other sounds. If these seem to be missing, run through the checklist of solutions for the previous problem, "No Sound from Speakers When an Audio CD Is Playing."

Background Music in Games and Multimedia Sounds More Like a Kazoo than a Symphony

There are two different kinds of sound technologies for playing synthetic MIDI sounds. One is called *FM synthesis* and is used in older and less expensive sound cards. It tends to make all of the instruments sound the same. The better technology is called *wavetable synthesis*. If you are really particular about the quality of your sound in games and multimedia, you may want to upgrade to a wavetable sound card or see if a wavetable add-on is available for your current card.

Is your $200 sound card connected to $5 speakers? A better set of speakers may be the answer. ●

CHAPTER 17

Scanners

In this chapter, you learn about the basic types of scanners, how to set them up, and some tips on how to make the most of your scanner. ■

What is a scanner?

Understand the technology behind scanners, what they can and can't do, and explore the various types available.

How to set up and use a scanner

Installing and using a scanner is relatively easy. This section will walk you though the basics you need to know to get the best results.

What is OCR?

Ever wish you could wave a magic wand and have those 50 typewritten pages instantly appear as a text file inside your computer? It's not quite that simple, but OCR (Optical Character Recognition) can certainly make your life easier.

Defining Scanner Types

Scanners are peripheral devices used to *digitize* (convert to electronic format) artwork, photographs, text, or other items from hard copy. In a sense, a scanner works as a pair of eyes for your PC. Your eyes see an image and translate the image into electrical impulses that travel to and are interpreted by your brain. Similarly, a scanner captures images and converts them to digital data that travel to and are interpreted by the computer.

A scanner works by dividing an image into microscopic rows and columns and measuring, like the film in a camera, how much light (or lack thereof) reflects from each individual intersection of the rows and columns. Each reflection is recorded as a dot, or picture element (pixel). After the scanner collects information from each dot, it compiles the result into a digital file on the computer.

There are a wide variety of scanners that work in a number of different ways, but the technology behind them is essentially the same. The following sections discuss the more popular types of scanners available today.

ON THE WEB

Two excellent Internet resources for more information on scanners and scanning techniques can be found at:

http://www.scanshop.com

http://www.cis.ohio-state.edu/~sking/Scanners.html

Flatbed Scanners

Flatbed scanners (shown in Figure 17.1) look and behave a lot like a photocopier. You lay the item to be scanned on a glass plate and the scanning head passes below the glass.

Flatbed scanners are very versatile: you can scan objects in a variety of sizes and shapes, including pages from a book, without damaging the original. While flatbed scanners are the best choice for a wide variety of uses, if you plan to do a lot of text scanning (called *OCR* for *Optical Character Recognition*) work, keep in mind that flatbeds only accommodate one page at a time. Scanning multi-page documents can be a slow, tedious process, because you have to manually remove one page and insert the next.

Sheetfed Scanners

Sheetfed scanners look and act more like fax machines. The page or item is fed into the machine, scanned, then spit out on the other end (see Figure 17.2). A sheetfed scanner is a good choice for large volumes of text, but not for handling delicate original photographs. Scanning directly from a book or other three-dimensional object is impossible.

FIG. 17.1
A flatbed scanner looks
and works like a copy
machine.

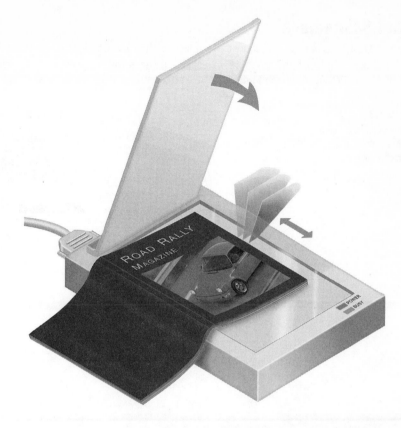

FIG. 17.2
A sheetfed scanner is
a good choice for
scanning text and
simple documents.

Hand Scanners

Hand scanners are a low-cost alternative to their larger, more sophisticated cousins. As their name implies, hand scanners are manual devices you move over a flat surface, just as you do your PC's mouse (see Figure 17.3).

FIG. 17.3
Hand scanners are great for small jobs and steady hands.

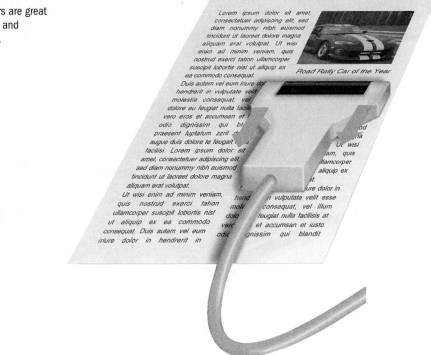

The hand scanner's advantages are many, but so are its disadvantages. Generally, hand scanners work best for small, uncomplicated images such as company logos or small black-and-white photographs. You might want a hand scanner if you don't plan to use it on a regular basis, because it usually doesn't require adding internal cards to your CPU, and it's easily disconnected and stored away. Most hand scanners can only scan a four-inch wide image at one time and require a steady hand. You're usually provided with software that helps you "sew up" a series of these 4-inch, side-by-side scans into one image, but this is obviously not as convenient as getting the full image at once.

N O T E   Other types of scanners also exist, such as barcode readers (like the ones at the grocery checkout) and slide scanners; however, because these are specialty items primarily used for commercial purposes, they are not covered here. ■

Color versus Grayscale Scanners

Scanners that can scan images in full color have become much more popular as their prices have dropped. Just a few years ago, color scanners cost several thousands of dollars, but can now be bought for a few hundred, depending on resolution and type.

Even so, grayscale (meaning shades of black and white only, no color) scanners are still available and are significantly cheaper. In many cases, they are perfectly adequate for the average user. Unless you have a color printer, or use your scanner to create artwork that will only be viewed on-screen (such as for a Web page), there's no point in having a color scanner. Consider this carefully before buying; however, what you think you'll never do now could change as you grow more experienced and interested in computer technology.

Understanding Resolution and Dots Per Inch

Like printers, the technical capability (*optical resolution*) of a scanner is measured in *dots per inch (dpi)*. The higher the dpi, the sharper your on-screen printable image will be. The reason for this is that the more dots that can be placed in the same area (in this case, one square inch), the smoother and more detailed the overall image will look.

On the other hand, the higher its resolution, the longer the scanner takes to scan the image, and the larger the resulting image's data file will be (more dots equals more information; more information equals a larger file). Typical flatbed scanners range from 300 dpi to more than 3,200 dpi; The most affordable resolution for the average consumer is 1,200–1,600 dpi.

NOTE Don't be fooled by ads touting astronomical resolutions like 6,400 dpi interpolated or enhanced resolution. *Interpolated resolution* (as opposed to optical or true resolution) is just another term for the scanner's ability to guess at how the image would look at a higher resolution by adding new dots in between the old ones. For most uses, this process adds no value—and can often actually reduce the scan quality. The exception is that interpolated resolution can improve the quality of scanned line art images that will be output at very high resolution, such as magazines or commercially produced documents.

System Requirements

Before you buy or try to install a scanner, make sure that your computer can actually run it. Scanners can really stretch the limits of a mid-range PC—and may not work at all on low-end ones. Carefully review the manufacturer's stated system requirements and verify that your system has at least the minimum amount of RAM, CPU speed, and hard drive space listed. For best results, *exceed* the minimum requirements by as much as possible. Most manufacturers require nothing less than a 486/33 processor (if you have a Pentium or better, you should be safe). Most experts recommend a minimum of 16–24M of RAM even if the manufacturer claims less.

Connecting a Scanner to Your PC

Like all peripheral devices, your scanner must be connected to your computer in some way. Most likely, your scanner came with all the equipment required to hook it up.

SCSI Cards and Cables

The vast majority of flatbed and sheetfed scanners use SCSI (Small Computer System Interface, pronounced "skuzzy") connections. If you're lucky, your computer already has a SCSI card installed and all you'll have to do is connect the provided cable to the SCSI port at the back of your computer. But most computers don't come that way, so you might need to open the system case and install a new card in one of your computer's expansion slots. If so, follow the instructions that came with the scanner, and check your computer system's manual to make sure you're installing it in the right place. See Chapter 27, "Upgrading Your Hardware," for details on how to install add-in cards.

N O T E   Hand scanners typically do not require SCSI connections; They usually connect to parallel ports, like the one used by your printer. ▪

The great thing about SCSI devices is that one SCSI card can support up to seven different devices connected together in a "SCSI chain." You might, for example, have a scanner plugged into the SCSI port, a Jaz drive connected to the scanner, an external hard drive connected to the Jaz drive, and a CD-ROM drive connected to the external hard drive. Not only does this give you more flexibility in configuring your system, it also saves the few expansion ports in your computer for other devices that aren't able to share.

CAUTION

Be careful when comparing scanners and the SCSI cards included with them. Some manufacturers cut corners (and offer lower prices) by including a *proprietary* SCSI card, or one that only works with that particular scanner and does not support other devices. The card will work, of course, but it's not a very efficient use of the technology. If you think the scanner is right for you but it comes with a proprietary card, you can always buy a general-purpose SCSI card separately.

N O T E   Most scanners and SCSI devices require a cable length of 12 feet or less—keep this in mind when you're setting up your system. ▪

TWAIN Drivers

Every hardware device, whether internal or external, requires a software program called a *driver* to help it communicate with your computer's operating system. For scanners, the standard driver type is a TWAIN driver (supposedly, *TWAIN* stands for *Technology Without An Interesting Name*). By using TWAIN drivers, scanners can communicate with any TWAIN-compatible applications. Most of today's popular drawing and graphics applications such as

CorelDRAW!, Paint Shop Pro, Adobe Photoshop, and even Microsoft Office 97 all support TWAIN, and thus use very similar steps, buttons, and the like. You don't have to learn a different method for every application you scan from. (If you're not sure, check the application's File menu for an item labeled Acquire, or look in the manual.)

Getting Windows 95 to Recognize Your Scanner

After you've made the physical connections, install the TWAIN driver according to the instructions that came with the scanner. If instructions for using the scanner under Windows 95 are not included, follow these steps:

1. Shut down the computer and wait 30 seconds. Power up the scanner, wait 10–15 seconds, then reboot your PC.

2. From the Start menu, choose Settings, Control Panel. When the Control Panel window opens, double-click Add New Hardware.

3. Click Next. The wizard will ask if you want Windows 95 to search for your new hardware; choose No and click Next again (see Figure 17.4).

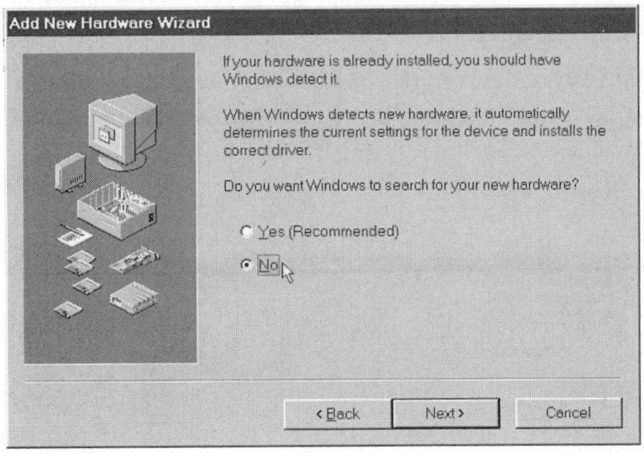

FIG. 17.4
If you know exactly where to point, it's faster to show Windows where the driver is rather than let it search for it.

4. At the next screen, click Other Devices from the list of items shown in Figure 17.5; click Next again.

5. Look through the Manufacturers list and the Models list. If you find your scanner (you probably won't), click Next. If not, click Have Disk.

6. In the Install from Disk dialog box, show the wizard where your install program is (usually on a floppy disk that came with the scanner), either by typing in the path name or clicking the Browse button and navigating to the proper location. Click Next twice.

7. When you get to the final wizard screen, click Finish. Windows will continue the setup process, and may ask you for your Windows 95 CD-ROM.

8. When the setup process is complete, restart your computer by choosing Shut Down from the Start menu, then choosing Restart the Computer?.

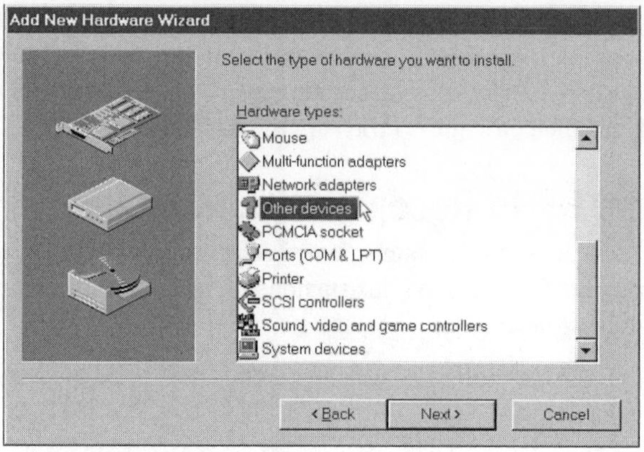

FIG. 17.5

Windows 95 currently doesn't support scanners directly like it does printers, mice, and other devices; but it does provide a provision for other devices you can add yourself.

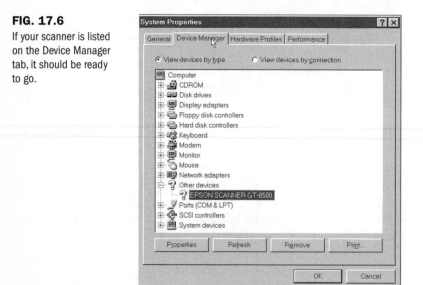

9. As Windows 95 restarts, you may notice a message on the screen indicating it has found a new device and is installing drivers for it, or other similar messages. Respond and follow any directions if necessary.

10. To confirm that Windows has found and set up your scanner, double-click the System icon in the Control Panel folder.

11. Click the Device Manager tab, and look for the Other devices entry on the list of devices. Click the + next to Other devices; your scanner should be listed, as shown in Figure 17.6. Click OK to clear the dialog box. Your scanner is now ready to use.

▶ **See** "Shutting Down Your Computer," **p. 45**

FIG. 17.6

If your scanner is listed on the Device Manager tab, it should be ready to go.

Scanning a Document

Most scanners come with some kind of image-editing software such as Adobe Photoshop or Photoshop LE. Even if not, there are some excellent programs available for a relatively inexpensive price—some you can even download from the Internet, such as Paint Shop Pro or Graphics Workshop.

If the program is TWAIN-compliant, its scanning features will work about the same no matter which program you choose. The main differences will come from the TWAIN driver supplied by your scanner's manufacturer. You'll want to review the program's documentation or check its online Help system to learn exactly how to use that particular program.

Regardless of the program, the general tips and techniques that follow will help you produce better scans and get the most out of your image-editing software:

- Always keep the glass on your flatbed scanner clean and free of smudges and fingerprints. Be sure to use special lens-cleaning cloths, not household tissues or paper towels—these can permanently scratch your scanner's glass. You can get lens-cleaning cloths at most computer or office supply stores.

- If you have to move your flatbed scanner, make sure you lock the scanning head in place first. If you don't, it can become dislodged from its track and be costly to repair. If the locking mechanism isn't obvious, check the scanner's documentation for help.

- Know the desired result before you scan. How will the image be used—for a letterhead? On a Web page? In a newsletter? Different jobs require different approaches, so plan ahead.

- Use the lowest resolution possible that will still provide the quality you want. "Overscanning" only serves to make larger files and slower scans.

- Scan photographs at about twice the resolution of the expected output. If you're not sure what that will be, ask your print shop. Magazines are traditionally printed at 133 lines per inch (lpi), so scan the photo at 266 dpi.

- For line art images (hand-drawn artwork, mechanical drawings, and so on), always use the highest resolution possible.

- Don't overscan an image if it's only going to a laser or inkjet printer. Laser printers generally output at about 50 or 100 lpi, so a simple 200 dpi scan will do just fine.

- Images intended only for on-screen viewing need even less: 80 to 100 dpi is adequate.

- For OCR (see the next section), use 300–400 dpi.

- Get to know your image-editing software. Experiment with the various filters and effects you can apply to your scanned images—they can make all the difference in the world. If you're really interested in mastering image editing or you need to learn a lot quickly, consider taking a class or buying a book especially on that software program. *Inside Adobe Photoshop* from New Riders Publishing would be one recommendation. An edition of the book is available for each of the two current releases (3 and 4).

OCR Software

Using OCR, scanners can also be used to convert hardcopy text to a text file you can then edit in your word processor, saving hours of retyping. In addition to stand-alone programs like IBM's TextBridge, many of the better fax/modem software programs such as Delrina WinFax PRO also include OCR capability.

Keep in mind that while most OCR programs have a 95 percent or higher accuracy rate, they are not perfect. For best results, you need to start with a clean hard copy (preferably on white paper), in a simple typeface, such as that produced by a typewriter. Handwritten words, unless very neatly printed, usually don't translate very well. If your original is messy, or the print is too small or fancy for the scanner to read easily, you might end up spending as much time cleaning up the scanned text as you would retyping it after all. ●

Connecting to the Internet

18   What Is the Internet?   189

19   Establishing an Internet Connection   199

20   Using Your WWW Browser   209

21   Sending and Receiving E-Mail   223

22   Sending and Receiving Files with FTP   233

23   Other Internet Options   241

What Is the Internet?

These days, it seems that everyone is talking about the Internet: on TV and radio, in schools, at work, even over the backyard fence. So it's not unnatural that even though you are just learning how to use your computer, that you're interested in learning what this Internet thing is all about. ▪

Learn about the Internet

Debunk the myths about the Internet, and learn the real truth about what it is and how it came to be.

Discover the World Wide Web

Learn about the World Wide Web and the treasures it contains.

Understand electronic mail

Discover how to send and receive e-mail over the Internet.

Learn the secrets of the Internet

Learn about other aspects of the Internet, including file transfers, terminal emulation, Gopher systems, and newsgroups.

What the Internet Isn't

Maybe, by talking to your kids or your coworkers, you've already begun to get some handle on this Internet thing, and maybe you're thinking that you should just skip this chapter. That's okay. But, if you think that the Internet is:

- Owned and operated by some large company or organization that maintains it
- The same thing as the World Wide Web
- Something Microsoft and Netscape invented
- Policed by the Secret Service, the FBI, and the CIA who want to spy on everything you do
- A great place to do your shopping, banking, and other private transactions

then you might want to read on.

What the Internet *Is*

The Internet is comprised of a bunch of interconnected *networks*. A network is a collection of computers that are connected to each other through a *server*. The Internet connects these servers to each other, forming a massive network in and of itself.

You connect to the Internet through one of these Internet servers, then make your way to the particular server that contains what you need. There are various types of servers on the Internet, each providing a particular service, or sometimes, a group of services. For example, an Internet server might provide access to documents that a user can view. The same server may also provide access to files for downloading to the user's system, and to electronic mail services, as well as other functions. The servers that form the backbone of the Internet are located within universities, businesses, government offices, and research facilities all over the world.

When you're connected to the Internet, you can:

- Read information on a wide range of topics, including recent news events, bass fishing, music, weather, poetry, government reports, and just about anything else you can name.
- Send and receive electronic mail messages (e-mail).
- Download (copy to your system) useful programs such as virus detectors and file compression/decompression utilities. You might also download updates or bug fixes for some program on your computer.
- Share your opinions and your knowledge on a variety of topics through various *newsgroups* (discussion groups).
- "Chat" in real time with other people who share your interests—by basically typing what you want to say.
- View interesting videos, listen to music, or wander though a three-dimensional world.

How Hypertext Weaves the World Wide Web

The Internet is a collection of interconnected networks. The data that travels through the Internet is text-based, and the commands that operate the Internet's key programs are UNIX-based. To make the Internet more graphical and easier to use (like Windows), the World Wide Web (WWW) was formed. The WWW is a group of Internet servers that support a *protocol* called HTTP *(HyperText Transfer Protocol)*. Protocol is a standard for transmitting data between computers. Because not all Internet servers support HTTP, the Web could be thought of as a subset of the larger Internet itself.

HTTP provides a method for transmitting a professionally laid out page (one with graphic images, formatted text, lines, frames, and animations) over the text-based Internet (see Figure 18.1). The laid out page is described in text using a language called *HTML (HyperText Markup Language)*. A Web page is basically text with special HTML codes to indicate special formatting. For example, the codes `<B>` and `</B>` that surround some of the text indicate that it should be bold. Some HTML codes indicate where a graphic file should be inserted, or a Java animation.

These codes tell Web *browsers* how to display the elements of the page: text, graphics, animations, sounds, lines, video, and so on. A Web browser, such as Netscape Navigator or Internet Explorer, is a program that allows you to browse the World Wide Web. Browsers translate the HTML codes they receive and use them to assemble a Web page for presentation on-screen.

Part
V

Ch
18

FIG. 18.1
Data is presented
graphically on the Web.

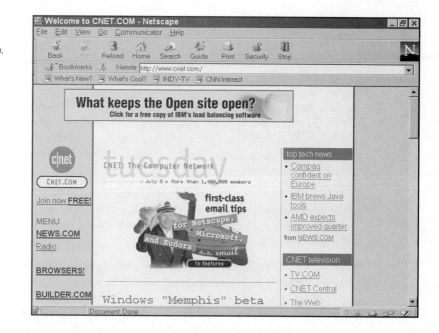

Each Web page is interconnected to other Web pages through links called *hypertext links*. When you click hypertext, you jump to a different Web page. You can think of the links that connect all these pages together as forming a giant "web," which is where the World Wide Web got its name.

When you visit a Web site (for example, the CNN Web site) you typically start out on what's called the *home page*. From there, you'll find links to other pages on the site—other pages related to CNN (visit their newsroom Web site at **http://www.nmis.org/NewsInteractive/ CNN/Newsroom/contents.html**).

Now, because of its graphical, dynamic nature, the Web has become the perfect showplace for all kinds of information. On the Web you will find pages for most large companies, and a lot of small ones. A lot of government agencies are represented on the Web, providing quick and simple access to the information you need. You'll find personal Web pages as well, usually with links to a person's favorite places on the Web. Web sites devoted to popular actors, singers, models, television shows, and movies are plentiful. There are also news sites, weather sites, and visitor information sites that can help you quickly get acquainted with another country, state, or province. And to help you find all these pages, there are many, many search sites.

Electronic Mail and the Internet

Besides locating information on anything from tools to tornadoes on the World Wide Web, another reason that a lot of people get connected to the Internet is to send electronic mail messages (e-mail).

E-mail messages are basically text messages that you type and then send to another person by using that person's e-mail address. An e-mail address identifies the mailbox that belongs to a particular person. It operates much like a postal address or a telephone number. When a message arrives at an e-mail address, the recipient can connect and download (copy) the message to her system. The person then can respond to the message, as shown in Figure 18.2.

You can include more than just text with your message. For example, you can attach a file such as a sales spreadsheet to a message, and then send it along to a colleague. That person can then detach the file, save it to his system, and display it in his own spreadsheet program, such as Lotus 1-2-3 or Microsoft Excel. Chapters of this book, for example, were sent between authors, editors, and technical editors as e-mail attachments.

Some programs such as Netscape Messenger allow you to attach electronic business cards (virtual cards, or *v-cards*) to your e-mail messages as well. These business cards can contain your e-mail address, along with other personal information such as your address, business and home phone numbers, and company name.

With most e-mail programs, you can attach Web pages to e-mail messages as well. So if you find something interesting out on the World Wide Web, you can share a copy of it with a colleague or a friend. Both Netscape Communicator and Internet Explorer contain e-mail programs. You'll learn more about e-mail in Chapter 21, "Sending and Receiving E-Mail."

FIG. 18.2

You can download your e-mail messages, then read and respond to them.

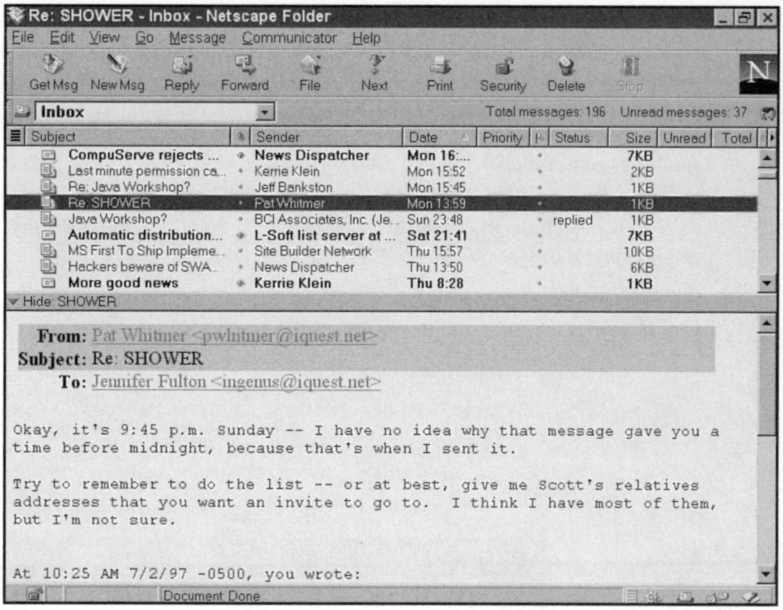

Other Information Sources on the Internet

The Internet supports many protocols, or methods for transmitting information. One method, *HTTP*, is used on the World Wide Web. But the most basic protocol used over the entire Internet is *IP*, or *Internet Protocol*. IP defines the addresses assigned to each connection. Each IP address represents a *gateway* through which data is sent and received. If you connect to the Internet through your modem (a dial-up connection), then you're assigned a temporary IP address by the server to which you connect. This allows the server to manage the data that you want to send and receive. You're not directly connected to the Internet, but simply connected to your ISP (Internet service provider), which is connected to the Internet, with its own IP address such as **indy.net**.

If you connect to the Internet though a company network, then you're not assigned an individual IP address. Instead, the network server, acting as a single user for all the employees connected to the network, is assigned an IP address such as **www.BigCo.com**. The server then manages the data going to and coming from each network user.

TIP Your service provider manages only so many of these addresses, so sometimes you're locked out until somebody logs off the Internet and frees up an IP address. If logging on becomes a serious problem, you can always look for another service provider. Or, you can request a private IP address (for a higher service charge), ensuring immediate access at all times.

Part
V

Ch
18

IP addresses are made up of numbers, such as 123.75.124.164. In order to make addressing easier, domain names—such as **www.microsoft.com**—are often used. A handful of servers on the Internet called *Domain Name Servers (DNS)* perform the task of translating domain names into IP addresses for all the client requests on the Internet.

Another common protocol is *TCP/IP (Transport Control Protocol for Internet Protocol)*. TCP/IP controls the way in which data is sent from one Internet server to another. The content of the data and the actual communication between IP hosts is controlled not by TCP/IP, but by something called a *transfer protocol*. There are many transfer protocols (or languages, if you will) being used on the Internet:

- HTTP servers support HTML, the language that enables the graphical presentation of data using simple text codes. HTTP is the protocol used on the World Wide Web.

- SNMP, POP, and IMAP4 servers process electronic mail (e-mail).

- FTP servers support *file transfer protocol*, which enables files on the Internet to be uploaded (sent) and downloaded (received). An FTP site is shown in Figure 18.3.

FIG. 18.3
You can download files from an FTP site.

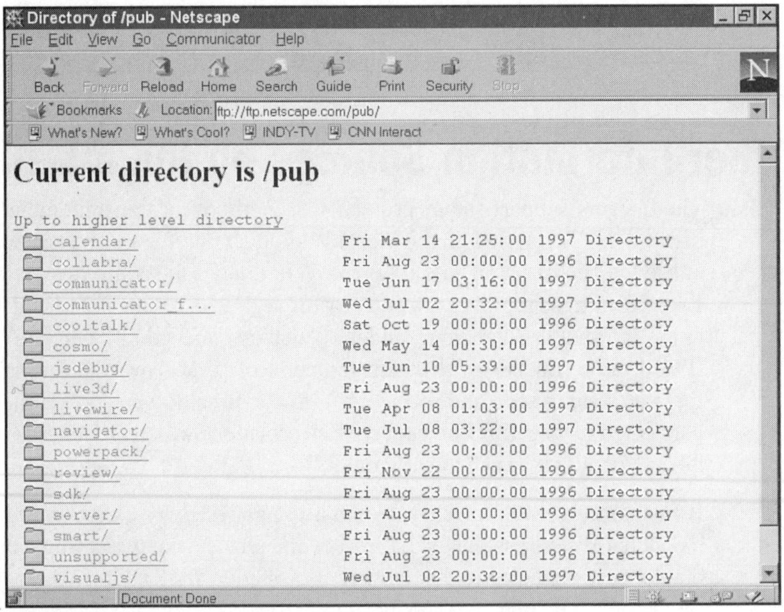

- Telnet servers support *terminal emulation*. This means that you can connect to them manually, and using the UNIX prompt they provide, issue specific commands to request information and then log back off. A Telnet site is shown in Figure 18.4.

FIG. 18.4

Your computer acts as a terminal when you connect to a Telnet site.

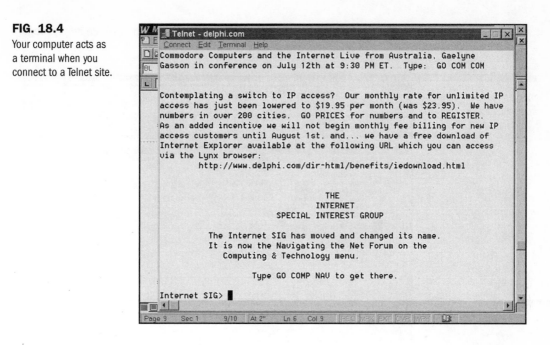

■ Gopher servers provide a menu system that enables a user to quickly locate the documents and files stored on them. Gopher was the first successful attempt to make the Internet more accessible. Most Gopher servers are located on university campuses. Gopher, by the way, was developed at the University of Minnesota and was named after the college's team mascot. A Gopher site is shown in Figure 18.5.

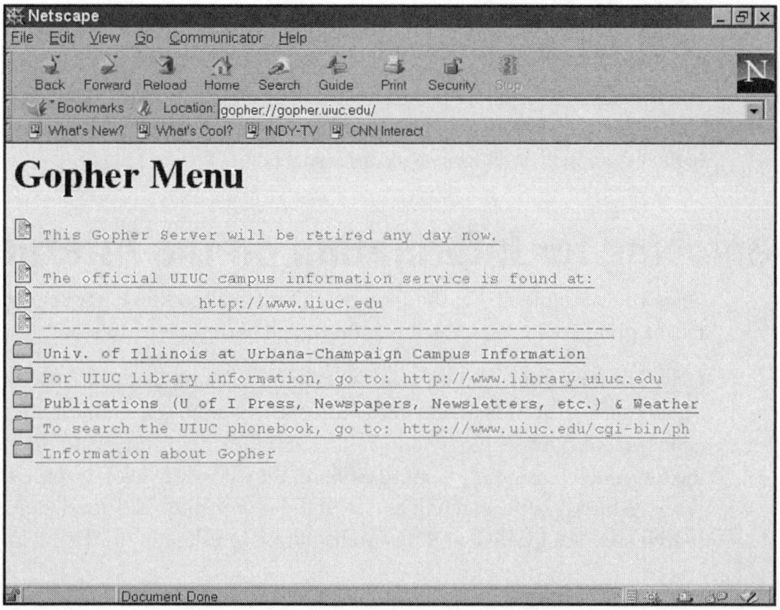

FIG. 18.5

Gopher sites provide a menu system.

Part
V

Ch
18

■ UseNet servers provide a messaging system for online discussion through newsgroups. A newsgroup is shown in Figure 18.6.

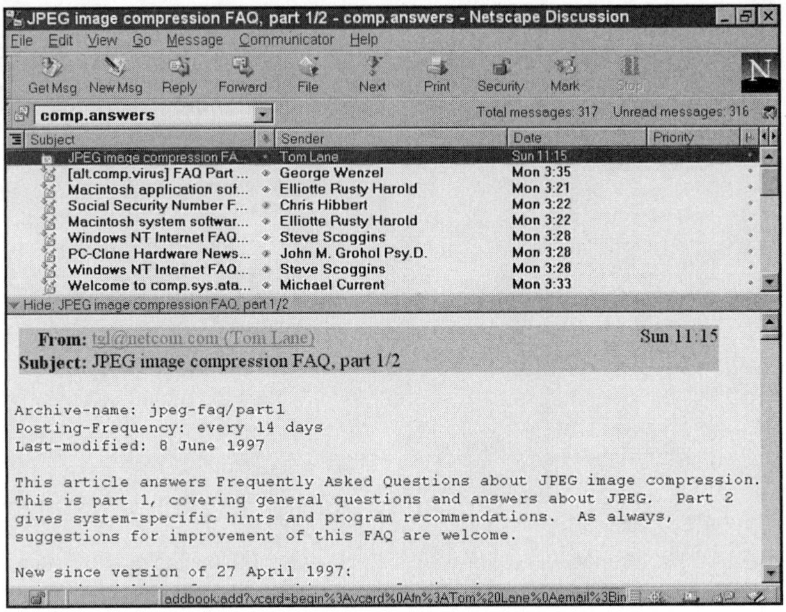

FIG. 18.6
You can discuss interesting topics within newsgroups.

You only need one program to connect to all these different servers, and that's a Web browser. You'd think that a Web browser could only navigate the World Wide Web, but today, that's just not true. With a Web browser such as Netscape Communicator or Internet Explorer, you can visit HTTP sites (World Wide Web sites), FTP sites, Gopher sites, Telnet sites, and UseNet sites. And, of course, you can send and receive e-mail from SNMP, POP3, and IMAP sites.

You can also use separate programs, such as FTP programs, Gopher programs, Telnet programs, e-mail programs, and newsreaders. These programs all perform at least as well (if not better) than their Web browser counterparts.

Searching for Information on the Internet

Once you're connected to the Internet, it's difficult to know where to start. First of all, you'll need a good Web browser, such as Netscape Navigator or Internet Explorer.

Once you have your Web browser installed, you're ready to explore. But where to start? Well, a good place to start is at one of the Internet's search sites. There are many search sites to choose from, such as Excite and Yahoo! and they help you locate the information you're looking for. And if you simply want to explore, they provide links to some of the best places on the World Wide Web. So, starting at one of the search sites is a good idea. You'll learn where these search sites are located, and how to use them in Chapter 20, "Using Your WWW Browser."

But the Internet, as you know right now, is more than just the World Wide Web. There are other things you can do on the Internet besides visit Web sites, although they are the best places for information. For example, you might need to locate a file, such as a program upgrade or bug fix, that might repair some problem you've been having with your PC. Many companies have Web sites that provide links to files you can download to fix problems you've been having. For example, Microsoft has an extensive Web site full of information and help. These files are typically located on FTP (file transfer protocol) sites. Once you find the file you want, it's a simple process to download (copy) it to your PC. See Chapter 22, "Sending and Receiving Files and FTP," for help. By the way, you don't need a special program to download files, your Web browser will do just fine.

Another great source of information and opinions on the Internet is *newsgroups*. Newsgroups are discussion groups devoted to a particular topic, such as fly tying, space exploration, gardening, computer hardware, bird watching, or computer clip art. When you find the newsgroups that interest you, it's easy to view the information they contain, and to make contributions of your own. You'll need a good newsreader to view newsgroup messages, but that's not a problem because both Netscape Communicator and Internet Explorer include one with their Web browser. ●

Part

V

Ch

18

CHAPTER 19

Establishing an
Internet Connection

In this chapter, you'll learn how to locate a good Internet service provider. You'll also learn how to get connected through your online service (such as America Online or CompuServe) or through a dial-up connection (such as your modem). This chapter will also acquaint you with the various Web browsers available, and what's right for you. ■

Prepare for your Internet connection

Learn what hardware your PC will need in order to connect to the Internet.

Choosing the right service provider

Understand how to pick the right Internet service provider to fit your needs.

Using an online service to connect

Learn about connecting to the Internet through your online service provider.

Connecting directly with your modem

Prepare your system for use with a dial-up connection to the Internet.

Making Sure You Have the Right Hardware

In order to connect to the Internet, your computer will need some basic equipment. This includes the following:

- *A modem.* You need a modem if you plan on connecting through a dial-up connection and not through your company's network.

- *A sound card.* You must have this in order to play any sound files that might be embedded within the Web pages you view.

- *At least 8M of RAM (memory).* Most Internet programs require this.

- *At least a 486 CPU (microprocessor).* Although you might be able to get by with less, you won't be happy with the results because they will be too slow to enjoy.

- *At least 20–30M of free space.* You need this to install your Web browser and other Internet programs.

Even if your PC meets these minimum requirements, there are some upgrades you might want to consider in order to get the most out of your Internet connection.

Upgrades to Consider

The Internet is a vast resource of information—literally, a treasure waiting to be plundered. But to do your best "plundering," you're going to need to get prepared. All of the graphics, sound, video, and animation on most popular Web pages today create huge files; you're going to need the fastest connection you can get, so you can spend more time browsing and less time waiting for downloads.

If you plan on connecting to the Internet through your company's network, then prepare to be spoiled. The direct connection that these networks provide are among the fastest available. However, if you plan on connecting to the Internet through a modem, there are some things you can do to make your connection as fast as possible:

- *Invest in a fast modem.* Get a modem with at least 28,800 baud—although 56,600 baud is preferable. You may also want to consider an ISDN connection—that is, if it's available in your area, and if you can afford it.

- *Clear some hard disk space for use as a cache.* A *cache* is a temporary storage area that your Web browser can use to keep copies of the Web pages that you visit. Then, when you want to visit them again, instead of downloading them from the Internet (which takes time), your Web browser can simply pull them from the hard disk and display them on-screen. A cache is always set to some particular size; when it becomes full, then the oldest data in the cache is deleted to make room for newer data. If you can make your cache larger, then you'll be able to speed up your Internet transactions. That's why clearing some hard disk space *now* is worth the effort.

- *Upgrade your computer or its components.* Of course, a faster computer can display the graphics, animations, and video files that crowd most Web pages much more quickly than a slower one. If upgrading to a faster PC is out of the question, perhaps you can consider upgrading to a better video card, a better monitor, or simply increasing the video RAM in your PC. These are relatively inexpensive upgrades that will make a huge difference in the speed and quality of your display.

Selecting an Internet Service Provider

The Internet service provider (ISP) you choose will be the stand-in for the direct network-to-network connection that you would otherwise need in order to link to the Internet. The ISP is persistently linked to the Internet; your computer, on the other hand, will be linked to the ISP intermittently, by phone. Deciding how you will link to the Internet requires that you consider quite a few factors, such as the following:

- Worldwide online services that act as ISPs, such as America Online and CompuServe, offer their own services to you outside of the Internet. The fees they charge you take into account both their exclusive features and their Internet access. America Online and other online services may be initially easier to use, but connecting to the Internet through them is slower than connecting directly.

- Other North American ISPs, such as AT&T WorldNet, NETCOM, and WorldCom (formerly UUnet), offer strictly-Internet access, perhaps with a few extra services that are Internet-based. Their prices may beat those of the major online services, and they may be structured for the type and level of service you require.

- Regional ISPs, such as IQuest (based in Indiana, though also servicing Illinois) and others, offer basically a dial-up connection and limited customer support. Their fees are typically low, however, and the reliability of their phone lines and Internet connection is surprisingly high, especially when compared to the worldwide services which frequently suffer brownouts, outages, and e-mail losses.

- Many cable television (CATV) providers in North America are offering high-speed Internet connections through the same coaxial lines that supply you with cable channels. These services require that you rent or lease from the CATV provider a *cable modem*, which is generally an external adapter box that works like an ordinary telephone modem. Data sent from the Internet to you comes through at speeds many times faster than those of telephone modems (56Kbps); however, data sent from you travels through a separate phone line linking you to the CATV provider at about 26Kbps—about as fast as the average telephone modem commonly used today. Keep in mind here that CATV fees are somewhat higher and, depending on your level of Internet use, may be prohibitive.

- Local telephone services in many major North American cities are offering direct, persistent Internet lines, including fiber-optic (ISDN) service. Such lines are generally for small and home-based businesses, perhaps with their own Web sites, which require online access throughout the business day, if not overnight as well. This is the most expensive type of Internet service to which you can subscribe; and for ISDN connections, you may need to rent, lease, or purchase a special ISDN "modem" (not really a modem), which is an added expense.

Part
V

Ch
19

▓ Private ISPs all over the continent have sprouted in small businesses and even home garages. The Internet dial-up services they offer may be primitive, and customer support may be severely limited, but access fees may range from a pittance to nonexistent (say, if the proprietor is your friend). Many private ISPs are the only reasonably affordable Internet access for rural areas.

To locate an ISP in your area, check the Yellow Pages under "Internet," "Internet Access," or "Internet Service Providers."

Connecting with an Online Service

Both America Online (AOL) and CompuServe are accessible to most geographical regions in North America through a local telephone call. When you dial up these services, the program you use is not a Web browser, and the first content you see is not the Internet. (This will reportedly no longer be the case with CompuServe in 1998, after that service migrates entirely to the Internet.) The first menus you see on these services lead you to their exclusive services or divert you to the Internet. When that happens, the most recent versions of their software bring up Web browsers that call up their Internet home pages. AOL's software will bring up Microsoft Internet Explorer; CompuServe's will bring up Netscape Navigator.

When you use CompuServe or AOL as your ISP, your Internet e-mail is routed to that service's electronic mailbox. You receive e-mail from other CompuServe or AOL users, plus Internet e-mail, at the same address. The e-mail you send will include the ISP mail service's address as its default reply address. Using one of these major providers for your e-mail is a bit like routing all air traffic through Chicago O'Hare airport. When things work well, things work *very* well; but when the smallest thing goes wrong, the snowball becomes an avalanche and the entire network can be affected. Deciding whether you want your e-mail handled by a major service is a crucial factor when you're thinking about subscribing to a value-added provider like AOL or CompuServe.

Dial-Up Connections to the Internet

If you're considering an Internet-based, dial-up ISP such as a regional or national provider, one factor to consider is whether the ISP differentiates between Serial Line Internet Protocol (SLIP) and Point-to-Point Protocol (PPP) connections. ISPs often charge more for the PPP connection, although the only technical difference between the two protocols has to do with the logon procedure. The handshaking procedure for PPP is more formalized, and in theory, more expensive for the ISP. As PPP becomes more commonplace, the need for special server software to handle PPP connections diminishes, so the extra fee becomes less justified. Once you're online, the quality of a SLIP and PPP connection to the same ISP should be equivalent. So, if your ISP wants to charge more for a PPP connection, go with SLIP.

Connecting to Your Service Provider

Not all Internet-based ISPs such as NETCOM are entirely national or continental in scope; as a result, some more remote areas may have to dial long distance just to log on. The quality of long distance connections is no longer a negative factor, as long distance lines in North America have become almost entirely digital fiber-optic. But long distance fees on top of Internet access fees often make CompuServe—as well as private, rural ISPs—seem that much more attractive.

Downloading the Basic Files from Your Service Provider

Many ISPs today offer their own collection of software on CD-ROM. In the setup process, you'll see a list of local phone access numbers for the various coverage areas; there, you choose the number that pertains to you. The software may use an exclusive program or a Web browser to take you to the ISP's Internet site, where you set up the specifics of your account.

Other ISPs don't offer their access software through disk media, but instead as a large download package. But because you need this software to get onto the Internet, how then does one go about downloading this software? You'll need a conventional telecom program, of the type you'd use to log on to a BBS, such as Procomm, Procomm Plus, or Telix. You can also use HyperTerminal, which comes free with Windows 95.

Procomm and Telix are shareware packages, and are available through many retail channels on single disks for small prices. Procomm Plus, however, is commercial software that costs considerably more than the shareware fees for your Internet software combined. So, if you're using this software just to obtain your Internet package, the commercial package should be out of the question.

When you use HyperTerminal, Procomm, or Telix to download the access package from the ISP, you'll be using a character-based terminal screen, most likely with single-character menus. To select an item from such a menu, you simply press the corresponding number or letter. Chances are, there will be very few steps to this process. You may also be setting up your Internet account through these menus. Most likely, however, you'll be setting up your account in a telephone conversation with a live person.

Part
V

Ch
19

Configuring Your System for TCP/IP

Transmission Control Protocol/Internet Protocol (TCP/IP) is a set of networking protocols (computer languages) that makes possible all Internet transactions. If your computer is connected to the Internet directly (through your company's network), or if you use a dial-up connection, it needs to be able to manage TCP/IP.

Using Windows 95, your first order of business will be to make certain you have Dial-Up Networking capability installed. The TCP/IP "stack" (the set of protocols) will need to have access to Dial-Up Networking while it's being set up. Here's how you set up Dial-Up Networking:

1. From the Windows 95 Start menu, select Settings, Control Panel. Windows 95 displays the Control Panel window.

2. Double-click the Add/Remove Programs icon. Windows displays the Add/Remove Programs Properties dialog box.

3. Click the Windows Setup tab (see Figure 19.1).

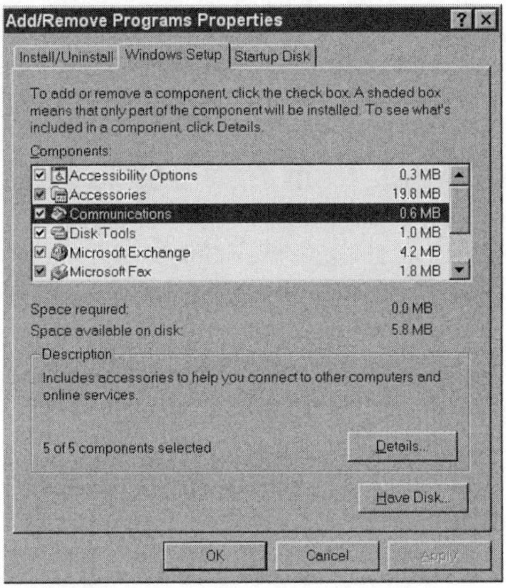

FIG. 19.1

The Windows Setup tab lists the space requirements of components and tells you how much disk space you have available.

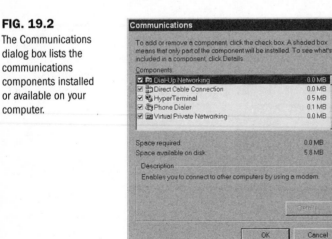

4. From the Components list, choose Communications, and then click the Details button. Windows displays the Communications dialog box shown in Figure 19.2.

FIG. 19.2

The Communications dialog box lists the communications components installed or available on your computer.

5. Dial-Up Networking will appear in the Components list here. If it's actually installed, the box to the left of the entry will be checked. In that case, you can click Cancel, then Cancel again, and go on to check whether TCP/IP is installed. If the box is not checked, then click Dial-Up Networking so that the box *is* checked, and then click OK. Windows *might* ask for the installation disk (or disc); if it does, insert it and click OK.

6. When installation is complete, click OK, and then click OK again to finish.

Next, you'll need to guarantee that TCP/IP has been enabled and, if it hasn't, you'll need to install it. For this process, you'll need your original Windows 95 installation disks or CD-ROM. With those in hand, here's what you do:

1. From the Windows 95 Start menu, choose Settings, Control Panel. Windows 95 displays the Control Panel window.

2. Double-click the Network icon. Windows displays the Network dialog box, shown in Figure 19.3.

FIG. 19.3
The Network dialog box displays the installed network components.

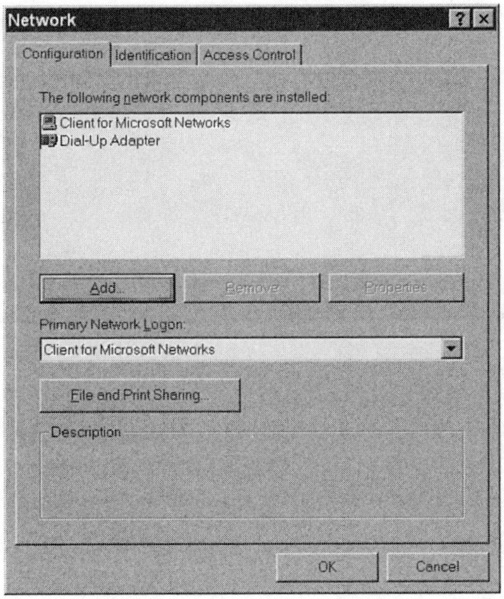

3. The list at the top, The Following Network Components Are Installed, shows those protocols that Windows currently recognizes. If TCP/IP is in this list, you don't need to install anything here; just click OK and skip to step 7. If it's not in the list, click the Add button. Windows displays the Select Network Component Type dialog box, shown in Figure 19.4.

4. Because TCP/IP is a *protocol*, choose Protocol from the list, and click Add. Windows displays the Select Network Protocol dialog box (see Figure 19.5).

Part
V
Ch
19

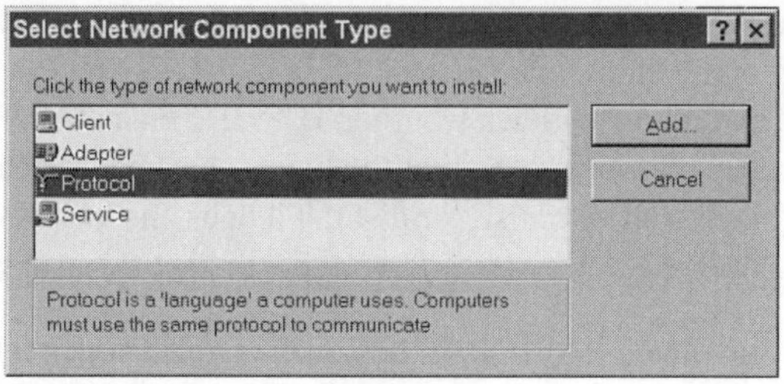

FIG. 19.4

Add TCP/IP by selecting Protocol in the Select Network Component Type dialog box.

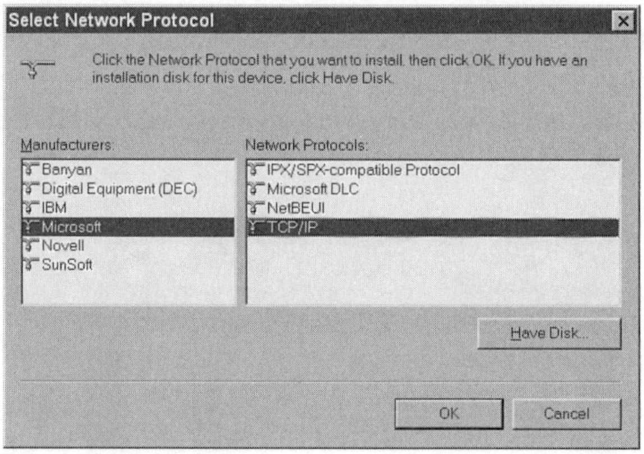

FIG. 19.5

Network protocols and their manufacturers are listed in the Select Network Protocol dialog box.

5. From the Manufacturers list at the left, choose Microsoft. A list of Microsoft protocols appears in the list at the right.

6. From the Network Protocols list, choose TCP/IP, and then click OK. The installation process will proceed, and Windows will bring back the Network dialog box. There, TCP/IP should be featured in the Components list. But you're not done yet.

7. Select Dial-Up Adapter in the Components list. Click the Properties button. Windows displays the Dial-Up Adapter Properties dialog box, shown in Figure 19.6.

8. Click the Bindings tab. Make sure that the box beside TCP/IP is checked, and click OK.

9. Back in the Network dialog box, click OK. Windows *might* ask you to insert your installation disk/disc again; if it requests this, do so and click OK.

10. Finally, Windows will request that you restart your computer. TCP/IP won't work until you do this, though you do not have to restart your computer right this moment. It's up to you.

FIG. 19.6

To complete the TCP/IP installation, you need to select a dial-up adapter.

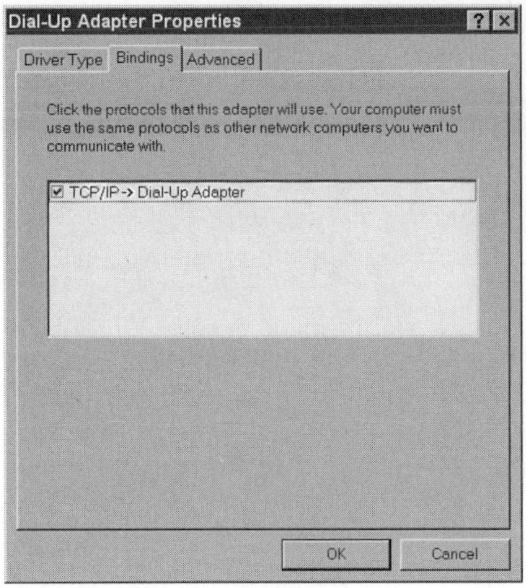

Dial-Up Adapter Properties

Driver Type | Bindings | Advanced

Click the protocols that this adapter will use. Your computer must use the same protocols as other network computers you want to communicate with.

☑ TCP/IP -> Dial-Up Adapter

OK   Cancel

CHAPTER 20

Using Your WWW Browser

In Chapter 19, you learned how to get connected to the Internet and how to download and install a Web browser. In this chapter, you'll learn how to use your new Web browser to explore the World Wide Web. ■

Introducing Web browsers

Discover what Web browsers do, how they work, and which are the most popular.

Navigating on the World Wide Web

Learn how to use your Web browser to surf the Web.

Using the elements of a Web page

Discover how to play sound files, view videos, complete forms, work with frames, and explore virtual worlds.

Locating information on the Web

Learn how to use the most popular Internet search engines.

Augmenting your Web browser

Introduce yourself to plug-ins and helper applications that can be used to enhance the capabilities of your Web browser.

Understanding Web Browsers

As you learned in Chapter 18, the World Wide Web is unlike other parts of the Internet because it supports the use of a graphical display for the presentation of information. On the WWW, textual data can be displayed with graphics, animation, sound, and video.

The Internet was designed for the transmission of text, so in order to transmit a graphically designed Web page complete with pictures, embedded sound, and animation, a special language had to be devised. That language is *HTML*, or *HyperText Markup Language*. HTML uses special text codes to define the various elements of a Web page. A Web browser translates the text and the HTML codes it receives, and assembles the associated Web page in memory. It then displays this page on-screen for you to view, as shown in Figure 20.1.

FIG. 20.1

A Web browser translates HTML text to present graphical, interactive Web pages.

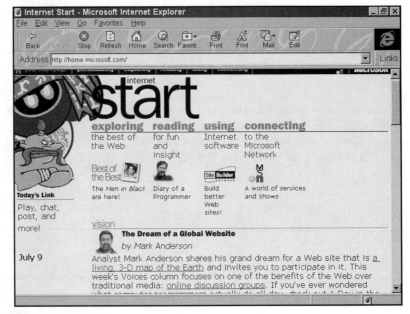

Which Web Browser?

Although the ISP you've chosen may have provided you with a Web browser already, the one you end up using every day is still your own choice. The most popular Web browsers are Internet Explorer and Netscape Navigator (which is part of the Netscape Communicator package). Some Web sites have been optimized for viewing by one brand or the other, but this optimization is not dramatic enough to require that you use one brand over the other. In fact, if you have the space on your hard drive, you might consider installing both major brands and alternating between the two.

Netscape Navigator

Now part of the Netscape Communicator suite of programs, Netscape Navigator is the most widely used browser on the Web today. On its own, the Communicator 4.0 package supports the most popular graphics, sound, and video file formats. *Plug-ins* (program extensions) are available for adding support for compressed animations and streaming "live" audio/visual presentations.

Over the past few years, Netscape Communications Corporation has been the leading developer of the HTML language. Although the World Wide Web Consortium has yet to endorse even the longest-running and most well-accepted Netscape extensions to HTML, including frames and tables, the modern Web page generally contains at least one Netscape extension.

Microsoft Internet Explorer

Introduced as a competitor to Netscape, Microsoft Internet Explorer (currently on version 3.02) has yet to gain the wide acceptance of Netscape products. It is a vastly capable Web browser, however, and is comparable feature-for-feature with Navigator.

Microsoft has been working to boost the acceptance of Internet Explorer (IE) by integrating it into the Windows operating system, beginning with IE version 4.0. Until that version emerges from its "public beta" period, IE 3.02 still cooperates very closely with Windows. If you use Microsoft Office 97 or any of its components (Word, Excel, PowerPoint), IE 3.02 can be integrated with that component so that they work in tandem. Two results of this collaboration are as follows:

- Word 97 can look to the Web for its documents nearly as easily as it looks to your own computer or network. This way, you can load a DOC file from the Web into Word 97, or import an HTML file from the Web. IE does the work, but the results show up in Word 97.

- Internet Explorer can load a DOC file into its main window nearly as easily as it loads an ordinary HTML page. With a DOC file, the toolbars and menu bar of Word 97 pop up in the IE window, just below its own controls.

While Netscape Navigator's functionality is extended with dedicated plug-ins, IE's functionality is extended with something called *ActiveX Controls*. These are programs that are designed to run in cooperation with other Windows programs, not necessarily IE. As a result, there are a wide variety of controls designed for Office 97 and Microsoft Visual Basic that will also work as part of a Web page specialized for Internet Explorer.

Exploring the World Wide Web

When you first start your Web browser, it takes you to your *home page*. This page is typically associated with the Web browser you installed. For example, if you installed Netscape Navigator, then you're taken to the Netscape home page.

Part
V

Ch
20

TIP You can usually change the default home page to something else if you want.

From your home page, you can begin exploring the Internet. You can move from page to page in one of two basic ways: by clicking a link, or by typing in the address of the page you want to visit. A link is usually some underlined text, typically blue, although it can be any color (see Figure 20.2). When you click a link, you're automatically taken to the Web page to which it refers. If you later return to that page, you'll notice that the link you clicked has changed color, typically from blue to purple, but it could change to any color. The change lets you quickly identify the links you've already visited.

A link can also be a graphic image. If you move the mouse over a graphic and it changes to a hand, then that graphic is acting as a link. If you click it, then you'll once again be taken to the page to which it refers. With both Web browsers, when you pass the mouse over a link, the address of its associated page appears in the status bar at the bottom of the screen.

FIG. 20.2

You can change to a new Web page using several methods.

Type in a new address to move to a new Web page

Some graphics are links to other sites

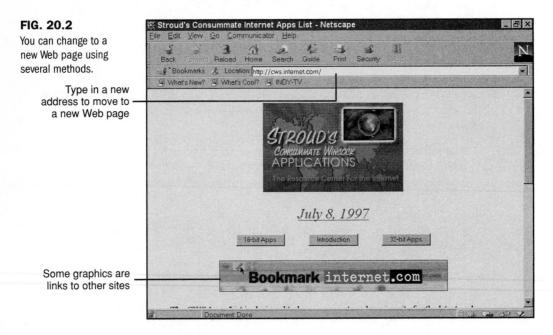

Another way to change to a different Web page is to enter its address. To do this, you type the address in the Location (Navigator) or the Address (Internet Explorer) text box. You might get the address of a Web page from a friend, from a television ad, from the newspaper, or in a magazine. After typing the address, press Enter, and the page located at the address you typed will appear.

A typical address (or URL—Uniform Resource Locator) looks something like this:

http://events.ticketmaster.com/ev_home.html

The **http://** part tells the Web browser that this page is located on the Web, because HTTP is the protocol of the Web. Other protocols include FTP (file download sites), Gopher (Gopher sites), and news (UseNet newsgroup sites).

The next part of the address, **/events.ticketmaster.com**, tells the Web browser the DNS address of the server that contains the page you want to display. The address in this example is an HTTP server called **events.ticketmaster.com**. The .com part tells you that this site is basically a commercial one, as opposed to .gov for government sites, .edu for educational sites, .org for non-profit organizations, or .net for an Internet service provider site.

The last part of the address, **/ev_home.html**, is the name of the file or page you want to display. If the address you have doesn't list a file name to display, don't worry about it. Your Web browser will display the files index.html or default.html instead. They represent the default home page for a site.

CAUTION

If you get an error message after typing in a URL, try checking what you've typed. Make sure you use / and not \ slashes, then press Enter again or click Reload. If that doesn't work, delete the file name from the address and see if you can connect to the site's home page. The link may simply be old; sites often move or close down completely. If you think you may have the wrong URL, you can search for the site's address (see "Searching for Information on the Web" later in this chapter).

Table 20.1 describes other ways to move from page to page.

Table 20.1 Navigation Buttons

To Do This	Click This in Navigator	Click This in Internet Explorer
Back to a previous page	Back	Back
Forward to original page	Forward	Forward
Return to home page	Home	Home
View cool pages	What's Cool?	Best of the Web
View hot, new pages	What's New?	Today's Link

If you find a page you like, you can bookmark it so you can return to it time and again. To create a bookmark in Netscape Navigator, follow these steps:

1. Jump to the page whose address you want to save.
2. Click the Bookmarks button.
3. Select Add Bookmark.

In Internet Explorer, follow these steps to add an entry for the page in Windows' Favorites folder:

1. Jump to the page whose address you want to save.

2. From the Favorites menu, select Add to Favorites.

3. In the Add to Favorites dialog box, accept or edit the name of the site as you want it to appear in Favorites.

4. To add the page to a folder, click Create In and select a folder, then click OK.

> **TIP** In Navigator, you can add buttons to the Personal toolbar (the one with the What's New? and What's Cool? buttons) by dragging the link icon in front of the Location text box onto the toolbar.

Understanding the Elements of a Web Page

You're already familiar with some of the elements of Web pages. Text, pictures, and sound are typical Web page components that need little explanation. But you may benefit from an introduction to elements such as frames, forms, and embedded video. The following section describes these common Web elements and the ways in which you can use them to enjoy the best in interactive Web viewing.

Dealing with Frames

Frames divide a Web page into sections, as shown in Figure 20.3. Each section can be designed to work as a page within a page, enabling you to scroll one part of a Web page while another part remains stationary.

In this figure, an index has been placed in the left-hand frame, and the contents of the currently selected page appear in the right-hand frame. Each frame contains its own Web page, with its own URL address. Sometimes the complete contents of the Web page will not show within the frame; in that case, scroll bars will appear. Use them to scroll the contents of the frame. You may also be able to change the size of a frame by dragging its border.

To select something in a frame such as a link, just click it like you would within any other Web page. When you click a link, the contents within that frame or within another frame may change, or you may be taken to a completely different Web page—what happens depends on how the framed Web page was designed.

If the contents of a frame change and you want to return to its previous contents, you simply click the Back button. Sometimes a link you choose in one frame will update the contents of another; if that happens, you can click the Back button to return the updated frame to its former state.

FIG. 20.3

Frames create sections on a Web page. Each section can contain its own element that can be addressed, scrolled, and used independently of other page elements.

This frame keeps the table of contents on-screen even after the text frame has been scrolled down

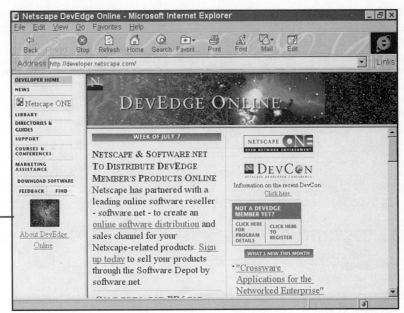

If you like a page that's contained in a frame, and you think you might want to return to it often, you can bookmark it, or what Internet Explorer calls "saving as a favorite." To save a bookmark for the Web page contained in a frame, in Navigator, right-click inside the frame and select Add Bookmark from the pop-up menu. In Internet Explorer, right-click inside the frame and select Add to Favorites.

To bookmark the framed Web page (and not the contents of a frame), follow the normal procedure. In Navigator, click the Bookmarks button and select Add Bookmark. In Internet Explorer, from the Favorites menu, select Add to Favorites, then name the page's entry in the dialog box that follows.

Completing Forms

Forms are used on Web pages to obtain information from you. Forms look a lot like dialog boxes—they can contain the following elements:

- *Text boxes*. These are used for textual information (such as your name or address).
- *Option buttons* and *check boxes*. You can use these to select various options such as Search the Web or Search the Entire Internet.
- *Drop-down list boxes*. These enable you to make a selection from a list.

A typical form is shown in Figure 20.4.

Part
V

Ch
20

FIG. 20.4

Forms are used to obtain information; complete forms using many of the same techniques you use to enter commands and selections in dialog boxes.

Choose options from drop-down lists

Type text in text boxes

Click buttons to issue commands

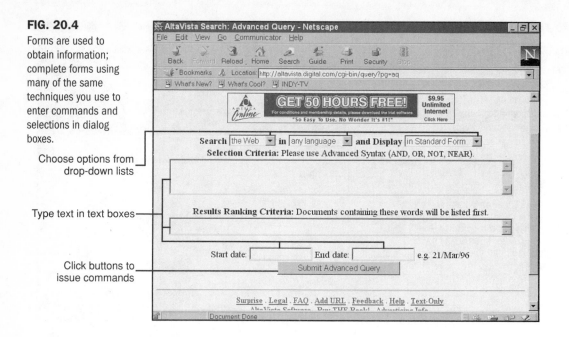

To complete a form, follow the same steps you would use to make selections in a dialog box. To type text into a text box, click in it, then type. To select an option or a check box, click it. To select an item from a drop-down list box, click its down arrow to display the list, then click an item to select it.

When you're finished, you submit the information in a form by clicking some kind of command button, such as Submit or Search Now. There's usually a Reset or Cancel button as well, in case you want to start over or forget the whole thing.

CAUTION

If a form asks you for private information, you may want to skip it, or at the very least, you may want to make sure that the Web site is secured. In Navigator, a glowing closed padlock appears in the lower-left corner of a secured page. In Internet Explorer, a small lock icon appears in the right-hand corner of the status bar.

Playing Embedded Sound or Video

Some Web pages contain embedded sound and video files that you can listen to or view. Your Web browser should be able to play most sound files without you doing anything at all. Simply click the link to the sound file, and after the file is downloaded, it will start playing (assuming your PC is equipped for sound). If you click and nothing happens, you'll have to install a program to help your Web browser play the sound file. See the section "Enhancing the Capabilities of Your Web Browser" for more help.

When the sound file starts playing, a sound console like the one shown in Figure 20.5 appears.

Click to stop the sound

FIG. 20.5
A sound console
appears when you play
embedded aound files
in a Web page; use the
console to control the
sound file playback.

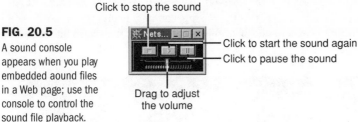

Click to start the sound again
Click to pause the sound

Drag to adjust
the volume

Some Web pages will contain embedded streaming audio files. With streaming audio, you don't have to wait until the entire file is downloaded before it begins playing on your system. A leader in streaming audio is *RealAudio*. You need to install RealPlayer to play RealAudio files. RealPlayer also handles streaming video files. See the section "Enhancing the Capabilities of Your Web Browser" later in this chapter.

There are four major types of video files: MPEG, AVI, MOV, and QT (QuickTime). In most cases, you need to install a program to play these files with your Web browser. See the section "Enhancing the Capabilities of Your Web Browser" for help.

To play the video file, you click its link. The file is then downloaded to your system, where it appears in its own box. To start the video file, double-click it. The video window usually contains the controls shown in Figure 20.6, which you can use to control the file's playback. The controls disappear after the video has played. To restart the video, right-click the window and select Play from the pop-up menu.

FIG. 20.6
The video file is
displayed in its own
window. To play the
video a second time,
right-click the window
and choose Play from
the pop-up menu.

Part
V

Ch
20

Click to play the video

Click to stop the video

N O T E If you play a QuickTime video, the controls will look a bit different than the ones shown here. But, left to right, they include the volume control, the Pause/Play button, the trackbar, as well as the Jump to the Start of Video, and Jump to the End of Video buttons. ▪

Exploring a Virtual World

Some Web sites are just for fun, like the new VRML (virtual world) Web sites. The idea is that you can explore these three-dimensional worlds by walking, running, flying, and so on— something that helps to make the experience of visiting that particular Web site a bit more interactive. See Figure 20.7.

FIG. 20.7

A virtual world makes your visit to a Web site truly interactive.

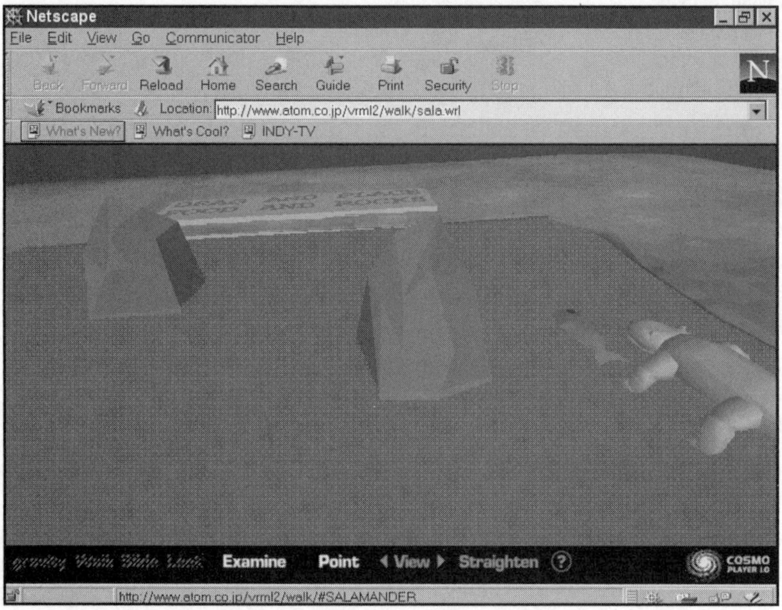

To visit a 3-D Web site, your Web browser will need the assistance of another program such as Live3D (which used to be the default VRML browser for Netscape, but now it is Cosmo Player), Quarterdeck's Qmosaic, TGS' Webspace, and Intervista's WorldView. If you use Navigator, you'll want to make sure that the plug-in, Cosmo Player, is installed. For Internet Explorer, one of the popular VRML-oriented ActiveX Controls is ActiveWorld, available as shareware. See the section "Expanding the Capabilities of Your Web Browser" for help.

To move around a virtual world, you can walk by following these steps:

1. Click Walk.

2. Drag the mouse pointer in the direction you want to move yourself. To move forward, you drag the pointer up; to back up, you drag down.

3. To stop walking, release the mouse button.

To spin the object in front of you:

1. Click Spin.

2. Drag the mouse pointer in the direction you want the object to spin. If you drag to the left, the object spins counterclockwise; drag to the right, and it spins clockwise. If you drag the mouse up, the object appears to move toward the top of your head. Drag down, and it moves drops toward your chin.

3. To stop spinning, release the mouse button.

To change your view, you look:

1. Click Look.

2. Drag the mouse pointer in the direction you want to turn your head.

You can also fly:

1. Click Slide.

2. Drag the mouse pointer in the direction you want to fly. To fly over an object, drag up. To fly below, drag down.

N O T E The difference between Slide and Walk is that you are moving along different axes. With Slide, you move along the vertical axis; with Walk, you move along the horizontal axis.

Running Java

Java is a programming language that can be used to create interactive programs—programs that can respond to the user's actions by displaying particular data or running a particular animation. Java programs run on both PC and Mac computers. You'll encounter Java on a lot of Web pages, most notably in the form of animated billboards that typically appear at the top of a Web page. Luckily, both Navigator and Internet Explorer provide built-in Java support, so there's nothing you need to do to run a Java application embedded in a Web page.

Searching for Information on the Web

To locate information on the Web, you should use a *search engine*. There are many popular search engines from which you can choose. Their Web addresses are listed in Table 20.2.

Part
V

Ch
20

Table 20.2	Popular Web Search Engines
Search Engine	**Web Address**
AltaVista	http://altavista.digital.com
Excite	http://www.excite.com
Lycos	http://www.lycos.com
InfoSeek	http://www.infoseek.com
Yahoo!	http://www.yahoo.com

T I P Click Navigator's or Internet Explorer's Search button to get connected to the most popular search engines quickly.

Search engines search the Web for pages, analyzing their contents and cataloging them in huge databases. After you enter your search criteria, the search engine looks through its database and finds as many matches as it can find. It then displays a list of Web pages that match your criteria. You can then click a link to one of these Web pages and display it on-screen. Pages are typically arranged with the pages that most likely match your search criteria appearing at the top. If the page does not prove helpful, you can return to the search results page and click a different link, or try searching again. A popular search engine, Excite, is shown in Figure 20.8.

FIG. 20.8

Excite is one of many search engines that you can use to search for Web pages.

Enter search criteria here

Click this button to start the search

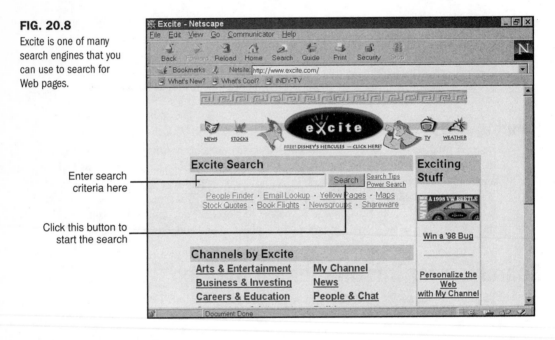

Most search engines function in basically the same manner: Type the words you want to search for in the text box, then click the Search, Seek, or Submit button. Some search engines such as Yahoo! allow you to choose a category first to narrow down the search. To search for a phrase such as bass fishing or French poetry, surround them with quotations, as in "**bass fishing**". Otherwise, Excite will search for any documents that contain either bass or fishing, but not necessarily the two together, or in that order.

As you type your search criteria, do not include common words such as to, the, an, who, and so on. The search engine will just ignore them. If you type **safety record**, for example, most search engines will look for documents that contain safety *AND* record. The AND, in this case, is understood. (Of course, because you might be looking for the phrase `safety record`, you may want to include it in quotes as in `"safety record"`.) You can also use an `OR` in your criteria, as in

`Indiana OR Illinois`

This will match all documents that contain either the word `Indiana` or the word `Illinois`. You can search for a phrase and a word, as in

`"infant car seat" AND safety`

If you want to make sure that some word is not included in the search results, use the operator `NOT`, as in

`Indian NOT American`

which will search for documents on people from India and not American Indians.

Some search engines allow you to use wildcards. For example, if you type **stock***, you'll get matches for `stockbroker`, `stockyard`, and `stocks`. With other search engines, you can create a *rule* by combining several commands together with parentheses, as in

`("infant car seat" OR "baby seat") AND safety`

Still other search engines allow you to enter *search busters*, words that either must (or must not) be found within the page's title or description in order to be included in the search results. A plus or a minus sign is used to indicate the search busters, as in `+civil`.

Words, characters, and symbols that trigger specific search parameters are called *search operators*. Learning how to use search operators will help you conduct faster and more efficient searches. Table 20.3 lists the search operators for each of the most popular search engines. N/A indicates that a particular option is not supported by that engine.

Table 20.3 Search Operators

Operator	AltaVista	Excite	Lycos	InfoSeek	Yahoo!
AND	AND, &	AND	Assumed	+	N/A
OR	OR, |	OR	N/A	-	N/A
NOT	NOT	NOT	-	N/A	N/A
Quotes	""	""	N/A	""	""
Rule	()	()	N/A	N/A	N/A
Wildcard	*	N/A	$	N/A	N/A
Must include	+	+	N/A	N/A	+
Must not include	-	-	-	N/A	-

Part

V

Ch

20

Enhancing the Capabilities of Your Web Browser

A Web browser can be enhanced by the capabilities of other programs. For example, Navigator can call upon the resources of Microsoft Word to display the contents of a Word document, when needed. Because you never know what you might encounter on a Web page, this ability can come in handy.

Navigator can use two different types of enhancers. One is called a *helper application*. A *helper application* is a separate program that can be used alone, such as Microsoft Word, but which can be called upon by Navigator when needed to display the contents of an associated file within its own window. To designate something as a helper app, you don't need to do a thing. Navigator automatically uses any program you have installed under Windows as a helper application when needed.

A *plug-in* is the second kind of enhancer used by Netscape. A plug-in is not a separate program—it cannot be run outside of Navigator—and you have to install it. Unlike a helper application, a plug-in displays the file within the Navigator window. Popular Navigator plug-ins include:

> Media Player—Streaming audio
>
> LiveAudio—Audio files such as .WAV, .AU, .AIFF, and MIDI
>
> QuickTime—QuickTime videos
>
> Cosmo Player—VRML (3-D) worlds
>
> Macromedia Shockwave—Shockwave animations
>
> Adobe Acrobat Reader—Acrobat formatted documents
>
> RealPlayer—Streaming audio and video

To install a plug-in, download it from the Web and then follow its normal installation procedure. Typically, this involves nothing more complicated than double-clicking the file you download, and then double-clicking the SETUP.EXE or INSTALL.EXE file that appears.

For Internet Explorer, versions of Macromedia Shockwave, Adobe Acrobat, and RealPlayer are available as ActiveX Controls. Regular sound files are handled by the ActiveX facilities that are already built into Windows (or that are enhanced within Windows when you install Internet Explorer). Apple's QuickTime stand-alone player program is still necessary if you want to play QuickTime videos. Because Internet Explorer relies on the Windows System Registry to determine which program handles what type of file, QuickTime and other non-ActiveX Controls can be enrolled as *de facto* helper applications for IE. The process of installing an ActiveX Control is generally no more involved than that for installing a Navigator plug-in. ●

CHAPTER 21

Sending and Receiving E-Mail

Understanding e-mail

Discover what e-mail is and how it works.

Sending electronic messages

Learn how to send messages to colleagues over the Internet.

Receiving electronic messages

Discover how to retrieve your mail, read it, and respond to it.

Attaching files to your messages

Find out how to include more than just text with your messages.

One of the most frustrating aspects of doing business is communication, or lack of it. More and more, the key to success is having information when you need it. Faxing is okay, but not always convenient. And telephones are not always a dependable means of communication because it's all too easy for someone to be away from their phone, and you can't exactly leave a 10-page document on someone's voice mail. With electronic messaging, you don't have to waste time playing telephone tag. You can get information to those who need it, when they need it, with the least amount of wasted time and effort on your part. ■

What Is E-Mail?

The term *e-mail* is short for *electronic mail*. E-mail is the process of sending a message from one computer to another *electronically*. Over the Internet, you can send an electronic message to someone across the street, in another city, state, or even another country. This process may take only a few minutes, or as long as an hour, depending on Internet traffic. But even so, using e-mail is still faster than the post office, or even special delivery services.

The process of sending an e-mail message works something like this:

1. You type your message into an e-mail program, then you enter the e-mail address of the person to whom you want to send it.

2. In your e-mail program, you issue the Send command, which causes the program to transmit your message over the Internet to your e-mail server. This e-mail server is located either on your company's network (if you connect to the Internet through your network), or at the offices of your Internet service provider (if you connect to the Internet via modem).

3. Your message is then routed over the Internet from server to server, until it reaches the server that handles the mail for the intended recipient. There the message sits until the recipient connects to the mail server, and requests his mail.

N O T E   You can send a message to anyone connected to the Internet, and even to people who are indirectly connected, such as people who use America Online or CompuServe for Internet access. ▇

Using E-Mail Addresses

The process of sending an e-mail message is as simple as typing your text, entering an address, and clicking Send. The key, of course, is correctly addressing the message, so that it finds the correct recipient.

 TIP   Save addresses you use often in the address book that comes with your e-mail program. That way, you can simply select the address you want to use, and avoid the mistakes you might make in typing it in.

Internet e-mail addresses, like postal addresses, follow a specific format. Here's an example of an Internet e-mail address:

> **jlsmith@sales.BigCo.com**

The first part of the address is the *user name*, which is the name by which that person is known to his mail server. Typically, the user name is comprised of the person's first initial and last name, although it could be a whole name, as in **johnsmith@sales.BigCo.com**, or a nickname, such as **nightwriter@speedy.net**.

If you connect to the Internet though your company's network, then your system administrator will assign a user name to you. If you connect through a service provider, you can choose your own user name when you sign up for service.

The second part of the Internet e-mail address, sales.BigCo.com in our example, identifies the mail server that handles that person's e-mail. The .com extension on the end tells you that the server is a commercial enterprise, meaning some kind of business.

If the second part of the address was something like speedy.net, then that might indicate that the person connects through a service provider known as Speedy. The .net extension indicates an *Internet service provider (ISP)*. There are other extensions (called *domain identifiers*) that are commonly used as well, including .gov for government offices, .org for non-profit organizations, .mil for military services, and .edu for educational institutions such as schools and universities.

TIP Be sure that you use proper case (upper and lower) when entering an e-mail address. It's not always an issue, but sometimes (for example), **JFulton@speedy.net** is not the same as **jfulton@speedy.net** or **Jfulton@Speedy.net**.

When sending an e-mail message to someone who is not connected to the Internet directly (in other words, they are connected through an online service), then the address you should use may be a bit different than the one they give you. For example, if I had a CompuServe account and someone on CompuServe wanted to send me an e-mail message, then they might send it to this address:

79041,2110

But, if you wanted to send me a message through the Internet, you'd have to change my address to this:

79041.2110@compuserve.com

The comma that CompuServe uses in its addresses is changed to a period because the Internet doesn't recognize commas in e-mail addresses. Table 21.1 lists the common online services and their equivalent Internet address formats.

Table 21.1 Internet Addresses Formats for Popular Online Services

Online Service	Address Format
CompuServe	**79041.2110@compuserve.com**
America Online	**nightwriter@aol.com**
Microsoft Network	**tjones@msn.com**
Prodigy	**alicesmith@prodigy.com**

Sending E-Mail

You can use a separate e-mail program to send electronic messages, or you can use the e-mail program that comes with your Web browser. Netscape Communicator's e-mail program is called Messenger. To send an e-mail message with Messenger, follow these steps:

1. Start Messenger by clicking the Mailbox icon on the Component bar, which is located at the bottom right-hand corner of the Navigator screen.

2. Click the New Msg button on the Navigation toolbar. The Composition window appears, as shown in Figure 21.1.

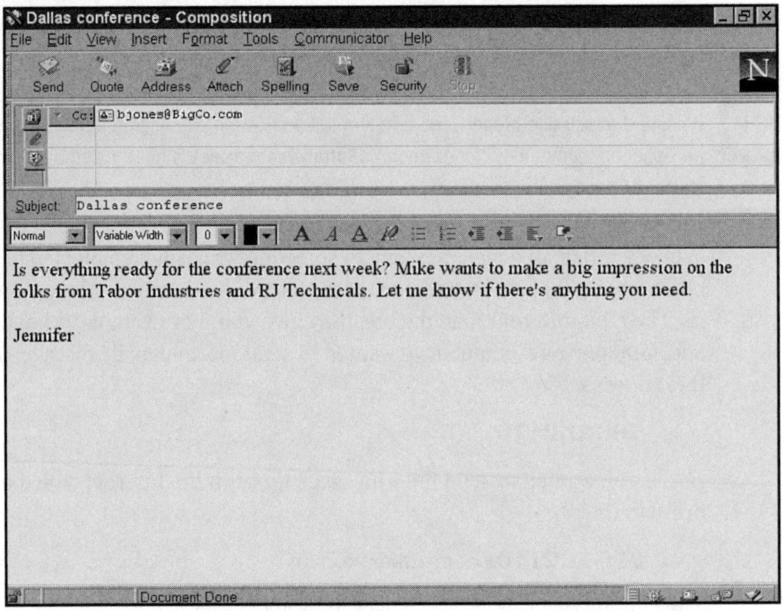

FIG. 21.1

Create an e-mail message with Netscape Messenger.

3. Click in the To box and type the address of the person to whom you want to send your message.

4. To send this message to a second person as well, press Enter. Another To box appears. Type the address of the second person in this box. Repeat this process to address the message to additional people.

5. Press Tab to move to the Subject box, and type a description of your message.

6. Press Tab to move to the text area, and type your message.

7. Make sure you're connected to the Internet, then click Send to send the message.

TIP Messenger allows you to spell check your messages before you send them; just click the Spelling button. You can also format the text in your messages with the buttons on the Formatting toolbar.

N O T E   If for some reason your message could not be delivered, you'll be notified via e-mail. ▨

Internet Explorer includes its own e-mail program as well, called Internet Mail. To send an e-mail message using Internet Mail, you follow a similar process:

1. Start Internet Mail by clicking the Mail button on the Internet Explorer toolbar. Select New Message from the menu that appears. The New Message window appears, as shown in Figure 21.2.

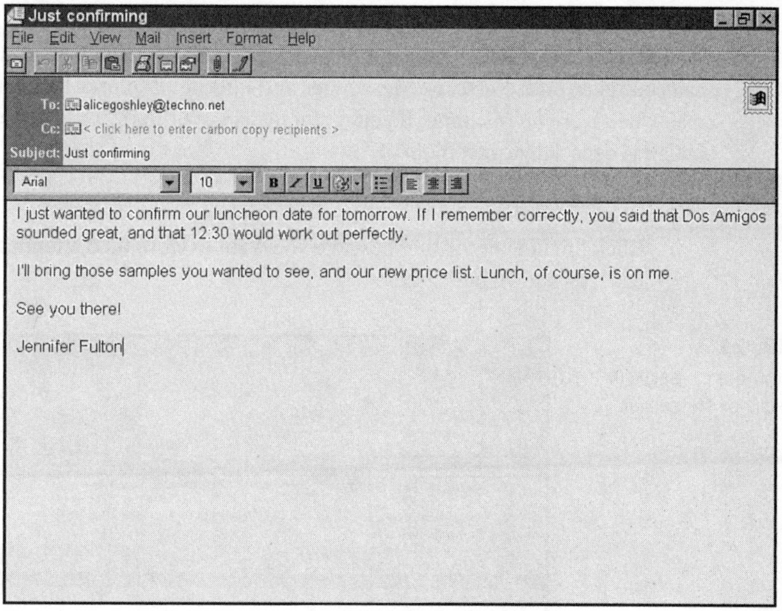

FIG. 21.2
Create an e-mail message with Internet Mail.

Just confirming

File Edit View Mail Insert Format Help

To: alicegoshley@techno.net
Cc: < click here to enter carbon copy recipients >
Subject: Just confirming

Arial   10   B / U   :=   :=

I just wanted to confirm our luncheon date for tomorrow. If I remember correctly, you said that Dos Amigos sounded great, and that 12:30 would work out perfectly.

I'll bring those samples you wanted to see, and our new price list. Lunch, of course, is on me.

See you there!

Jennifer Fulton

2. In the To box, type the address of the person to whom you want to send your message. To add the address of a second person, type a semicolon (;), followed by the second address. Repeat for additional people. If you want to copy others on the message, click the Cc box and type the name(s).

3. Click in the Subject box and type a description of your message.

4. Press Tab to move to the text area, and type your message.

5. Make sure you're connected to the Internet, then click Send to send the message (the envelope icon).

Part
V

Ch
21

T I P   Like Messenger, Internet Mail also allows you to spell check your messages before you send them; simply press F7. You can also format the text in your messages with the buttons on the Formatting toolbar. (To display the toolbar, open the View menu and select Formatting Toolbar.)

Receiving E-Mail

With e-mail, instead of walking out to the mailbox to get your mail, you connect to your mail server. The mail server checks your mailbox for messages, and if there are any, your e-mail program issues the command to have them downloaded (copied) to your PC.

The messages are then placed in your Inbox, a special folder in which your e-mail program places your incoming mail. You then open the Inbox and view any new messages. At that point, you can reply to any messages you want. You can also forward a copy of a message you receive to someone else.

To check for new mail messages in Messenger, you click the Get Msg button on the Navigation toolbar. To check for new mail in Internet Mail, click the Mail button and select View Mail. You can configure both Netscape Messenger and Internet Explorer to automatically check for new mail whenever you're online. If you're online all the time (through a network connection), this option is especially convenient.

To review and reply to messages in Messenger, follow these steps:

1. Click the header for the message you want to view. Its contents appear in the Message pane, as shown in Figure 21.3.

FIG. 21.3

View your messages in Netscape Messenger.

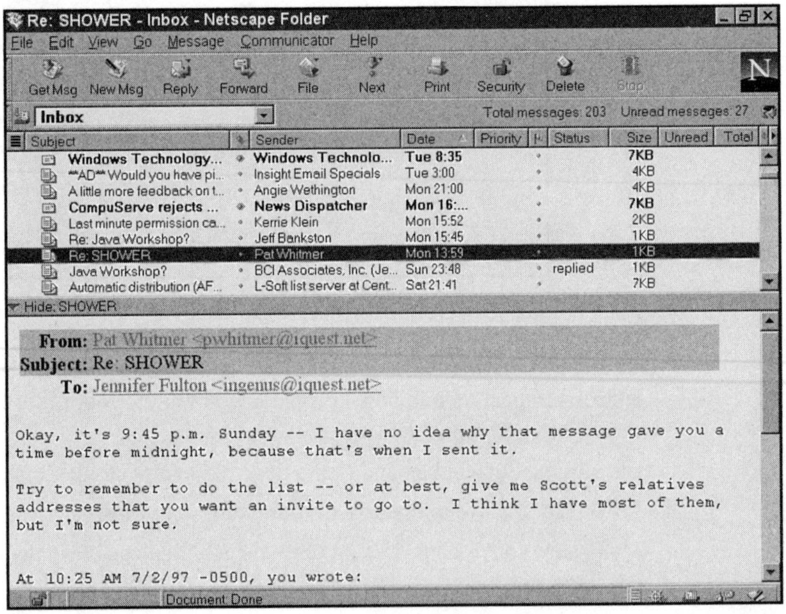

2. To reply to the message, click the Reply button and select either Reply to Sender, or Reply to Sender and All Recipients (to reply to everyone who received a copy of the original message). To forward the message to someone, click Forward instead.

3. The Composition window opens. In a reply, the text of the original message is automatically copied for you into the text area. You can type your reply under this text. If you're forwarding the message, then it is attached as a file. Type any comments you want to add in the text area.

4. In a reply, the message is automatically addressed to the sender (and all recipients, if you selected that option). Click Send to send the reply. If you're forwarding the message, then type an address in the To box and click Send.

To review and reply to messages using Internet Mail, follow these steps instead:

1. Click the header for the message you want to view. Its contents appear in the Preview pane, as shown in Figure 21.4.

FIG. 21.4

View your messages in Internet Mail.

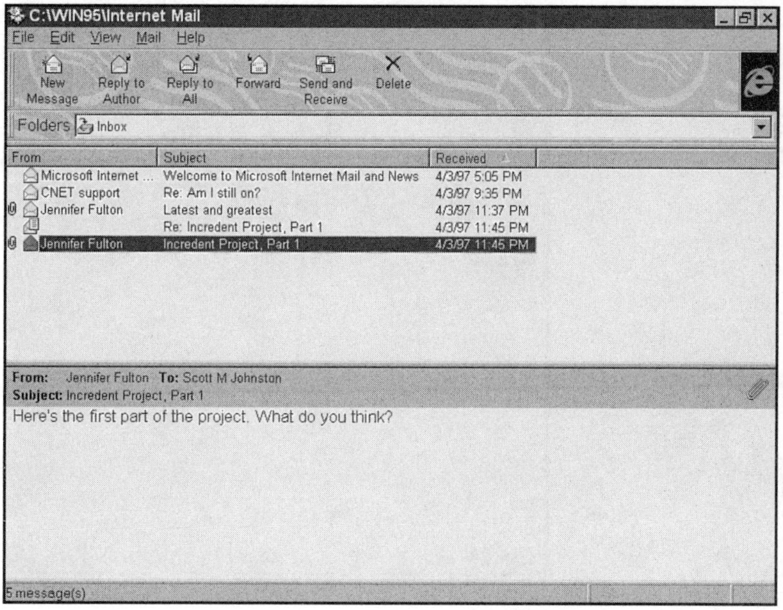

2. To reply to the message, click either the Reply to Author button or Reply to All (to reply to everyone who received a copy of the original message). To forward the message to someone, click Forward instead.

3. The New Message window opens. The text of the original message is automatically copied for you into the text area. You can type your reply or your comments on the forwarded message above this text.

4. In a reply, the message is automatically addressed to the sender (and all recipients, if you selected that option). Click Send to send the reply. If you're forwarding the message, then type an address in the To box and click Send (the envelope icon).

Attaching Files to Your E-Mail

E-mail messages can carry more than just message text. You can also attach a file such as a spreadsheet, a document, a graphic, or a chart to an e-mail message. You can attach more than one file to a message, if needed.

To attach a file to a message in Netscape Messenger, follow these steps:

1. Create the message in the usual manner. Then click the Attach button on the Message toolbar.

2. Select File from the drop-down menu that appears (see Figure 21.5).

3. In the Enter File to Attach dialog box, select the file you want to attach to the message and click Open.

4. The name of the file you selected appears on the Attach Files and Documents tab. Click Send to send your e-mail message.

To attach a file to an Internet Mail message, follow these steps instead:

1. Create your message as usual. Then click the Insert File button (the paperclip icon).

2. In the Insert Attachment dialog box, select the file you want to attach to the message and click Attach.

3. The file appears as an icon at the bottom of the message (see Figure 21.6). Click Send to send your message.

FIG. 21.6
This Internet Mail message has an attached file and is ready to send.

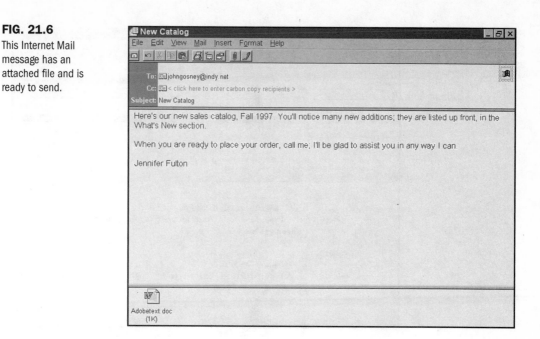

Saving an Attached File You've Received

If someone has attached a file to a message she originally sent to you, you must first save that file to your hard disk. Then you can start up the appropriate program and open the file to view, print, or change as needed.

If you use Netscape Messenger, follow these steps to save an attached file to your hard disk:

1. Click the message header to view the contents of the message. The file appears in the message as a link (a bit of underlined text, typically blue). See Figure 21.7.
2. Press and hold the Shift key as you click the link.
3. The Save As dialog box appears; change to the drive and directory in which you want to save the file.
4. Click Save to save the file to the selected directory.

If you use Internet Mail, follow these steps to save your file to the hard disk:

1. Click the message header to view the contents of the message. A paperclip icon appears on the right (see Figure 21.8).
2. Press and hold the Ctrl key as you click the paperclip icon. From the menu that appears, select the name of the file you want to save to your PC's hard disk.
3. The Save Attachment As dialog box appears; change to the drive and directory in which you want to save the file.
4. Click Save to save the file to the selected directory.

Part
V

Ch
21

FIG. 21.7

Save an attached file using Netscape Messenger.

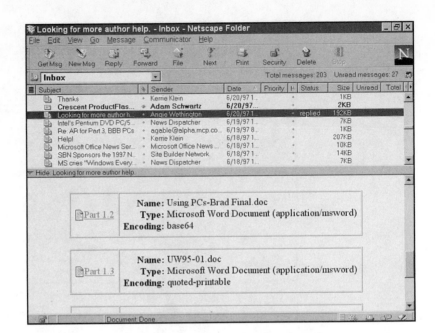

FIG. 21.8

Save an attached file using Internet Mail.

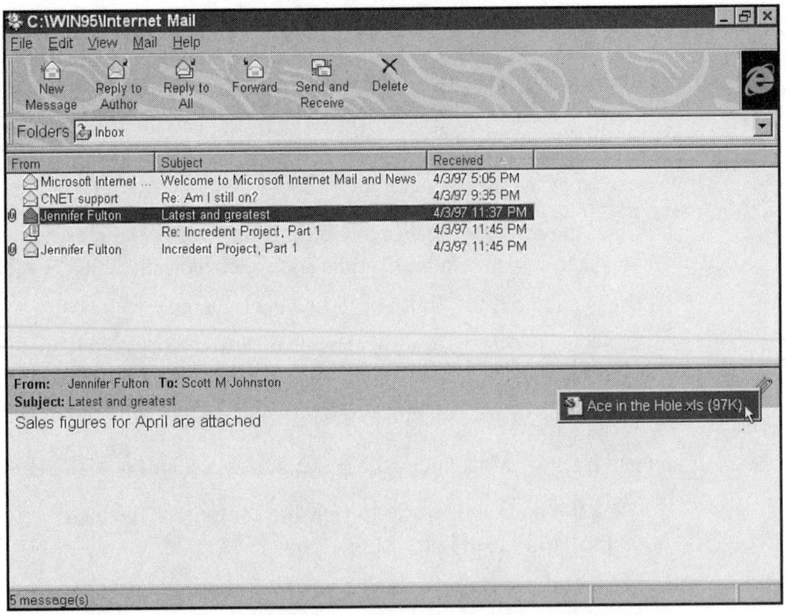

Sending and Receiving Files with FTP

The system used by the Internet to transfer a general file from server to client is File Transfer Protocol. The Internet's FTP breaks a file into packets, and routes those packets to your address as though the file were an e-mail message. At the receiving end, the packets are then re-organized in sequence.

Originally, FTP was a command that an Internet user in a Telnet connection would type at the command prompt in order to request a file. Servers that "speak" FTP still expect to see "FTP" as a typed command during the user's Telnet session. The Telnet session was, at one time, the protocol for communicating with other servers through the Internet. Telnet is still in use; in fact, the way the Internet is structured, it cannot really be replaced. ■

Understanding FTP
Uncover the purpose of FTP.

Popular download sites
Discover the best sources of downloadable files on the Internet.

Copying files to your PC
Learn how to download (copy) files from the Internet to your computer using FTP.

Sharing your files
Learn how to upload (send) files to various sites on the Internet.

FTPing with your Web browser
Find out how to download files using your Web browser.

What Is FTP?

FTP programsprovide a graphical environment that translates your selections into Telnet commands. So, you rarely have to type anything; instead, you can navigate an FTP directory almost as if it were a directory window for your own system. The examples here use a graphical FTP program for all Windows platforms, called CuteFTP. Figure 22.1 shows CuteFTP's main window.

FIG. 22.1

This directory is CuteFTP 1.8 by Alex Kunadze, currently in shareware.

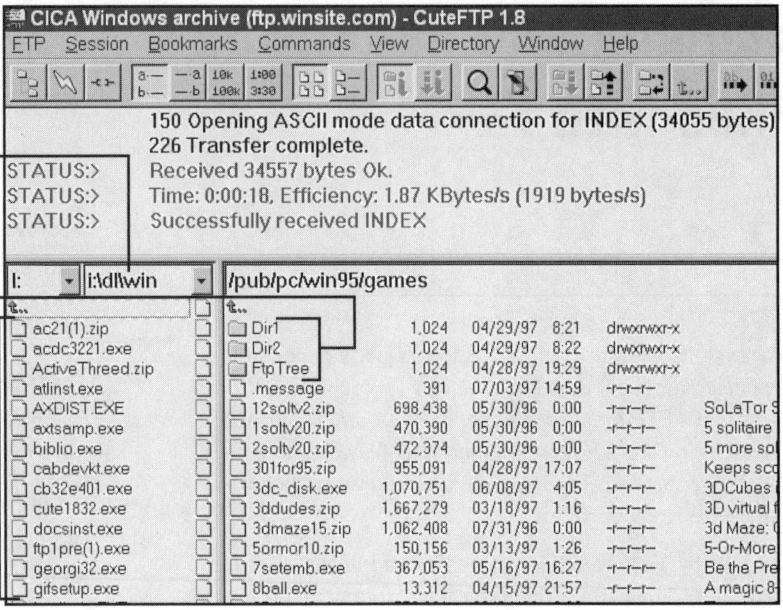

Current directory

Directories on your PC

Files in your current directory

```
CICA Windows archive (ftp.winsite.com) - CuteFTP 1.8
FTP   Session   Bookmarks   Commands   View   Directory   Window   Help

                  150 Opening ASCII mode data connection for INDEX (34055 bytes)
                  226 Transfer complete.
STATUS:>          Received 34557 bytes Ok.
STATUS:>          Time: 0:00:18, Efficiency: 1.87 KBytes/s (1919 bytes/s)
STATUS:>          Successfully received INDEX

I:  ▼  i:\dl\win          /pub/pc/win95/games

ac21(1).zip             Dir1           1,024      04/29/97   8:21    drwxrwxr-x
acdc3221.exe            Dir2           1,024      04/29/97   8:22    drwxrwxr-x
ActiveThreed.zip        FtpTree        1,024      04/28/97  19:29    drwxrwxr-x
atlinst.exe             .message         391      07/03/97  14:59    -r-r--r--
AXDIST.EXE              12soltv2.zip   698,438    05/30/96   0:00    -r-r--r--   SoLaTor 9
extsamp.exe             1soltv20.zip   470,390    05/30/96   0:00    -r-r--r--   5 solitaire
biblio.exe              2soltv20.zip   472,374    05/30/96   0:00    -r-r--r--   5 more sol
cabdevkt.exe            301for95.zip   955,091    04/28/97  17:07    -r-r--r--   Keeps sco
cb32e401.exe            3dc_disk.exe   1,070,751  06/08/97   4:05    -r-r--r--   3DCubes
cute1832.exe            3ddudes.zip    1,667,279  03/18/97   1:16    -r-r--r--   3D virtual f
docsinst.exe            3dmaze15.zip   1,062,408  07/31/96   0:00    -r-r--r--   3d Maze: (
ftp1pre(1).exe          5ormor10.zip   150,156    03/13/97   1:26    -r-r--r--   5-Or-More
georgi32.exe            7setemb.exe    367,053    05/16/97  16:27    -r-r--r--   Be the Pre
gifsetup.exe            8ball.exe      13,312     04/15/97  21:57    -r-r--r--   A magic 8-
```

What you are seeing in Figure 22.1 is *not* the product of File Transfer Protocol at work. In fact, after you've logged on to the server **ftp.winsite.com** and retrieved this directory, nothing you've done involves FTP at all. CuteFTP here manages the Telnet session between you and **ftp.winsite.com**. A series of text commands placed to UNIX programs running on the server are issued by CuteFTP, the result being the directory listing in the lower-right pane, which includes the detailed index in the right column of that pane.

The uppermost pane contains CuteFTP's account of the Telnet session. Again, you don't type anything here; all the textual commands are entered on your behalf by CuteFTP. You'll learn the exact steps for using CuteFTP later in this chapter in the section "Downloading a File."

Finding Files to Download

CuteFTP already contains a list of the major FTP anonymous download sites, from which you may choose. Table 22.1 shows the DNS addresses of the most frequented FTP sites in the world, which you can also access by way of a Web browser if you don't want to use an FTP program like CuteFTP. You will learn how to use your Web browser to FTP later in this chapter.

Table 22.1   Common FTP Download Sites

DNS Address	Description
ftp.winsite.com	Formerly the CICA Windows Archive
ftp.ncsa.uiuc.edu	National Center for Supercomputing Applications, home of the first Web browser
oak.oakland.edu	Oak Software Repository, Oakland University
ftp.coast.net	EagleQuest Mirror, coast-to-coast software repository
garbo.uwasa.fi	Garbo Software Repository, University of Vaasa, Finland
ftp.cdrom.com	Walnut Creek CD-ROM, home of FreeBSD operating system
ftp.sunet.se	Swedish University Network

All of these are massive software repositories, containing Windows programs arranged in UNIX directories by category. There are shareware applications, utilities, almost every imaginable game, and perhaps most abundantly, programmers' tools.

N O T E   Shareware is based on a try-before-you-buy concept. If you download a shareware program and like it, you can register it by paying a small fee. Check the program's Help system for details.

Downloading a File

In CuteFTP, the FTP download sites are maintained in a database by the Site Manager—similar to the bookmark system on a Web browser. The Site Manager pulls up DNS addresses of commonly visited FTP sites, or other such sites previously visited by you. Figure 22.2 shows the Site Manager dialog box. The Site Manager dialog box automatically appears when you start CuteFTP. But if you need to display it, click the Site Manager button.

To download a file from an FTP site:

1. Initiate the logon process by double-clicking one of the FTP site's names in the list on the right side of the Site Manager dialog box. CuteFTP contacts the DNS address for the chosen site.

2. When the server asks for a user name and password, type the user name **anonymous** (you don't need to have a private account on the major FTP sites in order to download files from them). Type your e-mail address as your password.

3. After you're online, CuteFTP searches for a file in the FTP site's current directory named INDEX.* (where the extension can be anything). If it finds that file, CuteFTP asks if you want to continue the download (sometimes it can take a long time). Verify that you want the download to continue.

FIG. 22.2
You log on by double-clicking a site name in CuteFTP's Site Manager dialog box.

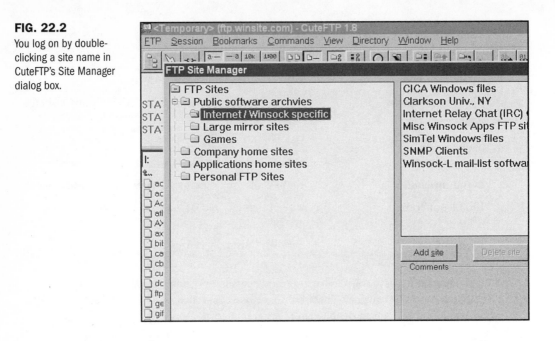

The index file is generally a text file that contains the file name of each downloadable file in that directory, along with a one-line description of its contents, which can be pretty helpful in identifying the actual file you want to download.

CuteFTP matches this downloaded index against its own previously downloaded directory of the FTP site's files, and attaches the descriptions from the index to the file names in the window. These descriptions enable you to have some idea of what each file contains before you download it.

The download process in CuteFTP is actually quite academic. CuteFTP has two directory panes, the one on the left representing a directory on your own system, and the one on the right of the FTP site you're perusing (refer to Figure 22.1). To switch to a subdirectory, you double-click its folder icon, just as you would in Windows Explorer; to back up one directory, double-click the up arrow icon. You can download a single file by double-clicking its file name. Or, you can download a series of files by highlighting them in the FTP directory list, then dragging them to the directory (on your system) shown in the left pane to which you want the files downloaded.

Uploading a File

Not all software archives require, request, or even allow you to upload (post) files to them. But some of the smaller archives run on the honor system, where you agree to trade so many downloads for one upload.

To upload a file in CuteFTP:

1. Highlight the file or files you want to upload.
2. Right-click one of the selected files. A pop-up menu appears.
3. Select Upload from the pop-up menu.

If you cannot upload files to this FTP site, you'll find out soon enough. You might have to navigate to a predetermined upload directory before your upload can be received; this is probably explained in the rules of the FTP site. If the rules are included within the site's logon screen, then CuteFTP will display them whenever you log on to the site.

Using Archie to Locate a File

Outside of the Web, there are not many tools available to help you find a file. One of the legacy systems in place on the Internet for helping you find a particular file by name is Archie, named after the comic strip character. The Archie system relies on a set of so-called Archie servers, which maintain a list of files that are downloadable from FTP directories.

For Windows users, the shareware program fpArchie, shown in Figure 22.3, manages a Telnet session between you and an Archie server.

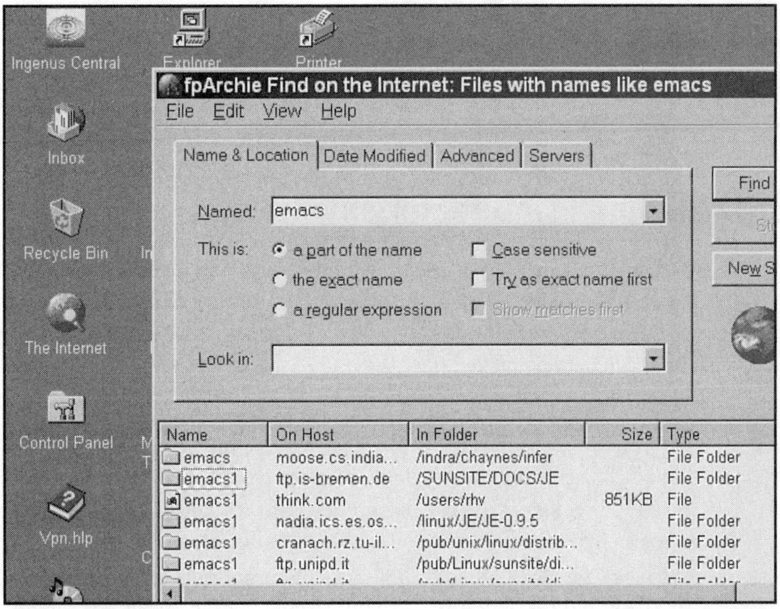

FIG. 22.3
fpArchie, by Peter Tanis and Frank Fesevur, helps you find files on the Internet.

fpArchie looks like the Windows 95 File Find dialog box. Here, you're given four tabs full of options for conducting your search. The Servers tab lets you choose which Archie server you want to contact; the list literally shows all the Archie servers currently active throughout the world. A file not listed in the database of one Archie server may be listed in another; servers don't share their data with one another.

Using Your Web Browser for FTP

A Web browser, such as Netscape Navigator in Figure 22.4, manages an FTP session much like it does an HTTP session (the displaying of a Web page). It logs on, gets its data, displays it or stores it, and immediately logs off.

FIG. 22.4
An FTP directory is displayed by Netscape Navigator 4.0.

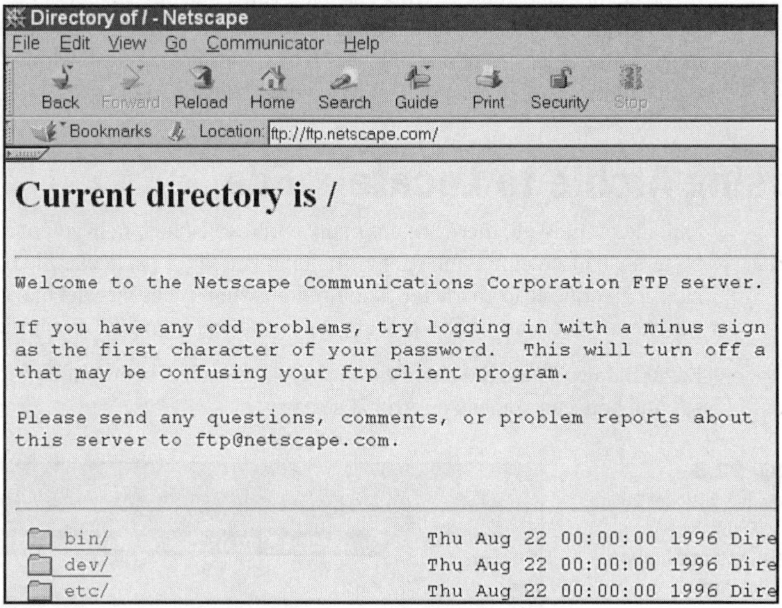

Downloading FTP Directories and Files

With a Web browser, you dial up an FTP site using an URL address, almost like you were calling up a Web page. To download the root directory of **ftp.winsite.com**, you would enter the URL **ftp://ftp.winsite.com** into the Location or Address text box. Any subdirectories such as /pub/pc could be tacked onto the end of the URL, as in **ftp://ftp.winsite.com/pub/pc**.

Figure 22.5 shows an FTP directory displayed in Microsoft Internet Explorer 3.02.

As you can see from the previous two figures, a Web browser assembles an HTML page out of the FTP directory it has received. Files and directories are formatted within these dynamic pages as hyperlinks, which you can click to download the file or navigate to another directory. Netscape Navigator attaches folder icons to its directories, and document icons to its files. Microsoft Internet Explorer, by comparison, leaves off the icons and simply boldfaces its links to directories.

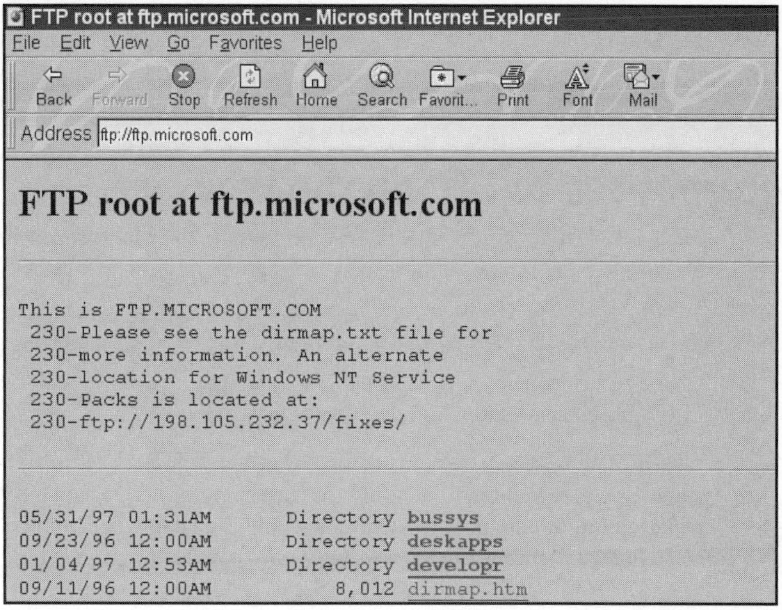

FIG. 22.5

Note the hyperlinks available in Internet Explorer's view of an FTP directory.

```
FTP root at ftp.microsoft.com - Microsoft Internet Explorer
File   Edit   View   Go   Favorites   Help

  ⇦        ⇨       ⊗       🗘       🏠       Q        📑▾      🖨       🅰       🗂▾
 Back   Forward   Stop   Refresh   Home   Search   Favorit...  Print   Font   Mail

 Address  ftp://ftp.microsoft.com
```

FTP root at ftp.microsoft.com

```
This is FTP.MICROSOFT.COM
 230-Please see the dirmap.txt file for
 230-more information. An alternate
 230-location for Windows NT Service
 230-Packs is located at:
 230-ftp://198.105.232.37/fixes/



05/31/97 01:31AM        Directory  bussys
09/23/96 12:00AM        Directory  deskapps
01/04/97 12:53AM        Directory  developr
09/11/96 12:00AM            8,012  dirmap.htm
```

N O T E The FTP "pages" generated by both major Web browsers don't provide you with links with which you can back up one directory, like the up-arrow icon in CuteFTP. Instead, browsers expect you to click the Back or Forward button in their own toolbars. But this will only work if the directory you're backing up to is one that you've seen before.

So, if your FTP browsing process began at a subdirectory—for example, **ftp://ftp.winsite.com/pub/ pc/win95**—to back up one directory and see the server's directory list for other supported platforms, you would need to place your cursor into the Location box and edit out the /win95 part manually. Clicking the Back button would simply take you to the Web page you were viewing before you typed in the FTP address. ▓

Neither Web browser makes use of the index files found on most FTP sites' directories, as CuteFTP does. Nevertheless, when you find a file you want to download, single-click the link of the file you want to download.

At this point, the Web browser isn't certain of whether you're downloading this file so that it can try to display it, or whether you're downloading it so you can store the file to disk. (With CuteFTP, all downloads are presumed to be stored to disk; you don't have the option of opening files you download for viewing.) FTP sites' files are generally mathematically compressed; you could choose to have your decompressor program, such as WinZip, open these files immediately after download, thus saving you one step. If you choose instead to store your downloaded file to disk, the Web browser will immediately prompt you for a location. Enter the location in the prompt dialog box; from this point, the download is the same as that for any Internet file.

N O T E   You cannot perform a batch download of files using a Web browser, like you can with
CuteFTP. Also, you can't upload files with a Web browser; it's designed to be a receiver, not
a sender. If you're planning an upload transaction, you need to use a dedicated FTP program. ■

Alternatives to FTP on the Web

The FTP program has recently taken a backseat to the widespread use of the Web browser,
because more archives and file repositories are moving their services over to HTTP and the
World Wide Web.

As this transfer of service takes place, the number of dedicated FTP sites operating in the
world has become fewer. In their place are elaborate Web sites with easy-to-understand menus
and comprehensive file-searching capabilities, which FTP alone completely lacks.

The CICA Windows Archive, once the powerhouse FTP server for Windows users, has been
taken over by a commercial venture that has spawned a Web counterpart, **http://www.
winsite.com**. From there, you can access any and all the files from your Web browser that you
could find by perusing FTP directories. Other popular Web repositories include ClNet's
SHAREWARE.COM, and the ZD*Net Software Library, both of which use sophisticated search
techniques to help you locate a program or file by its content, purpose, or characteristics.

If you're looking for Internet-related programs exclusively, the most comprehensive and up-to-
date repository anywhere on the globe is Stroud's Consummate Winsock Applications, located
at **http://cws.internet.com**. At least five times per week, a handful of dedicated professionals
maintain a stock of shareware and commercial programs that are provided, and often replaced
daily, by their manufacturers. You can purchase some products directly online. Stroud's also
provides reviews and user comments on all of its files available for download.

Although FTP will always have a place in the actual file transfer transactions that take place
every day on the Internet, continued use of the conventional Telnet methods for FTP downloads and uploads is waning, and HTTP is taking over. The key reason you might still want
to use a dedicated FTP program such as CuteFTP is not because you're looking for a
particular file, but because you trust certain FTP sites such as Finland's long-standing
garbo.uwasa.fi. ●

CHAPTER 23

Other Internet Options

What made the Internet widely popular around the world was the World Wide Web. To most users, the Internet and the Web are virtually the same beast, or at least permanently intertwined. Yet prior to the advent of the Web, the Internet was a burgeoning information center for scientists (especially physicists), programmers, and the more digitally inclined. The first part of this chapter explores two of the mainstay applications of the Internet that are older than the Web: Internet Relay Chat (IRC) and the public discussion (newsgroup) system UseNet.

The last part of the chapter will switch gears and talk about some of the new directions in which Internet technology is headed. ▪

Understanding newsgroups

Learn about newsgroups: what they are, what they contain, and how you can participate in their discussions.

Talking on the Internet

Discover Internet Relay Chat and the wonder of talking live to other people through the Internet.

Keeping up with new developments on the Internet

Discover ways in which you can keep up with the rapidly changing world of the Internet.

Exploring Newsgroups

A *newsgroup* is an electronic address for messages designed and intended to be read by many people. The name *newsgroup* was chosen because at the time of this system's creation, it was intended mainly for university students to post news events related to their field of study. Today's newsgroups are part of an informal system called *UseNet*, which is the term given to the collection of servers that support *Network News Transport Protocol (NNTP)*.

In the UseNet system, Internet service providers (ISPs) agree to carry—or in a sense, to syndicate—the past few days' worth of messages addressed to a set of newsgroups. The content of these newsgroups is provided by NNTP servers.

The UseNet Mechanism

A person reading the content from one of these newsgroups sees messages written by anyone on the Internet, regarding the subject matter for which that newsgroup specializes. For example, the newsgroup **comp.infosystems.www.browsers.ms-windows** features messages written mainly about the operation of Web browsers for the Windows platform. People who discover interesting features about their browsers, or who need help and might be frustrated by the normal manufacturer channels, will post open letters to anyone knowledgeable on this subject who might be willing to help.

A capable ISP can handle the last week's worth of messages from as many as 25,000 UseNet newsgroups at one time; and believe me, there are at least as many others that ISPs choose to leave out. Some of the more common UseNet newsgroups are available through so-called *public news servers*; here, users set their newsreaders to the DNS address of the server. More likely, however, you would access UseNet newsgroups either through a subscription account (for a nominal fee) with a *private news server*, or as part of the regular service you receive from your ISP.

UseNet is one area where your company network's direct connection is of no help to you at all. Unless your network's server has the immense capacity to be able to handle UseNet content, you're better off subscribing to UseNet privately. If you have a persistent connection through a network, contact your closest regional ISP to see if they offer private UseNet access.

Accessing UseNet Newsgroups

After you've established your account with an ISP—public or private—there are two ways you could go about accessing newsgroups. You could use the newsreader software that is shipped as part of your Web browser package (Netscape Communicator and Microsoft Internet Explorer both include UseNet newsreaders). Figure 23.1 shows the newsreader portion of Netscape's Message Center.

FIG. 23.1

Here is a list of UseNet newsgroups from Netscape Communicator's Message Center.

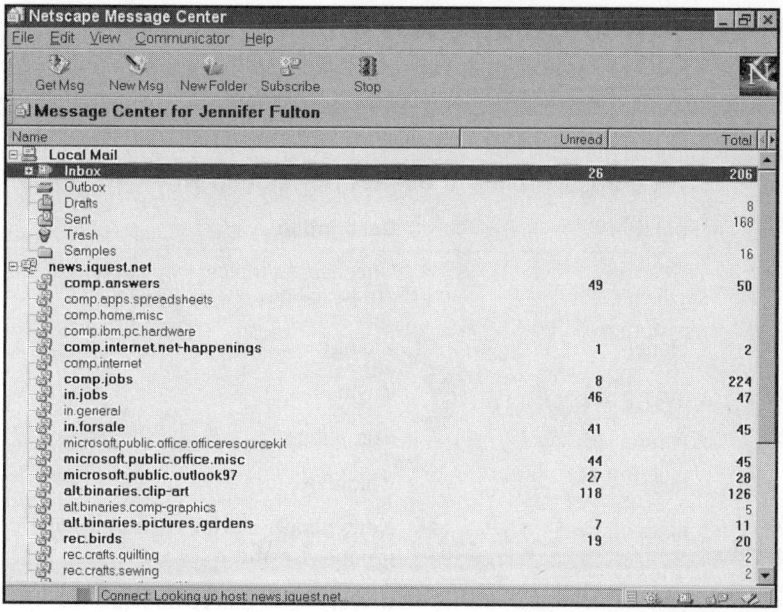

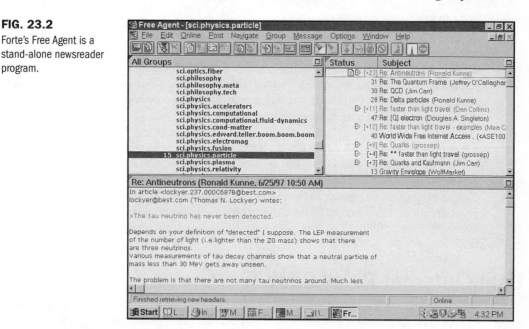

Alternatively, you could use an exclusive newsreader program such as Forte's Agent or Free Agent, which contain features that are tailored more for the not-so-casual user. Figure 23.2 shows a session with Free Agent, the freeware edition of Forte's shareware Agent product.

FIG. 23.2

Forte's Free Agent is a stand-alone newsreader program.

What the Newsgroup Titles Mean

The names of newsgroups are segmented into categories and subcategories, separated by periods. Table 23.1 lists some of the most common UseNet main categories.

Table 23.1   Common UseNet Newsgroup Title Categories

Category	Description
alt	Uncensored topics; may not necessarily be controversial or offensive, though they can be.
bionet	Biology
biz	Business
comp	Computing
misc	Unique topics
news	News about UseNet, such as discussions you might find on groups elsewhere.
rec	Recreation or entertainment
sci	Science (except biology)
soc	Sociology
talk	Politics and public opinion

As Figure 23.2 shows, the average UseNet message works pretty much like an e-mail message, except for the fact that it's not directed to a person but to the newsgroup itself. As with e-mail, many messages include binary attachments, especially graphics; for Netscape and IE (Internet Explorer) users, a message can be formatted with HTML, like a Web page. A UseNet message is designed to provoke comments, to bring people into the discussion and thus form a collective body of users who have at least one common interest.

NOTE Newsgroups such as the **sci** category helped establish the UseNet system, and continue to be revolutionary because they offer any individual the opportunity to converse on an even par with the world's most renowned physicists, and scientists from other fields. As an educational resource, these groups are priceless. Yet because some newsgroups include questionable material (especially of a graphic nature), you'll need to monitor how your children or adolescents use this system. ▪

Using Internet Relay Chat

Today, the Internet's standardized system for live conversation between multiple parties via keyboard is called *Internet Relay Chat (IRC)*. Here, you "talk" to other users by typing what you want to say on your keyboard. Through the IRC system, individuals linked to the Internet are able to initiate informal conference calls with one another, even on a whim. Figure 23.3 shows one of the most popular IRC clients in the shareware channel, *Visual IRC*.

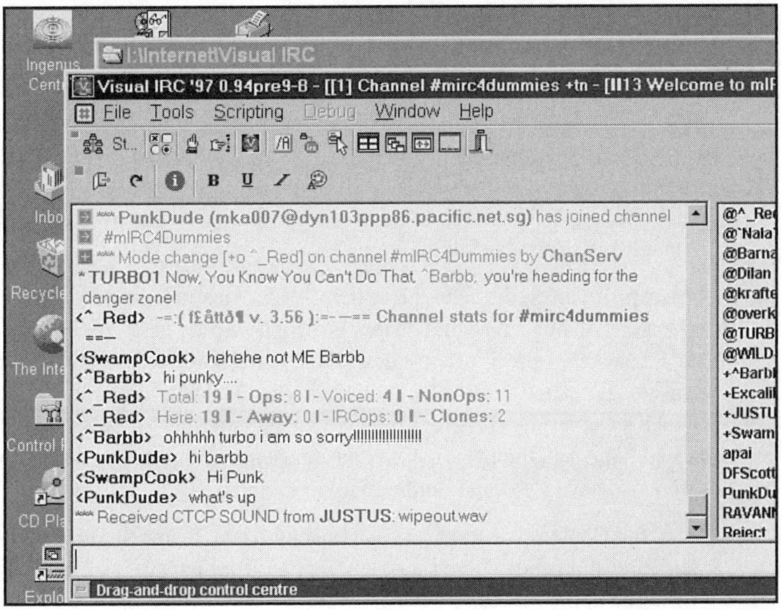

FIG. 23.3
Here, a live conversation via relay chat takes place on Visual IRC.

Part
IV
Ch
23

To participate in IRC chat, you first need the client software. Visual IRC, mIRC, and PIRCH are just a few of the IRC client programs available for downloading from the Internet. These programs should be available on most Internet software archives. When you've downloaded the program, spend some time playing around with it to learn how to use its features.

Accessing Chat Channels

In addition to having IRC "client" software, you also must connect with an IRC server to participate in Internet chat. The *IRC server* is the equivalent of an online service chat forum; it carries information between IRC participants. Most IRC programs provide lists of IRC servers from which you can choose. To log onto the server, select it from the list and connect by using the command provided in the dialog box that contains the list.

With Visual IRC, you're given a list of IRC servers that act as centralized relay points for all the messages that people send one another. You log on to one of these servers (if you find an open slot, that is), then acquire from the server its current list of channels. This list could number from 12 to 5,000 depending on the server. While you're online with the server, your user name is visible to other users; so someone could query you personally, say hi, then if you respond, you've established a private channel just between you and the sender. You can also join an established channel, whose name by protocol begins with a pound sign (#)—for example, **#Colorado**.

After you've joined the persistent channel, Visual IRC pulls up a separate window containing the ongoing transcript of the discussion in progress. You have a text box with a blinking cursor that works somewhat like a command prompt; whatever you type there, after you press Enter, is echoed to the group. You can send commands to the IRC server itself by prefixing your command with a forward slash (/). This way, you can ask the server for a list of who is in this group, or who else is logged on to the server.

CNN and MSNBC run two of the most well-moderated chat services on the Internet, completely outside of IRC. (*Moderated* here means that someone is listening to the conversations and excluding comments that seem out of line.) Yahoo!, the Web directory service run by Ziff Communications, has its own Yahoo! Chat page, too. And one of the originators of computer conferencing, Delphi Internet Services, continues its chat tradition with a Java applet available through **http://www.delphi.com**.

Netscape, to its credit, recognizes that Internet users have good reasons to chat with one another outside of normal chat channels. The Netscape Conference tool, part of its Communicator 4.0 package and shown in Figure 23.4, is designed to work more like a global intercom console. You place a call to someone using his e-mail address as a reference. If that other person's Conference program is active, he'll get a ring—it even sounds like a telephone. If he answers the call, then you have a chat session in progress, and either of you can call others (who also have Netscape Conference) to join in.

Once the Conference session is established, you can use the program's tools to send information other than text. There's also a whiteboard, which acts as a collective Paintbrush screen. Any or all of the conference participants can use the screen to draw diagrams, or to import existing presentation graphics as though it were a projection screen. You can also transfer files over the session to *all* of the participants simultaneously.

FIG. 23.4

Conference is Netscape's more sensible alternative to IRC chat.

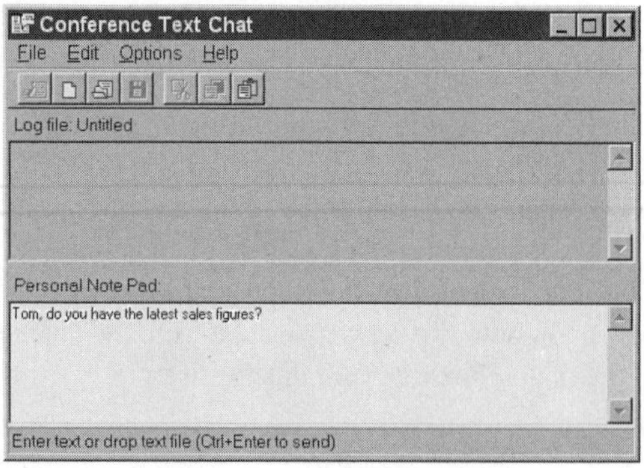

When the Conference session is closed, the "circuit" is terminated. So you don't have to worry about your conversations being listened to (or joined by) other people on the Internet.

Staying Abreast of the Internet's Evolution

Over the next few years, many of the protocols that have supported, and even come to symbolize, the Internet today will be superseded, or perhaps just outmoded. From just examining the suddenness of its popularity, one might get the impression that the Web is here to stay. It is not. This doesn't mean that the Internet is by any means passing; it is simply evolving. The Web as we know it is supported by a set of temporary standards, which will expire in due course. The older protocols—Gopher, Archie, FTP, IRC—are already becoming history.

Part
IV

Ch
23

TIP One good way to stay abreast of changes on the Internet is to stay informed. A good source of information is C|Net, located at **http://www.news.com**.

Netcaster and Push Technologies

The newest, most lucrative, and sometimes most controversial development in transport protocols concerns what is collectively called *push technology*. Here, rather than relying on the Web model where every resource is uploaded to you in response to your direct request, the "push" client subscribes to services that upload resources to you automatically, in the background, while you're doing other things. You can then request these downloaded resources or files at your leisure or convenience.

Figure 23.5 shows Netscape's latest entry in the push technology field, Netcaster.

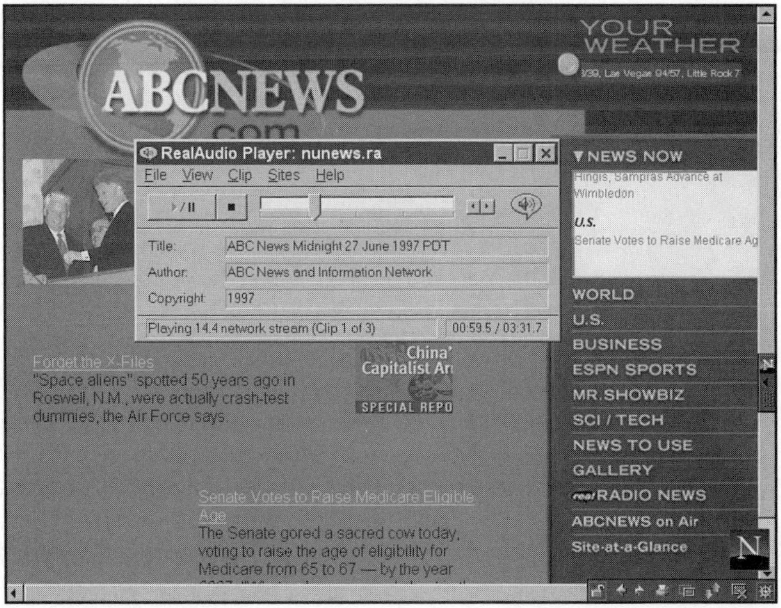

FIG. 23.5

Netscape Netcaster, a push technology client for Communicator 4.0, delivers the latest news and information to your system regularly and automatically.

Resources you receive from Netcaster are in HTML format, very much like what you would receive in Navigator. The exceptions are as follows:

▪ Netcaster resources are provided to you in the form of *channels*, to which you tune in like operating a remote control. Netcaster provides this remote control in a special floating window on the right of the screen, as shown in Figure 23.6.

FIG. 23.6
The "Channel Finder" control window for Netcaster floats on the right side of the window.

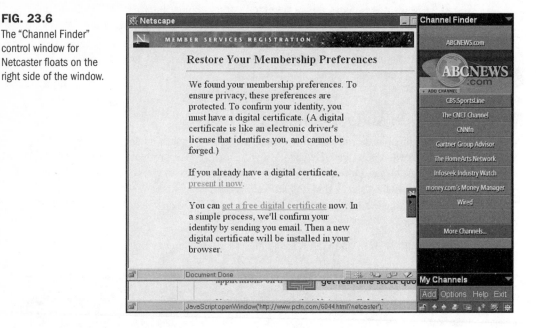

▪ Much of the content of Netcaster channels tends to float around in its own panels, as though it was being blown about by an unseen wind. The result looks a bit more like fancy television graphics than Web pages.

▪ Most channels formatted specifically for Netcaster expect to be displayed on top of your entire Windows desktop. As Figure 23.5 shows, channel contents can be shown in a "wall-to-wall" format, behind all of your other open windows but on top of the Windows desktop, in an area that Netcaster calls the *webtop*.

Another push technology provider, PointCast, has provided subscription services to its exclusive clients since 1996, and has proven at least that the idea of push can be profitable. Microsoft is currently formalizing its own competitive Channel Definition Format (CDF), and will be introducing it to the public with its formal release of Internet Explorer 4.0.

The Potential of the Internet as a Software Server

Built into Microsoft's CDF proposal is a system that will allow channel-based Internet services to provide software applications to subscribers. Imagine, if you will, pulling up a console of Internet controls, logging on, and dialing up Microsoft Office.

Already available as an experimental service through Netcaster, Corel has made available an all-Java edition of its Office suite—which includes WordPerfect—for Internet use. With this type of service, you don't download the software, install it, and use it until it expires or the next version comes along. Instead, you're connected to the software, it's downloaded to you, and once you disconnect, the software doesn't leave any remnants of itself on your system. If you need the software again, you connect to it again.

Now, modem technology at present is quite prohibitive to the concept of downloading entire applications on demand. But higher-speed connections through other media are becoming more commonplace. With such connections playing a more definitive role in Internet development, software manufacturers such as Corel and Microsoft are actively exploring the possibility of providing their products entirely online.

Microsoft's current experiment in Internet-based software component distribution is *ActiveX*, a standard that is based in the very roots of Windows. ActiveX Controls have been mentioned in some of the previous chapters. In Web pages, they act as little embedded programs that play a role in these pages' layout and use. Unlike Java applets, ActiveX Controls install themselves on your system permanently once you've downloaded them. This way, should another Web page use the same control, or should one page use the same control several places, your Web browser doesn't need to download the code for that control several times, wasting valuable bandwidth.

Microsoft has been working to develop ActiveX into a potential main system of software distribution for the corporation, should it decide to go that route. A future revision of the Windows operating system could expect all of its application software to be provided in component form. In such a system, each of those components could be amendable or replaceable through the Internet, perhaps as a background process that you don't even see. By simply connecting frequently to Microsoft's server, you could always be running the latest revision to your application software, even if those versions are updated *weekly*.

So as transmission speeds become higher, Internet services may become primary channels for software distribution. This evolution of the Internet would completely transform the software industry, weaning it from its dependence on factories and physical media such as CD-ROM, and dramatically reducing its costs. These reductions could make it more attractive and more feasible for new, smaller software companies to enter the market, providing their own application components in whole or in part. ●

Part
IV
Ch
23

Problem Solving

24 Getting Help with Software 253

25 Getting Help with Hardware 263

26 Upgrading Your Software 273

27 Upgrading Your Hardware 283

Getting Help with Software

If you're lucky, you'll be able to use your software programs right out of the box, with only a short learning curve to slow you down at the start. If you're not lucky, however, you could find yourself running into a variety of problems ranging from simply wondering if there's an easier way to get a job done, to losing valuable data because of a computer virus. Where do you go for information on how to get the most out of your software applications?

Windows 95—and most applications designed to run with Windows 95—comes with a variety of resources you can use to keep software problems to a minimum. Built-in help programs as well as online and telephone customer support make it a snap to get answers to your software questions. You can also learn how to solve problems yourself, and to take precautions to avoid problems before they happen. ■

Use the Windows 95 Help system

Learn how to navigate the Help program to get help while you work.

Troubleshoot problems

There are steps you can take to diagnose and resolve problems with Windows 95.

Protect your system from computer viruses

Viruses can damage or delete valuable data. Learn how to protect your system from these viral predators.

Get help over the phone

You can use your modem to get help on the Internet, or you can call for customer support.

Using the Help System

The Windows 95 Help system is a software program that includes information on just about every topic that has anything to do with Windows 95 and your computer. The Help system is installed automatically when you set up Windows 95.

The Windows 95 Help system provides general information about topics as well as step-by-step instructions for how to perform tasks. When you are working at your computer and you have a question about a particular feature, or even about what to do next, click the Start button and select Help from the menu. The Help system starts in the Help Topics window (see Figure 24.1).

The Help Topics window contains three tabs that offer options for finding the specific help information you need.

FIG. 24.1

You can use the three tabs in the Help Topics window to locate answers to your questions about using Windows 95.

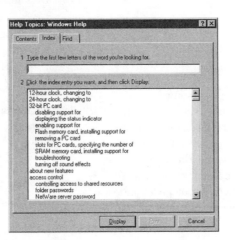

To locate help information using the Contents tab, follow these steps:

1. Click the Contents tab.
2. Double-click a main topic to display a list of subtopics.
3. Double-click the subtopic to display the list of actual help information. Double-click the help information listing of interest to you.

Each of the three Contents tab items is marked by an identifying icon: closed-book icons for main topics, open-book icons for subtopics, and document page icons for help information.

To locate help information using the Index tab, follow these steps:

1. Click the Index tab.
2. Start typing the topic for which you need help into the first text box at the top of the window.
3. When the topic you want is selected in the list, click Display.

To locate help information using the Find tab, follow these steps:

1. Click the Find tab.
2. Type the word or phrase you want to locate in the top text box.
3. Select a word to narrow the search in the second text box.
4. Select the topic in the third text box and click Display.

N O T E The first time you use the Find tab, you have to create a word list, which takes a few minutes. Click the Find tab in the Help Topics window, then click the Next button, then click the Finish button. ▪

Whichever method you use to locate the help topic, the help information is displayed in a Help window (see Figure 24.2).

In the Help window, you can:

▪ Click Options, select Print Topics, then click OK to print the current Help window.

▪ Click Help Topics to get back to the Help Topics window.

▪ Click Back to go back to the previous Help window.

▪ Click the Close button at the right end of the Help window title bar to close the Help system.

FIG. 24.2
Help information is displayed in a Help window like this one.

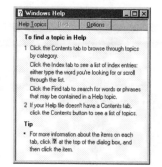

T I P Microsoft software applications that run with Windows 95 use similar help systems. This means you can use these same methods to get help with your application programs, not just with Windows 95.

Click hyperlinked buttons or text in a Help Topics window to jump to associated information. Hyperlinked text is shown in green text with a dotted underline. Hyperlinked buttons occur in the help text; your pointer changes to a pointing hand when it rests on a hyperlinked button.

Part
VI

Ch
24

TIP   To get help in a dialog box, click the Help icon (?) in the upper-right corner to change the mouse pointer into a Help pointer. With the Help pointer, click the item for which you need help. Windows 95 displays pop-up help describing the item. Click anywhere on the desktop to change back to the regular mouse pointer.

Using Software Wizards

Windows 95 introduced a feature called *wizards* designed to make it easy for you to accomplish complex tasks with your software applications. Wizards are little dialog boxes that pop up here and there to help you get through what might otherwise be a confusing situation.

In Windows 95, wizards simplify tasks like setting up shortcuts or installing new hardware. The wizards prompt you to answer questions, then, based on your responses, they take care of all the work. Best of all, other Microsoft applications use wizards, too. For example, if you use Microsoft Access, you can set up an entire database using a wizard!

When you see a wizard (such as Microsoft Word's Letter Wizard shown in Figure 24.3), follow the instructions and click the <u>N</u>ext button to switch pages. Click the <u>F</u>inish button when you reach the last page of the wizard, then sit back while the wizard completes the task.

See Chapter 6, "Working with Applications," for more information about using software programs.

FIG. 24.3

You can let your Microsoft software do the work for you by using a wizard. Here, Microsoft Word's Letter Wizard takes the guesswork out of setting up a letter.

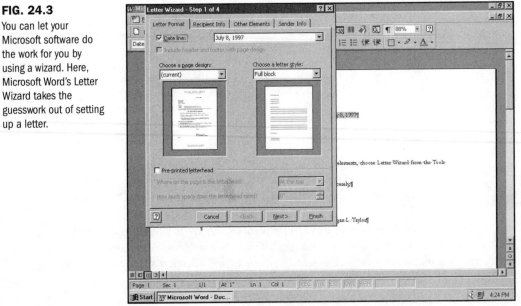

Troubleshooting Windows 95

Most of the time, Windows 95 will work just fine. However, you may run into problems from time to time, particularly when you install new hardware or software. Look for these signs that all is not well:

- Windows 95 slows down significantly
- Windows 95 is frozen
- Peripheral devices are not working
- Error messages are appearing on-screen
- Computer spontaneously reboots

Here are a few steps you can take on your own to try and set the problem right:

1. Close all open applications and open just the ones you need.
2. Make sure that you don't have more than one copy of the same application running at the same time. If you do, close one.
3. Shut down Windows 95.
4. Check all cables and wires to make sure the connections between the computer and peripherals are secure.
5. Restart Windows 95.

You can also use the Help system to troubleshoot common problems that arise while you are using Windows 95. For example, see the Print Troubleshooter window in Figure 24.4.

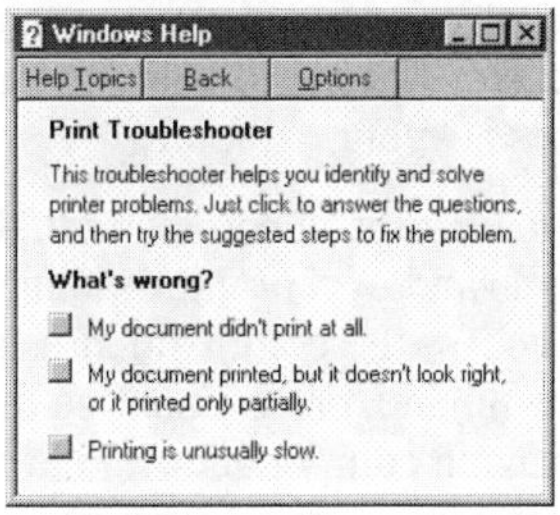

FIG. 24.4
The Print Troubleshooter helps you identify and resolve common printing problems associated with Windows 95.

To use a Help troubleshooter, follow these steps:

1. Click the Start button and select Help to start the Help system.
2. Click the Contents tab.
3. Double-click Troubleshooting.
4. Select the topic that describes the problem you're having, then click Open.
5. Follow the step-by-step instructions in the Help window to identify and resolve the problem.

Part
VI

Ch
24

If you still have problems starting your computer with Windows 95, follow these steps to start your computer in troubleshooting mode:

1. Start or restart your computer.

2. When you see the message Starting Windows 95... on your monitor screen, press the F8 key. A menu of options for starting the computer is displayed.

3. Type the number of the option you want. Table 24.1 describes the options.

Table 24.1   Troubleshooting Mode Menu Options

Menu Option	Description
Normal	Starts Windows normally.
Logged (\BOOTLOG.TXT)	Starts Windows normally, but creates a text file called Bootlog.txt located in your root directory. Use this option so you can consult the file for information about which files loaded correctly.
Safe mode	Starts Windows with a basic configuration instead of your usual configuration. Some of the features you usually use may not work correctly. Use this option to start Windows so you can make changes to your system configuration and restart your computer.
Safe mode with network support	Starts Windows with a basic configuration, but includes network capabilities. Use this option to start Windows if you are on a network. You can make changes to your system configuration and restart your computer.
Step-by-step confirmation	Displays each command in the startup process, followed by a prompt waiting for your response. To process the command, press Enter; to bypass the command, press Esc. Use this option to load only certain components, and to bypass the components you believe may be causing the problems.
Command prompt only	Starts your computer normally but does not start Windows. Use this option if you are comfortable using the DOS command prompt interface.
Safe mode command prompt only	Starts your computer with a basic configuration instead of your usual configuration; it does not start Windows.
Previous version of MS-DOS	Starts your computer using the version of MS-DOS that was in effect before you set up Windows 95.

If you are still having problems, contact your software dealer or the manufacturer. See the sections on getting online and telephone support at the end of this chapter.

Avoiding Viruses

Viruses are software programs that are designed to harm your computer. Some are more annoying than harmful, but others can destroy the contents of your computer system and render it useless. Viruses are most often transmitted via software files downloaded from the Internet, or copied from unauthorized sources. You can protect yourself from viruses by being careful about where you get the programs and files you put on your machine and by running anti-virus software regularly.

If you have a completely closed system—you never put new software on, you never copy files from a floppy, you never communicate with other devices, you're not hooked up to a network, and you never go online—then you don't need a virus checker. Because this is rarely the situation, you should add a virus checker to your Windows 95 Startup folder. This will check your system for viruses each time your system is booted. In addition, if you download files from the Internet or other online services, make sure you download them to a separate directory and scan all files before using them on your system.

Part
VI

Ch
24

You can protect your machine from viruses by performing each of the following tasks:

- Install an anti-virus software (such as Norton Anti-Virus) according to the directions included with the software. Run the program regularly, and update the software periodically according to instructions included with the software.

- Only accept or purchase software from known vendors.

- If you download files from the Internet, create a special download folder and have the antivirus software scan the folder each time you download any new files.

- Before you use a program or file from a floppy disk, have the anti-virus software scan the disk.

TIP AOL and other common providers offer a "flashmail" option that automatically dumps e-mail to the user's hard drive, then downloads and unzips anything attached to the e-mail. It's a good idea to look at the list of e-mail waiting in the mailbox before just starting flashmail, so files attached to e-mail from unknown sources don't get downloaded with flashmail.

Getting Online Support

If you are connected to an online service or to the Internet, you can get information about your software programs using your modem and a telephone line.

Online services such as CompuServe and America Online offer sites and forums for major software manufacturers like Microsoft. In addition, most software manufacturers and dealers maintain their own Web sites to provide online information about their products. For example, you'll find Microsoft on the World Wide Web at **http://www.microsoft.com/** (see Figure 24.5).

There are also central clearinghouse types of sites that offer access to information for just about every product. For example, you can access information from books published by Que at the Macmillan Information SuperLibrary Web site at **http://www.mcp.com**.

FIG. 24.5

On the Internet, you can get helpful information about software programs at sites such as this one.

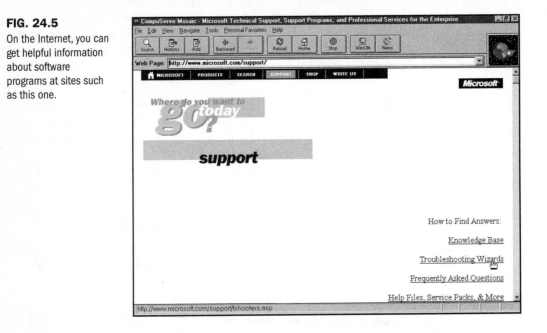

> **TIP** Look in the manual that came with the software program to find the Web address for software support. Also, many sites have an FAQ (Frequently Asked Questions) link that's worth browsing for information.

At most of these sites, you'll find:

- Downloadable fixes for common problems
- Information about new releases
- Tips and tricks for getting the most out of the software
- Access to trained technicians with whom you can discuss your specific problem

For more information about using an online service or the Internet, see Part V, "Connecting to the Internet."

Getting Help by Phone

You can also get help the old-fashioned way—by phone. When you need to talk to someone about how to solve a problem, pick up the phone and call the customer support line. You'll find the support phone numbers and the hours support is available in the manual that came with the program. For example, if you live in the United States and need help with Microsoft Windows 95, call (206) 635-7000, between 6 AM and 6 PM Pacific time.

TIP If you can't find the phone number for customer support in the software document, look for a readme.txt file in the folder where the software program is stored on your computer. You can open the file using Windows Notepad.

Software manufacturers offer different types of customer telephone support. Here are a few of the options you might come across:

- *Free support.* The manufacturer provides a toll-free number you can call for assistance with anything from installing the software, to tips on how to make it work better.

- *Free support, but you pay for the call.* The manufacturer provides free assistance, but no toll-free number. Because you tend to spend quite a bit of time navigating through automated telephone systems, then waiting on hold for a technician, the phone charges can add up. Some companies will call you back if they think the wait will be too long.

- *Support plans.* You can usually purchase "priority" type support plans. For a set fee, you get access to a telephone number and technicians who are supposedly easier to reach and more knowledgeable than those who staff the regular support lines.

To make sure you get the best help available, sit down at your computer before you call, and have the following information on hand:

- Exactly what happened to cause the problem, including the steps leading up to the problem, and what you did after the problem occurred.

- The exact wording of any messages that appear on the screen when the problem occurs.

- The name and version number of the software you are using.

- The documentation that came with the software.

- A list of the components of your computer system, including information like the type of processor, how much memory is installed, and other software programs that are installed.

Part
VI

Ch
24

CHAPTER 25

Getting Help with Hardware

Consider the components found in a PC, among them the power supply and fan, motherboard, memory, hard drives and floppy drives, video card, modem, sound card, CD-ROM, parallel and serial ports, and drive controller. Then there are the peripherals such as the keyboard, mouse, monitor, printer, scanner, and joystick, to name a few. With so many components, there are ample opportunities for problems to occur. ■

Learn the basics of trouble-shooting

Work through the simple procedures that solve the majority of hardware problems.

Perform preventive maintenance

Service your computer to keep it running reliably.

Make effective use of manufacturers' tech support

Learn about your system manufacturers' technical support programs and how they can help you.

Take advantage of the Internet

Find sites on the Internet that will help you solve hardware problems.

Simple Solutions First

At one time or another, most of us have been stumped by an apparently catastrophic computer glitch, only to have another user end the crisis with a few clicks of the keys or the throw of a switch. Even experienced users sometimes overlook the simple solutions and immediately begin taking more drastic measures. Any user—novice or expert—is better off starting with basic diagnostic procedures that take only a minute or two before going on to more exotic efforts. Remember two simple solutions before you begin dissecting your computer:

- Many hardware problems are the result of incorrect setup or settings.
- Sometimes a single-click or a reboot will solve a seemingly catastrophic problem.

The following sections discuss each of these approaches in more detail.

> **CAUTION**
>
> Do not open up your computer's power supply or monitor. Both can store enough energy to hurt or even kill you. Besides, there's little the average user can do to repair either of these components. Power supplies are inexpensive and normally are replaced when they fail. If you have a problem with your monitor, and reading the manual doesn't suggest a solution and the cables are firmly seated, take it to an authorized repair facility.

Getting the Settings Right

The best way to prevent annoying hardware problems from developing is to be sure the hardware is set up properly when you install it. While serious hardware problems—those where the hardware is damaged and in need of repair or replacement—can crop up occasionally, most hardware problems are related to improper settings that don't allow components to work together smoothly. These problems often occur when you make changes to the system's hardware. If you incorrectly install a new component or change a hardware setting, your well-behaved computer can become a monster.

A couple of quick tips for avoiding newly installed hardware problems:

- Read up on the system or component before you buy it. In particular, read the product reviews in computer magazines. These are good places to find out about a system's quirks or nonstandard design that can lead to hardware conflicts down the road. You can also find these product reviews on the Internet at such sites as ZDNet (**http://www.zdnet.com**), CINet (**http://www.cnet.com**), and TechWeb (**http://www.techweb.com**).

- If you are installing a new component, read the manual first. Reading manuals on motherboards, add-in boards, or CD-ROMs may be like reading a foreign language, but they're better than hours of guessing. The more you familiarize yourself with the terminology in these manuals, the easier it is to diagnose and solve problems as they arise.

Such components as motherboards, hard drives, and CD-ROMs use jumpers (see Figure 25.1) and DIP switches (see Figure 25.2) that must be set correctly to work with the other equipment in your system. On a new computer the manufacturer will set the jumpers, although sometimes an incorrect setting may be overlooked, causing glitches. Or, in adding a new device to your system—for example, if you add a second hard drive to your computer—you may set some jumpers incorrectly, and the machine can't detect the drive.

FIG. 25.1
Closed and open jumpers.

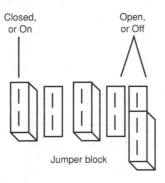

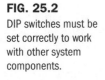
FIG. 25.2
DIP switches must be set correctly to work with other system components.

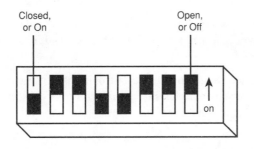

How do you know which jumpers or DIP switch settings to use? Start with the manuals for your motherboard and the component. These will show the proper settings for most circumstances.

Avoiding Problems with Device Drivers

Device drivers are another frequent source of hardware foul-ups. A device driver is a software program that acts as an interface between software and hardware (or between two software programs). Video display drivers and printer drivers are among those that most commonly cause frustration for new users. New users often aren't aware that drivers are necessary for these and other components to work, so they think they have a catastrophe on their hands when the video goes haywire, or when the printer doesn't work correctly.

All the drivers you'll ever need aren't automatically installed when you set up Windows 95. You may have to manually install driver upgrades or reinstall drivers if the driver files have been corrupted. You can change device drivers by way of the Add New Hardware Wizard or the Device Manager.

Most devices requiring drivers come with a disk that has the necessary drivers on it. However, if you need a driver, you can quickly find it on the Internet. Go to the Windows Sources page at **http://finders.zdnet.com/** and choose DriverFinder to search for the driver for the component you're using. Or, go to the device manufacturer's Web site.

Dealing with Interrupt Conflicts (IRQ)

Interrupt (IRQ) conflicts are another hardware problem that has wasted millions of man hours of effort. When a component needs a chunk of time from the computer's processor, it sends out its request on an interrupt line. Each device has its own interrupt, but there are a limited number of IRQs available on a PC. If two devices are competing for the same interrupt, conflicts can develop. As you cram your system with more devices, juggling hardware interrupts (and input/output addresses and DMA channels) becomes more difficult.

The problem is particularly acute when you have older add-in boards in the mix, because Plug and Play may not automatically sense these and reconfigure your machine. Instead, you have to make changes manually.

While IRQ conflicts are annoying rather than catastrophic, they cause more than their share of problems for both users and manufacturers. For manufacturers, Plug and Play is a way to reduce the amount of tech support spent helping users overcome IRQ conflicts.

ON THE WEB

For more information on IRQ conflicts, visit the NetPro Northwest Web page at:

http://www.geocities.com/SiliconValley/7047/irqfaq1.html

N O T E   You can disable a Plug and Play board and leave it in the computer. However, you may have to physically remove non-Plug and Play boards in order to free up such system resources as IRQs and ports. ▪

Wait, Escape, Reboot, and Other Simple Fixes

When a problem develops that your system doesn't quickly fix by itself, take a minute to think before you start hitting keys. If the system isn't smoking or making grinding noises, there's no reason to rush to shut down the system.

The solution might be to wait 10 or 20 seconds. Sometimes the computer's processor works on a task without letting you know it's working (it's working when it shows Windows 95's hour-glass icon). Then, when it's done, it allows you to regain control of the system.

In other circumstances, a single keystroke might be all that's needed to free up the logjam. For example, if you're on the Internet using the World Wide Web, the computer may spend a long time trying to access a busy site; hitting the Esc key will stop the attempt to access the file.

Don't rush. In Windows 95 you can use the Ctrl+Alt+Delete keystroke combination to close an application that seems to be giving you trouble. Then, if the system still shows signs of instability, try to exit Windows 95 normally. Don't push the computer's reset button until you're sure you've exhausted the possibilities for a graceful exit from Windows 95. If you exit Windows 95 with files still open, rebooting the system can result in corrupted files or lost data. Sometimes you don't have any choice, but don't hurry to reboot. If you do have to reboot with files open, start Windows 95 in Safe Mode (as explained in Chapter 24, "Getting Help with Software") after the reboot. This second startup may return the system to normal functioning.

Once you've exited Windows, reboot the system to see if a power fluctuation caused a temporary glitch.

Part
VI

Ch
25

Diagnosing Hardware Problems

When a PC starts up, it does a Power On Self Test (POST). A single short beep from the computer indicates all is well. Other beep patterns indicate there is a problem with the system. The beeps give you clues to the problem. For example, a repeating short beep indicates your power supply is going bad. One long and two short beeps tells you there's a video board/cable problem. (I have two computers hooked to one monitor via a switchbox, and I hear this pattern of beeps when I try to start one computer while I have the switchbox set to the other computer.)

TIP Document your troubleshooting efforts. Keep a notebook and pen on hand for recording events about your computer such as the settings you use when installing a new component, what software was running, what process you were trying to do when a problem occurred or an error message came up, and what type of problems arise when you try to do something on the computer. These notes can be helpful if you talk with a support technician.

Your motherboard manual may contain descriptions of its POST beep codes. If not, the UCS Knowledge Base at **http://sckb.ucssc.indiana.edu/kb/data/aaln.html** has information on the beep codes.

If restarting the computer doesn't solve the problem, here are some simple diagnostic procedures to try before you move to more drastic measures:

- *Verify the power strip is turned on.* You won't be the first person to think you've had a catastrophic hardware failure when in fact you've turned off your power strip for some reason.
- *Check the cables.* Be sure the power cables to the computer, monitor, printer, and other devices are plugged in properly. Then secure the cable connectors on all other cables.
- *Check the software.* Have you upgraded any software recently? Are you running a version of software that's not compatible with your computer? Have you provided the correct hardware information to the software? Does the software have any bugs? (You'll find discussions of buggy programs on the Internet.) Keep in mind that a computer's hardware and software work together, so when problems arise, it can be difficult to determine whether it is the hardware or the software causing the problem.
- *Have you changed anything?* Added components? If so, you may have created an IRQ conflict.
- *Run your diagnostic software.* Windows 95 Help has a hardware conflict troubleshooter. Go to the Help index and look through the list of topics for "hardware troubleshooter." You can read the "Overview of resolving conflicts" or start the troubleshooter. By choosing from the options the troubleshooter supplies, you can isolate and fix many problems. For example, you can choose "Troubleshooting Printing Problems," then choose the particular situation you're encountering. The wizard keeps supplying short lists of alternatives from which you can choose, until it can offer a solution.
- *Read the documentation.* Manuals for the motherboard, sound card, video card, CD-ROM, hard drive, and other components will usually accompany new computers. This documentation has the information you need to solve many problems.

Using Device Manager to Identify and Fix Problems

Windows 95's Device Manager (see Figure 25.3) lets you view information about your computer's hardware. It's a handy tool because it lets you see all the devices on your system. Carefully examining the Device Manager information can help you identify and undo conflicts. However, changing settings willy-nilly in Device Manager is a great way to get in over your head. This is where your notebook comes in handy; record the settings before you begin making changes.

To start the Device Manager, follow these steps:

1. Click the Start button, select Settings, Control Panel, and then click the System icon. This will bring up the System Properties dialog box.
2. Click the Device Manager tab on the System Properties dialog box.

FIG. 25.3

Windows 95 Device Manager lists every device on your system.

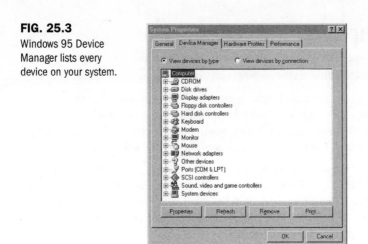

3. Click the plus sign (+) next to a device to display the actual devices in the system. Highlight a device and click the Properties button; this will bring up a dialog box with up to three tabs: General, Driver, and Resources. Each tab gives you more information about the device, and in some cases allows you to change the settings for the device.

Self-Service that Prolongs the Life of Your Hardware

There are a few things you can do to keep your computer equipment running reliably:

- With the computer turned off and unplugged, dust the back of the machine. Inside the computer, dust can build up on the add-in cards and hold in the heat, so it helps to periodically dust the innards of the machine. Carefully wipe the dust from the inner chassis surfaces, but not from the add-in cards. Use a can of compressed air (available at computer stores and camera stores) to dislodge the dust from the add-in cards, but you might want to have a vacuum cleaner handy to keep it from settling elsewhere in the machine. Be gentle; don't use the compressed air or the vacuum too close to the components.

- Keep liquids away from the computer so that nothing spills or leaks on it. The keyboard is the most common victim of spills.

- Be sure there's a fan on the system's processor. A fan keeps the processor cool, which helps prolong its life. And whenever you have the cover off the machine, check the fan to see that it is seated properly on the processor.

- Keep magnets away from the system; they can destroy data on floppy disks and hard drives.

Using Technical Support

When the manuals don't seem to have the information you need, it's time to turn to the manufacturer's tech support system.

Telephone tech support has been the main way to get quick solutions to hardware problems (and *quick* is a relative term; some diagnoses may take several calls over a period of days or weeks, although most solve the user's problem on the spot). Some people head for the phone whenever they have a question, while others don't call until they've run out of other options.

If phone support is important to you, you might want to find out which manufacturers offer quick, effective phone support. Read the computer magazines; for example, *PC World* magazine regularly reports on the quality of the tech support delivered by the major computer manufacturers. Large computer manufacturers such as Dell, Gateway, and Compaq employ hundreds of technical support people—but often that's not enough.

While phone support can be the quickest way to solve hardware problems, there can be drawbacks. You may have a long wait on the line for a technician, which can run up some hefty long-distance telephone charges.

TIP Even if a company has an adequate staff of support technicians, they're not all equally competent. A technician might have you remove components and send them back for replacements; then the replacements don't appear to work because the problem lies elsewhere in the computer. It's important to get a technician who knows what he's talking about. If you sense that the tech is not knowledgeable enough about the problem, ask to be switched to another technician or to a supervisor.

Manufacturers have various schemes for charging for support, but most computer owners feel their purchase entitles them to free phone support for some period of time. Some companies do charge if they provide a solution to your problem, and the problem isn't related to their hardware. For example, if you think you have a hardware failure, but it turns out to be incorrect settings in the operating system software, you may find a charge on your credit card for the tech support.

Many companies offer tech support by fax, where they fax answers to your specific questions. It may take several days to get an answer this way, but if you've given a good description of your problem, you may get the answer you need. It can involve a lot less hassle and expense than sitting on the line waiting for a technician.

Using the Internet as a Troubleshooting Tool

An increasing number of companies have turned to the Internet, and especially to the World Wide Web, to make vast amounts of information available to users so they can analyze their hardware problems at their own convenience.

There are hundreds of sites with hardware information on the Internet. One of the most comprehensive is ZDNet's HealthyPC.com Support Finder at **http://www3.zdnet.com/hpc/filters/suppfind.html**. There you can find the online tech support e-mail addresses, Web sites, and telephone and fax numbers for hundreds of companies. Many vendors have up-to-date FAQs (lists of frequently asked questions), tutorials, and product information on their Web sites.

Another huge database of information isthe Microsoft Technical Support Knowledge Base at **http://www.microsoft.com/kb/default.asp**. Using the Building a Query tool on the page, you can choose the Windows 95 option and search on the topic of your choice. The Knowledge Base has hundreds of megabytes of information dealing with problems encountered between Windows 95 and hundreds of hardware products. You may have to work your way through a number of unrelated topics, but you will often find the specific information you need to solve the problem.

If you've exhausted the resources the manufacturers provide on the Internet, you may want to try private sites that focus on hardware topics. For example, the Cyrix 6x86 FAQ page (**http://www.alternativecpu.com**) covers issues related to the Cyrix 6x86 processor. And the Modem Information page (**http://foothill.net/modems.html**) has all kinds of links to modem information. You can find similar sites by using a search engine like HotBot (**http://www.hotbot.com**), AltaVista (**http://www.altavista.digital.com/**), or InfoSeek Ultra (**http://ultra.infoseek.com/**) and searching for the manufacturer's name or product name.

The newsgroups that proliferate on the Net are another place to look for help. You're likely to find a newsgroup that focuses on the manufacturer or type of hardware with which you're having trouble. The group's FAQs may hold the solution to your troubles; if not, someone may answer your e-mail questions. If you haven't used newsgroups before, the easiest way to reach them is to use your Web browser (choose Window, Netscape News in Netscape Navigator or Go, Read News in Microsoft Internet Explorer). See also Chapter 10, "Working with Networks." ●

Part

VI

Ch

25

Upgrading Your Software

There are many reasons for upgrading your software. You may need to add different programs designed for different purposes than any of the software already installed on your computer. Or, you may prefer a program from another software developer to one of those programs you have. This might be because you like some particular features in another program or you need to use a specific program for compatibility with colleagues or with what you use at work.

One of the most common reasons for installing new software is to upgrade to a newer version of a program you are already using. Software developers are constantly improving their products, adding new features and capabilities and striving to make existing features easier to use. You'll need to upgrade to the new version of the program in order to take advantage of the new features.

Adding new software to your PC

Learn how to install new software on your computer.

Upgrading to new software versions

Find out why you might want to replace some of your software with newer versions of the same program.

Installing over older software versions

Check out your options for software upgrades.

Removing old software

Learn how to get rid of old, unneeded software programs.

Adding New Software to Your PC

You'll probably choose new software based largely on recommendations from friends and coworkers. However, you should also do some of your own research to ensure that your computer has enough RAM, hard disk space, and other facilities required to run the program.

Don't overlook the distinctions between the different operating systems for which the software is designed. Windows 95 can run almost any Windows program, but you'll get the best results from programs designed specifically for the Windows 95 environment. Programs designed for older versions of Windows will usually have a notation in the program's system requirements that they require Windows 3.x or above; the program may also be labeled *Windows 95 compatible*. These programs will work in Windows 95 but can't take full advantage of the Windows 95 operating system. For that, you'll need a program labeled *designed for Windows 95*; such programs are often referred to as *native 32-bit programs*. Make sure the program you're considering doesn't require Windows NT, the souped-up version of Windows for high-security networking.

After you select and purchase your new software, you can break open the shrink wrap package and get ready to install it on your computer.

Before You Install Software

Before you actually start installing your new software, there are a few things you should do:

- First, back up your system. Make backup copies of all your critical files, just in case something happens during the installation that corrupts some of your current programs. Such problems are relatively rare, but they do happen. A good backup enables you to recover from a disaster with a minimum of trouble. (See Chapter 9, "Making Backup Copies of Your Files," for instructions.)

- Exit any programs that are running before starting to install your new software. This includes things like e-mail and fax programs that might start automatically when you start Windows and run in the background all the time. Exiting all other programs is necessary because the installation program may need to update a file or Windows component that is shared by several Windows programs. But it won't be able to update the file if another program is using it.

- Carefully read and follow the installation instructions packaged with your new software. Reading the instructions can sometimes enable you to avoid or prevent trouble with the installation, and avoiding mistakes is always easier than fixing them later.

TIP   To start (or restart) Windows 95 without automatically running the programs in the Startup folder, press and hold down the Shift key as Windows 95 starts. This is a good way to start clean with no programs running in preparation for installing a new program.

Installing Software from the Control Panel

Windows 95 includes a built-in feature to assist you in installing software. It's always available with just a few mouse clicks and it works with almost any software installation. You'll find the Add/Remove Programs applet in the Control Panel window. To use it, follow these steps:

1. Click the Start button on the taskbar to display the Start menu.

2. Select Settings to display the Settings submenu and then click Control Panel. This will open the Control Panel window.

3. In the Control Panel window, double-click the Add/Remove Programs icon to open the Add/Remove Programs Properties dialog box with the Install/Uninstall tab selected, as shown in Figure 26.1.

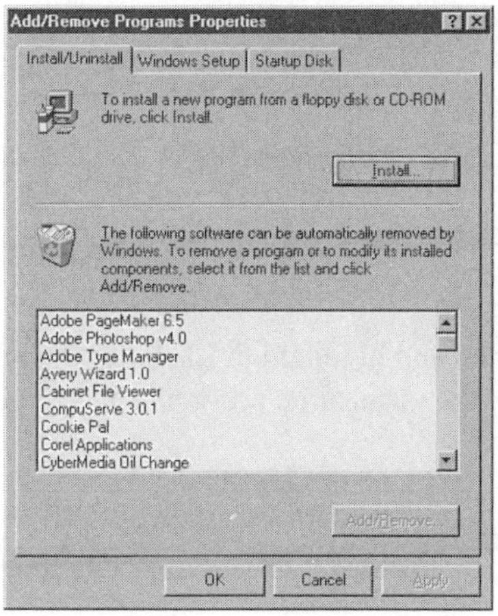

FIG. 26.1

The Add/Remove Programs Properties dialog box makes a convenient starting point for software installations.

4. In the Add/Remove Programs Properties dialog box, click the Install button. Windows 95 will launch the Program Installation Wizard as shown in Figure 26.2.

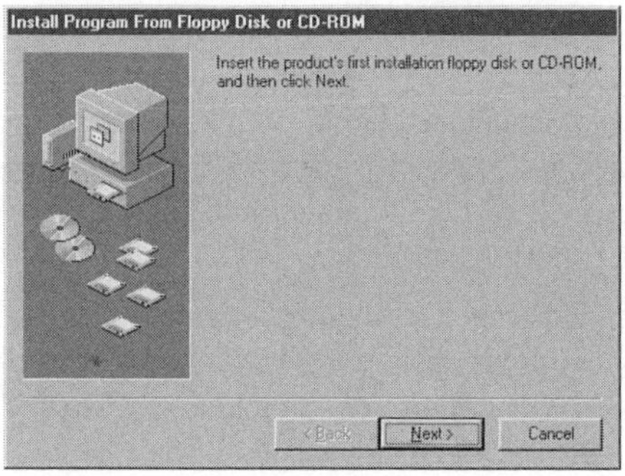

FIG. 26.2

The Program Installation Wizard gets things started.

Part
VI

Ch
26

5. Insert the first installation floppy disk or CD into the appropriate drive.

6. Click the Next button. When you do, the wizard searches for an Install or Setup program on the floppy disk or CD. If the wizard finds the installation program for your new software, it displays the file name in the Run Installation Program dialog box as shown in Figure 26.3.

FIG. 26.3

The wizard can usually find the installation program for your new software.

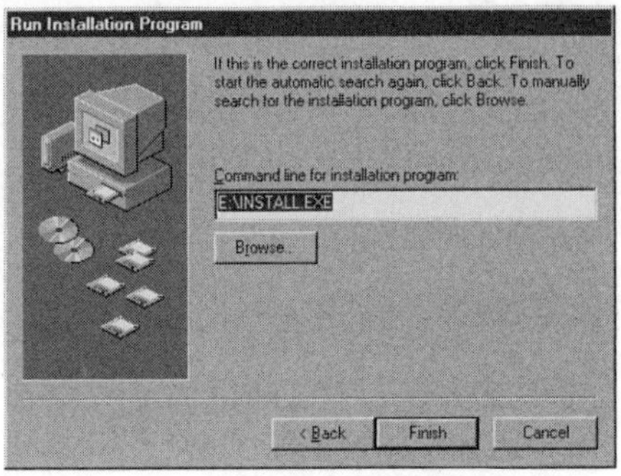

7. If the wizard fails to find the installation program automatically, click the Browse button to open the Browse dialog box.

8. Locate the installation program and highlight it. Click the Open button to close the Browse dialog box and place the installation program's file name in the Run Installation Program dialog box.

TIP Most software installation programs are named Setup.exe or Install.exe.

9. In the Run Installation Program dialog box, click the Finish button. The wizard will launch the software installation program.

10. When the software installation program appears, follow the on-screen instructions to proceed with the installation. You may need to supply information, select options, and confirm settings in a series of dialog boxes presented by the installation program.

    For example, you may need to specify or confirm the drive and folder where the software will be installed. If you're installing a large, complex program, you may need to select installation options such as accessory programs, default settings, and optional features to install as shown in Figure 26.4. On the other hand, simple programs may have few, if any, options for you to select during installation.

11. After you select the options you want to install, the installation program will copy the appropriate files from the floppy disk or CD to your hard drive. You may need to insert additional floppy disks or CDs when prompted to do so. Most of the files will be placed in the program's own folder, but some files are likely to be copied to the Windows folder. The installation program will also register your new software with Windows 95 and add the program to the Start menu.

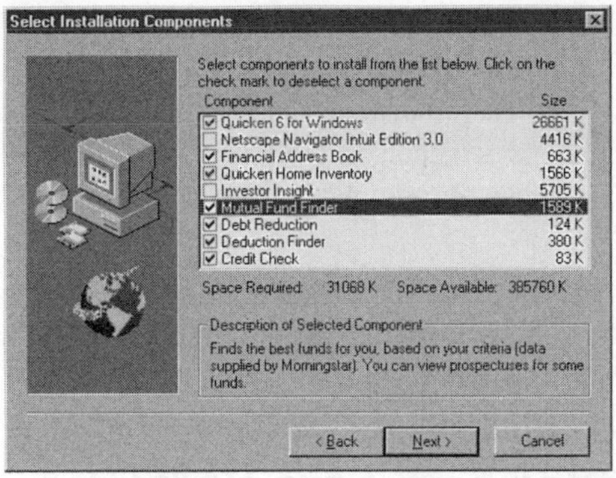

FIG. 26.4

Depending on the program you're installing, you may be able to select a variety of features and options.

12. The installation program may offer to register your new software with the software developer. If so, the installation program will prompt you to enter your name, address, and other information. Then, it may print the information for submission to the software developer via mail or fax. It's increasingly common for software installation programs to use your modem to submit your registration information electronically.

13. When the program setup is finished, the installation program will close and return you to the Windows 95 desktop. However, you shouldn't be surprised if the last step of software installation is to restart Windows 95. Restarting your computer is often required in order for changes in some behind-the-scenes settings to take effect.

T I P After installing software, you may want to rearrange the Start menu icons and folders to organize the new program entries according to your preferences instead of sticking with the default Start menu icons. You may have to create a shortcut and drag it to your Startup icon set.

▶ **See** "Customizing the Start Menu," **p. 57**

N O T E Sometimes, all you need to do to start installing a new software program is to insert the installation CD into your CD-ROM drive and wait a few seconds. If your system is configured to allow CDs to AutoRun, Windows 95 will automatically run the program on the CD—presumably the setup program for the software. If AutoRun is not installed on your system, you can install it from your Windows 95 CD. Simple instructions for installation are in your user manual. ■

Upgrading to New Software Versions

If the software you have is doing the job you need it to do, there may be no compelling need to upgrade to a new version just because a newer version is available. However, there are several reasons why you may want to consider upgrading your software:

■ You need or want some of the new features that the software developers are constantly adding to successive versions of their programs.

Part

VI

Ch

26

■ You may want to upgrade your software to take advantage of bug fixes and other improvements in the program.

■ You have to upgrade in order to maintain compatibility with coworkers and other users. If you need to exchange documents and data files with others who have begun using a newer version of a particular program, you may be forced to upgrade your own software to match.

■ You may need to upgrade your software to be guaranteed that you will be able to get technical support for the programs you use. Software developers normally support the current version of their programs and one or two previous versions.

Installing Over Older Software Versions

Normally, when you upgrade to a new version of a program you already have installed on your computer, the installation program will automatically detect the presence of the older version of the same software and will handle the installation as an upgrade instead of a completely new installation. Typically, an upgrade installation will replace the older version of the program with the new version and will maintain as much of your existing documents, data, and preference settings as possible. Occasionally, you must first remove your old software and then install the new version from scratch, but that's an unusual scenario.

Although the default software upgrade involves installing the new version to replace the older version, you almost always have two options for handling the upgrade:

■ You can replace the old version with the new version.

■ You can install the new version separately and keep the old version.

If you allow the installation program to replace the old version of the software with the new version, the old, familiar program you've been using will be unavailable. You're forced to quit cold turkey and commit to using the new version. The advantage is that the upgrade usually is able to pick up most macros, personal options, custom settings, data files and so on, and use them in the new version of the software.

The installation program will normally offer to install the new software in the same folder where the old version is installed. If you want to install the new software version to replace the older version on your hard drive, you can usually just accept the default installation settings.

If you want to keep the old version of the software as well as install the new version, you can usually do so by simply specifying a different folder for the new version of the software. The installation program will then install the new software in the new location and leave the old version of the software alone. The new version is installed as if you were starting from scratch instead of upgrading a previous installation.

> **CAUTION**
>
> Occasionally, having two versions of the same program installed on the same computer will cause some conflicts. Typically, it's nothing more serious than confusion about which version will automatically launch when you open a document file, but some conflicts may cause one, or both, versions of the program to behave strangely.

Removing Old Software

Software designed to run in Windows 95 insinuates itself into the operating system with Registry settings, and stores parts of the program scattered about in various folders. Some parts of the program may even be shared with other programs on your computer, and deleting those shared components could disable other programs. As a result, it's very difficult to manually remove a program from a Windows 95 computer.

The good news is that this difficulty in removing software manually has forced software developers to provide special tools to enable users to remove software easily. Any program that is designed for Windows 95 must include an uninstall program to remove the software.

You may find an icon for an uninstall program in the program's folder on the Start menu. To remove the software from your computer, you can just click that icon and follow the instructions.

> **CAUTION**
>
> Before removing a program, make sure you save any documents and data files you want to keep by copying them into another folder or creating backup copies on floppy disks or another removable media. Documents saved in the same folder with the program may be deleted along with the program.

Part VI
Ch 26

In addition to the uninstall programs you find listed on the Start menu, Windows 95 maintains a command center for software installation and removal in the Control Panel. To use the Add/Remove Programs applet in the Control Panel to remove a program from your computer, follow these steps:

1. Click the Start button on the taskbar to display the Start menu.
2. Select Settings to display the Settings submenu and then click Control Panel. This will open the Control Panel window.
3. In the Control Panel window, double-click the Add/Remove Programs icon to open the Add/Remove Programs Properties dialog box with the Install/Uninstall tab selected, as shown in Figure 26.5.

FIG. 26.5

The Add/Remove Programs Properties dialog box is your command central for removing unwanted or outdated software.

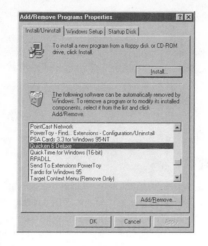

4. From the list in the lower portion of the Add/Remove Programs Properties dialog box, select the program you want to remove.

5. Click the Add/Remove button. The Add/Remove button doesn't launch a wizard to look for the uninstall program (as when you used the Install button in this same dialog box). Windows 95 already knows where to find the program because the information was recorded during the program installation. It launches the appropriate setup/uninstall program immediately.

6. When the uninstall program appears, follow the on-screen instructions to remove the software. Often the uninstall program is the same as the installation program for the software, and you can use it to add and remove various components of the program. To remove the program completely, you simply choose to remove all the components that make up the software. As with program installation, large complex programs may have many options that you need to select and simpler programs may have few, if any, options for removing the program.

7. After you select the options, the uninstall program will begin deleting the appropriate files and folders from your hard drive. The uninstall program will remove references to the software from the Windows Registry, and remove the program from the Start menu. You may need to confirm some of these actions when prompted by the uninstall program.

CAUTION

If you have rearranged the Start menu and moved the program's icons, the uninstall program probably won't be able to find the program icons in their new locations. Consequently, you'll probably need to manually edit the Start menu to remove the program icons after you remove the program from your computer.

▶ **See** "Customizing the Start Menu," **p. 57**

8. When the program removal is complete, the uninstall program will close and return you to the Windows 95 desktop. You may need to restart Windows 95 to remove the last traces of the program and reset some Windows settings.

After the uninstall program has done its work, the software is gone and the disk space it once occupied is recovered for other uses. In some cases, you may need to delete some files and folders manually—particularly if document or data files were left over after the uninstall program did its job. ●

Part
VI

Ch
26

Upgrading Your Hardware

For most of us, cost is a major consideration when deciding upon upgrading versus buying a new system. As you look at the cost of the new parts that you want to upgrade in your system, keep a running tab and compare that to the cost of buying a whole new system.

The cost of buying every part in your system and assembling it yourself (upgrading the whole thing) is much higher than the cost of a new system. PC manufacturers buy in bulk and pass their savings along. In addition, a new system will usually come with a complete warranty and software. If you upgrade your parts, the warranty will depend on the warranty for each part.

In general, if the cost of your upgrade starts to approach $1,000, you'll want to look carefully at the option of getting a new PC. There's always a fast new system that can be bought in the $1,000 to $2,000 range. If you decide a new PC is the way to go, be sure to read the later section "What to Look for in a New PC." ■

Upgrading hardware versus buying a new PC

Learn when to upgrade your existing system and when it's time to buy a new one. If you want to upgrade, learn what upgrades you can make yourself.

Hardware compatibility issues

When buying parts—especially drives, RAM, and expansion cards—be sure to get ones that will work with your existing system.

Tips for buying a new PC

Learn what to look for and where to buy one for desktop and notebook systems.

Plug and Play

Understand what this new catch phrase means and what to look for when buying new computers and add-ons.

Are You Uncomfortable Opening Your Computer Case?

If you aren't comfortable opening the case of your PC and adding or replacing things inside it, you won't want to consider upgrades to items such as hard drives, video cards, or RAM on your own. However, for a small service charge, most computer stores will perform these upgrades for you. So, if you choose to upgrade and have the service done for you, factor in that cost of the service to the total of the upgrade.

TIP Professional service should come with a warranty and a guarantee. If you perform your own video card upgrade and you break it or the motherboard, you'll have to pay for the replacement. Hiring a pro with a guarantee should mean that anything that goes wrong is fixed at their cost.

If you don't want to open the case and you aren't going to pay someone else to upgrade it, there still are a few items you can upgrade or add on to increase the life of your PC and what you can do with it:

- *Monitors*. Replacing a monitor is as easy as unplugging the old and plugging in the new.
  - ▶ **See** "Hooking Up Your New Monitor," **p. 116**

- *Printers*. A printer is another item you can add or replace by just plugging it in to the back of the PC.
  - ▶ **See** "Connecting Your Printer to your PC," **p. 149**

- *Modems*. An external modem can be added or replaced by hooking it up to an external serial port if you have a serial port that is not being used.
  - ▶ **See** "Connecting a Modem," **p. 160**

- *Keyboards, mice, and joysticks*. Keyboards can be replaced just by plugging them in to the back of the PC. If you buy a new mouse or joystick with the same connection time as the one on your PC, these can be replaced without opening the PC case.
  - ▶ **See** "Connecting a Joystick," **p. 141**

- *Tape drives*. Many tape drive models can be connected to your parallel port, and most even have a cable to have your printer and tape drive connected to the port at the same time.

- *Zip drives*. If you need more disk storage space, Zip drives come in a version that can be connected to your existing parallel port. This is an easy way to add storage space without opening the PC.

- *Speakers*. If you already have a sound card, adding and replacing speakers is an easy upgrade.

Upgrading Parts Inside Your PC

If you want to upgrade anything inside your PC, it is highly recommended that you read the book *Upgrading PCs Illustrated* by Que. This book has many drawings and photographs to show you step-by-step procedures for adding and replacing parts in your PC. Although most of the parts inside a PC are very easy to replace, they can also be very easy to damage if you don't follow the right steps. This book can save you a lot of time and frustration with those processes.

What type of upgrades can you make inside your PC?

- *Memory.* This is one of the easiest internal upgrades to make. It usually just involves snapping a new RAM or SIMM(s) into place. Your motherboard and BIOS should recognize the new memory when you restart the PC.

- *Processor.* This is another relatively easy but more delicate process. Usually you need to unplug the old processor and plug in the new one. Most PCs have a small lever that helps lift out the old processor and secure the new one in place. You may have to change settings on your motherboard by moving small connectors called *jumpers*, or making changes in the system BIOS.

- *Hard drive.* Adding a new hard drive can be more complicated. In addition to physically mounting the drive in place, you need to connect cables to the drive and configure it to work with an existing drive. Replacing your C drive is even more complicated because you need to have a way to get all of your old files onto the new drive. Once the new drive is installed, you have to set up the BIOS to recognize and format it before storing any data on it.

- *Video card.* Upgrading the video card means removing the old one from its slot and plugging in the new one. You also have to select the correct video card drivers in Windows.

- *Sound card.* Sounds cards simply plug into any empty expansion slot.

- *Other expansion cards.* Internal modems, an interface card for a SCSI drive or scanner, a video capture card, and any other type of interface card are added by installing them into an open expansion slot and installing any software that came with them.

- *BIOS.* Most computers built in the last few years have BIOSes that can be upgraded by installing a new software called a *flash* upgrade. However, if you ever have to replace the BIOS chip itself, be sure the replacement comes with good directions and that all of your data on your hard drives is backed up first.

- *System battery.* There's a small battery on your motherboard that runs the clock and helps your BIOS remember settings for your hard drives. These batteries usually last three years or more. There is usually a small clip that holds the battery in place. When replacing these, be sure you have a printed record of your BIOS settings (there's usually a BIOS utility to help with this). Also, make sure to get the right voltage battery and to get it in the correct direction.

Part
VI

Ch
27

IDE and SCSI Drives

Hard drives and CD-ROM drives come in two different varieties. If you want to add a second hard drive, a new CD-ROM drive, or replace a hard drive, you'll need to be sure to get one of the same type that is already in your system.

IDE drives are most common. Unless you specifically asked for SCSI drives when you bought your PC, you probably got it with IDE drives. Most PCs are capable of supporting four IDE drives at one time. So you could have any combination of four IDE hard drives and CD-ROM drives.

There was a time when IDE drives were slower than most SCSI drives. But IDE drives have evolved quickly, and for most uses are now just as fast as SCSI.

N O T E Some older IDE drives have compatibility issues working with other older IDE drives. If you have an IDE hard drive that is 250M or less and more than two years old, you'll want to consider replacing it with a newer drive rather than adding a second drive. If you do decide to add a second drive, your best bet to avoid incompatibilities is to buy a drive of the same brand as the first.

If your PC does have a SCSI drive connector (either built-in or as an adapter card), be sure to buy SCSI drives. These generally cost more than IDE drives of the same brand and size.

Matching Memory

When it's time to upgrade your computer's RAM, there are several memory type issues you need to be aware of. It's important to buy the right type of memory for your PC, or you will have all sorts of odd problems. Or, the PC may just refuse to boot.

A PC motherboard has slots for memory. (These are different than the expansion slots for cards.) The most common of these slots are called *SIMM (Single Inline Memory Module) slots.* SIMMs come in several different sizes; the most common are 72-pin. These are most common on any PC with a Pentium or faster processors. Some older PCs have 36- or 32-pin SIMMs.

▶ **See** "Determining How Much RAM You Have," **p. 24**

Most PCs have somewhere between four and eight SIMM slots. To decide what memory to buy to upgrade your PC, you should open the case and see how many memory slots are free. If you have no free slots, you will have to replace memory to upgrade. Unfortunately, this situation is common, because many PCs with four slots were sold with all of the slots full.

The most important question in dealing with memory is: "How many megabytes?" Regardless of the number of pins your memory needs to have, the SIMMs can be found in many megabyte sizes. These typically range from 4 to 32M for new RAM. Older RAM that you are replacing may be as low as 1M.

Buying RAM gets tricky at this stage. Even though a SIMM slot may have the right number of pins to accept a PIN, all motherboards have a limit to the number of megabytes that can be on any single SIMM. So, if your motherboard is limited to using 16M SIMMs, don't buy 32M even if they look like they'll fit.

Some motherboards require the SIMMs to be added in pairs called *banks*. If your motherboard has this limitation (check your computer's specifications or contact the vendor to determine), be sure to buy two matching SIMMs to add the RAM you want. For example, to add 16M, buy two 8M SIMMs.

The next complicating factor in buying RAM is choosing parity or non-parity RAM. Most new machines work with *non-parity RAM*. *Parity RAM* is used to check the RAM for internal errors. Again, check your computer specifications to determine which type of RAM your machine requires—then make sure you buy the right type.

Another RAM term you'll encounter is *EDO (Extended Data Output)*. This is a faster type of SIMM that has become very standard in PCs. If your motherboard supports it, buy it. It usually sells for the same price as standard (non-EDO) RAM.

If all of this isn't confusing enough, there are several new RAM types and terms you may encounter. Many new PCs are now shipping with slots for *DIMM memory (Dual Inline Memory Module)*. DIMMs pack more pins (168 instead of 72) and more RAM into just a slightly larger package. If you want to buy DIMMs, be sure to consult an expert first, usually a qualified technician where you bought your PC. DIMMs have a dizzying array of voltages and other specifications in addition to memory amounts, and buying the wrong type will cause problems.

CAUTION

Don't purchase "cheaper" slower additional RAM. Additional RAM must be at least the same speed or faster than the machine's original RAM. Mismatched speeds can cause system problems.

Another new type of RAM is called *SDRAM*. Like EDO, this is a faster kind of RAM. Unlike EDO, SDRAM is currently much more expensive than standard RAM; unless you are a hard-core computer speed addict, it isn't worth the extra money.

Part
VI

Ch
27

ISA, PCI, and Other Expansion Slots

If you are going to install a new card into your PC, you need to know what kind of slot it will go in.

There are two slots that you will find in most current PCs. The first is an *ISA slot*. This is an older standard and is slower than the other type. But, for many uses, it is still more than fast enough. Cards that you'll probably want to buy ISA versions of include:

- Internal modems
- Sound cards

N O T E If you have an older PC, you may find that you have two different types of ISA slots. One is a short 16-bit slot and the other is a longer 16-bit slot. If you have a system that has 8-bit slots, you can only use 8-bit cards in these. Eight-bit cards will work in either 8- or 16-bit slots, but you'll want to save your 16-bit slots for 16-bit cards. ▪

The other kind of slot is a *PCI slot*. Most PCs now have three of these. These slots are much faster at transferring information from the card to the processor than ISA. They also have the advantage of working better with Plug and Play. Cards that can take advantage of PCI slots include:

- ▪ Video cards
- ▪ Hard drive interfaces (SCSI or IDE), although most motherboards have IDE built in
- ▪ Network adapters

Before buying any card, be sure to check the PC to see that there is a free slot of the right type. If the card is a replacement, remember that you will be able to use the slot currently filled by the old card.

▶ **See** "How Many Open Slots Do You Have?" **p. 27**

N O T E Before there was PCI, there were two other types of fast slots. One was MCA and the other was Vesa Local Bus (VLB). You won't find these on any new PCs, and if you need to upgrade a card in one of these, you may have trouble finding them. If you are considering upgrading a machine with either of these, replacement is probably a better option. ▪

Understanding Plug and Play Technology

Adding and replacing expansion cards and peripherals in your PC is not easy. Most cards have small connectors called *jumpers* that determine what system resources the card will use to communicate with the PC. But no card can use all system resources. These resources are limited, and configuring more than two cards to work together can drive even experienced PC upgraders crazy.

So, Microsoft and several hardware vendors established a new system called *Plug and Play* (available with the release of Windows 95). The theory is that you plug the new card into a slot or plug in the new peripheral, and when you restart the computer, Windows and the motherboard BIOS find the new card and configures it for you.

In order for this to work, your PC has to support Plug and Play and you have to buy hardware add-ons that are labeled as Plug and Play (PnP) compatible. The bad news is that if your system is more than a couple of years old, it definitely won't support this. And while there are a lot of PnP devices available, there are also a lot of devices that aren't PnP. If you have several older non-PnP cards in your PC, these may cause Windows trouble when trying to configure PnP devices.

If you are shopping for new cards, there are a couple of things you'll want to be sure to look for PnP varieties of. First is sound cards. Sound cards can be the most difficult addition to a PC, and Plug and Play can be a huge help with them.

You should also look for PnP varieties of internal modems. If your PC has built-in serial ports and supports PnP, a PnP modem is much easier to install. There are also so many modem varieties that it can be hard to find the exact correct model in the Windows modem setup if you don't have a PnP modem that Windows can identify for you.

Some devices such as hard drives, keyboards, and mice don't need to be PnP. Printers, monitors, video cards, hard drive interface cards, CD-ROM drives, network cards, and scanners all come in PnP varieties.

What to Look for in a New PC

Unless you enjoy the work of upgrading your PC and adding on to it, be sure you get everything that you want in your new PC when you buy it. Here are some guidelines for what to look for.

All of the items in this first list are essential must-have items for your new PC:

- *Processor*. Get the fastest processor you can afford. Although Intel makes the processors sold in the majority of PCs, don't shy away from PCs with AMD or Cyrix processors. I'm writing this on a PC with a nice, new AMD processor, and it's every bit as good as PCs I've had with Intel brains.

- *Memory*. Consider 16M to be the minimum for a new machine. If you can afford the upgrade to 32M, get it now. If not, you'll probably end up buying more later anyway.

- *Hard drive*. You won't find many new PCs with drives smaller than 1G. It is common now to have 2–4G drives. Although it may seem that you would never use all of this space, it will fill up fast, especially if you plan to load a lot of software, games, or files from the Internet.

  Most machines will come with IDE drives. Unless you plan to use the machine for copying or mastering CD-ROMs (with a CD-ROM recorder), an IDE drive will suit you fine. If you do plan to make your own CDs, go ahead and upgrade to a SCSI hard drive now.

- *Monitor*. Don't buy anything less than a 15-inch monitor unless you can't afford it. In fact, you're better off skimping elsewhere to be able to afford a better monitor. For example, the cost difference between a 14-inch and 15-inch monitor is probably about $75–100. That's usually the same difference between 16M of RAM and 32M. If that difference is what is breaking your budget, get the better monitor. You can always upgrade the RAM later if you have more money and that will still only cost you around $75–100. But to upgrade the monitor, you'll have to replace it, which will cost around $300. Your eyes will thank you.

  ▶ **See** "Monitor Sizes," **p. 112**

Part
VI

Ch
27

- *CD-ROM drive*. Every new system should come with a CD-ROM drive. Almost all new software that you want to install will come on CDs. And any multimedia game or educational software will require a CD. If you want to make your own CDs, see if you can find a PC that comes with a CD recorder.

- *Keyboard*. If you will be using your PC a lot, invest in a good ergonomic keyboard and avoid any chance that you will develop a medical problem like carpal tunnel syndrome.

  ▶ **See** "Avoiding Keyboard-Related Injuries," **p. 131**

- *Mouse*. The new Microsoft IntelliMouse with the roller for scrolling Web pages is a nice addition, but I wouldn't pay extra for it. Look for a mouse that fits your hand comfortably.

  ▶ **See** "Using the IntelliMouse Wheel," **p. 138**

- *Floppy drive*. You still need one of these. It should be a 3 1/2-inch model.

- *Case*. Your computer needs a case. Most makers make systems with desktop (flat) and tower (upright) cases. The choice is really a matter of personal preference and the layout of the space where you use the PC.

- *Windows 95*. Your new system should come with Windows 95 preinstalled and ready to run. It should also include the installation CD and documentation. Some vendors save a few dollars by not including a printed manual.

In addition, here's what to look for in other optional equipment:

- *Tape drive or other removable drive*. You probably won't buy a tape drive until after the first time you have a bad system crash and lose data, but you should. Many new systems include these. The Zip and Jaz drives are also good alternatives for backing up data or moving large files. Zip drives cost about $200, but I've seen new PCs with these as an option for about $100. You'll get similar savings by buying the PC with a tape drive instead of adding one later.

  ▶ **See** "Making Back Up Copies of Your Files," **p. 91**

- *Sound card and speakers*. Although not essential for your PC to operate, almost every new PC comes with a sound card. Be sure it is Sound Blaster-compatible. If you want booming bass, upgrade to speakers with a subwoofer.

  ▶ **See** "Sound Cards," **p. 166**

- *Modem*. Don't buy anything less than a 33.6K modem. If you want to use the Internet a lot, consider an upgrade to a 56K modem. If buying a 56K modem, be sure that you can get 56K service and that your brand modem will work with the provider.

  ▶ **See** "Making Sure You Have the Right Hardware," **p. 200**
  ▶ **See** "Selecting an Internet Service Provider," **p. 201**

- *Printer*. These are easy enough to add on your own, but you can usually get a good deal on one if you buy it with the PC. If you just need to print black and white business documents, an inexpensive laser printer is your best bet. For color printing, ink jets and bubble jet color printers have great output quality and low prices. But be prepared to spend money on refills for the ink.

■ *Joysticks, steering wheels, and other game input hardware.* Buying these amounts to matters of personal taste and what games you like to play. If you want to be a master of *Quake* or *Duke Nukem*, don't expect to do it with a bargain-basement $10 joystick. Likewise, there's a reason real racecars have steering wheels and gas pedals. If you live to play *Indy Car Racing* or *Sega Rally Championship* on your PC, buy a PC steering wheel with pedals if your games support it.

■ *Optional software.* If you use Microsoft Office (Word, Excel, PowerPoint, Access) at work, look for a PC that has these preinstalled if you want to use your PC to work on these types of files. Many vendors offer lots of preinstalled software on PCs. If the software is something you'll use, it's a great deal. If not, you'll just end up uninstalling it at some later date.

Where to Buy New PCs and Upgrades

There are two main options to look at when buying PCs or parts. You can buy them from any local store that sells them, or you can buy them from a mail-order (direct) outlet.

The advantages of buying from a local store usually involve convenience. If you want the security of seeing the PC or part before you buy it, or knowing that you can return it or have it serviced by simply driving to the local store at the mall, buying locally is for you.

TIP When shopping for a new monitor, I almost always recommend buying it locally rather than mail-order. You'll want to see what the picture looks like on-screen as monitors with all of the same technical specifications can have dramatically different picture quality. You can't see that in a magazine ad or over the phone.

Buying locally usually gives you a chance to test-drive the system in the store and ask a helpful sales representative questions about the hardware. A little common sense goes a long way here. A lot of stores sell PCs now. Chances are the salesperson at the local PC store will be able to answer more of your PC questions than the salesperson at an electronics store who also sells refrigerators and TVs, or the salesperson at a department store selling everything from underwear to computers. The bottom line is, shop where you feel most comfortable.

The big advantage of buying from a mail-order or direct outlet is usually price. You will be hard pressed to find a local retail store that can sell you a new system with all of the same features as a mail-order outlet for the same price.

Buying direct also has the advantage of having a much larger selection. If you like to have a lot of choices, call several mail-order outlets and compare their offerings. You'll always find a better selection than at the local stores.

A final advantage that most major mail-order retailers have is a better trained sales staff. For example, when you call Gateway or Dell's order lines, the person that answers the phone does nothing but sell computers. Before they ask you technical questions about what type of

Part
VI

Ch
27

processor you need or how much RAM you want, they do a good job of finding out how you plan to use the system so that they understand your needs. Gateway and Dell aren't the only ones; any of the major PC vendors who sell direct can help you a lot when buying a new system.

When buying parts through a direct channel, I recommend picking up a copy of *Computer Shopper* magazine before buying. Any computer store carries this massive magazine, and you can find dozens of reputable dealers listed there. For about $5, this is a great investment in the most up-to-date information about who's selling what for how much.

Special Tips for Buying a Notebook Computer

There are several things about buying a new notebook that are different than buying a PC. Here's a quick list of additional or different features you'll want to look at in a notebook.

■ *Processor.* The processor should be a special *mobile* processor. These are made to run cooler and use less power so your battery will last longer. Some notebook makers put desktop processors in their notebook to save money. I recommend avoiding notebooks that use desktop processors.

When buying a notebook, buy one with the processor you intend to use for the life of the notebook. You'll never upgrade the processor.

■ *Video card and display.* These are built into the system in the notebook and can't be upgraded. Be sure to get ones you'll be happy with as long as you own the notebook.

  ▶ **See** "Special Considerations for Notebook Displays," **p. 115**

■ *PC Card slots.* This is a different type of expansion slot for notebooks. Be sure to get one with two PC Card slots. The newest technology for these is Cardbus and Zoomed Video. Get one that supports these standards if you can.

■ *Battery.* Battery life is critical if you travel with your notebook. Lithium Ion (LiO) batteries are the best for life. Nickel-Metal Hydride (NmH) are also good. Nickel-Cadmium is an old battery type that you should avoid. Look for a notebook that uses standard battery types so replacements will be inexpensive and easy to find. If possible, get one with *hot swappable* batteries so you can buy a second battery and switch without rebooting.

■ *Power management.* Only buy a notebook that supports power management to save battery life.

■ *CD-ROM drive.* Most notebooks now have internal CD-ROM drives standard or at least as an option. Many times, these are removable and can be swapped with the floppy drive and second battery. You won't be able to install new CD-based software without a CD-ROM drive, so your notebook really should have one.

■ *RAM.* Expect to pay a little more for RAM in a notebook than in a desktop system. Most notebooks use proprietary RAM modules, but a few use standard desktop SIMMs. In some notebooks, upgrading RAM will be more difficult than in a desktop system, so you may want to buy it with all the RAM you think you'll ever need.

■ *Keyboard.* The closer to full size and regular key spacing, the easier it will be to use.

■ *Pointing device.* Most of the time, you won't use a mouse with the notebook. Most notebooks now come with a small, built-in *track pad* that you drag your finger across for mouse options. I prefer the pointing stick that you find on IBM ThinkPads and a few off-brands, but these are hard to find outside of IBM. Trackballs are very rare now.

■ *Hard drives.* Expect to pay a little more for your notebook hard drive, too. Capacities are a little smaller than desktop drives and they can be harder to replace. Most notebooks can't take a second drive.

■ *Sound card and speakers.* Most notebooks include a basic Sound Blaster-compatible card and speakers as a standard feature.

■ *Weight.* If you travel with a notebook, buy the lightest-weight model you can with all of the features you need. Consider the weight of a carry case, extra battery, charger, and anything else you plan to carry.

■ *External ports.* There should be ports for connecting a mouse, keyboard, printer, and external monitor. Optional ports may include speakers and serial plugs (for an external modem).

■ *Port replicator.* If you plan to use the notebook as a replacement for a desktop system, you'll want to see if a port replicator is available. The port replicator has all of the same external ports as the notebook. You plug the monitor, keyboard, and mouse into the replicator and the notebook snaps into the replicator. Leave the external devices plugged in to the replicator, and you can plug and unplug the notebook without having to attach the monitor, keyboard, and mouse individually.

■ *Docking station.* This is the big brother to the port replicator. A docking station has all of the same features as the replicator with additional features such as bays for added drives and slots for expansion cards.

Reference Information

28 Glossary of Common Terms and Phrases 297

29 Computer Company Listing 325

30 Top Internet Sites 339

31 Suggested Reading 355

CHAPTER 28

Glossary of Common Terms and Phrases

Although this list of definitions doesn't include every new word you'll encounter regarding computers, it should help you clear up the meanings of some you'll see a lot, and some others that might otherwise remain a mystery.

One of the most frustrating things you encounter when talking to others about computers is how to pronounce these terms. Acronyms are especially tricky—sometimes you're supposed to spell it out, sometimes say it as a word. This glossary includes pronunciation guides for those acronyms that you treat as words, like ASCII (AS-kee). Otherwise, the correct way to say it is one letter at a time, as in A-O-L. ■

Symbols and Numbers

@ (at)   The "at" symbol separates the user ID from the domain name of an Internet address, such as **wagner@who.net**. See *domain*.

*   See *asterisk, wildcard*.

?   See *question mark, wildcard*.

16-bit (operating system)   An operating system, such as Windows 3.1, that uses a central processing unit (CPU) with a 16-bit data bus and processes 2 bytes (16 bits) of information at a time.

32-bit (operating system)   An operating system, such as Windows 95, that uses a central processing unit (CPU) with a 32-bit data bus and processes 4 bytes (32 bits) of information at a time.

14,400 bps   A medium-speed modem. If you're buying a new computer or modem, however, look for one that is faster, such as 28,800 or 33,600. Sometimes written as 14.4Kbps (kilobytes per second). See *bits per second*.

2,400 bps   A very slow modem speed by today's standards. (See *bits per second*.) Unless you plan on only occasional use and don't want to download or upload files, avoid this speed modem or anything slower.

28,800 bps   Among the faster modems available for the average consumer. (See *bits per second*.) Sometimes written as 28.8Kbps (kilobytes per second).

33,600 bps   The fastest modem currently available that does not require special phone lines or additional equipment. Sometimes written as 33.6Kbps (kilobytes per second). Faster modems (56Kbps, also called X2) are increasing in popularity, but if you buy a new computer today, it will likely include a 33.6 modem.

9,600 bps   Slow modem speed, compared to current standards.

A

abend   An abnormal end to processing that stops the network, usually the result of a software or hardware problem.

access time   Measurement of the speed at which it takes a device (such as a disk drive) to find a piece of data. Access time is measured in milliseconds (ms). The lower the access time, the faster or better the drive quality. Anything under 10ms is very good.

adapter   A connector that converts one type of cable to another (such as 9- to 25-pin adapter for modems). If the plug on your computer doesn't match the plug that came with your peripheral device, you probably need one of these. When speaking of networks, the term means a network interface card.

address   A unique number assigned to every component on the network. The address identifies the sender and receiver of each machine's messages (packets).

America Online (AOL)   A popular commercial online service that also provides a gateway to the Internet. AOL is probably the fastest growing of the big three services—CompuServe, AOL, and Prodigy—and appeals to a wide variety of users.

American Standard Code for Information Interchange (ASCII)   Pronounced AS-kee. The set of 128 characters, consisting of the standard upper- and lowercase English letters, the digits 0–9, and 32 other nonprinting control characters. ASCII is the standard for most computing devices.

anti-virus program   A program or application that scans your computer's files for potentially damaging viruses. See *virus*.

AOL   See *America Online*.

application   See *program*.

archive   A file that has been compressed to save space on a computer or file server. To use these files, you must first decompress them using a utility such as PKZIP or WinZip.

ASCII   See American Standard Code for Information Interchange.

ASCII file   Generally, a plain-text file without any formatting, which can be read by a wide variety of applications.

asterisk (*)   A wildcard character generally used to take the place of one or more specific characters. When chatting or composing e-mail, also used to give emphasis to words by adding inflection to your online "voice," much like italics do in print. Example: "Man, it is *really* cold outside!!" Also called a star. See *question mark, wildcard*.

asynchronous   Varying, uneven length transmissions wherein characters are separated from the message by means of start and stop bits.

AT command set   The standard language spoken by most modems. Any modem that uses the AT command set is said to be Hayes compatible. See *Hayes-compatible modem*.

attachments   Files that are sent along with e-mail messages or other online communications, much like one piece of paper attached to another.

attenuation   The amount of signal that is lost over a distance.

AUTOEXEC.BAT   A file your computer reads when you boot or reboot the system. AUTOEXEC.BAT runs specific commands needed to get the computer up and running properly. This file can be altered with a text editor, but don't change it unless you know what you are doing.

Part

VII

Ch

28

B

backbone   The cable connecting the main server, in the case of a dedicated network, to other components.

background task   In multitask computers, a low-priority task (such as printing or file downloading) which is carried out "behind the scenes" while the computer is actively engaged with an application in the foreground. The foreground task is usually the one the user sees in operation. See also *foreground task*, *multitasking*.

backup   A copy of the files or programs on your computer. Creating frequent backups is an important safety precaution against system crashes and helps prevent data loss.

bandwidth   Technically, the amount of information that can flow through a channel at one time, measured in bits per second (bps) or cycles per second (Hz). A higher frequency means a higher bandwidth. If you see this mentioned online, however, it's probably someone complaining about wasted bandwidth, meaning he's annoyed by someone else who's taking up space in cyberspace. In the context of networks, the term refers to how many simultaneous transmissions a cable can carry.

bang   Another name for an exclamation point (!).

Basic Input Output System (BIOS)   Pronounced BYE-ose. Startup instructions built into the computer's microprocessor that tell it how to deal with input and output. The computer reads the BIOS before it even loads the operating system.

baud rate   The number of signal changes per second on a channel. Baud rate is often used incorrectly to refer to modem speed, which is really measured in bits per second.

BBS   See *bulletin board system or service*.

bells and whistles   The features included in a software program or application.

binary file   A non-text file, such as a graphics or compressed file. A user can't read a binary file as it is. Usually, users can't send binary files between online services (such as from AOL to Prodigy), but they work fine when sent from within the same service. Internet users may need a special program or program capability to read binary files if they have been encoded.

bindery   A database maintained by a NetWare network containing all users, their passwords, and associated information.

BIOS   See *Basic Input Output System*.

bit   Short for binary digit, the smallest unit of information used in computing. Eight bits make up one byte. See *byte*.

bits per second (bps)   The measurement for the speed at which a modem can transfer data. The higher the number, the faster the modem. 2,400 bps and under is slow. For best results, use a modem with a speed of 14,400 bps or higher.

bps   See *bits per second*.

boot   The process of starting or restarting your computer. When you turn on the computer, it's called *booting up the system*. Likewise, restarting is known as *rebooting*.

break   A signal you send to the computer to cancel a command, process, or data transfer. The common keystroke is Ctrl+C for DOS and Windows computers.

broadcast   A message sent to all users on the network.

browser   A program you use to navigate a server or network of servers. Usually used in reference to the World Wide Web (WWW). See *Web browser, World Wide Web*.

buffer   A computer's temporary storage area. The larger the memory buffer, the faster your computer can work.

bug   An error in a computer program. A bug can cause minor problems such as miscalculated figures, or serious ones resulting in system crashes or loss of data.

bulletin board system or service (BBS)   Like commercial online services such as AOL, you can use BBSes for e-mail, file downloading, chatting, and so on. The difference is they're usually much cheaper than commercial services, and often have more of a local "flavor."

bus   The pathway inside the computer along which information signals are sent. There are three basic types of buses in a personal computer:

- *Address bus*. Identifies which memory location will be used next.
- *Control bus*. Carries signals from the control unit, making sure the bus traffic flows smoothly.
- *Data bus*. Transfers data to and from the microprocessor and the memory. The data bus includes both internal and external data buses.

There are several different bus architectures (designs). The most common terms you will hear are *ISA*, *EISA*, and *PCI*. PCI is the standard architecture for Pentium computers, although ISA and EISA are often included as well to support older hardware devices you may already own.

byte   Pronounced bite. A collection of 8 bits; 1 byte represents one character. Computer files, memory, and storage capacities are usually measured in bytes. See *bit, megabyte*.

C

cache   Pronounced cash. A portion of memory built into the microprocessor. This extremely fast memory stores the most recently accessed data from a disk or file and helps speed up your computer because the computer does not have to go looking for it on the disk again—it's right there in the cache. The most cache memory a computer has, the better off you'll be (256K and 512K are average).

capacity   The amount of data a disk can store. The common floppy disk stores 1.44M of data; most hard disks on the market today store between 800M and 4G of data.

card   Same as network interface card, or NIC. One card is installed in each computer connected to the network; it provides the gateway between the network cable and the PC itself.

case-sensitive   If your software is case-sensitive, it means that uppercase letters are read differently than lowercase letters. For example, a case-sensitive search for "Smith" would find only "Smith," not "SMITH," "SMith," or "smith." Most programs will tell you whether or not they are case-sensitive, or give you an option one way or the other.

CD-ROM   See *Compact-Disc Read-Only Memory*.

central processing unit (CPU)   See *microprocessor*.

CGM   See *Computer Graphics Metafile*.

channel   Much like the channels on a television, areas in Internet Relay Chat (IRC) or the online services for specific topics or people of like interests. See *Internet Relay Chat*.

characters per second (cps)   Another type of measurement of modem or data transfer speed. More specifically, the amount of effective throughput, or meaningful information that's transferred. See *bits per second*.

chat   One of the most popular uses of online services and BBSes is chatting, or conversing (through typing) with other people who are online when you are. They see your comments immediately.

CIS   See *CompuServe Information Service*.

Class 1, Class 2   Standards rating the type of modem you have. Class 2 modems tend to do more of the work that the computer used to do, making the communication process faster and more efficient. If you also see Group 3, it means the modem has fax capabilities.

client   A program or computer that seeks files or information from another program or computer (called the server). Also, a user on the network. See *file*.

client/server   A method of networking wherein the processing of a given application is shared between a client's PC and a central server.

clip art   Electronic artwork you can use in most documents and graphics files. You will find lots of clip art available online for downloading.

Clipboard   A special Windows file that lets you temporarily store text or graphics for use elsewhere. If you cut or copy data, the data is stored in the Clipboard, enabling you to paste it somewhere else in that or another document. If you later cut or copy different data, it replaces the contents of the Clipboard.

CMOS   See *Complementary Metal-Oxide Semiconductor*.

coax   Also known as *coaxial cable*, a solid wire surrounded by insulation and wrapped in conductive metal mesh. Due to its flexibility and adaptability, it is a favored cable for networking.

collision   A network disruption caused by two messages corrupting each other.

COM port Abbreviation for *communications port.* Your computer's COM ports are serial ports. These are the things at the back of your computer you connect your modem or phone line to.

command Tells your computer what to do, such as "print this document," or "quit this program."

command line The place where you type in commands on your computer. In a DOS window, for example, the command line starts at the c:> prompt (or something similar). In Windows 95, the command line is Start, Run.

Compact-Disc Read-Only Memory (CD-ROM) Pronounced see-dee-RAHM. A CD-ROM looks identical to the CDs you play on your stereo system, but is used to hold computer files instead of music. Most CD-ROMs can store up to 600M of data. Most CD-ROM drives can also read and play music (audio) CDs.

Complementary Metal-Oxide Semiconductor (CMOS) Pronounced SEE-moss. The CMOS is a battery-operated memory chip in your computer that feeds basic information about the system to the microprocessor during boot up.

compression program Programs that squeeze the data in a file down to a smaller size to save space or shorten transfer time. For Windows and DOS, PKZIP is the most common; for Macintosh, StuffIt and CompactPro are the most popular. They are always accompanied by a decompression program, which you use to blow the file back up again. Because most files you'll find online are compressed archives, you'll usually need a copy of the program to decompress the file before you can read or work with it. See *archive, file compression, PKZIP, self-extracting archive, StuffIt, .ZIP.*

CompuServe Information Service (CIS) A popular commercial online service for e-mail, file downloading, chatting, business and technical discussions, and Internet access. CompuServe is especially popular for business users. See *America Online, Prodigy.*

Computer Graphics Metafile (CGM) A graphics file format that can be read by a variety of graphics programs.

conferencing Similar to chatting, but usually a more sophisticated or organized effort. Most of the commercial services offer conferences, where members meet online at a specified time to discuss a specific issue or chat with a special guest. See *chat.*

CONFIG.SYS A file your computer reads when you boot or reboot the system. CONFIG.SYS contains specific details about your hardware and software that are needed to get the computer up and running properly. This file can be altered with a text editor, but don't change it unless you know what you are doing.

cps See *characters per second.*

CPU (Central Processing Unit) See *microprocessor.*

cursor A horizontal or vertical line or box, sometimes flashing, that appears next to or below characters on the screen. The cursor indicates the insertion point—whatever you type next appears at the cursor.

cyberspace   Generally refers to the entire online computing world, especially the Internet. See *Internet, surfing*.

D

D connector   A multiple-pin connector that has a D-shaped shell encompassing the pins. RS-232C serial connections commonly use a 25-pin D connector.

daisy chain   A physical topology for connecting workstations to a network.

data   Any type of information stored or processed by a computer.

database   A collection of information organized so that the data can easily be searched, sorted, printed, or organized. Information from your address book or video collection might best be contained in a database, for example.

database program   A computer application designed to create or process databases. Popular database programs include Access, Paradox, dBASE, FileMaker Pro, and others.

decryption   Returning an encrypted file to a readable state. See *encryption*.

default   The settings or instructions a computer or computer program automatically uses if no others are specified.

demo   A sample program designed (usually as a sales/marketing tool) to give the user an overview of the software's capabilities and features. To protect the manufacturer, a demo program usually lacks the capability to perform certain vital functions such as printing or saving. See *shareware*.

demodulation   The second part of modulation/demodulation (upon which the term *modem* was derived). This is what the receiving computer does to the signal it receives over a modem so it can read the information. It translates the incoming signal into something the computer can understand.

density   The amount of data storage space, in square inches, available on a disk. The greater the density, the more space available. A high-density floppy disk, for example, can store more data than a low-density or double-density floppy disk.

desktop   In Windows 95, the main screen. When you start your computer, Windows 95 takes you to the desktop from which you can launch programs or do other work.

desktop computer   A computer that is designed to literally sit on a desktop. The term generally refers to a system unit (case) that is long and wide, as opposed to a tower, which is tall and narrow. Compare also to a laptop computer, which is portable.

desktop publishing (DTP) program   An application that lets you use text and graphics to create professional-looking documents such as resumes, newsletters, and business cards. Popular programs include Adobe PageMaker, QuarkXPress, and Microsoft Publisher.

dialog box   Part of a graphical user interface (GUI), a dialog box allows you to send commands to the computer or program by choosing certain options, entering specific information, and otherwise "conversing" with the computer. When you're finished working with the dialog box, you usually click OK or press the Enter key to issue the command.

directory   An area on the system for storing files. Using directories to organize your data is a very good idea, just like it's a good idea to use filing cabinets to organize your paper files. Each directory is like a drawer in the filing cabinet. You can also create subdirectories to further divide and organize your data. In Windows 95 and Windows NT, directories are called folders. In network terminology, the term refers to next level of division beneath a volume. Volumes are broken into directories, which are then divided into subdirectories.

disk   A device used to store data, based on electromagnetics. Disks come in various sizes and formats, from floppy disks that hold a few kilobytes of data to large hard disks that store several gigabytes of data.

disk drive   A device that reads and writes data to and from a disk. A disk is useless without a disk drive, just like an audio CD is useless without a CD player.

disk duplexing   The action of storing the same information on separate disks, with a controller card for each. When the primary system fails, the secondary system comes into action without interrupting processing.

disk mirroring   The action of storing the same information on the same controller (but separate disks). If the disk fails, the secondary disk comes into action without interrupting processing. If the controller fails, however, then the system is completely down. Therefore, duplexing is a superior fail-safe to mirroring.

display   See *monitor*.

DMA (Direct Memory Access)   One method by which NIC cards communicate between workstations and the network.

DNS   See *Domain Name Service*.

domain   The part of an Internet address (node name) that designates who the address belongs to or, if not a U.S. address, the country of origin. In the address **que.mcp.com**, the com domain means that the address belongs to a commercial organization (in this case, Macmillan Computer Publishing).

Common domain indicators include:

.com	Commercial
.org	Usually a nonprofit organization
.mil	Military
.gov	Government
.net	Network
.edu	Educational institution

Because the Internet was developed in the U.S., foreign addresses usually carry a domain name designating their country, as in .uk for the United Kingdom or .de for Germany.

Domain Name Service (DNS)   The naming system used to assign plain-name Internet addresses to computers. Computers read a numeric address (the IP address) such as **198.137.240.100**, but the DNS allows humans to use the more memorable address **whitehouse.gov**. Both addresses link to the same site. See *Internet Protocol*.

DOS (Disk Operating System)   Usually in reference to MS-DOS, a Microsoft product. MS-DOS is the master control program for the majority of personal computers in the world.

dot   Nickname for a period (.), especially when said aloud as part of a file name, Internet URL, or e-mail address. Example: "My e-mail address is wagner at who dot net" (**wagner@who.net**).

download   What you do when you copy or transfer a file from another computer to yours over a modem. See *file transfer protocol*.

drawing program   A program that enables you to render from scratch a drawing or piece of artwork. The most popular commercial drawing program is arguably CorelDRAW!, a robust application that includes sophisticated special effects capabilities. For the less ambitious, a basic drawing program called Paint comes free with Windows 95.

driver   A file your computer needs to understand and work with your hardware devices, something like a German/English translation dictionary. It's generally not something you need to mess with; it usually installs automatically when you install your software.

E

EISA bus   See *bus*.

electronic mail (e-mail)   Messages sent and received over a network or between networks through a modem or other type of link. Although e-mail is like a postal letter from one person to another person, or one person to a few other people, the term is often used loosely when referring to public areas of online services.

encryption   The process of converting data to a non-human readable form so that it can only be read by people who can decipher or decrypt it on the other end.

Ethernet   The original network standard from which the IEEE 802.3 protocol standard developed.

executable file   A file containing vital information to run a program. A program may consist of a single executable file, or the executable file may be just one of many files needed to run a large, robust application. Most executable files have the extension .exe, .com, or .bat.

expansion slot   An expandable computer system can be upgraded to newer or more powerful parts, such as a larger disk drive (providing more capacity for storage) or more memory. The more expansion slots your system has, the more flexible it will be when you want to upgrade it in the future. Expansion slots can be used to add sound cards, internal modems, SCSI adapters, and more.

Explorer   A program that comes with Windows 95 that helps you view and manage your files.

extension   See *filename extension*.

external disk drive   A hard disk drive that is not inside the system unit case. Often added to the system as a peripheral device at a later time. See *disk drive*.

F

FAQ (Frequently Asked Questions)   Pronounced fack. A file found in most newsgroups and online service forums to help you familiarize yourself with the area, how it works, and the general "rules of the road." Always read the FAQ before you jump in head first to a newsgroup. Otherwise, you'll be an easy target for flaming. See *flame, newsgroup*.

fault   An error in transmission.

fault tolerance   The ability to use redundancy to reduce the number of faults.

fax/data modem   A modem that works as both a fax machine and a regular data modem. Usually just called a faxmodem.

fiber optics   A type of telephone line made of thin glass fibers that is especially well-suited for long-distance data transmission.

file   A collection of data stored on the computer as one unit. Most files are measured in bytes or (more often) kilobytes, but some files—especially graphics or video files—may be dozens or hundreds of megabytes in size.

file server   A computer attached to a local area network (LAN) that stores the files used by all the computers on the network. See *local area network*.

file transfer protocol (FTP)   A standard for sending and receiving files over phone lines. Generally, file transfer protocols include ZMODEM, XMODEM, Kermit, and others (ZMODEM is the best of these). Both your modem and the computer you're calling must support the same protocol; check your modem's software manual for available protocols.

filename extension   The three characters that follow the period in a DOS-based file name. The extension often gives you a clue as to what type of file it is. For example, the file name MYFILE.DOC is likely to be a word processing file; CONFIG.SYS is an important system file you shouldn't mess with unless you know what you're doing. In Windows 95, extensions are usually hidden, but they still exist.

firewall   Term for a device or setting that helps deter outsiders from accessing your Internet server, or to prevent users from accessing the Internet from your LAN.

flame   An insult, terse remark, or other derogatory message sent via e-mail, usually as a result of asking dumb questions or questions you could have learned from the FAQ. Also sent in response to controversial or insulting remarks. See *FAQ*.

Part
VII

Ch
28

floppy disk A small, removable disk used to store data. Older floppy disks were 5 1/4-inch square, very thin, and very delicate (hence the name floppy). The standard today is the 3 1/2-inch floppy disk, which comes in a thicker plastic case with a sliding metal door. The smaller disks are not only less vulnerable to damage, but also more convenient to handle and store.

flow control The method computers use to process incoming data. Hardware flow control is faster and more efficient; use it if you can. Software flow control (usually a setting called Xon/Xoff) is the other method, but only works at modem speeds up to 2,400 bps.

folder See *directory*.

footprint The amount of space a system or peripheral takes up on a desktop. A device with a small footprint is desirable if you don't have a lot of room to work with.

foreground task In multitask computing, the high-priority task in which the computer and computer user are actively engaged; the task that takes priority status over lower-level background tasks. See also *background task, multitasking*.

forum An area of an online service or BBS where people of like interests can chat, post messages and files, and otherwise share information. Also called SIG (derived from the term *special interest group*).

freeware Copyrighted software that is available to the general public for personal use at no charge. Freeware usually starts as a program, game, or utility program the creator wrote for his or her own purpose. With freeware, you can't alter the original program, while with public domain software you can. See *public domain software*.

FTP See *file transfer protocol*. FTP refers to two other things: a program you use to transfer files to and from the Internet, and the specific UNIX protocol used on the Internet for transmitting data. See *FTP server*.

FTP server A computer dedicated to storing files that Internet users can download. See *file transfer protocol*.

G

G See *gigabyte*.

gateway A hardware device or software program that connects non-compatible networks so that users can share files or e-mail between the networks. For example, CompuServe offers a mail gateway to the Internet so that CompuServe users can exchange e-mail with non-CompuServe Internet users. In networking, a router devoted to a single task, very often the action of moving electronic mail from one network to another.

GIF See *Graphics Interchange Format*.

gigabyte (G) A measurement of capacity. One gigabyte equals 1,000 megabytes, or 1,073,741,824 bytes.

Gopher A program developed by the University of Minnesota that helps you locate and retrieve files on Internet servers. Ironically, this program "goes fer" files, and the U of M mascot just happens to be a gopher.

graphical user interface (GUI) Pronounced gooey. The "face" a program presents on the screen to the user. A GUI used by Windows and Macintosh programs, for example, features pictures, icons, menus, and so on. GUIs tend to be more user-friendly and easy to use than cold, unfriendly, command-line interfaces (such as the DOS command lines), which usually look something like this:

```
C:>
```

See also *icon*.

Graphics Interchange Format (GIF) Pronounced giff. A type of computer graphics file developed by CompuServe, Inc. that can be read by many different types of computers.

graphics program An application designed to create, edit, and otherwise manipulate graphics files such as photographs or clip art files for use with desktop publishing programs, World Wide Web pages, and other purposes. Popular programs include Adobe Photoshop, Microsoft Image Composer, and JASC, Inc.'s PaintShop Pro.

GUI See *graphical user interface*.

guru Nickname for an expert in his or her field of computing.

H

hacker This used to refer to an exceptionally skilled person, but has evolved to generally mean a computer expert who attempts to break into networks or servers without authorization by decrypting user IDs or passwords, or other methods. Most states have laws against computer hacking.

hard disk A large electromagnetic disk used to store data. Most hard disks reside inside the computer and generally store large quantities of data, including the operating system and your application programs. Some hard disks reside in a removable disk drive, such as Iomega's Jaz drive, and can be used in more than one computer, much like a floppy disk.

home page A document or page on the World Wide Web that is dedicated to a particular subject. It usually contains hyperlinks to related pages. You can use a home page you've designed yourself, or use one owned by another person or organization. See *hyperlink, HyperText Markup Language, World Wide Web*.

host The computer you call and connect to using a modem. The host is usually a file server of some kind. See *file server*.

hot fix A method by which NetWare performs fault tolerance. If it fails to write the contents of memory to a block, it moves the memory contents to another storage area on the disk set aside for just such an occurrence. It then remembers the address of the original block and marks it in memory as being bad.

Part
VII
Ch
28

HTML See *HyperText Markup Language.*

HTTP See *HyperText Transport Protocol.*

hub A centralized hardware component that repeats data signals sent on the network. These can also be used as bridges and routers, and are also known as *repeaters.*

hyperlink An active link to another document, or to another location in the same document. Usually, you simply click a word to jump to the linked document. Also called a hypertext link or an anchor. See also *hypertext.*

hypertext A technology used to add links to other documents. Usually, you simply click a word to jump to the linked document. World Wide Web browser programs as well as Windows and Mac help files all use hypertext extensively. See *hyperlink.*

HyperText Markup Language (HTML) The language used to create links to other Internet sites on World Wide Web browser pages. See *hypertext, World Wide Web.*

HyperText Transport Protocol (HTTP) The World Wide Web's communications protocol. Almost all Internet URLs begin with **http://**. See *hypertext, protocol, World Wide Web.*

I

icon A small picture that appears on your desktop or program screen; you click an icon to activate a program or send a command to your computer.

IEEE (Institute of Electrical and Electronics Engineers) Authors of several networking standards, primarily those used in token-ring networks.

IMAP See *Interactive Mail Access Protocol.*

impedance The amount of resistance, usually measured in ohms, that cable is providing to the transmission it is carrying.

insertion point See *cursor.*

Integrated Services Digital Network (ISDN) A very expensive special phone line that supports very high-speed digital modems (up to 64Kbps), which are faster than the common analog modems most people have. Also, the standard for all digital communications networks, whether they carry data, video, or any other digital messages.

Interactive Mail Access Protocol (IMAP) Pronounced EYE-map. A newly emerging electronic mail storage and retrieval protocol.

internal disk drive A hard disk drive that is always inside the system unit case. See *disk drive, hard disk.*

Internet Simply put, a network of networks. Networks owned and operated by companies, universities, government agencies, and others are all linked together via phone lines, satellite links, and other methods. The Internet of today is an outgrowth of a U.S. Department of Defense system known as ARPAnet. See *network.*

Internet Explorer   A popular Web browser made by Microsoft. See *Web browser.*

Internet protocol (IP)   The main data transmission protocol used by Internet computers.

Internet Relay Chat (IRC)   A global network service specifically designed for real-time chatting. See *chat, real-time.*

interrupt   A signal to suspend a program temporarily while another job runs. When that jobs finishes, the first job continues processing from the point that it left off.

interrupt request line (IRQ)   In layman's terms, the path a peripheral device (like a modem, a mouse, or a printer) uses to send a message to the computer to get its attention. The important thing to know here is that two devices cannot share an IRQ, or neither one of them will work.

IP   See *Internet protocol.*

IP address   Internet protocol address. The four-part numeric address, such as **123.45. 678.90**, that identifies a specific Internet site, much like a phone number, and connects to only one location. Rather than try to remember these long numbers, most people use the more useful plain-name address, such as **que.mcp.com**. See *Domain Name Service.*

IPX (Internetwork Packet eXchange)   A protocol that sends packets to requested destinations on the network.

IRC   See *Internet Relay Chat.*

IRQ   See *interrupt request line.*

ISA bus   See *bus.*

ISDN   See *Integrated Services Digital Network.*

ISO (International Standardization Organization)   The originators of the OSI network protocol model that is widely accepted today.

J

Joint Photographic Experts Group (JPEG)   A file compression technique used specifically for some graphics files. It removes certain "unimportant" parts of the graphic file's data in order to compress the file to a fraction of its original size without much noticeable loss in image quality.

joystick   An input device used as an alternative to a keyboard or mouse, mpss often used for games.

JPEG   See *Joint Photographic Experts Group.*

Part
VII

Ch
28

K

K   See *kilobyte*.

keyboard   The primary input device you use to send commands to your computer. Although various configurations are available, by far the most popular is the QWERTY configuration which, like a typewriter keyboard, is so designated by the first six keys on the left side of the top row. When you press a key, a signal is sent to the computer, which in turn displays a character on the screen. May applications take advantage of special keys not found on a typewriter, such as Ctrl, Alt, and function keys such as F1, F2, and so on. Each program uses these special keys for different purposes.

kilobyte (K)   A unit of measurement, usually in relation to memory or disk capacity. One kilobyte equals 1,024 bytes.

L

LAN   See *local area network*.

laptop computer   A small, portable computer that literally fits in your lap. Laptop computers generally cost $1,000 or so more than a desktop computer of equal power. Also called a notebook computer, because many are about the size of a notebook and easily fit in a briefcase.

legacy device   An older hardware device that does not support Windows 95's Plug and Play specifications. See *Plug and Play*.

LISTSERV   A software program from LSoft, Inc., that manages Internet mailing lists. Also used to generically refer to any mailing list. See *mailing list*.

local   Your computer, as opposed to a network server or an Internet or network host.

local area network (LAN)   A group of computers, usually in close proximity to one another (such as within the same building) connected by cables. LANs are usually controlled by special software such as NetWare or Windows NT. Compare to *wide area network*.

logical drive   See *partition*.

lurk   To sit back and watch the action in a forum or newsgroup without participating. Lurking is not necessarily a bad thing; in fact, it is highly recommended for newbies. See *newbie*, *newsgroup*.

M

M   See *megabyte*.

MAC (Media Access Control)   The rules that LANs use to avoid data collisions. These rules may be the type used in token ring or CMSA (Carrier Sense Multiple Access).

macro   A program of recorded instructions, usually used to automate frequently performed or complex tasks. You might record a macro, for example, to add the return address, salutation, closing, and signature lines of a letter, because this information is almost always the same.

mailing list   A list of users or subscribers who automatically receive postings from newsgroups. See *newsgroup, UseNet.*

megabyte   Roughly 1 million bytes. Usually abbreviated M, sometimes referred to as a "meg." Because they're usually pretty substantial, the amount of space software programs take up on your hard drive is usually measured in megabytes. It sounds less painful that way: Would you rather have a program use a trim 4M of disk space, or hog up a whopping 4,194,304 bytes of that precious real estate? (This term was obviously conceived by someone in marketing.) See *byte.*

memory   An area inside the computer used to temporarily store data or instructions while the computer is using them. Memory is generally referred to as RAM, or random-access memory. When you shut down your computer, the memory is cleared and anything that was not saved to disk is lost.

menu   An organized presentation of available commands. Much like a restaurant menu, you choose which command you want, and the computer proceeds with the operation. Menus make it much easier to use a computer because you don't have to remember the name of every command and type it in each time you want to use it.

MHz (megahertz)   A unit of measurement equal to one million electrical vibrations or cycles per second; commonly used to compare the clock speeds of computers.

microprocessor   Also called the central processing unit (CPU), the microprocessor chip is the real brain of the computer, where all information is processed and calculations performed.

Microsoft Exchange   A program that helps you send, receive, and organize your e-mail, faxes, and other things you've sent or received using your modem. The client-side version is included in Windows 95. The server-side version runs on network servers. In later versions of Windows 95, it is also called Windows Messaging.

Microsoft Fax   A program included with Windows 95 you can use to send and receive faxes.

The Microsoft Network (MSN)   A commercial online service from the software giant. See *America Online, CompuServe Information Services, Prodigy.*

MIME   See *Multipurpose Internet Mail Extensions.*

mirroring   See *disk mirroring.*

MMX   Intel's successor to the Pentium microprocessor chip. MMX (which stands for *MultiMedia eXtensions*), though not limited to multimedia, give the microprocessor additional capabilities that speed graphics, sound, animation, and 3-D rendering. MMX uses a technique called single instruction, multiple data (SIMD); this technology allows the CPU to perform one calculation simultaneously on two, four, or even eight data elements without any decrease in speed.

modem The device you use to connect your computer to cyberspace via telephone lines. The word modem is derived from modulator/demodulator. See *cyberspace, demodulation, modulation*.

modulation The first part of modulation/demodulation (upon which the term modem was derived). This is what the sending computer does to the signal it sends over a modem so it can be read by the receiving computer.

monitor The TV-like screen attached to your computer that displays your work.

Motion Picture Experts Group (MPEG) Also called Motion JPEG. A data compression technique used to reduce the size of video files, much like JPEG works for graphics files. See *Joint Photographic Experts Group*.

mouse A hand-held input device, used primarily with GUIs, that make it easier to work with menus, dialog boxes, and so on. As you push the mouse across your desktop, a small ball bearing inside the mouse sends a signal to the computer to move the pointer (also called a cursor) across the screen.

MPEG See *Motion Picture Experts Group*.

multimedia The combination of graphics images, audio, and moving video in a computer presentation.

Multipurpose Internet Mail Extensions (MIME) One type of format the Internet uses to process non-text files, such as graphics or binary files, that are attached to e-mail messages. See *binary file*.

multitasking Windows 95 is a multitasking operating system, meaning that you can run more than one application at a time. Older operating systems, such as MS-DOS, were not capable of multitasking.

N

netiquette The Ps and Qs of the cyberworld. If you aren't a responsible Net citizen and don't practice proper netiquette, you're likely to get flamed a lot. For example, DON'T TYPE IN ALL CAPITAL LETTERS, as this is considered SHOUTING and is very RUDE! See *flame*.

Netscape A popular Web browser. Netscape Navigator is the full name of the product (or for the newest release, Netscape Communicator). See *Web browser*.

NetWare A brand of network operating system used to link computers together in a local area network. See *local area network*.

network A collection of hardware and software working together to enable the sharing of computers, files, printers, and other resources.

network interface cards (NIC)   Provide the physical connection between each workstation and the network cable. All communication between the server and every workstation is carried across the cable and into every NIC. It is the responsibility of the card to determine if the packet is intended for the workstation and continue processing, or ignore it.

network operating system (NOS)   The master control program that enables computers to work together on a network. NetWare and Windows NT are the most popular, but there's also Banyan VINES, LANtastic, and many others. Also, the shell that surrounds the Command.Com file and receives network commands before they pass through to DOS or another operating system.

newsgroup   A group of like-minded users who use the Internet to share information, discuss topics, and find camaraderie. See *forum*, *UseNet*.

newsreader   A software program that enables you to read, file, and otherwise work with newsgroup postings. See *newsgroup*.

NIC   See *network interface cards*.

node address   A unique number that identifies each network board on a network. Every station must contain at least one unique node number to distinguish it from the other workstations.

NOS   See *network operating system*.

notebook computer   See *laptop computer*.

Notepad   A no-frills Windows text editor used primarily to write and edit programming code.

O

OCR   See *optical character recognition*.

offline   When you are offline, you are not connected to any other computers or networks.

online   If your computer is communicating with another computer via a modem, you're online.

online service   Companies that provide users with news, information, and other types of services such as e-mail. Almost all of these are commercial services, so there is usually a fee. CompuServe, MSN, and AOL are among the most popular online services in the U.S.

operating system   The master control program that allows your computer to work with itself and other programs. Think of it as the language the computer speaks. There are many flavors of operating systems, including MS-DOS, Windows, Macintosh, UNIX, and so on.

optical character recognition (OCR)   Software that enables your computer to read a document that has been faxed or scanned in and convert it to a text file that you can later edit. It's really handy if you don't want to retype the information you already have on hard copy. Many of the better fax/modem software programs such as Delrina WinFax Pro include OCR capability.

Part VII
Ch
28

P

page   A location on the World Wide Web that contains information. A Web page usually contains hyperlinks to other pages. To go directly to a specific page, you can type in its URL address.

parallel port   Connections on your computer you use to hook up certain devices, the most common of which are printers. Parallel ports are usually identified as LPT1, LPT2, and so on.

partition   Hard disks can be partitioned into smaller sections, or partitions, to help you better organize your data, or to enable you to use more than one operating system on the same computer (but not at the same time). A partition is also called a logical drive. My hard drive, for example, is partitioned into logical drives; drive C contains the Windows 95 operating system, drive D contains the Windows NT operating system, drive E is used to store my applications, and drive F holds all my data files such as word processing documents and spreadsheets.

path   The map or route to a particular file or program, starting at the root directory and working down through any subdirectories to the actual file name itself. The path to run Microsoft Word, for example, might be C:\OFFICE97\WINWORD\WINWORD.EXE.

PCI bus   See *bus*.

Pentium   The Intel microprocessor that, with more than three million transistors, has twice the processing speed of its predecessor, the 486 DX2. The gains were made possible by a design that allows the microprocessor to carry out two instructions simultaneously. The MMX chip is the successor to the Pentium chip.

peripheral device   Any piece of equipment attached to your computer that is not part of the main system. Printers, scanners, and removable storage devices are generally considered peripherals, while keyboards and monitors are not.

Personal Information Manager program (PIM)   A program used to manage information such as appointments, addresses, and other personal information. Popular applications include Corel Sidekick, Lotus Organizer, and Microsoft Outlook.

pixel   The smallest unit of measurement relating to a computer monitor or screen. A pixel (short for "picture element") equals one screen dot. The number of pixels that appear on a screen is called the screen resolution.

PKZIP   A popular file compression utility for DOS-based computers. You should have the PKZIP utility collection if you plan to upload or download files (it also comes with PKUNZIP, which you use to decompress files that have already been compressed). See *file compression*.

Plug and Play   A specification supported by Windows 95 that makes it easy to install new hardware. What this means to most people is that they no longer have to worry about all those technical details like IRQs and ports. Windows 95 does everything behind the scenes, and just lets you get to work. Devices that aren't Plug and Play compatible are called legacy devices because they were around before the release of Windows 95.

Point-to-Point Protocol (PPP) A type of Internet connection you might have if you use an Internet service provider rather than, say, your office LAN's Internet connection. PPP and SLIP connections allow your computer to act like a full-fledged Internet site. See *Serial Line Internet Protocol*.

port The place(s) in the back of your computer where you plug in external devices, such as modems and printers.

PPP See *Point-to-Point Protocol*.

presentation program An application used for creating slide shows and business presentations, usually combining graphics and text to convey information or entertain viewers. Popular presentation programs include Microsoft PowerPoint, Corel Presentations, and Lotus Freelance Graphics.

printer A peripheral device attached to your computer that is used to transfer the contents of data files onto paper or hard copy. There are various types of printers; the most popular among typical consumers are the laser, bubble-jet, and inkjet.

Prodigy A popular commercial online service offering news, weather, special interest topics, e-mail, and more. See *America Online, CompuServe Information Services, The Microsoft Network*.

program A collection of instructions and commands (often spread across multiple files) that tells the computer what to do. Word processors, games, and databases are all types of programs.

protocol A set of standards, such as those used by two computers to communicate with each other. See *file transfer protocol*.

public domain software Software you can use, modify, or distribute without charge. Similar to freeware, but not copyrighted. See *freeware, shareware*.

Q

question mark (?) A wildcard character generally used to take the place of one specific character. See *asterisk, wildcard*.

R

random-access memory (RAM) Temporary memory your computer uses to store the data it is currently using. The more RAM you have (measured in megabytes), the more powerful and productive your computer is. Windows 95 requires no less than 4M of RAM to run, but you'll likely find it much more satisfying with no less than 8M or 16M of RAM. Very expensive computers can use hundreds of megabytes of RAM.

Part
VII

Ch
28

read-only memory (ROM)   As opposed to RAM, this type of memory is not erased when the computer is shut down. Essential system programs that neither you nor the computer can erase are stored in ROM.

README file   As its name implies, usually contains important information about the program it accompanies. You will almost always find a README file on the first disk of a software program. Always read the README file before you install the software, for it might contain instructions or last-minute information that was written too late to go in the user manual (if there is one).

remote control software   Software you can use to control your computer and all its files from a different location. This is especially handy for people who work both at an office and from their home.

removable disk drive, removable storage device   A hard disk drive, tape drive, or other device intended for mass storage, but removable and transportable between more than one computer. Devices such as SyQuest drives (44M and higher capacities) and Iomega's Zip drive (100M capacity) and Jaz drive (1G capacity) have become increasingly popular as the demand for larger and more flexible storage capabilities grows. Tape drives are also considered in this category, but are mostly used only for system backups because they are not as fast, flexible, or convenient to use.

resolution   Collectively, the number of pixels displayed on the monitor's screen. Most monitors run at 640×480 pixels resolution (meaning 640 dots across and 480 dots down the screen) or 800×600. Newer computers, however, usually allow you to select a variety of settings, as much as 1,280×1,024 pixels or higher. Higher resolutions offer crisper, clearer displays, but everything also appears smaller. (The more pixels that fit on the same size screen, the smaller each individual dot has to be.) Your available resolutions depend on the size of your monitor and the type of video adapter card you have inside your computer. See *pixel*.

RJ-11   Standard telephone line cable connector—the familiar clear plastic clip. Virtually all modern modems use RJ-11 cable connections.

ROM   See *read-only memory*.

RS-232   An RS-232 cable is the common cable you use to connect external serial devices, like modems and scanners, to your computer.

S

scanner   A peripheral device used to digitize (convert to electronic format) artwork, photographs, or other items from hard copy. A scanner works very much like a photocopy machine: You place the hard copy on or into the scanner, and the scanner reads the material and converts it to a data file. From there, you can use or manipulate the file like you would any other data file. Using technology called optical character recognition (OCR), scanners can also be used to convert hard copy text to a text file, saving hours of retyping. See *optical character recognition*.

SCSI See *Small Computer System Interface*.

self-extracting archive (SEA) A compressed file that is designed to automatically decompress itself when executed or started. Depending on which utility was used to compress the file, the SEA may have an extension like .SEA, .BAT, or .EXE (although other programs use these extensions as well, so don't assume that's what it is).

Serial Line Internet Protocol (SLIP) A protocol used to connect a computer to the Internet, generally over a telephone line. SLIP connections are generally being phased out in favor of PPP.

shareware Copyrighted software programs that you are welcome to try out for a certain period of time, then send the creator or distributor a fee if you plan to continue using the program, usually in exchange for future updates and upgrades to the program. Most shareware programs suggest a 15–45 day trial period before you send in your registration fee or erase it from your computer. See *demo, freeware, public domain software*.

site The location of a host computer hooked up to the Internet.

SLIP See *Serial Line Internet Protocol*.

Small Computer System Interface (SCSI) Pronounced scuzzy. A special type of interface or connection used on peripheral devices (and some internal devices). You can connect as many as seven SCSI devices to the same SCSI port with no loss of performance among any of them. Common devices that use SCSI technology (or work better if they are designed for SCSI) include scanners, CD-ROM drives, printers, removable storage devices, and even hard disk drives.

snail mail The good old U.S. Postal Service and its international counterparts; so nicknamed due to the relative speed of Internet e-mail.

sneakernet Before the days of high-speed modems and world-wide networks, the file transfer process was this: Users had to copy a disk to a file, walk down the hall, and hand the disk to the person who needed it (or mail it, if they were far away). That's sneakernet (assuming the person is wearing sneakers, of course).

sound card A PC board or adapter card inside your computer that gives your system the capability to reproduce sound digitally. The vast majority of sound cards are Sound Blaster-compatible, based on the early standards made popular by Creative Labs, Inc., the makers of Sound Blaster sound cards and related devices.

spreadsheet program A program that simulates an accountant's worksheet on-screen. A spreadsheet uses rows and columns (which are intersected at points called cells). You can create formulas to automatically do a wide variety of calculations, from simple row or column totals to complex amortization schedules or scientific equations. Most of the more popular spreadsheet programs (such as Microsoft Excel or Lotus 1-2-3) offer additional features, such as the capability to create stunning charts and data maps based on numbers and calculations taken directly from the spreadsheets.

Part
VII

Ch
28

subdirectory See *directory*.

surfing Generally refers to browsing, searching, or visiting a number of Internet (especially World Wide Web) sites in one session. See *browser, World Wide Web*.

surge protector A device that helps protect your computer (and anything else you plug into it) from power surges, which could seriously damage your computer. You really need one of these, especially if you live in an area prone to blackouts or brownouts. A surge protector also protects your modem line, and one that accepts both power cords and phone cords, is highly recommended.

T

T-1, T-3 Types of very high-speed connections used for the Internet and other hookups. Even a 56Kbps modem is slow in comparison. They are, of course, very expensive, and are mostly used only by big companies who can afford them.

tape The format most commonly used for creating and storing backups.

TAPI See *Telephony Applications Programming Interface*.

TCP/IP (Transport Control Protocol and Internet Protocol) A set of standards that form the basis of most network and Internet functions.

Telephony Applications Programming Interface (TAPI) Pronounced TAP-ee. A program interface that allows modems and programs to work together without having to deal with the modem hardware or your actual telephone. TAPI is like having your own personal translator for every step of your trip to Paris instead of carrying around a French/English dictionary everywhere you go.

Telnet An Internet program that allows you to log in to remote computers connected to the Internet.

text editor A program you use to create or change computer files, usually text files. Notepad is a typical example of a Windows-based text editor. Because they are primarily designed for writing computer programs, text editors generally do not have a lot of the special features (for text formatting, and so on) you find in word processors such as WordPerfect.

text file Generally, the same thing as an ASCII file and the opposite of a binary file. You can read a text file without any special decoders or translators. See *ASCII, binary file*.

tower computer As opposed to a desktop computer, which is generally wider than it is tall, a tower computer stands vertically on the floor or desktop. Although the two function identically, tower computers are more popular among computer experts because they are easier to work on internally—devices tend to be stacked on top of each other rather than side by side, allowing more room for fingers and tools to move around. Tower computers are also popular because they can be placed on the floor, leaving more room on the desktop.

U

UART   See *Universal Asynchronous Receiver/Transmitter*.

Uniform Resource Locator (URL)   Pronounced earl. The means of addressing sites and pages on the World Wide Web, like the street address for your house. A URL usually looks something like this:

> **http://www.mcp.com**

Universal Asynchronous Receiver/ Transmitter (UART)   Pronounced YOU-art. The integrated circuit that translates data between serial and parallel form. The data is in serial format when it is sent through the phone lines; it is in parallel format inside the computer.

UNIX   The operating system used by many Internet hosts.

upload   To upload is to transmit a file to a server or host. Compare to *download*.

URL   See *Uniform Resource Locator*.

UseNet   A service, accessed over the Internet, that is dedicated to supporting the thousands of special interest groups (newsgroups). See *forum, newsgroup, SIG*.

user ID   Your specific account name for accessing a network or Internet account, usually an assigned number (like **74404,3307**) or a derivative of your actual name, such as **lwagner** or **balucas**. In the real world, this equates to the street address for your house. Also called user name.

user group   A group of people who share the same interests in a particular software application, computer type, and so on. Most cities have a variety of user groups. They may focus on a particular application such as Adobe PageMaker, or a type of computer-related activity such as desktop publishing. User groups are a great source for networking with others, getting free software, and learning more about using your computer. Check with your local computer stores or the newspaper local events section to find them in your area.

user name   See *user ID*.

V

virus   A computer program written specifically to cause serious damage or mischief to computer files or data. A virus can replicate itself and attach itself to other programs, thus it is easy for viruses to spread very quickly, especially within an office environment where files and disks are regularly shared. Viruses are known to sneak in on files you download from BBSes or the Internet, although most places are pretty good about scanning for viruses before files are made available for downloading. Surprisingly, commercial software disks are the place you'll most likely pick up a virus (thanks to generous return policies and shrink-wrap machines hidden in the back room of the store). Also, beware of computer repair technicians, who go sticking their diagnostic disks into dozens of different computers all day, every day. To protect yourself from computer viruses, scan every single disk or file with an antivirus program before you use it. See *anti-virus program*.

Part

VII

Ch

28

W

WAIS   See *Wide Area Information Server*.

WAN   See *wide area network*.

WAV files   A file that contains a digitized sound. You can play a WAV file through Media Player or a similar program if you have a sound card and speakers.

Web browser   A program you use to view Web pages on the Internet's World Wide Web. See *browser*.

Wide Area Information Server (WAIS)   Pronounced ways. An Internet-connected network of full-text databases. You supply search criteria for WAIS to use to search all its databases for information.

wide area network (WAN)   A group of computers linked together by satellite signals or telecommunications and other links. WANs can connect computers that are thousands of miles apart, as opposed to LANs, which connect computers that are usually in close proximity to one another. See *local area network*.

wildcard   Special character that can be used to represent one or more characters, especially when searching directories or documents. They are named for the wildcards in games like poker, where one particular card can be used to represent any card the player chooses. The most common wildcards are * and ?. The * (asterisk) can take the place of one or more characters. If you are searching for all instances and forms of the word "compute," you could search for "compu*." This search might find "compute," "computer," "computing," "computed," and "CompuServe." The question mark (?) usually represents a single missing character. Searching for "?andy" would result in matches of "candy," "handy," and "Randy," but not "Andy" or "brandy."

Windows   A popular operating environment that features a friendly graphical user interface, from Microsoft Corporation. Windows is the dominant GUI on personal computers across the world. Windows 95 is the current version available, although older Windows 3.1 is also still very popular. See *graphical user interface*.

Windows Messaging   See *Microsoft Exchange*.

Windows NT   A popular network operating system from Microsoft Corporation.

WinZip   The Windows version of the popular compression program, PKZIP. See *PKZIP*, *file compression*.

word processor   A program used to enter, edit, format, print, and otherwise manipulate text. Microsoft Word, Corel WordPerfect, and Lotus WordPro are popular word processors. These programs also include a robust collection of related features such as mail-merge capabilities, desktop publishing features, and spelling and grammar checking.

World Wide Web (WWW)   The fastest growing part of the Internet, and the easiest to use. The Web is exactly that—an endless collection of images and sounds from thousands of different Web sites, all of which are linked together via hyperlinks. You can start on a home page for Indiana University and within minutes be looking at a home page on a computer in Bangladesh. See *hyperlink*, *HyperText Markup Language*.

write-protection   Disks can be write-protected, which prevents the data on them from being erased, modified, or overwritten. On 3 1/2-inch floppy disks, turn on write-protection simply by sliding the small switch on the back of the disk to the "open" position (so you can see through the little window behind the switch).

WWW   See *World Wide Web*.

X-Y-Z

.ZIP   File extension used to indicate a file that has been compressed using PKZIP. See *PKZIP*.

CHAPTER 29

Computer Company Listing

The following is an alphabetic list of the most popular computer hardware and software vendors and their Internet and FTP addresses. FTP sites are locations where you can find software, updates, and drivers; WWW sites are locations where basic company information can be found.

3Com

FTP Site: **ftp.3com.com**

WWW Site: **www.3com.com**

Accolade

FTP Site: **ftp.netcom.com**

WWW Site: **www.accolade.com**

Acer

FTP Site: **ftp.acer.com**

WWW Site: **www.acer.com**

Adaptec

FTP Site: **ftp.adaptec.com**

WWW Site: **www.adaptec.com**

Adobe

FTP Site: **ftp.adobe.com**

WWW Site: **www.adobe.com**

Advanced Micro Devices (AMD)

FTP Site: **ftp.amd.com**

WWW Site: **www.amd.com**

ALR

FTP Site: **ftp.alr.co**

WWW Site: **www.alr.com**

American Megatrends (AMI)

FTP Site: **ftp.megatrends.com**

WWW Site: **www.megatrends.com**

Apple

FTP Site: **ftp.austin.apple.com**

WWW Site: **www.apple.com**

Artisoft (Lantastic)

FTP Site: **ftp.artisoft.com**

WWW Site: **www.artisoft.com**

AST

FTP Site: **ftp.ast.com**

WWW Site: **www.ast.com**

ATI

FTP Site: **ftp.atitech.ca**

WWW Site: **www.atitech.ca**

Autodesk

FTP Site: **ftp.autodesk.com**

WWW Site: **www.autodesk.com**

Berkeley Systems

FTP Site: **ftp.berksys.com**

WWW Site: **www.berksys.com**

Blizzard Entertainment

FTP Site: **ftp.blizzard.com**

WWW Site: **www.blizzard.com**

Boca Research

FTP Site: **ftp.boca.org**

WWW Site: **www.bocaresearch.com**

Borland

FTP Site: **ftp.borland.com**

WWW Site: **www.borland.com**

CA-Associates

FTP Site: **mf.cai.com**

WWW Site: **www.cai.com**

Cirrus Logic

FTP Site: **ftp.cirrus.com**

WWW Site: **www.cirrus.com**

Cisco

FTP Site: **ftp.cisco.com**

WWW Site: **www.cisco.com**

Compaq

FTP Site: **ftp.compaq.com**

WWW Site: **www.compaq.com**

Conner

WWW Site: **www.conner.com**

Corel

FTP Site: **ftp.corel.com**

WWW Site: **www.corel.com**

Creative-Labs

FTP Site: **ftp.creaf.com**

WWW Site: **www.creaf.com**

Cyrix

FTP Site: **ftp.cyrix.com**

WWW Site: **www.cyrix.com**

D Link

FTP Site: **ftp.dlink.com**

WWW Site: **www.dlink.com**

Dell

FTP Site: **dell1.dell.com**

WWW Site: **www.dell.com**

Delrina

FTP Site: **ftp.symantec.com**

WWW Site: **www.delrina.com**

Diamond

FTP Site: **ftp.diamondmm.com**

WWW Site: **www.diamondmm.com**

Digital Equipment (DEC)

FTP Site: **ftp.digital.com**

WWW Site: **www.dec.com**

Electronic Arts

FTP Site: **ftp.ea.com**

WWW Site: **www.ea.com**

Epic MegaGames

FTP Site: **ftp.epicgames.com**

WWW Site: **www.epicgames.com**

Epson

FTP Site: **ftp.epson.com**

WWW Site: **www.epson.com**

Everex

FTP Site: **ftp.everex.com**

WWW Site: **www.everex.com**

Gateway 2000

FTP Site: **ftp.gw2k.com**

WWW Site: **www.gw2k.com**

Gravis

FTP Site: **advanced.gravis.com**

WWW Site: **www.gravis.com**

Hayes

FTP Site: **ftp.hayes.com**

WWW Site: **www.hayes.com**

Hercules

FTP Site: **ftp.hercules.com**

WWW Site: **www.hercules.com**

Hewlett-Packard

FTP Site: **ftp.hp.com**

WWW Site: **www.hp.com**

IBM Corporation

FTP Site: **ftp.austin.ibm.com**

WWW Site: **www.pc.ibm.com**

id Software

FTP Site: **ftp.idsoftware.com**

WWW Site: **www.idsoftware.com**

Intel

FTP Site: **ftp.intel.com**

WWW Site: **www.intel.com**

Interplay

FTP Site: **ftp.interplay.com**

WWW Site: **www.interplay.com**

Intuit

WWW Site: **www.intuit.com**

Iomega

FTP Site: **ftp.iomega.com**

WWW Site: **www.iomega.com**

Logitech

FTP Site: **ftp.logitech.com**

WWW Site: **www.logitech.com**

Lotus

FTP Site: **ftp.ccmail.com**

WWW Site: **www.lotus.com**

LucasArts

FTP Site: **ftp.lucasarts.com**

WWW Site: **www.lucasarts.com**

Macromedia

FTP Site: **ftp.macromedia.com**

WWW Site: **www.macromedia.com**

MAG Innovision

FTP Site: **ftp.maginnovision.com**

WWW Site: **www.maginnovision.com**

Matrox

FTP Site: **ftp.matrox.com**

WWW Site: **www.matrox.com**

Maxis

FTP Site: **ftp.maxis.com**

WWW Site: **www.maxis.com**

Maxtech

FTP Site: **ftp.maxtech.com**

WWW Site: **www.maxtech.com**

Maxtor

FTP Site: **ftp.maxtor.com**

WWW Site: **www.maxtor.com**

McAfee Associates

FTP Site: **ftp.mcafee.com**

WWW Site: **www.mcafee.com**

Micron

WWW Site: **www.mei.micron.com**

MicroProse

FTP Site: **ftp.microprose.com**

WWW Site: **www.microprose.com**

Microsoft

FTP Site: **ftp.microsoft.com**

WWW Site: **www.microsoft.com**

Mitsubishi

FTP Site: **www.mitsubishi.co.jp**

WWW Site: **www.mitsubishi.com**

NEC

FTP Site: **ftp.nec.com**

WWW Site: **www.nec.com**

Netscape

FTP Site: **ftp.netscape.com**

WWW Site: **www.netscape.com**

Nokia

FTP Site: **ftp.nokia.com**

WWW Site: **www.nokia.com**

Novell

FTP Site: **ftp.novell.com**

WWW Site: **www.novell.com**

Number Nine

FTP Site: **ftp.nine.com**

WWW Site: **www.nine.com**

Oracle

FTP Site: **ftp.oracle.com**

WWW Site: **www.oracle.com**

Packard Bell

FTP Site: **ftp.packardbell.com**

WWW Site: **www.packardbell.com**

Panasonic

FTP Site: **ftp.mitl.research.panasonic.com**

WWW Site: **www.panasonic.com**

Phoenix Technologies

FTP Site: **ftp.ptltd.com**

WWW Site: **www.ptltd.com**

Practical Peripherals

FTP Site: **ftp.practinet.com**

WWW Site: **www.practinet.com**

Promise Technology Inc.

FTP Site: **ftp.promise.com**

WWW Site: **www.promise.com**

Seagate

FTP Site: **ftp.seagate.com**

WWW Site: **www.seagate.com**

Sequent

FTP Site: **ftp.sequent.com**

WWW Site: **www.sequent.com**

Sharp Electronics

FTP Site: **www.sharplabs.com**

WWW Site: **www.sharp.co.jp**

Sony

FTP Site: **ftp.sony.com**

WWW Site: **www.sony.com/pc**

Standard Microsystems (SMC)

FTP Site: **ftp.smc.com**

WWW Site: **www.smc.com**

Sun Microsystems

FTP Site: **ftp.sun.com**

WWW Site: **www.sun.com**

Supra

FTP Site: **ftp.supra.com**

WWW Site: **www.supra.com**

Symantec

FTP Site: **ftp.symantec.com**

WWW Site: **www.symantec.com**

Texas Instruments

FTP Site: **ftp.ti.com**

WWW Site: **www.ti.com**

WWW Site (for laptops): **www.acer.com/aac**

Toshiba

FTP Site: **pcsupport.tais.com**

WWW Site: **www.computers.toshiba.com**

US-Robotics

FTP Site: **ftp.usr.com**

WWW Site: **www.usr.com**

Virgin Interactive Entertainment

FTP Site: **ftp.vie.com**

WWW Site: **www.vie.com**

Western Digital

FTP Site: **ftp.wdc.com**

WWW Site: **www.wdc.com**

Westwood Studios

FTP Site: **ftp.westwood.com**

WWW Site: **www.westwood.com**

Xircom

FTP Site: **ftp.xircom.com**

WWW Site: **www.xircom.com**

Ziff-Davis Publishing

FTP Site: **ftp.zdnet.com**

WWW Site: **www.zdnet.com**

Zoom Technologies

FTP Site: **ftp.zoom.com**

WWW Site: **www.zoom.com**

CHAPTER 30

Top Internet Sites

Computers and the Internet

C|Net

www.cnet.com

This is another complete computer news site, this time from the makers of the C|Net TV shows. There are reviews of hundreds of software and hardware products here. The "How To" section has a great collection of tips and tricks for getting the most out of your software and making your own hardware upgrades.

DejaNews

www.dejanews.com

This is a search site that indexes all of the articles posted in UseNet newsgroups. You can use this to search for and read any recent UseNet article.

Dell

www.dell.com

If you've ever thought about ordering a PC online, Dell's site is a great place to put those thoughts to work. You can completely customize any Dell offering on this site and get an exact price quote for your new system. Then order it online or call them and talk to a sales rep.

Download.com

www.download.com

The Internet is home to thousands of pieces of software that you can download and use for free. Some you try and pay for if you keep them (shareware). Others are free for as long as you use them (freeware). Download.com is one of the biggest directories of downloadable software on the Web. If you want to look for software for almost any use, this is the place to start. Software is sorted by application category and by operating system, which makes it very easy to find the software you need. The site also includes reviews and ratings as well as lists of the most frequently downloaded programs.

Excite

www.excite.com

While Yahoo is based mainly on a directory of sites that are hand-picked and entered into categories, Excite is a huge database of sites that you can search. Excite has an automated program that visits Web pages and catalogs them into a database. When you search Excite, it may return a list of hundreds or even thousands of sites that match your topic.

Geocities

www.geocities.com

This is an Internet "homestead" site where you can put up a Web page with a community of others with pages about similar interests.

HotBot

www.hotbot.com

There are dozens of these sites that act as databases of Web sites. Everyone who uses the Web a lot has a personal favorite. HotBot is mine. I make a living knowing about the Internet and the Web, and this site is always helpful to me when I need to find something.

HotWired

www.hotwired.com

This is the online sibling of the trendy Wired magazine. (No, your browser isn't broken. This site is just strange.)

Intel

www.intel.com

This site has all the inside information on Intel processors, the brains of most PCs.

Lycos

www.lycos.com

Lycos is another site that runs a huge (tens of millions) database of Web pages that it has automatically searched and indexed. Type in what you want to look for and click Search. All of the sites like Lycos and Excite return long lists of possibly matching sites with the most likely matches first.

NetBuyer

www.netbuyer.com

NetBuyer is ZDNet's comparison shopping section for hardware and software. You can find reviews for the products you want to buy, and then when you are ready to make a purchase, order them online.

Microsoft

www.microsoft.com

Come to this site to get the latest news about any Microsoft software product. You can download many free products, including the Internet Explorer Web browser, as well as updates and extras for other popular programs, such as the Microsoft Office suite of applications and Windows.

Netscape

www.home.netscape.com

This is the home of the Netscape Web browser, which made this company famous in record time. Read about their other products and services here. You can buy copies of their software online or download them for a free trial.

Que

www.quecorp.com

The Que Web site is where to go to get information about computer books on every computing topic. You can preview the entire contents of many of these books online.

Part
VII

Ch
30

Stroud's Consummate Winsock Apps

www.cws.internet.com

This is another site listing hundreds of pieces of software that you can download. This site specializes in software for use with the Internet, such as browsers, plug-ins, and add-ons. Stroud has been reviewing Internet software as long as anyone, and this is considered to be one of the best lists around.

SuperSeek

www.mcp.com/superseek/index.cgi

With so many search sites on the Web, you might hope there was just one place you could go to search them all. In fact, there are several of them, including SuperSeek. Type what you want to find at the SuperSeek site, and it searches several other search sites for you and returns results from all of them.

Symantec

www.symantec.com

Symantec is the company that makes the popular Norton Anti-Virus software. Stop by their site to download monthly updates for your virus definitions to keep your PC virus-free. You'll also want to read about their Norton Secret Stuff program for keeping e-mail private and download it for free.

TuneUp

www.tuneup.com

Try this service for 60 days for free. Here, you can find answers to thousands of frequently asked computer questions. The site also features one-on-one answers to your specific questions from trained PC technicians. After the 60-day free trial, the service does cost a few dollars a month.

Windows 95.com

www.windows95.com

This site has a ton of information about using Windows 95 and about many shareware programs you can download and install to enhance it.

Yahoo

www.yahoo.com

Yahoo is probably the best-known Web directory. Even though it isn't the biggest, it is one of the best. Yahoo has a huge directory-style list of categories with hundreds of thousands of Web sites listed. If you are looking for a Web site about a certain topic, this is a great place to start.

To use Yahoo, just click a link for one of the category topics, and it will open a page with a list of subcategories and Web pages for that topic.

Yahooligans

www.yahooligans.com

Yahooligan's is an offshoot of Yahoo. This is a directory of Web sites for kids and it's organized into topics of interest for them.

ZDNet

www.zdnet.com

ZDNet is a great comprehensive computer resource on the Web. ZDNet has all of the news about the newest hardware and software, product reviews and recommendations, and links to downloading software. A favorite area for shoppers here is the ratings of PC hardware and software vendors for quality, customer satisfaction, service and repair, technical support, and other key measures. If you are thinking about buying a new PC anytime soon, look here to see how fellow consumers rate the products. Check out the Healthy PC area for tips on keeping your PC running in tip-top shape and for troubleshooting advice when something goes wrong.

NOTE There are dozens of sites for searching the Web, and this chapter lists only a few. If you are still looking for more, try out some of these:

- AltaVista: **www.altavista.digital.com**
- WebCrawler: **www.webcrawler.com**
- InfoSeek: **www.infoseek.com**

Other Popular Web Sites

Check out these Web sites for interesting and useful services, information, and references.

123 Greetings

www.123greetings.com

Thanks to the Web and e-mail, it's never too late to send your Christmas cards, birthday cards, and notes for other holidays and celebrations. With this, you can send a free customized electronic card for any occasion to any friend or relative with an e-mail account.

Amazon.com

www.amazon.com

Billed as the "world's largest bookstore," this is a great place to buy books online. You can read reviews and get book recommendations, too.

AT&T Toll Free Directory

www.tollfree.att.net

AT&T runs this comprehensive searchable directory of toll-free numbers. With their simple search page you can enter a business name. If they have a toll-free number, this site will find it for you. You can also look for companies with toll-free numbers by looking up a business category.

BigBook

www.bigbook.com

One of the most useful and distinctive features of this directory is the Search Close By option. While the Internet is worldwide, sometimes you do want to find something next door, and this helps you find local businesses.

Big Yellow

www.bigyellow.com

As the name suggests, this site's specialty is a Yellow Pages-style directory of business information. They have useful category listings like you would find in a printed Yellow Pages directory to help you find businesses. This site has a great interface to search their 16 million (and growing) listings.

CBS

www.cbs.com

CBS presents an eye-catching directory on its home page, which makes it easy for you to find updates of CBS News, CBS Sports, The CBS Store, Daytime, CBS Kids, Specials, Primetime, *The Lateshow with David Letterman*, and a featured in-depth news report (*The Class of 2000*). You can use the RealAudio Player to hear the CBS theme, catch movie reviews, and go to the David Letterman link to see famous Top Ten Lists.

CBS SportsLine

cbs.sportsline.com

CBS Sports on TV and radio hosts some of the premier sporting events in the world, including the NCAA Men's Basketball Championships. Their Web site draws from their long experience with some of the Web broadcasters and reporters in the game to bring you scores, stories, fantasy sports leagues, and more.

CNN

www.cnn.com

If you count on CNN to be on top of the events reported on television, you can count on CNN for that same coverage on the Web. Check out CNN Interactive, a huge site that gives you access to some of the best pictures, stories, and sound bytes in the world of news gathering. There's a lot of fresh content here; this isn't just recycled news from the cable station and news wires.

The Dilbert Zone

www.unitedmedia.com/comics/dilbert/

Catch up on the antics of America's most well-known cubicle dweller with daily doses of Dilbert at the Dilbert Zone.

The Discovery Channel

www.discovery.com

Are you ready for an adventure? Climb Mount McKinley, scuba dive, take an African safari, vacation in Hawaii, or travel to another planet all in one day by exploring the Discovery Channel Online. Every day you can discover new technology, history, nature, animals, and science. You can even link to the Learning Channel from this site.

Disney

www.disney.com

This is one that you and your kids will enjoy. There are lots of games and downloadable snippets from many Disney favorites here. (My favorite, *Toy Story*, actually has its own site and address at **www.toystory.com**.) This site will provide hours of family fun.

Edmund's

www.edmunds.com

Edmund's knows the automobile industry—they've been publishing automobile buying guides since 1966. So if you're in the market for a new or used car, don't even think about stepping onto a dealer's lot without visiting the Edmund's Web site first. For new cars, they list the base price, prices for all of the options, and most importantly, what the dealer really paid for the car. You'll also find exact details on the car's interior and exterior dimensions, safety features, performance data, fuel efficiency, warranties, and how much it costs to insure it. Once you've found the car you want, Edmund's will even help you locate a dealer near you.

Epicurious

www.epicurious.com

Epicurious is the site "for people who eat." Actually it's for more than just eating; it's for drinking and playing with your food as well. You'll find everything from tips for outdoor grilling, with a grill guide and more than 150 recipes, to directions to dozens of festivals around the country where you can sample your favorite food and drink.

ESPNet SportsZone

espn.sportszone.com

Fans of all sports will want to make "The Zone" one of their first bookmarks. If you are looking to catch up and keep up on all the scores, they've got it. You will find a constantly updated scoreboard with all of the scores of games and events in progress. (You can even put it on your desktop so that you don't have to keep their Web page open.) But this site is about more than just scores. All the sports news, all the inside scoop, interviews with players and coaches—it's all here.

FedWorld

www.fedworld.gov

FedWorld is a huge government site that distributes all kinds of government documents. The FedWorld files libraries have more than 15,000 documents about health, safety, and business online, and that's just the beginning. There are federal job announcement postings and the full text of every Supreme Court case for the last 60 years.

HealthFinder

www.healthfinder.gov

HealthFinder is a government service to help you find health and medicine information on the Web. In addition, it can help you get in touch with government offices and private agencies for your health questions.

Hollywood Online

www.hollywood.com

You would expect a site about Hollywood to be full of glitz, and this site doesn't disappoint. In addition to a movie guide and show times, be sure to check out their *Buzz* forums for fun online chats with other movie fans.

Intellicast

www.intellicast.org

The Web is a great place to get all kinds of weather and meteorological information, and one of the best sites around is Intellicast. Intellicast is easy to navigate and has clear maps that are updated frequently from a variety of satellites, seismographs, and Doppler radar data. More adventuresome, scientific types looking for hard-core meteorological data should check out the Space Science and Engineering Center listed later. Intellicast enables you to zoom in on any part of the world for detailed current weather conditions and anticipated low and high temperatures. Want more? Check out where the jet stream is, get a surface analysis, or get a 24- to 48-hour forecast. If you're a real weather buff, check out the Dr. Dewpoint section, which has articles on a variety of topics, from summaries of past weather patterns to the effects of sunspots on global temperatures.

Internet Gaming Zone

www.zone.com

For years, playing games online usually meant hours setting up your modem so you could play Doom with your friend across the country. It was a tedious and expensive proposition at best. Now, Microsoft has joined a half dozen other companies to bring you the thrill of playing some of your favorite games over the Internet. In the *Internet Gaming Zone*, you can play board and card games such as backgammon, bridge, and chess. If you've played such Microsoft games as Close Combat or Monster Truck Madness at home, you can test your skills against hundreds of others.

The Internet Movie Database

us.imdb.com

The Internet Movie Database was one of the very early major sites on the Web that you could actually do something with. It has grown from a humble labor of love to a major force in the online entertainment world. So what's here? Just a completely searchable database of facts and figures for nearly every movie ever made. Not interested in who played the T1000 character in Terminator 2? Are reviews of current theatrical releases and new videos more what you need? They're all here too. This site also has movie and Hollywood news and links to local movie theater schedules. You can even buy tickets online from participating theaters.

The Internet Underground Music Archive

www.iuma.com

This is a huge database of sounds and music that you can download and play on your PC (with the right software, which you can find links to here as well).

The IRS

www.irs.ustreas.gov

This is a site you almost have to see to believe. The same folks who give us beautiful and fun literature like the 1040 and Schedule C can't be responsible for a truly great Web site. Right? But they are. Here, the IRS has shed its stodgy, pain-inflicting image and built a Web site that actually helps taxpayers. There are tax tips and hints from the real masters, all of the current year's forms online in a form you can download and print for use (you'll need to install the free Adobe Acrobat Plug-in for your Web browser to use any of these), and much more. But beyond that, the site is actually fun, well-presented, and it has a sense of humor.

Kids' Space

www.kids-space.org

This site is a collaborative effort of organizers and kids around the world. Much of the content here is in the form of stories and pictures that children contribute. There is a collaborative "Beanstalk" project where children can actually work with other children on the net to build a story. Guide Bear's Guide Tour offers help for kids learning to use the Internet and the Kids' Space site. The on-air concert section has cute musical selections performed by children.

Microsoft Expedia

www.expedia.com

If you thought Microsoft only made computer software, check out this site. Bill Gates and company are making a big splash into the travel services industry with Expedia. With a couple of vacation or business destinations in mind, click to the site's magazine, aptly named *Expedia*, and take a 360-degree surround video tour of a location. Find out what the online experts think of it and go to the relevant forum to hear what ordinary travelers are saying. Once you have picked your site, go to the Travel Agent and find out the lowest fares, book your vacation, and away you go for some R&R.

The Monster Board

www.monster.com

They don't call it The Monster Board for nothing. This site is busting at the seams with more than 50,000 U.S. and international job postings. You can search the site for specific careers, or just choose the Personal Job Search Agent to do the work for you. The Monster Board lists thousands of jobs in virtually every area possible, including both trade and nontrade positions. You'll find listings by location, discipline, and keywords. This site is guaranteed to save you hours of digging through the classifieds or making cold calls.

MTV Online

www.mtv.com

The world's first music video network is online with all the flash and style that comes through in televisions worldwide. MTV's site is the place for the latest in what's happening in the world of popular music.

NASA (National Aeronautics and Space Administration)

www.nasa.gov

You shouldn't be too surprised that the world's oldest and largest active space agency has not only a Web site but a comprehensive one at that, possibly the most comprehensive site on the Web. The site has almost as many links as the night sky has stars, including an immense number of downloadable movies, images, and sounds. All of NASA's latest missions are updated daily, including countdowns to shuttle launchings. Their well-honed site design will have you light-clicking your way through as you explore areas such as Aeronautics, Space Science, Human Space Flight, and Education.

NBA.com

www.nba.com

The NBA season and playoffs may only run eight months a year, but the NBA.com Web site is available to you 24 hours a day, 365 days a year to provide you with your pro hoops fix. In season, you find highlights, scores, game summaries, previews, interviews, and more basketball news than you could possibly read. In the off-season, be sure to check here for draft news, player trades and signings, as well as news from the training camps. If you want to join the action, you'll find a variety of interactive forums, including chats with other fans (even players and coaches stop in sometimes).

NBC.com

www.nbc.com

NBC.com is a "must-see TV" Web site rich in graphics, yet surprisingly easy to download. The site contains direct links to MSNBC Online News and NBC Sports sites, a home-page layout similar to a magazine cover with featured links, and a directory of important links within the site, such as online programs with information about the show and excerpts. You can shop, search, send e-mail, check out a site map, and even chat. NBC.com is effective in using their brand recognition to attract your attention by using recognizable marketing slogans (such as "must-see TV"), the network mascot, the NBC peacock, and the music used in their television network promos.

The New York Times

www.nytimes.com

On the Web or in print, it's still "all the news that's fit to print." Read the Op/Ed and editorials, check out Arts and Leisure for reviews, or scan the heralded classifieds for job listings. You'll need to register, but it's free.

Paramount

www.paramount.com

The major movie studios have all taken to the Web in a big way, and Paramount is no exception. Home to blockbuster hits such as *Mission Impossible,* and the entire series of *Star Trek* movies, this is a fun site for movie fans to visit. Look for sound clips, videos, and even interactive games relating to new releases and blockbuster favorites. There's a whole additional off-shoot of this site for fans of the *Star Trek* movies. And because Paramount is into television as well, be sure to look for parts of the site related to their great shows, including *Duckman* and of course the current *Star Trek* series. (*Star Trek* fans will want to look at **startrek.msn.com** for even more officially sanctioned *Star Trek* goodies.)

Parenthood Web

www.parenthoodweb.com

Find out information on a variety of topics at the Parenthood Web site's pick-of-the-week topics. To name a few, there may be topics on children's health or behavioral issues, early childhood mental and physical development, or even family-related matters. Be adventurous.

Pathfinder

www.pathfinder.com

This is easily one of the largest and most well-known sites on the Web, and certainly the best starting point to explore magazines. Pathfinder is run by Time Warner, publishers of over a dozen of the most popular magazines. This site is a central jumping-off point for access to all of their magazines that are online, including *People, Money, Time, Sports Illustrated, Fortune,* and *Life.* In addition to providing links to the magazine, the main site itself keeps track of news and current events in many topics. With each of the magazines, expect to find headlines and sample stories from the print edition at a minimum. With most, you'll find additional features including, stories not available in print, daily (or more frequent updates), and archives of past issues.

Quote.com

www.quote.com

Use this site to get live, continuous stock quotes and other market information. There's a 30-day free trial, but after that you need to pay to subscribe.

Roll Call Online

www.rollcall.com

"Hill Rats" who can't get enough of Congress go to Roll Call's Web site to share in its insiders' reporting on Capitol Hill. Roll Call takes you behind the usual headlines to what is really going on behind closed doors of the House of Representatives and Senate. Get a ringside seat to find out who is fighting whom (often within the same political party) for power. You'll find news scoops, commentary, policy briefings, and other roll call files.

Senior.com

www.senior.com

This is a leading site on the Web for the 50+ crowd. There is health and travel information here as well as links to professional services for seniors. The chat area is very active and well-populated.

Star Wars

www.starwars.com

This is the official *Star Wars* site on the Web, complete with an introductory letter from George Lucas himself.

Switchboard

www.switchboard.com

Not every phone directory site will find every person or all of the same businesses. So it's good to know where several of these are when you are looking for someone. Switchboard is another of the best directories and it's one you'll want to use.

Thomas: The U.S. Congress

thomas.loc.gov

If you're a C-Span junkie, a political activist, or just want to be a knowledgeable citizen, then aim your browser at Thomas, the legislative tracking service provided by the Library of Congress. Named after Thomas Jefferson, this service tracks bills before the House of Representatives and the Senate. You can search for bills, sorted by topic, title, and number, and follow the bill of your choice through the various committees that have jurisdiction over it. The Web site also contains historical documents, such as the Constitution and the Federalist Papers. Thomas supplies Congressional member names the complete with phone numbers and office addresses.

USA Today

www.usatoday.com

Experts predicted *USA Today* would not last long on newsstands when the paper first published in the early 1980s. Not only has it survived and thrived, but now it has a Web site that continues to break news. You'll find the familiar four colored sections—NEWS, SPORTS, MONEY, and LIFE—like the morning paper, but now these sections are updated 24 hours a day on the Web. Track your stocks, read up-to-the-minute sports scores, and plan trips with the Travel Extra Bonus Section. Follow every known weather development in the special yellow Weather section. Teachers can enroll in a Classline feature designed to make today's headlines relevant to students. USA Today even reports winning lottery numbers for every state that plays to win.

The Wall Street Journal

www.wsj.com

The Wall Street Journal Interactive edition boasts an incredible 50,000 pages of content, much of which is refreshed 24 hours a day. There is an annual subscription cost here, but it's much cheaper than subscribing to the print edition.

Warner Bros. Movies

www.movies.warnerbros.com/main.html

In addition to current movies, there are links to the part of their site about movies out on home video.

The White House

www.whitehouse.gov

Here you will find not only what Bill and Al are up to, but the entire executive branch as well. All sorts of government information including access to social security, student aid, small business assistance, and countless other federal programs can be accessed from this Web site.

WhoWhere

www.whowhere.com

The number of sites where you can look up someone's phone number or address has exploded over the last year. The one site I find myself coming back to over and over again is WhoWhere. I haven't done systematic research on this, but it seems like I find more of what I'm looking for here than at other sites. This site has one of the broadest offerings of lookup services, including personal phone, address, and e-mail addresses, as well as business directories, toll-free numbers, and those hard-to-find government offices. It's all easy to use and all you have to do is type in a person's name (or business's name), and you'll be presented with all of the information that is available about that person. Keep in mind that certain information, such as unlisted numbers, is still not available here.

The X-Files

www.thex-files.com

This is the official site for this amazingly popular TV series. There's an episode guide and information on characters. If you are looking for more detailed (but unofficial) sites, search Yahoo for **x-files**, and you'll find links to at least 500 other sites. ●

CHAPTER 31

Suggested Reading

Que Corporation offers a wide variety of technical books for all levels of users. Following are some recommended titles, in alphabetical order, which can provide you with additional information on computer operations and networking.

> **TIP** To order any books from Que Corporation or other imprints of Macmillan Computer Publishing (Sams, New Riders Publishing, Ziff Davis Press, and others), call 800-428-5331, visit Macmillan's Information SuperLibrary on the World Wide Web (**http://www.mcp.com**), or check your local bookseller.

The Complete Idiot's Guide to Networking

Author: Dan Bobola

ISBN: 1-56761-590-2

Millions of offices are now equipped with network systems and millions of users are confused by network jargon and tasks. Finally, there's a book that makes sense of it all and provides lighthearted steps to getting a network up and running and using it effectively. This book covers various software packages for IBM and compatibles.

- Provides straightforward instructions on configurations, software issues, interconnectivity, security, and more.
- Humorous, friendly approach makes an intimidating topic easy and even fun.
- Includes Oops! notes, Techno Nerd Teaches tips, and Speak Like a Geek definitions.

Introduction to Networking, Third Edition

Author: Barry Nance

ISBN: 1-56529-824-1

Readers will get a thorough introduction to the world of networking from this new edition, which covers the fundamentals as well as more advanced skills of computer connectivity. This book covers IBM and compatibles.

- How to mix and match networking technologies to meet any need.
- Covers TCP/IP, WANs, LANs, workgroups, and more.
- Includes a complete vendor reference.

Managing Multivendor Networks

Authors: John Enck and Dan Blacharski

ISBN: 0-7897-1158-3

With all of the changes in networking and operating systems, the need for a complete reference becomes essential. This updated book delivers information on the fundamentals of how to design the perfect system and add new capabilities to networks.

- Defines the fundamental network architectures of four key computer manufacturers and gives MIS personnel sufficient information to understand the basics for making informed, intelligent decisions about their own networks and networking strategies.

- Provides information on standards and architectures for the major types of network configurations, covers LANs and WANs, and addresses security concerns.

- Discusses using the Internet and the World Wide Web with a network, and working with high-speed networking solutions.

Platinum Edition Using Windows 95

Author: Ron Person, et al.

ISBN: 0-7897-0797-7

With two CD-ROMs, this is the most comprehensive collection of techniques and tools anywhere. It features coverage of hot topics like Registry and customization, Dial-Up Networking, and the World Wide Web. A "must-have" resource for accomplished to expert users who want information precisely targeted to their needs and delivered in a clear, focused, "content dense" manner.

- Complete coverage of all of the new Windows 95 service pack updates.

- Expert tips on integrating MS Exchange, Fax, and telephony features with the Internet, all major online services as well as company networks.

- CD #1 contains hundreds of the best connectivity, Internet, customization, performance tuning, backup, security, and training tools available—the best of which are pre-registered, full-working copies.

- CD #2 contains full working versions of *PC Magazine*'s WinBench '96 and Winstone '96—the industry's best system benchmarking and performance evaluation programs.

Que's Computer User's Dictionary

Author: Bryan Pfaffenberger, Ph.D.

ISBN: 1-56529-881-0

An authoritative dictionary, containing more than 2,500 terms, acronyms, jargon, and technobabbles; all translated into easy-to-understand English. This is the most up-to-date dictionary available, covering everything from accelerator boards to Zapf Dingbats.

Special Edition Using NetWare 3.12

Author: Bill Lawrence, et al.

ISBN: 1-56529-627-3

Part
VII

Ch
31

This comprehensive reference guide is overflowing with information and advice on networking fundamentals and advanced techniques. This book will provide the tools necessary for readers to manage and enhance the operation of local area networks using NetWare 3.12.

- Shows readers how to install a LAN, organize the server, manage and enhance the network, and more.
- All the up-to-date features and advice for the latest release—covers releases 3.11 and 3.12.
- Tips, cautions, notes, and troubleshooting sections lead to thorough understanding of NetWare 3.12.

Special Edition Using NetWare 4.1, Second Edition

Authors: Bill Lawrence and Vangie Bazan

ISBN: 0-7897-0810-8

As an updated edition to a proven best-seller, no matter what the task at hand, all the information needed to be productive with NetWare 4.1 can be found in this book. A recognized expert is the guide through the intricacies of managing a network.

- Covers use of NetWare Directory Services (the tool that sets NetWare 4.1 apart from its predecessors), design and building of a directory tree, and working with any workstation operating system—Windows 95, Windows NT, or Macintosh System 7.
- Discusses the power of the Novell Web Server, NetWare security, activation of TCP/IP on your NetWare Servers, and upgrading from previous NetWare versions 3.x and 2.x.
- Includes expert coverage of the most important networking topics—including Internet, TCP/IP, high-performance server hardware, and data communications technology—this book is a must-have for serious users and administrators.

Upgrading and Repairing Networks

Authors: Craig Zacker and Paul Doyle

ISBN: 0-7897-0181-2

Network professionals will find this an indispensable tool when it comes to making the right decisions when troubleshooting a network. The book includes "buyer's guide" information on software and hardware, brand contrasts and comparisons, expert advice and solutions, and much more!

- Includes a complete collection of reviews and comparisons of popular network solutions, both software and hardware.
- Comprehensive coverage of products and troubleshooting not found anywhere else.
- Recommendations and reviews enable users to make the right choices when upgrading or repairing networks.

Windows 95 Communications Handbook

Authors: Jim Boyce, Robin Hohman, Kate Chase, D. Rorbaugh

ISBN: 0-7897-0675-X

This guide shows readers how to efficiently and effectively communicate with Windows 95, covering the wide array of built-in communication tools. Readers will discover the power of the Internet and learn how to work with the most popular online services.

- CD-ROM contains Internet tools, 32-bit communications software, and utilities, as well as working versions of CompuServe and America Online.
- Demystifies the installation and configuration of Windows 95's tremendous communications tools.
- Covers the use and integration of Microsoft Exchange, fax and telephony features with the Internet, all major online services, company networks, and more.

Part
VII

Ch
31

Index

Symbols

, (comma), 225
! (exclamation point), 300
(pound sign), 245
* (asterisk), 221, 298
+ (plus sign), 86, 269
- (minus sign), 86
. (period), 225
  see also dot
/ (forward slash), 213, 246
\ (backward slash), 213
110v alternating current (AC), 28
12v direct current (DC), 28
14,400 bps, 298
16-bit
  cards, 288
  operating system, 298
2400 bps, 298
28,800 bps, 298
3 1/2 inch floppy disks, 6
3-D Web sites, visiting, 218
32-bit (operating system), 298
33,600 bps, 298
3Com FTP site, 326
3Com Web site, 326
5 1/4 inch floppy disks, 6
5v direct current (DC), 28
8-bit cards, 288
9600 bps, 298

A

abend, 298
access time, 298
Accessories folder, 50
Accolade
  FTP site, 326
  Web site, 326
Acer
  FTP site, 326
  Web site, 326
ActiveX Controls, IE (Internet Explorer), 211
Adaptec
  FTP site, 326
  Web site, 326
adapters, 298
  power supplies, 33
Add
  Bookmark command (pop-up menu), 215
  button, 127, 205
  Hardware Wizard, 142
  Language dialog box, 127
  New Hardware Wizard, 162
  Printer Wizard, starting, 151
Add to Favorites
  command (Favorites menu), 214-215
  dialog box, 214
Add/Remove
  button, 280
  Programs dialog box, 94
  Programs icon, 275, 279
  Programs Properties dialog box, 204, 275, 279
Address bus, 26
addresses, 299
  e-mail, parts of, 224-225
Adobe
  FTP site, 326
  Web site, 326
Advanced button, 171
Advanced Micro Devices
  FTP site, 326
  Web site, 326
alphanumeric keys, *see* typewriter keys
ALR
  FTP site, 326
  Web site, 326
AltaVista Web site, 219, 271
Amazon.com Web site, 343
America Online, *see* AOL
American Megatrends
  FTP site, 327
  Web site, 327
anti-virus programs, 299
AOL (America Online), 202, 299
  Internet address, 225
Apple
  FTP site, 327
  Web site, 327

applets, Add/Remove Programs, 275

applications
bundles, 66
databases, 65
frozen
closing, 46
restarting, 46
graphics, 65-66
Personal Information
Managers, 66
presentations, 65-66
spreadsheets, 63-64
suites, 66
switching between, 43
taskbar, 43
types, describing, 62-66
word processors, 62-63
see also programs

Archie, FTP files, locating, 237

architectures, bus, 26

archive attribute, 92

archives, 299

Artisoft
FTP site, 327
Web site, 327

ASCII
(American Standard Code for
Information Interchange), 299
files, 299

AST
FTP site, 327
Web site, 327

asterisk (*), 221, 298-299

**asynchronous transmissions,
299**

at (@), 298

AT command set, 299

**AT&T Toll Free Directory Web
site, 344**

ATI
FTP site, 327
Web site, 327

Attach button, 230

**Attach Files and Documents
tab, 230**

attachments, 299

attenuation, 299
cables, 107

attributes, archive, 92

**audio, nondirectional
sound, 35**

**audio files, streaming,
embedded, 217**

Audio Out port, 35

audio, *see* sounds

Autodesk
FTP site, 327
Web site, 327

AUTOEXEC.BAT, 299

B

Back button, 213-214

Back or Forward button, 239

backbone, 300

Background tab, 121

background tasks, 300

backing up
files, 77-78, 274
archive attribute, 92
CD-ROMs (recordable), 101
floppy disks, 100
full, 92-93
full backups, performing,
94-97
hard drives
(removable), 101
incremental, 92-93, 97
media (removable), 101
Microsoft Backup,
installing, 94
options, 96
other methods, 100-101
strategies, 93-94
tapes, 100
Windows 95, 94-97
ZIP disks, 101
systems, 80, 274

Backup
dialog box, 99
icon, 94
message box, 96
tab, 94
window, 94, 98
Wizard, 94

backup utility, 92

backups, 300

backward slash (\), 213

bandwidth, 300

bandwidth cables, 107

bang, 300

**Basic Input Output System,
see BIOS**

batteries, 292

baud rates, 300

**BBS (Bulletin Board System or
Service), 300**

bells and whistles, 300

**benchmarking, video cards,
ZiffDavis Benchmarks, 115**

Berkeley Systems
FTP site, 327
Web site, 327

Best of the Web button, 213

Big Yellow Web site, 344

BigBook Web site, 344

binary files, 300

bindery, 300

Bindings tab, 206

**BIOS (Basic Input Output
System), 300**
upgrading, 285

bit, 300

blackout, 28

Blizzard Entertainment
FTP site, 328
Web site, 328

Boca Research
FTP site, 328
Web site, 328

bookmarks
creating, 213
frames, creating, 215

Bookmarks button, 215

boots, 301
warm, 45

bootup routines, 40

Borland
FTP site, 328
Web site, 328

bps (bits per second), 300

break, 301

brightness setting, monitors, 119

broadcast, 301

brownouts, 28

Browse
button, 53, 117, 168, 183, 276
dialog box, 276

browsers, Web, 191

bubble jet printers, 16

buffers, 301

bugs, 301

Building a Query tool, 271

bundles, 66

bus, 106, 301, 304
architectures, 26
types of, 26

Buttons tab, 139

byte, 301

C

CINet, SHAREWARE.COM, 240

CINet Web site, 247, 339

CA-Associates
FTP site, 328
Web site, 328

cables
attenuation, 107
backbone, 300
bandwidth, 107
coax, 302
connectors, RJ-11, 318
impedance, 107
networks, topologies, 107
RS-232, 318
serial, 36

cache, 200, 301

Cache RAM (Randon-Access Memory), 21

capacity, 301

Capacity drop-down list, 77

cards, 302
8-bit, 288
16-bit, 288
expansion, upgrading, 285
PCI slots, 288

sound, 166, 290, 293, 319
upgrading, 285
video, 292
upgrading, 285

case-sensitive, 302

cases, 290

CATV (Cable Television) ISPs, 201

CBS SportsLine Web site, 344

CBS Web site, 344

CD-ROMs (Read-Only Memory) drives, 81-82, 302
disks
inserting, 81
read-only, 81
drives, 12-13, 76, 290, 292
Drive D, 81
recordable, files, backing up, 101

CDs
control, 171
headphones, listening to, 171-172
installing, software, 277

cells, ranges, selecting, 66

centering setting, monitors, 119

Central Processing Unit, see CPU

CGM (Computer Graphics Metafile), 302

Change button, 117

Change Display Type
button, 117
dialog box, 118

channels
bandwidth, 300
baud rates, 300

Character Map application font list, 126

character-based terminal screen, files, downloading, 203

characters, special, keyboards, 126-127

Characters to Copy box, 127

chat, 302

chat channels
accessing, 245-246
Netscape Conference tool, 246

chat services
CNN, 246
MSNBC, 246

Check Now button, 79

Check Port State Before Printing check box, 151

chips
microprocessors, numbers and letters combinations, 22
Pentium, 22
speeds, 22

CICA Windows Archive, 240

Cirrus Logic
FTP site, 328
Web site, 328

CIS (CompuServe Information Service), 302

Cisco
FTP site, 328
Web site, 328

Class 1, Class 2 standards, 302

Click here for icon, 42

client/server, 302

clients, 302

clip art, 302

Clipboard, 302

Close Program dialog box, 46

clusters
files, storing, 80
hard disks, 80-81

CMOS (Complementary Metal-Oxide Semiconductor), 302

CNN
chat services, 246
Web site, 192, 345

coax, 302

coaxial cables, 107

collision, 302

color scanners, 181

colors
capabilities, terms for, 113-114
numbers of, changing, 119-120
printers, 147
RGB (Red, Green, Blue), 113
video cards, 113-114

COM port, 303

comma (,), 225

command line, 303

commands, 303
Edit menu
Copy, 68-69
Cut, 68
Paste, 68-69, 127
Paste Special, 69
Favorites menu, Add to
Favorites, 214-215
File menu
Delete, 152
Empty Recycle Bin, 89
New, 86
Open, 71
Open File Set, 96
Print, 72, 153
Print Preview, 72
Save, 70, 172
Save As, 70-71, 96
Format, 77
My Computer
Delete, 89
Properties, 24
Rename, 90
pop-up menu
Add Bookmark, 215
Properties, 117, 120-121
Recycle Bin, Restore, 89
Settings menu
Control Panel, 161
Options, 96, 99
shortcut menu
Create Shortcut(s) Here, 90
Minimize All Windows, 43
Properties, 25
Rename, 87
Send To, 78
Start menu
Programs, 172
Restart the Computer?, 183
Settings, 117, 127, 151, 167,
183, 203, 205
Shut Down, 183
submenu, Properties, 79
View menu, Details, 26
Windows Explorer
Delete, 89
Rename, 90

Communications dialog
box, 204

communications
software, modems, 159
speed, modems, 157

Compaq
FTP site, 328
Web site, 328

The Complete Idiot's Guide to
Networking, 356

components
networks, 104-105
sounds, 166-167

Components list, 206

Composition window, 229

compression
programs, 303
standard, modems, 159

CompuServe, 202
Internet address, 225

computers
bootup routines, 40
boxes and packing materials,
saving, 32
cases, 284
desktop, 8, 304
disk drives, 12-13
electrical damage,
protecting, 36
error messages, 47
extension cables, 36
floppy drive light, 11
functions, 8
game ports, 14
hard drive light, 11
inspecting, 32
joysticks, 14
connecting to, 141-142
keyboards, 14
laptop, 9, 312
locks, 10
modems, 16-17
monitors, 13
mouse, 14
connecting to, 136-137
networks, 104
notebooks, 9
palmtops, 9
parallel (LPT) ports, 14
peripherals, scanners, 178-181
power off, 47
power switches, 10
printers, 16
connecting to, 36, 149-150

purchasing, 291-292
Reset button, 11
resetting, 45-46
scanners, connecting, 182-184
SCSI ports, 14
serial (COM) ports, 14
serial numbers, matching, 32
shutting down, 45
speakers, 15
shielded, 123
starting, 40-41
troubleshooting, 47-48
tower, 8, 320
trackballs, 14
troubleshooting
crashes, 46-47
shutdowns, 46-47
Turbo
button, 11
light, 11
unpacking, 32
upgrading, 289-291
warm boots, 45

conferencing, 303

CONFIG.SYS file, 303

Configure Port button, 151

connections, T-1, T-3, 320

Conner Web site, 328

Contents tab, help,
locating, 254

contrast setting, monitors, 119

Control bus, 26

Control Panel, installing
software, 275-277

Control Panel command
(Settings menu), 161

Control Panel window, 279
opening, 275

controllers
EIDE (Enhanced Integrated
Device Electronics), 78
hard drives, 78
IDE (Integrated Device
Electronics), 78
SCSI (Small Computer Systems
Interface), 78

controls
ActiveX, IE
(Internet Explorer), 211
CD, 171
error indicator, modems, 161
Line In, 171

MIDI (Musical Instrument
Digital Interface), 170
modems
mode indicator, 161
power on light, 161
speed indicator, 161
printers, 150-151
Wave, 170

Copy
button, 68, 127
command (Edit menu), 68-69

copying
data, 68-69
files, 88
to floppy disks, 77-78
folders, 88

Corel
FTP site, 329
Web site, 329

costs
modems, 159
printers, 146

**cps (characters per second),
302**

**CPU (Central Processing Unit),
21-22, 302**
bus, 26
plugging in, 33
positioning, 33
see also microprocessors

crashes, troubleshooting, 46-47

**Create Shortcut(s) Here
command (shortcut menu),
90**

Creative-Labs
FTP site, 329
Web site, 329

**Ctrl+Alt+Delete key
combination, 46-47, 267**
computer not responding, 47

**Ctrl+paperclip icon key
combination, 231**

**Ctrl+Windows+F key
combination, 129**

cursor, 303, 310
keys, 126

Cut
button, 68
command (Edit menu), 68

CuteFTP, 234
files, downloading, 235
Site Manager, 235

cutting, data, 68-69

cyberspace, 304

Cyrix
FTP site, 329
Web site, 271, 329

D

D connector, 304

D Link
FTP site, 329
Web site, 329

D-shaped connector, 34

daisy chain, *see* bus

data, 304
copying, 68-69
cutting, 68-69
modems, transferring, 156-157
pasting, 68-69

data
communications software, 157
format, modems, 159

data bus, 26

databases, 65, 304

dates, current, checking, 44

decryption, 304

default, 304

Defragment Now button, 81

Defragmenter program, 80

**defragmenting, hard disks,
80-81**

Deguass button, 119

Deguass setting
monitors, 119

DejaNews Web site, 339

Delete command
File menu, 152
My Computer, 89
Windows Explorer, 89

**deleting, files and folders,
88-89**

Dell
FTP site, 329
Web site, 329, 340

**Delphi Internet Services Web
site, 246**

Delrina
FTP site, 329
Web site, 329

demodulation, 304

density, 304

desktop
computers, 8, 304
publishing, 304

Details
button, 204
command (View menu), 26

**device drivers, problems,
avoiding, 266**

Device Manager
problems, handling, 268-269
tab, 184, 268

**Dial-Up Adapter Properties
dialog box, 206**

**dial-up connections, Internet,
202-206**

Diamond
FTP site, 329
Web site, 329

Digital Equipment (DEC)
FTP site, 329
Web site, 329

Dilbert Zone Web site, 345

**DIMM (Dual Inline Memory
Module), 23**
slots, upgrading, 287
FTP
backing up, 239
Web browsers,
downloading, 238-240

directory, 305

**Discovery Channel Web
site, 345**

**Disk Defragmenter dialog
box, 81**

disk drives, 12, 24-25, 305
external, 13
floppy disks, 25
hard disks, 25, 78-81, 309
clusters, 80-81
Defragmenter, 80
defragmenting, 80-81
space, checking, 79
systems, backing up, 80

disks, 305
    CD-ROM, inserting, 81
    duplexing, 305
    floppy, 76-78, 308
        3 1/2-inch, 25
        5 1/4-inch, 25
        drive A, 76
        drive B, 76
        files, backing up, 100
        files, copying, 77-78
        formatting, 76-77
    magnetic, 29
    maintaining, 82
    mirroring, 305
    read-only, 81
    space
        determining amount of,
          25-26
        freeing up, 89
    write-protection, 323
    ZIP files, backing up, 101
Disney Web site, 345
Display icon, 117
**Display Properties dialog box,
  117, 120-121**
Display Type dialog box, 118
**DMA (Direct Memory Access),
  305**
**DNS (Domain Name Service),
  305**
DNS Servers, 194
docking stations, 293
documents
    opening, 71
        starting a program by, 53
    printing, 72
    saving, 69-70
    scanning, 185
domain, 305
domain names, 194
**DOS (Disk Operating System),
  306**
dot, 306
**dot-matrix printers, 16, 146,
  148-149**
dots per inch, *see* **dpi**
**double-clicking speed, mouse,
  configuring, 139**
download, 306

Download.com Web site, 340
**downloading, FTP files,
  235-236**
**dpi (dots per inch),
  scanners, 181**
**DRAM (Dynamic Random-
  Access Memory), 23**
drawing programs, 306
Drive Space dialog box, 26
Driver tab, 269
drivers, 306
    software, modems, 157
    TWAIN (Technology Without
      An Interesting Name),
      scanners, 182-183
drives, 76
    A, floppy disks, 76
    B, floppy disks, 76
    C, hard drives, 78
    CD-ROM (Read-Only Memory),
      12-13, 76, 81-82, 290, 292
    contents, viewing, 86
    D, CD-ROMs, 81
    disks, 12, 24, 305
        external, 13, 307
        floppy disk drive, 25
        hard disks, 25
        internal, 310
    floppy disks, 12, 77-78, 290
        inserting, 76
    floppy drive light, 11
    hard drives, 76, 79-81, 289, 293
        controllers, 78
        speed, 78
        files, restoring to, 97-100
        G (gigabytes), 78
        light, 11
        M (megabytes), 78
        ms (milliseconds), 78
        removable, files, backing up,
          13, 101
        ScanDisk, 79-80
        sizes, 78
        upgrading, 285
    IDE, 289
        upgrading, 286
    maintaining, 82
    My Computer, 85
    removable disk, 318
    SCSI, upgrading, 286
    speed, 78
    tape, 13, 290
        replacing, 284
    Windows Explorer, 85-86
    Zip, replacing, 284

drop-down list boxes, 215
**DTP (DeskTop Publishing)
  programs, 304**

E

e-mail
    addresses, formats, 224-225
    defined, 306
    electronic business cards,
      attaching to, 192
    files
        attaching, 192, 230
        saving, 231
    flashmail, 259
    Inbox, 228
    Internet, 192
    Internet Mail, messages
        checking, 228
        replying, 229
        reviewing, 229
        sending, 227
    mail servers, 228
    messages
        forwarding, 228
        sending, 224, 226-227
        spell checking, 226
    Messenger, messages
        checking, 228-229
        replying, 228-229
        reviewing, 228-229
        sending, 226
    receiving, 228-229
Edit menu commands
    Copy, 68-69
    Cut, 68
    Paste, 68-69, 127
    Paste Special, 69
Edmund's Web site, 345
EDO (Extended Data Out), 23
**EIDE (Enhanced Integrated
  Device Electronics) controller,
  78**
Eject button, 81
**electrical damage, computers,
  protecting, 36**
Electronic Arts
    FTP site, 330
    Web site, 330
**electronic business cards,
  attaching e-mail to, 192**

electronic mail, *see* e-mail

Empty Recycle Bin command (File menu), 89

encryption, 306

End Task button, 46

Enhanced Integrated Device Electronics, *see* EIDE

Enter File to Attach dialog box, 230

Epic MegaGames
    FTP site, 330
    Web site, 330

Epicurious Web site, 346

Epson
    FTP site, 330
    Web site, 330

ergonomic keyboards, 131

error indicator
    control, modems, 161
    printers, 151

error messages, computers, 47

Esc key, 126

ESPNet SportsZone Web site, 346

Ethernet, 306

Everex
    FTP site, 330
    Web site, 330

Excite Web site, 219, 340

exclamation point (!), 300

executable files, 306

exiting
    programs, 274
    Windows 95, 48

expansion
    cards, upgrading, 285
    slots, 21, 27, 306
        upgrading, hardware, 287-288

Explorer, 307

extension, 307

extension cables, 36

external
    disk drives, 13-17, 307
    modems, 157
    ports, 293

F

FAQ (Frequently Asked Questions), 260, 307

fault, 307

fault tolerance, 307

Favorites
    folder, Web pages, entering, 214
    menu commands, Add to Favorites, 214-215

fax/data modems, 307, 159-160

FedWorld Web site, 346

fiber optics, 307

fiber-optic cables, 107

fiber-optic (ISDN) ISPs, 201

File
    button, 230
    Find dialog box, 237
    menu commands
        Delete, 152
        Empty Recycle Bin, 89
        New, 86
        Open, 71
        Open File Set, 96
        Print, 72, 153
        Print Preview, 72
        Save, 70, 172
        Save As, 70-71, 96
    Name box, 70

file servers, 307

File Transfer Protocol, *see* FTP

filename extensions, 307

files, 84, 307
    ASCII, 299
    attachments, 299
    AUTOEXEC.BAT, 299
    backing up, 77-78, 274
        archive attribute, 92
        CD-ROMs (recordable), 101
        floppy disks, 100
        full backups, performing, 94-97
        hard drives (removable), 101
        incremental, 97
        media (removable), 101
        Microsoft Backup, installing, 94

    options, 96
    other methods, 100-101
    strategies, 93-94
    tapes, 100
    Windows 95, 94-97
    ZIP disks, 101
    backups, 300
    binary, 300
    clusters, storing, 80
    CONFIG.SYS, 303
    copying, 88
    corrupted, replacing, 99
    deleting, 88-89
    disks, maintaining, 82
    downloading, 197
        character-based terminal screen, 203
        shareware packages, 203
    e-mail
        attaching to, 192, 230
        saving files, 231
    executable, 306
    finding to download, 234-235
    floppy disks, copying to, 77-78, 88
    folders, creating, 86
    formats, saving, 70-71
    FTP (File Transfer Protocol), 234
        sites, downloading, 235-236
        Web browsers, downloading, 238-240
    hard drive, restoring to, 97-100
    INDEX.*, 235
    moving, 87
    names, 84
        characters, number allowed, 70
        truncated, 86
    organizing, 84
    README, 318
    Recycle Bin, undeleting, 89
    renaming, 87
    shortcuts to, creating, 90
    sound
        embedded, playing, 216-217
        WAV, playing, 168
    streaming audio, embedded, 217
    system, viewing, 84-86
    text, 320
    video
        embedded, playing, 216-217
        types of, 217
    WAV, 322

Find tab, help, locating, 255

Finish button, 256

firewalls, 307

flashmail, 259

flatbed scanners, 178

floppy disk drives, 12, 25, 76-78
A, 76
B, 76
inserting, 76

floppy disks, 76-78, 308
3 1/2-inch, 25, 76
5 1/4-inch, 25, 76
files
backing up, 100
copying, 88
copying to, 77-78
formatting, 76-77

floppy drives, 290
light, 11

flow control, 308

folders, 84, 308
Accessories, 50
collapsing, 86
contents, viewing, 86
copying, 88
creating, 86
deleting, 88-89
expanding, 86
moving, 87
My Computer, 85
naming characters, limited number of, 86
organizing, 84
Recycle Bin, undeleting, 89
renaming, 87
shortcuts to, creating, 90
Windows, 51
Windows Explorer, 85-86

fonts, printers, 147

footprints, 308

foreground tasks, 308

Format
command, 77
dialog box, 77

formats
data, modems, 159
files, saving, 70-71
floppy disks, 77

formatting
floppy disks, 76-77
numbers, 67
text, 67

forms
check boxes, 215
completing, 215-216
drop-down list boxes, 215
elements, 215
Option buttons, 215
text boxes, 215

forums, 308

Forward button, 213, 228

forward slash (/), 213, 246

frames
bookmarking, 215
links, 214
previous contents, returning to, 214
Web pages, 214-215

freeware, 308

FTP (File Transfer Protocol), 213, 307
alternatives to, 240
Archie, files, locating, 237
CICA Windows Archive, 240
CuteFTP, 234
Site Manager, 235
directories, backing up, 239
files
Archie, locating, 237
downloading, 235-236
finding to download, 234-235
uploading, 236-237
hyperlinks, 238
INDEX.* file, 235
servers, 194, 308
sites
Accolade, 326
Acer, 326
Adaptec, 326
Adobe, 326
Advanced Micro Devices, 326
ALR, 326
American Megatrends, 327
Apple, 327
Artisoft, 327
AST, 327
ATI, 327
Autodesk, 327
Berkeley Systems, 327
Blizzard Entertainment, 328

Boca Research, 328
Borland, 328
CA-Associates, 328
Cirrus Logic, 328
Cisco, 328
Compaq, 328
Corel, 329
Creative-Labs, 329
Cyrix, 329
D Link, 329
Dell, 329
Delrina, 329
Diamond, 329
Digital Equipment, 329
download sites, 235
Electronic Arts, 330
Epic MegaGames, 330
Epson, 330
Everex, 330
files, downloading, 235-236
ftp.cdrom.com, 235
ftp.coast.net, 235
ftp.ncsa.uiuc.edu, 235
ftp.sunet.se, 235
ftp.winsite.com, 234, 235
garbo.uwasa.fi, 235
Gateway 2000, 330
Gravis, 330
Hayes, 330
Hercules, 331
Hewlett-Packard, 331
IBM Corporation, 331
id Software, 331
Intel, 331
Interplay, 331
Iomega, 331
Logitech, 332
Lotus, 332
LucasArts, 332
Macromedia, 332
MAG Innovision, 332
Matrox, 332
Maxis, 332
Maxtech, 333
Maxtor, 333
McAfee Associates, 333
MicroProse, 333
Microsoft, 333
Mitsubishi, 333
NEC, 333
Netscape, 334
Nokia, 334
Novell, 334
Number Nine, 334
oak.oakland.edu, 235

Oracle, 334
Packard Bell, 334
Panasonic, 334
Phoenix Technologies, 335
Practical Peripherals, 335
Promise Technology
    Inc., 335
Seagate, 335
Sequent, 335
Sharp Electronics, 335
Sony, 335
Standard Microsystems, 336
Sun Microsystems, 336
Supra, 336
Symantec, 336
Texas Instruments, 336
3Com, 326
Toshiba, 336
UNIX directories, 235
US-Robotics, 336
Virgin Interactive
    Entertainment, 337
Western Digital, 337
Westwood Studios, 337
Xircom, 337
Ziff-Davis Publishing, 337
Zoom Technologies, 337
Telnet, 234
URLs (Uniform Resource
    Locators), 238
Web browsers
    directories, downloading,
        238-240
    files, downloading, 238-240
    index files, 239
ftp.cdrom.com (FTP site), 235
ftp.coast.net (FTP site), 235
ftp.ncsa.uiuc.edu
    (FTP site), 235
ftp.sunet.se (FTP site), 235
ftp.winsite.com (FTP site),
    234-235
full backups, 92-93
    performing, 94-97
function keys, 126

G

G (gigabytes), 78, 308
game ports, 14
garbo.uwasa.fi (FTP site), 235

Gateway 2000
    FTP site, 330
    Web site, 330
gateways, 308
General tab, 25, 269
Geocities Web site, 340
Get Msg button, 228
GIF (Graphics Interchange
    Format), 308-309
gigabytes, see G (gigabytes)
Gopher, 309
    protocol, 213
    servers, 195
graphics, 65-66
graphics programs, 309
Gravis
    FTP site, 330
    Web site, 330
grayscale scanners, 181
guru, 309

H

hackers, 309
hand scanners, 180
hard disks, 25, 78-81, 309
    clusters, 80-81
    Defragmenter, 80
    defragmenting, 80-81
    drives, 12-13
    partitions, 316
    removable storage devices, 25
    space, checking, 79
    systems, backing up, 80
hard drives, 76, 81, 289, 293
    controllers, 78
    drive C, 78
    drive speed, 78
    errors, checking, 79-80
    files, restoring to, 97-100
    G (gigabytes), 78
    light, 11
    M (megabytes), 78
    ms (milliseconds), 78
    removable, files, backing
        up, 101
    ScanDisk, 79-80

sizes, 78
upgrading, 285
hardware, 19-20
    cases, 290
    CD-ROM drives, 290
    computers
        case, 284
        upgrading, 289-291
    device drivers, problems,
        avoiding, 266
    Device Manager, problems,
        handling, 268-269
    expansion slots, upgrading,
        287-288
    floppy drives, 290
    hard drives, 289
    help, newsgroups, 271
    IDE drives, 289
        upgrading, 286
    installing, problems, avoiding,
        264-265
    Internet, 200-201
        problems, troubleshooting,
            270-271
        upgrading, 200-201
    IRQ (interrupt conflicts), 266
    ISA slots, upgrading, 287-288
    joysticks, 291
        calibrating, 143
    keyboards, 290
    legacy device, 312
    memory, 289
        SDRAM, 287
        upgrading, 286-287
    modems, 156-157, 290
    monitors, 289
    mouse, 290
    PCI slots, upgrading, 287-288
    Plug and Play technology,
        upgrading, 288-289
    POST (Power On Self Test),
        267
    printers, 290
    problems
        diagnosing, 267-268
        troubleshooting, 264
    processors, 289
    RAM (Random-Access
        Memory), upgrading, 286-287
    SCSI drives, upgrading, 286
    self-servicing, 269
    software, working together, 29
    sound cards, 290
    speakers, 290
    steering wheels, 291

tape drives, 290
technical support, 270
upgrades, purchasing, 291-292
upgrading, 283-284
  PC, parts inside of, 285
Windows 95, 290
  troubleshooting, 257-259

Have Disk button, 117, 151, 162

Hayes
  FTP site, 330
  Web site, 330

headphones, CDs, listening to, 171-172

HealthFinder Web site, 346

help
  Contents tab, locating, 254
  Device Manager, problems, handling, 268-269
  dialog boxes, locating, 256
  Find tab, locating, 255
  hardware
    AltaVista Web site, 271
    Cyrix Web site, 271
    device drivers, 266
    HotBot Web site, 271
    InfoSeek Ultra Web site, 271
    installing correctly, 264-265
    Internet, troubleshooting problems, 270-271
    IRQ (interrupt conflicts), 266
    Microsoft Technical Support Knowledge Base Web site, 271
    Modem Web site, 271
    newsgroups, 271
    problems, diagnosing, 267-268
    problems, troubleshooting, 264, 267
    self-servicing, 269
    technical support, 270
    ZDNet HealthyPC.com Support Finder Web site, 271
  Help system, troubleshooting, 257
  Help Topics window, hyperlinks, 255
  Index tab, locating, 254
  manufacturers support, 261
  Mode menu, options, troubleshooting, 258

online support, 259-260
POST (Power On Self Test), 267
software
  Macmillan Information SuperLibrary Web site, 260
  Microsoft Web site, 260
  Web sites, FAQ (Frequently Asked Questions), 260
  wizards, locating, 256
by telephone, 261
viruses, avoiding, 259
Web sites, FAQ (Frequently Asked Questions), 260
Windows 95
  Help system, 254-256
  troubleshooting, 257-259

Help
  button, 152
  icon, 256
  system, troubleshooting, 257
  Topics window, 254
    hyperlinked text, jumping to, 255
  window, locating, 255

Hercules
  FTP site, 331
  Web site, 331

Hewlett-Packard
  FTP site, 331
  Web site, 331

Hollywood Online Web site, 346

Home button, 213

home pages, 192, 211, 309
  links
    addresses, entering, 212
    graphic images, 212
    underlined text, 212

horizontal and vertical sizing, monitors, 119

host, 309

hot fix, 309

HotBot Web site, 271, 340

HotWired Web site, 340

HTML (HyperText Markup Language), 191, 310
  Web pages, 210

HTTP (HyperText Transfer Protocol), 191, 213, 310
  servers, 194

hub, 310

hyperlinks, 238, 310
  Help Topics window, 255

hypertext, 310
  Web pages, linking, 191

HyperText Markup Language, see HTML

HyperText Transfer Protocol, see HTTP

I

IBM Corporation
  FTP site, 331
  Web site, 331

icons, 310
  Add/Remove Programs, 204, 275, 279
  Backup, 94
  Click here for, 42
  Display, 117
  Help, 256
  identifying, 41-42
  Inbox, 42
  Internet (The), 42
  Keyboard, 127
  Mailbox, 226
  Modems, 161
  Mouse, 139
  My Computer, 42, 77, 79, 85
  Network, 205
  paperclip, 230-231
  Recycle Bin, 42, 89
  shortcuts, renaming, 90
  Sounds, 167
  Speaker, 171
  System, 268

id Software
  FTP site, 331
  Web site, 331

IDE (Integrated Device Electronics) controller, 78

IDE drives, 289
  upgrading, 286

IE (Internet Explorer), ActiveX Controls, 211

IEEE (Institute of Electrical and Electronics Engineers), 310

IMAP (Interactive Mail Access Protocol), 310

impedance, cables, 107

Inbox, 228
  icon, 42

incremental backups, files,
  92-93

index files, Web browsers, 239

Index tab, help, locating, 254

INDEX.* file, 235

information
  input, 29
  linking, automatically, 69
  updating, automatically, 69

InfoSeek
  Ultra Web site, 271
  Web site, 219

injuries, keyboard-related,
  avoiding, 131

inkjet printers, 16, 146-148

input device, 29

Insert Attachment dialog
  box, 230

insertion point, see cursor

Install from Disk dialog box,
  117, 183

Install New Modem Wizard,
  161

Install/Uninstall tab, 275, 279

installing
  hardware, problems, avoiding,
    264-265
  modems, 160-161
  software, 274-277
    with CD, 277
    from Control Panel, 275-277
    over older versions, 278-279
    precautions before, 274
  Windows 95
    modems, 161-162
    printers, 151-152

Integrated Device Electronics,
  see IDE

Intel
  FTP site, 331
  Web site, 331, 341

Intellicast Web site, 347

IntelliMouse wheel, 138

interlacing, monitors, 113

internal
  disk drives, 310
  modems, 157

Internet, 190, 310
  changes, keeping up-to-date,
    247-249
  chat channels, accessing,
    245-246
  dial-up connections, 202-206
  DNS Servers, 194
  domain names, 194
  e-mail, 192
  files, downloading, 197
  FTP (File Transfer Protocol),
    234
    servers, 194
  Gopher, servers, 195
  hardware
    problems, troubleshooting,
      270-271
    upgrading, 200-201
  HTML (HyperText Markup
    Language), 191
  HTTP (HyperText Transfer
    Protocol), 191
    servers, 194
  information
    searching for, 196-197
    sources, 193-196
  IP (Internet Protocol), 193
  IRC (Internet Relay Chat),
    244-246
  ISP (Internet Service Provider),
    193
    AOL (American Online), 202
    CATV (Cable Television),
      201
    CompuServe, 202
    connecting to, 203
    establishing, 202
    files, downloading, 203
    ISDN (fiber-optic), 201
    local telephone, 201
    North American, 201
    PPP (Point-to-Point
      Protocol), 202
    private, 202
    regional, 201
    selecting, 201-202
    SLIP (Serial Line Internet
      Protocol), 202
    telephone (local), 201
    worldwide online
      services, 201
  modems, connecting, 200

networks, interconnected, 190
  newsgroups, 197, 242-244
  online services, addresses, 225
  PPP (Point-to-Point Protocol),
    202
  push technologies, 247-248
  search sites, 196
  servers
    connecting, 190
    locations of, 190
  SLIP (Serial Line Internet
    Protocol), 202
  SNMP servers, 194
  software, distributing, 248-249
  TCP/IP (Transmission Control
    Protocol/Internet Protocol),
    configuring for system, 194,
    203-205
  Telnet, servers, 194
  UseNet, servers, 196
  WWW (World Wide Web), 191
    browsers, 191, 210
    pages, 191
    sites, home pages, 192

Internet (The) icon, 42

Internet Explorer (IE), 311

Internet Gaming Zone Web
  site, 347

Internet Mail, e-mail
  files, saving, 231
  messages
    checking, 228-229
    replying, 229
    reviewing, 229
    sending, 227
    spell checking, 227

Internet Movie Database Web
  site, 347

Internet Protocol, see IP

Internet Relay Chat, see IRC

Internet Service Providers, see
  ISPs

Internet Underground Music
  Archive Web site, 347

Interplay
  FTP site, 331
  Web site, 331

interrupt, 311

interrupts, see IRQs

IntraNetWare, 105

Introduction to Networking, Third Edition, 356

Intuit Web site, 331

Iomega
FTP site, 331
Web site, 331

IP (Internet Protocol), 193
address, 311

IPX (Internetwork Packet eXchange), 311

IRC (Internet Relay Chat), 244, 246, 311
servers, 245
software, 245

IRQ (interrupt conflicts), hardware, 266

IRQ (Interrupt ReQuest line), 311

IRQs (interrupts), 106

IRS Web site, 348

ISA
bus, 311
slots, 27
upgrading, 287-288

ISDN (fiber-optic) ISPs, 201

ISDN (Integrated Services Digital Network), 310

ISO (International Standardization Organization), 311

ISPs (Internet Service Providers), 193, 242
AOL (American Online), 202
CATV (Cable Television), 201
CompuServe, 202
connecting to, 203
files, downloading, 203
ISDN (fiber optic), 201
local telephone, 201
locating, 202
North American, 201
PPP (Point-to-Point Protocol), 202
private, 202
regional, 201
selecting, 201-202
SLIP (Serial Line Internet Protocol), 202
worldwide online services, 201

J

Java, running, 219

Joint Photographic Experts Group (JPEG), 311

joysticks, 14, 291
calibrating, 142-143
connecting to PC, 141-142
replacing, 284
types of, 141

JPEG (Joint Photographic Experts Group), 311

K

K (kilobytes), 312

key combinations
Ctrl+Alt+Delete, 46, 267
computer not responding, 47
Ctrl+paperclip icon, 231
Ctrl+Windows+F, 129
Left Alt+Shift, 128
Shift+Windows+M, 129
WINDOWS, 129
WINDOWS+Break, 129
WINDOWS+E, 129
WINDOWS+F, 129
WINDOWS+F1, 129
WINDOWS+M, 129
WINDOWS+R, 129
WINDOWS+Tab, 129

Keyboard
icon, 127
Properties dialog box, 127

keyboards, 14, 290, 293, 312
Character Map application font list, 126
characters, special, 126-127
cleaning, 130
ergonomic, 131
injuries, avoiding, 131
languages, typing in other, 127-129
layout, 126
maintaining, 130
notebooks, 131-132
plugging in, 35
positioning, 34-35
problems, troubleshooting, 132-133

replacing, 284
software, 129-130
static electricity, 130
symbols, special, 126-127
Windows 95
keys, special, 129
logo keys, 129
Menu key, 129

keys
cursor, 126
Esc, 126
function, 126
logo, 129
Menu key, 129
numeric keypad, 126
Print Screen, 126
Scroll Lock, 126
typewriter, 126
Windows 95, keyboards, 129

Kids' Space Web site, 348

kilobytes (K), 312

L

LAN (local area network), 104, 312

Language tab, 127

languages
programming, Java, 219
typing in other, 127-129

laptop computers, 9, 312

laser printers, 16, 146-147

layouts, keyboards, 126

Left Alt+Shift key combination, 128

Left-handed button, 139

legacy device, 312

Legend button, 81

lights
floppy drive, 11
hard drive, 11
Turbo, 11

Line In control, 171

links
addresses, entering, 212
frames, 214
graphic images, 212
underlined text, 212

list boxes
drop-down, 215
Manufacturers, 151
Printers, 151

lists
Character Map application font list, 126
Components, 206
Manufacturers, 206
Network Protocols, 206

LISTSERV, 312

local, 312

local area network, *see* **LAN**

local telephone ISPs, 201

Location box, 239

Location or Address text box, 238

locking up, troubleshooting, 47

locks, 10

logical drive, *see* **partition**

Logitech
FTP site, 332
Web site, 332

logo keys, 129

Look In drop-down list, 71

Lotus
FTP site, 332
Web site, 332

LucasArts
FTP site, 332
Web site, 332

lurk, 312

Lycos Web site, 219, 341

M

M (megabytes), 78, 312-313

MAC (Media Access Control), 312

Macmillan Information SuperLibrary Web site, 260

Macromedia
FTP site, 332
Web site, 332

macros, 313

MAG Innovision
FTP site, 332
Web site, 332

magnetic disk, 29

mail, snail mail, 319

Mail button, 227-228

mail servers, 228

Mailbox icon, 226

mailing lists, 313

maintenance, printers, 147

Managing Multivendor Networks, 356

manufacturers, software, help support, 261

Manufacturers list, 206

Manufacturers list box, 151

math coprocessor, 21

Matrox
FTP site, 332
Web site, 332

Maxis
FTP site, 332
Web site, 332

Maxtech
FTP site, 333
Web site, 333

Maxtor
FTP site, 333
Web site, 333

McAfee Associates
FTP site, 333
Web site, 333

media, removable, files, backing up, 101

megabytes, *see* **M (megabytes)**

memory, 289, 313
DIMM (Dual Inline Memory Module), 23
DIMM memory slots, upgrading, 287
DRAM (Dynamic Random-Access Memory), 23
EDO (Extended Data Out), 23
motherboards, memory slots, 286
RAM (Random-Access Memory), 23
SIMM (Single Inline Memory Modules) slots, 23, 286
upgrading, 285-286
SDRAM, 287

Menu key, 129

menus, 313
Start, 42-43

message boxes
Backup, 96
Operation Complete, 97, 100
Restore, 99

messages, e-mail
sending, 224, 226-227
spell checking, 226

Messenger, e-mail
files
attaching to, 230
saving, 231
messages,
checking, 228-229
replying, 228-229
reviewing, 228-229
sending, 226

MHz (megahertz), 313

Micron Web site, 333

microphones, sounds, recording, 172-174

microprocessors, 21, 313
chips
numbers and letters combinations, 22
speeds, 22
Pentium chip, 22
systems, speeds, 22
types of, 22

MicroProse
FTP site, 333
Web site, 333

Microsoft
Backup, 92
installing, 94
Backup dialog box, 97
Exchange, 313
Expedia Web site, 348
Fax, 313
FTP site, 333
MSN, 313
Network, Internet address, 225
Technical Support Knowledge Base Web site, 271
Web site, 127, 260, 333, 341
see also IE (Internet Explorer)

MIDI (Musical Instrument Digital Interface), 170

milliseconds, *see* **ms**

MIME (Multipurpose Internet Mail Extensions), 313

Minimize All Windows command (shortcut menu), 43

minus sign (–), 86

mirroring, 313

Mitsubishi
FTP site, 333
Web site, 333

MMX (MultiMedia eXtensions), 313

mode indicator
control, modems, 161
printers, 150

Mode menu, options, troubleshooting, 258

Modem Web site, 271

modems, 16-17, 156-157, 290, 314
2400 bps, 298
9600 bps, 298
14,400 bps, 298
28,800 bps, 298
33,600 bps, 298
adding, 284
AT command set, 299
choosing, 157-159
Class 1, Class 2 standards, 302
communications
software, 159
speed, 157
compression standard, 159
connections, making, 157
controls, 161
cost, 159
data
communications
software, 157
format, 159
transferring, 156-157
error indicator control, 161
external, 157
fax capabilities, 159-160
fax/data, 307
installing, 160-161
internal, 157
Internet, connecting, 200
mode indicator control, 161
parameters,
communications, 159
power on light control, 161
replacing, 284
speed indicator control, 161
speeds, 17

telephone lines, 157
transfer protocols, 159
transmission speed, 159
troubleshooting, 162-164
Windows 95, installing, 161-162

Modems
icon, 161
Properties dialog box, 161

modes, Safe, Windows 95 restarting, 47-48

modulation, 314

modulator-demodulator, *see* **modems**

monitors, 13, 289, 314
brightness setting, 119
centering setting, 119
cleaning, 123
colors
capabilities, terms for, 113-114
numbers of, changing, 119-120
contrast setting, 119
D-shaped connector, 34
Deguass setting, 119
display problems, troubleshooting, 123-124
horizontal and vertical sizing, 119
interlacing, 113
notebooks
active matrix displays, 115
display resolution, 116-119
displaying, 115-116
passive matrix displays, 115
size displays, 115
pixels, 112
plugging in, 33-34
positioning, 33
protecting, 123
replacing, 284
resolutions, 13
changing, 120-121
colors, maximum number displayed, 114
pixels, 112
recommended, 112
SVGA video card, 113
VGA video card, 113
XGA video card, 113
setting up, 116-117
settings, adjusting, 119
sizes, 112
speakers, shielded, 123

SVGA, 112
VGA, 112
video cards, 111
colors, 113-114
graphics speeds, 115
RAM (Random-Access Memory), 114
Windows 95
patterns, changing, 121-123
setting up, 117-118
wallpaper, 121-123

Monster Board Web site, 348

motherboards
bus, 26
components, 20-21
disk space, determining, 25-26
floppy disks, 25
hard disks, 25
memory slots, 286
microprocessors, 21-22
power, supplies, 28-29
RAM (Random-Access Memory), 23
determining amount of, 24
slots
determining number of, 27-28
expansion, 27
software and hardware, working together, 29

Motion Picture Experts Group, *see* **MPEG**

Motion tab, 140

mouse, 14, 290, 314
buttons
left, 137-138
right, 138
cleaning, 141
connecting to PC, 136-137
double-clicking speed, configuring, 139
IntelliMouse wheel, 138
plugging in, 35
pointer shapes
Help pointer, 256
pointing hand, 255
pointer speed, adjusting, 139-140
positioning, 34-35
properties, adjusting, 139
replacing, 284
right- or left-hand preferences, configuring, 139
three-button, 139

Mouse
  icon, 139
  Properties dialog box, 139-140
MPEG (Motion Picture Experts Group), 314
ms (milliseconds), 78
MSNBC, chat services, 246
MTV Online Web site, 349
multimedia, 314
Multipurpose Internet Mail Extensions, *see* MIME
multitasking, 314
music, playing on PC, 169
Musical Instrument Digital Interface, *see* MIDI
Mute
  box, 170
  check box, 171
My Computer, 85
  commands
    Delete, 89
    Properties, 24
    Rename, 90
  icon, 42, 77, 79, 85
  programs, starting, 51
  window, 25
    views, changing, 26

N

Name box, 168
nanoseconds, RAM (Random-Access Memory), 23
NASA Web site, 349
NBA.com Web site, 349
NBC.com Web site, 349
NEC
  FTP site, 333
  Web site, 333
NetBuyer Web site, 341
Netcaster, push technologies, 247-248
netiquette, 314
NetPro Northwest Web site, 266
Netscape, 314
  Conference tool, 246
  FTP site, 334

Navigator
  enhancers, 222
  Personal toolbar, buttons, adding, 214
  plug-ins, 211, 222
  Web site, 334, 341
NetWare, 105-106, 314
Network
  dialog box, 205
  icon, 205
network interface cards, *see* NIC
Network News Transport Protocol, *see* NNTP
Network Operating System, *see* NOS
Network Protocols list, 206
networking
  The Complete Idiot's Guide to Networking, 356
  Introduction to Networking, Third Edition, 356
  Special Edition Using NetWare 3.12, 357
  Special Edition Using NetWare 4.1, Second Edition, 358
networks, 314
  cables, 107
  components, 104-105
  connections, arrangement of, 106-107
  IntraNetWare, 105
  IRQs (Interrupts), 106
  Managing Multivendor Networks, 356
  NetWare, 105-106
  NICs (network interface cards), 104, 106
  peer-to-peer, 105
  peripherals, sharing, 104
  printers, sharing, 104
  servers, dedicated, 105-106
  software, sharing, 104
  topologies
    cables, 107
    daisy chain, 106
    ring, 107
    star, 107
  Upgrading and Repairing Networks, 358
  Windows NT Server, 105-106
New command (File menu), 86

New Message window, 229
New Msg button, 226
New York Times Web site, 350
newsgroup protocols, 213
newsgroups, 244, 315
  accessing, 242-243
  hardware, help, 271
  Internet, 197
  ISPs (Internet Service Providers), 242
  NNTP (Network News Transport Protocol), 242
  titles, meanings of, 244
  UseNet, 242
newsreaders, 315
Next button, 256
Next Step button, 95, 98
NICs (network interface cards), 104, 315
  IRQs (interrupts), 106
NNTP (Network News Transport Protocol), 242
No button, 81
node addresses, 315
noise, printers, 146
Nokia
  FTP site, 334
  Web site, 334
nondirectional sound, 35
North American ISPs, 201
NOS (Network Operating System), 315
notebooks, 9, 315
  active matrix displays, 115
  display resolution, 116-119
  features, purchasing, 292-293
  keyboards, 131
    standard, using with, 132
  monitors, displaying, 115-116
  passive matrix displays, 115
  size displays, 115
Notepad, 315
  window, 51
Novell
  FTP site, 334
  Web site, 334
Number Nine
  FTP site, 334
  Web site, 334

numbers
formatting, 67
selecting, 66-67
numeric keypad, 126

0

oak.oakland.edu (FTP site), 235
OCR (Optical Character Recognition), 315
software, scanners, 186
offline, 315
Ohio State University Web site, 178
123 Greetings Web site, 343
online
light, printers, 150
online services, 315
addresses, 225
AOL (America Online), 202
CompuServe, 202
connecting, 202
Open command (File menu), 71
Open File Set command (File menu), 96
opening, documents, 71
operating systems, 274, 315
16-bit, 298
32-bit, 298
Operation Complete message box, 97, 100
Option buttons, 215
Options command (Settings menu), 96, 99
Oracle
FTP site, 334
Web site, 334
organizing, files and folders, 84

P

Packard Bell
FTP site, 334
Web site, 334
pages, 316

palmtop computers, 9
Panasonic
FTP site, 334
Web site, 334
paperclip icon, 230, 231
parallel (LPT) ports, 14, 316
parameters, modems, communications, 159
Paramount Web site, 350
Parenthood Web Web site, 350
partitions, hard disks, 316
Paste
button, 68-69
command (Edit menu), 68-69, 127
Special command (Edit menu), 69
pasting, data, 68-69
Pathfinder Web site, 350
paths, 316
patterns, Windows 95, changing, 121-123
PC Card slots, 292
PCI
bus, 316
slots, 27
cards, 288
upgrading, hardware, 287-288
PCs, see computers
peer-to-peer networks, 105
Pentium, 316
Pentium chip, 22
period (.), 225
see also dot
peripheral devices, 316
peripherals
scanners, 178-181
sharing, 104
Personal Information Manager program, see PIM
Personal toolbar, buttons, adding, 214
Phoenix Technologies
FTP site, 335
Web site, 335
phone, see telephone

pixels, 112, 316
interlacing, 113
PKZIP, 316
Platinum Edition Using Windows 95, 357
Play button, 168, 171-172
Plug and Play, see PnP (Plug and Play)
plug-ins
installing, 222
Netscape Navigator, 211, 222
plus sign (+), 86, 269
PnP (Plug and Play) technology, 288-289, 316
Point-to-Point Protocol, see PPP
PointCast, push technologies, 248
pointing devices, notebooks, 293
pop-up menu commands
Add Bookmark, 215
Properties, 117, 120-121
ports, 317
Audio Out, 35
COM, 303
external, 293
game, 14
parallel, 316
parallel (LPT), 14
replicators, 293
SCSI, 14
serial, 36
serial (COM), 14
POST (Power On Self Test), 267
pound sign (#), 245
power
management, 292
supplies
110v alternating current (AC), 28
12v direct current (DC), 28
5v direct current (DC), 28
adapters, 33
electrical damage, 36
extension cables, 36
interruptions, 28

spikes, 36
surge protectors, 28-29
surges, 36
three-prong outlets, 33
UPS (Uninterruptible Power Supply), 28-29
watts, 28
surges, 28

power on light control, modems, 161

Power On Self Test, *see* POST

power switches, 10

PPP (Point-to-Point Protocol), 202

Practical Peripherals
FTP site, 335
Web site, 335

presentations, 65-66
programs, 317

Print
button, 153
command (File menu), 72, 153
dialog box, 72, 153

Print Manager, opening, 153

Print Preview
button, 72
command (File menu), 72

Print Screen key, 126

Print Troubleshooter window, 257

Printer Name text box, 151

printers, 290, 317
adding, 284
bubble jet, 16
colors, 147
computers, connecting to, 36
connecting to PC, 149-150
controls, 150-151
cost, 146
dot-matrix, 16, 146, 148-149
error indicator, 151
fonts, 147
inkjet, 16, 146-148
laser, 16, 146-147
maintenance, 147
mode indicator, 150
noise, 146
online light, 150
other considerations, 153
parallel (LPT) ports, 14
positioning, 35

purchasing, factors to consider, 146-147
replacing, 284
resolution, 146
serial cables, 36
serial ports, 36
sharing, 104
software, support, 146
speed, 146
Windows 95, installing, 151-152

Printers list box, 151

printing
documents, 72
Print Manager, opening, 153

private ISPs, 202

processors, 289, 292
upgrading, 285

Prodigy, 317
Internet address, 225

Program Installation Wizard, 275

programming languages, Java, 219

programs, 317
anti-virus, 299
compression, 303
Defragmenter, 80
demo, 304
drawing, 306
DTP (DeskTop Publishing), 304
exiting, 274
Explorer, 307
Gopher, 309
graphics, 309
LISTSERV, 312
Microsoft Exchange, 313
Microsoft Fax, 313
presentation, 317
spreadsheets, 319
starting, 50-53
by opening a document, 53
with My Computer, 51
with Run command, 53
with shortcut icons, 53
with Start menu, 50-51
with Windows Explorer, 51-53
text editor, 320
uninstalling, 279
Web browsers, 322

Programs command (Start menu), 172

Promise Technology Inc.
FTP site, 335
Web site, 335

Properties
button, 206, 269
commands
My Computer menu, 24
pop-up menu, 117, 120-121
shortcut menu, 25
submenu, 79
dialog box, 25, 79, 151, 173

protocols, 317
FTP (File Transfer Protocol), 213, 234
Gopher, 213
HTTP (HyperText Transfer Protocol), 191, 213
IP (Internet Protocol), 193
newsgroup, 213
NNTP (Network News Transport Protocol), 242
PPP (Point-to-Point Protocol), 202
push technology, 247-248
SLIP (Serial Line Internet Protocol), 202
TCP/IP (Transport Control Protocol / Internet Protocol), 194
transfer, modems, 159

public domain software, 317

push technologies
Internet, 247-248
PointCast, 248

Q

Que Web site, 341

Que's Computer User's Dictionary, 357

question mark (?), 152, 298, 317

Quote.com Web site, 350

R

RAM (Random-Access Memory), 21, 292
determining amount of, 24
DIMM (Dual Inline Memory Module), 23

DRAM (Dynamic Random-Access Memory), 23
EDO (Extended Data Out), 23
monitors, video cards, 114
nanoseconds, 23
SIMMs (Single Inline Memory Modules), 23

Random-Access Memory, *see* **RAM**

read-only disks, 81

Read-Only Memory, *see* **ROM**

README files, 318

Record button, 172

recording, sounds, 172-173

Recording Control dialog box, 174

Recycle Bin
commands, Restore, 89
disks, spaces, freeing up, 89
files, holding, 89
folders, holding, 89
icon, 42, 89

regional ISPs, 201

remote control software, 318

removable
disk drive, 318
hard disk drive, 13
storage devices, 25

removing, software, 279-281

Rename commands
My Computer, 90
shortcut menu, 87
Windows Explorer, 90

Reply button, 228

Reply to All button, 229

Reply to Author button, 229

Reset button, 11, 45-47, 216

resetting, computers, 45-46

resolutions, 318
colors, maximum number displayed, 114
monitors, 13
changing, 120-121
recommended, 112
SVGA video card, 113
XGA video card, 113
printers, 146
scanners, 181

Resources tab, 269

Restart button, 46

Restart the Computer?
check box, 45, 48
command (Start menu), 183

Restore
command (Recycle Bin), 89
message box, 99
tab, 98-99

RGB (Red, Green, Blue), 113

Right-handed button, 139

ring, 107

RJ-11, cable connectors, 318

Roll Call Online Web site, 351

ROM (Read-Only Memory), 21, 318

RS-232, cables, 318

Run
command, programs, starting, 53
dialog box, 53
Installation Program dialog box, 276

Safe mode, Windows 95, restarting, 47-48

Save As
command (File menu), 70, 71, 96
dialog box, 96, 231

Save Attachment As dialog box, 231

Save command (File menu), 70, 172

Save In drop-down list, 70

saving
documents, 69-70
files, formats, 70-71

Scan Shop Web site, 178

ScanDisk
dialog box, 79
hard drives, errors, checking, 79-80

scanners, 318
color, 181
computers, connecting to, 182-184
documents, scanning, 185
dpi (dots per inch), 181
flatbed, 178
grayscale, 181
hand, 180

OCR software, 186
resolution, 181
SCSI (Small Computer System Interface), 182
sheetfed, 178
systems, requirements, 181
TWAIN (Technology Without An Interesting Name), drivers, 182-183
types of, 178-181
Windows 95, recognizing, 183-184

screens
Verify Modem, 161
Windows, taskbar, 43

Scroll Lock key, 126

SCSI (Small Computer System Interface), 319
scanners, 182
chain, 182
controller, 78
devices, scanners, cable length, 182
drives, upgrading, 286
ports, 14

SDRAM, upgrading, 287

Seagate
FTP site, 335
Web site, 335

search busters, 221

Search button, 220

search engines, 219
search busters, 221
search criteria, 220
search operators, 221
wildcards, 221

Search Now button, 216

search operators, 221

Seek button, 220

Select Device dialog box, 117

Select Network Component Type dialog box, 205

Select Network Protocol dialog box, 205

selecting
cells, ranges, 66
numbers, 66-67
text, 66-67

Send To command (shortcut menu), 78

Senior.com Web site, 351

Sequent
  FTP site, 335
  Web site, 335

serial (COM) ports, 14

serial cables, 36

Serial Line Internet Protocol,
  see SLIP

serial numbers, computers,
  matching, 32

serial ports, 36

servers
  DNS (Domain Name Servers),
    194
  file, 307
  FTP, 308
  Internet
    connecting, 190
    FTP (File Transfer
      Protocol), 194
    Gopher, 195
    HTTP, 194
    SNMP, 194
    software, distributing,
      248-249
    Telnet, 194
    UseNet, 196
  IntraNetWare, 105
  IRC (Internet Relay Chat), 245
  locations of, 190
  mail, 228
  NetWare, 105-106
  networks, dedicated, 105-106
  Web browsers,
    connecting to, 196
  Windows NT Server, 105-106

Servers tab, 237

Settings - Options dialog box,
  96, 97, 99

Settings command (Start
  menu), 117, 127, 151, 167,
  183, 203, 205

Settings menu commands
  Control Panel, 161
  Options, 96, 99

Settings tab, 117, 120

shareware, 319
  packages, 203

SHAREWARE.COM,
  C|Net, 240

Sharp Electronics
  FTP site, 335
  Web site, 335

sheetfed scanners, 178

shielded speakers, 167

shielded twisted pair
  cables, 107

Shift button, 45

Shift+WINDOWS+M key
  combination, 129

shortcuts
  files, creating, 90
  folders, creating, 90
  icons
    renaming, 90
    starting, programs, 53
  menu commands
    Create Shortcut(s) Here, 90
    Minimize All Windows, 43
    Properties, 25
    Rename, 87
    Send To, 78

Show Details button, 81

Shut Down
  button, 46
  command (Start menu), 183

Shut Down the Computer?
  check box, 45

Shut Down Windows dialog
  box, 45, 48

shutdowns, troubleshooting,
  46-47

shutting down, computers, 45

SIMMs (Single Inline Memory
  Modules), 23, 286

Site Manager
  button, 235
  CuteFTP, files,
    downloading, 235
  dialog box, 235

sites, 319
  FTP
    Accolade, 326
    Acer, 326
    Adaptec, 326
    Adobe, 326
    Advanced Micro Devices,
      326
    ALR, 326
    American Megatrends, 327

Apple, 327
Artisoft, 327
AST, 327
ATI, 327
Autodesk, 327
Berkeley Systems, 327
Blizzard Entertainment, 328
Boca Research, 328
Borland, 328
CA-Associates, 328
Cirrus Logic, 328
Cisco, 328
Compaq, 328
Corel, 329
Creative-Labs, 329
Cyrix, 329
D Link, 329
Dell, 329
Delrina, 329
Diamond, 329
Digital Equipment, 329
download sites, 235
Electronic Arts, 330
Epic MegaGames, 330
Epson, 330
Everex, 330
files, downloading, 235-236
ftp.cdrom.com, 235
ftp.coast.net, 235
ftp.ncsa.uiuc.edu, 235
ftp.sunet.se, 235
ftp.winsite.com, 234-235
garbo.uwasa.fi, 235
Gateway 2000, 330
Gravis, 330
Hayes, 330
Hercules, 331
Hewlett-Packard, 331
IBM Corporation, 331
id Software, 331
Intel, 331
Interplay, 331
Iomega, 331
Logitech, 332
Lotus, 332
LucasArts, 332
Macromedia, 332
MAG Innovision, 332
Matrox, 332
Maxis, 332
Maxtech, 333
Maxtor, 333
McAfee Associates, 333
MicroProse, 333
Microsoft, 333
Mitsubishi, 333

NEC, 333
Netscape, 334
Nokia, 334
Novell, 334
Number Nine, 334
oak.oakland.edu, 235
Oracle, 334
Packard Bell, 334
Panasonic, 334
Phoenix Technologies, 335
Practical Peripherals, 335
Promise Technology
  Inc., 335
Seagate, 335
Sequent, 335
Sharp Electronics, 335
Sony, 335
Standard Microsystems, 336
Sun Microsystems, 336
Supra, 336
Symantec, 336
Texas Instruments, 336
3Com, 326
Toshiba, 336
US-Robotics, 336
Virgin Interactive
  Entertainment, 337
Western Digital, 337
Westwood Studios, 337
Xircom, 337
Ziff-Davis Publishing, 337
Zoom Technologies, 337
Web
  Accolade, 326
  Acer, 326
  Adaptec, 326
  Adobe, 326
  Advanced Micro
    Devices, 326
  ALR, 326
  AltaVista, 219, 271
  Amazon.com, 343
  American Megatrends, 327
  Apple, 327
  Artisoft, 327
  AST, 327
  AT&T Toll Free
    Directory, 344
  ATI, 327
  Autodesk, 327
  Berkeley Systems, 327
  Big Yellow, 344
  BigBook, 344
  Blizzard Entertainment, 328
  Boca Research, 328
  Borland, 328

ClNet, 247, 339
CA-Associates, 328
CBS, 344
CBS SportsLine, 344
Cirrus Logic, 328
Cisco, 328
CNN, 192, 345
Compaq, 328
Conner, 328
Corel, 329
Creative-Labs, 329
Cyrix, 271, 329
D Link, 329
DejaNews, 339
Dell, 329, 340
Delphi Internet
  Services, 246
Delrina, 329
Diamond, 329
Digital Equipment, 329
Dilbert Zone, 345
Discovery Channel, 345
Disney, 345
Download.com, 340
Edmund's, 345
Electronic Arts, 330
Epic MegaGames, 330
Epicurious, 346
Epson, 330
ESPNet SportsZone, 346
Everex, 330
Excite, 219, 340
FAQ (Frequently Asked
  Questions), 260
FedWorld, 346
Gateway 2000, 330
Geocities, 340
Gravis, 330
Hayes, 330
HealthFinder, 346
Hercules, 331
Hewlett-Packard, 331
Hollywood Online, 346
HotBot, 271, 340
HotWired, 340
IBM Corporation, 331
id Software, 331
InfoSeek, 219
InfoSeek Ultra, 271
Intel, 331, 341
Intellicast, 347
Internet Gaming Zone, 347
Internet Movie
  Database, 347

Internet Underground
  Music Archive, 347
Interplay, 331
Intuit, 331
Iomega, 331
IRS, 348
Kids' Space, 348
Logitech, 332
Lotus, 332
LucasArts, 332
Lycos, 219, 341
Macmillan Information
  SuperLibrary, 260
Macromedia, 332
MAG Innovision, 332
Matrox, 332
Maxis, 332
Maxtech, 333
Maxtor, 333
McAfee Associates, 333
Micron, 333
MicroProse, 333
Microsoft, 127, 260, 333, 341
Microsoft Expedia, 348
Microsoft Technical Support
  Knowledge Base, 271
Mitsubishi, 333
Modem, 271
Monster Board, 348
MTV Online, 349
NASA, 349
NBA.com, 349
NBC.com, 349
NEC, 333
NetBuyer, 341
NetPro Northwest, 266
Netscape, 334, 341
New York Times, 350
Nokia, 334
Novell, 334
Number Nine, 334
Ohio State University, 178
123 Greetings, 343
Oracle, 334
Packard Bell, 334
Panasonic, 334
Paramount, 350
Parenthood Web, 350
Pathfinder, 350
Phoenix Technologies, 335
Practical Peripherals, 335
Promise Technology
  Inc., 335
Que, 341
Quote.com, 350

Roll Call Online, 351
Scan Shop, 178
Seagate, 335
Senior.com, 351
Sequent, 335
Sharp Electronics, 335
Sony, 335
Standard Microsystems, 336
Star Wars, 351
Stroud's Consummate
    Winsock Applications, 240
Stroud's Consummate
    Winsock Apps, 342
Sun Microsystems, 336
SuperSeek, 342
Supra, 336
Switchboard, 351
Symantec, 336, 342
TechWeb, 264
Texas Instruments, 336
Thomas: The U.S.
    Congress, 351
3-D, 218
3Com, 326
Toshiba, 336
TuneUp, 342
UCS Knowledge Base, 267
US-Robotics, 336
USA Today, 352
Virgin Interactive
    Entertainment, 337
Wall Street Journal, 352
Warner Bros. Movies, 352
Western Digital, 337
Westwood Studios, 337
White House, 352
WhoWhere, 352
Windows 95.com, 342
Winsite, 240
X-Files, 353
Xircom, 337
Yahoo!, 169, 219, 342
Yahooligans, 343
ZDNet, 264, 266, 343
ZDNet HealthyPC.com
    Support Finder, 271
Ziff-Davis Publishing, 337
Zoom Technologies, 337
Web, for laptops
    Texas Instruments, 336

slashes
    / (forward), 213, 246
    \ (backward), 213
Slide, VRML, 219

**SLIP (Serial Line Internet
    Protocol), 202, 319**
slots
    determining number of, 27-28
    expansion, 27, 306
    ISA, 27
    PC Card, 292
    PCI, 27
**Small Computer System
    Interface, *see* SCSI**
snail mail, 319
sneakernet, 319
SNMP, servers, 194
software
    communications, modems, 159
    data communications, 157
    drivers, modems, 157
    freeware, 308
    hardware, working together, 29
    help, by telephone, 261
    installing
        from Control Panel, 275-277
        over older versions, 278-279
        precautions before, 274
        with CD, 277
    Internet, distributing, 248-249
    IRC (Internet Relay Chat), 245
    joysticks, calibrating, 142
    keyboards, 129-130
    manufacturers, help
        support, 261
    networks
        peer-to-peer, 105
        servers, dedicated, 105-106
    OCR, scanners, 186
    online support, 259-260
    operating systems, 274
    optional, 291
    printers, support, 146
    public domain, 317
    remote control, 318
    removing, 279-281
    shareware, 319
    sharing, 104
        software wizards,
            locating, 256
    uninstalling programs, 279
    upgrading, 273, 277-278
    viruses, avoiding, 259
    Windows 95
        Help system, 254-256
        troubleshooting, 257-259
    wizards, help, locating, 256

Sony
    FTP site, 335
    Web site, 335
**sound cards, 166, 290, 293,
    319**
    upgrading, 285
Sound Recorder, opening, 172
sounds
    CDs, listening to on
        headphones, 171-172
    components, 166-167
    embedded, playing, 216-217
    files, WAV, playing, 168
    icon, 167
    microphone and input levels,
        adjusting, 173-174
    microphones, 172-174
    music, playing on PC, 169
    new sounds, getting, 169
    nondirectional, 35
    problems, troubleshooting,
        174-175
    Properties dialog box, 167
    sound cards, 166
    speakers, 166
        shielded, 167
        subwoofer, 167
        tone, adjusting, 170-171
        volume, adjusting, 170-171
    testing, 168
    volume
        CD control, 171
        Line In control, 171
        MIDI (Musical Instrument
            Digital Interface),
            controlling, 170
        Wave control, 170
    WAV sound files, playing on
        PC, 168
    Windows 95
        events, playing for, 167-168
        recording, 172-173
Speaker icon, 171
speakers, 15, 290, 293
    Audio Out port, 35
    connecting, 35
    nondirectional sounds, 35
    positioning, 35
    replacing, 284
    shielded, 123, 167
    sounds, 166-167
    subwoofer, 167
    tone, adjusting, 170-171
    volume, adjusting, 170-171

Special Edition Using NetWare 3.12, 357

Special Edition Using NetWare 4.1, Second Edition, 358

speed
  indicator control, modems, 161
  printers, 146

spell checking
  e-mail messages, 226
  Internet Mail messages, 227

Spelling button, 226

spikes, 36
  voltage, 28

Spool MS-DOS Print Jobs check box, 151

spreadsheets, 63-64
  cells, ranges, selecting, 66
  programs, 319

Standard Microsystems
  FTP site, 336
  Web site, 336

star, 107

Star Wars Web site, 351

Start Backup button, 96

Start button, 42-43, 50, 79

Start menu, 42-43
  commands
    Programs, 172
    Restart the Computer?, 183
    Settings, 117, 127, 151, 167,
      183, 203, 205
    Shut Down, 183
  programs, starting, 50-51

Start Restore button, 99

starting
  computers, 40-41
    troubleshooting, 47-48
  programs, 50-53
    by opening a document, 53
    with My Computer, 51
    with Run command, 53
    with shortcut icons, 53
    with Start menu, 50-51
    with Windows Explorer,
      51-53

static electricity, keyboards, 130

steering wheels, 291

strategies, files, backing up, 93-94

streaming audio files, embedded, 217

Stroud's Consummate Winsock Applications Web site, 240, 342

subdirectory, *see* **directory**

Subject box, 226-227

submenu commands, Properties, 79

Submit button, 216, 220

subwoofer, 167

suites, 66

Sun Microsystems
  FTP site, 336
  Web site, 336

SuperSeek Web site, 342

Supra
  FTP site, 336
  Web site, 336

surfing, 320

surge
  protectors, 320
    power button, 40
  suppressers, 36

surges, 36
  power, 28

SVGA
  monitors, 112
  video cards, 113

Switchboard Web site, 351

Symantec
  FTP site, 336
  Web site, 336, 342

symbols, special, keyboards, 126-127

System
  backing up, 274
  batteries, upgrading, 285
  files, viewing, 84-86
  icon, 268
  Properties dialog box, 24, 268
  Tray, 44

systems
  backing up, 80
  requirements, scanners, 181
  TCP/IP (Transmission Control
    Protocol/Internet Protocol),
    configuring for, 203-205

T

T-1, T-3 connections, 320

tabs
  Attach Files and
    Documents, 230
  Background, 121
  Backup, 94
  Bindings, 206
  Buttons, 139
  Contents, help, locating, 254
  Device Manager, 184, 268
  Driver, 269
  Find, help, locating, 255
  General, 25, 269
  Index, help, locating, 254
  Install/Uninstall, 275, 279
  Language, 127
  Motion, 140
  Resources, 269
  Restore, 98, 99
  Servers, 237
  Settings, 117, 120
  Tools, 79
  Windows Setup, 94, 204

tape drives, 13, 290
  replacing, 284

tapes, backing up files, 100

TAPI (Telephony Applications Programming Interface), 320

taskbar, 43
  System Tray, 44

tasks
  background, 300
  foreground, 308

TCP/IP (Transmission Control Protocol/Internet Protocol), 194, 203-205, 320
  enabling, verifying, 205-206
  system, configuring for, 203-205

technical support (hardware), 270

technologies, push (Internet), 247-248

Technology Without An Interesting Name, see TWAIN

TechWeb Web site, 264

telephones
  lines (modems), 157
  wire cables, 107

Telnet, 320
  FTP (File Transfer Protocol), 233
  servers, 194
Texas Instruments
  FTP site, 336
  Web site, 336
text
  editor, 320
  files, 320
  formatting, 67
  selecting, 66-67
text boxes, 215
  Location or Address, 238
  Printer Name, 151
Thomas: The U.S. Congress Web site, 351
three-prong outlets, 33
titles, newsgroups, meanings of, 244
To box, 226, 227
Today's Link button, 213
tools (Building a Query), 271
Tools tab, 79
ToolTips, 44
topologies (networks), 106-107
  cables, 107
  daisy chain, 106
  ring, 107
  star, 107
Toshiba
  FTP site, 336
  Web site, 336
tower computers, 8, 320
trackballs, 14
transfer protocols (modems), 159
transmission speed (modems), 159
troubleshooting
  computers, starting up, 47-48
  crashes, 46-47
  hardware problems, 264, 267
  keyboard problems, 132-133
  modems, 162-164
  monitors (display problems), 123-124
  shutdowns, 46-47
  sound problems, 174-175
  Windows 95, 257-259

TuneUp Web site, 342
Turbo button, 11
Turbo light, 11
TWAIN (Technology Without An Interesting Name), 182-183
  scanner drivers, 182-183
twisted pair cables, 107
typewriter keys, 126

U

UART (Universal Asynchronous Receiver/Transmitter), 321
UCS Knowledge Base Web site, 267
Uniform Resource Locator, see URL
Uninterruptible Power Supply, see UPS
UNIX, 321
UNIX directories, 235
Up One Level button, 70
upgrading
  BIOS, 285
  expansion cards, 285
  hard drives, 285
  hardware, 283
    expansion slots, 287-288
    ISA slots, 287-288
    PC, outside of, 284
    PC, parts inside of, 285
    PCI slots, 287-288
  memory, 285-287
    DIMM memory (Dual Inline Memory Module) slots, 287
  processors, 285
  purchasing, 291-292
  RAM (Random-Access Memory), 286-287
  software, 273, 277-278
  sound cards, 285
  system batteries, 285
  video cards, 285
uploading FTP files, 236-237
UPS (Uninterruptible Power Supply), 28-29

URLs (Uniform Resource Locators), 212-213, 238, 321
  error handling, 213
US-Robotics
  FTP site, 336
  Web site, 336
USA Today Web site, 352
UseNet, 321
  ISPs (Internet Service Providers), 242
  mechanisms, 242
  newsgroups, 242
    accessing, 242-243
  NNTP (Network News Transport Protocol), 242
  servers, 196
user groups, 321
user IDs, 321
utilities
  backup, 92
  Microsoft Backup, 92

V

v-cards, see electronic business cards
Verify Modem screen, 161
VGA
  monitors, 112
  video cards, 113
video
  cards, 292
    colors, 113-114
    files (types of), 217
    graphics speeds, 115
    monitors, 111
    RAM (Random-Access Memory), 114
    resolutions, colors, maximum number displayed, 114
    RGB (Red, Green, Blue), 113
    SVGA, 113
    upgrading, 285
    VGA, 113
    XGA, 113
    ZiffDavis Benchmarks, 115
  embedded, playing, 216-217

View menu commands (Details), 26

viewing system files, 84-86

Virgin Interactive Entertainment
FTP site, 337
Web site, 337

virtual cards, see electronic business cards

viruses, 321
avoiding, 259
flashmail, 259

voltage spikes, 28

Volume Control dialog box, 170, 173
bass and treble settings, adjusting, 171
sound sources
volume, controlling, 170-171

VRML (Virtual Reality Modeling Language)
Virtual World, exploring, 218-219
Slide, 219
Walk, 219

W

WAIS (Wide Area Information Server), 322

Walk (VRML), 219

Wall Street Journal Web site, 352

wallpaper, Windows 95, changing, 121-123

WAN (wide area network), 322

warm boot, 45

Warner Bros. Movies Web site, 352

watts (power supplies), 28

WAV sound files, 322
playing, 168

Wave control, 170

Web browsers, 322
cache, 200
capabilities, enhancing, 222
displaying elements, 191

FTP (File Transfer Protocol), 238-240
directories, downloading, 238-240
files, downloading, 238-240
index files, 239
home pages, 211
HTML (HyperText Markup Language), 210
IE (Internet Explorer), 211, 311
Netscape Navigator, 211, 314
enhancers, 222
plug-ins, 222
servers, connecting to, 196
WWW (World Wide Web), exploring, 211-214

Web pages, 191
bookmarks, creating, 213
cache, 200
elements, 214-219
Favorites folder, entering, 214
forms, completing, 215-216
frames, 214-215
bookmarking, 215
links, 214
previous contents, returning to, 214
HTML (HyperText Markup Language), 210
hypertext links, 191
Java, running, 219
navigating, 213
secured (closed padlock), 216
sounds, embedded, playing, 216-217
streaming audio files, embedded, 217
URL (Uniform Resource Locator), 212-222
videos, embedded, playing, 216-217
VRML (Virtual Reality Modeling Language)
Virtual World, exploring, 218-219
see also home pages

Web sites
3-D Web, visiting, 218
3Com, 326
Accolade, 326
Acer, 326
Adaptec, 326
Adobe, 326
Advanced Micro Devices, 326

ALR, 326
AltaVista, 219, 271
Amazon.com, 343
American Megatrends, 327
Apple, 327
Artisoft, 327
AST, 327
AT&T Toll Free Directory, 344
ATI, 327
Autodesk, 327
Berkeley Systems, 327
Big Yellow, 344
BigBook, 344
Blizzard Entertainment, 328
Boca Research, 328
Borland, 328
ClNet, 247, 339
CA-Associates, 328
CBS, 344
CBS SportsLine, 344
Cirrus Logic, 328
Cisco, 328
CNN, 192, 345
Compaq, 328
Conner, 328
Corel, 329
Creative-Labs, 329
Cyrix, 271, 329
D Link, 329
DejaNews, 339
Dell, 329, 340
Delphi Internet Services, 246
Delrina, 329
Diamond, 329
Digital Equipment, 329
Dilbert Zone, 345
Discovery Channel, 345
Disney, 345
Download.com, 340
Edmund's, 345
Electronic Arts, 330
Epic MegaGames, 330
Epicurious, 346
Epson, 330
ESPNet SportsZone, 346
Everex, 330
Excite, 219, 340
FAQ (Frequently Asked Questions), 260
FedWorld, 346
Gateway 2000, 330
Geocities, 340
Gravis, 330
Hayes, 330
HealthFinder, 346

Hercules, 331
Hewlett-Packard, 331
Hollywood Online, 346
home pages, 192
HotBot, 271, 340
HotWired, 340
IBM Corporation, 331
id Software, 331
InfoSeek, 219
InfoSeek Ultra, 271
Intel, 331, 341
Intellicast, 347
Internet Gaming Zone, 347
Internet Movie Database, 347
Internet Underground Music
    Archive, 347
Interplay, 331
Intuit, 331
Iomega, 331
IRS, 348
Kids' Space, 348
for laptops (Texas
    Instruments), 336
Logitech, 332
Lotus, 332
LucasArts, 332
Lycos, 219, 341
Macmillan Information
    SuperLibrary, 260
Macromedia, 332
MAG Innovision, 332
Matrox, 332
Maxis, 332
Maxtech, 333
Maxtor, 333
McAfee Associates, 333
Micron, 333
MicroProse, 333
Microsoft, 127, 260, 333, 341
Microsoft Expedia, 348
Microsoft Technical Support
    Knowledge Base, 271
Mitsubishi, 333
Modem, 271
Monster Board, 348
MTV Online, 349
NASA, 349
NBA.com, 349
NBC.com, 349
NEC, 333
NetBuyer, 341
NetPro Northwest, 266
Netscape, 334, 341
New York Times, 350

Nokia, 334
Novell, 334
Number Nine, 334
Ohio State University, 178
123 Greetings, 343
Oracle, 334
Packard Bell, 334
Panasonic, 334
Paramount, 350
Parenthood Web, 350
Pathfinder, 350
Phoenix Technologies, 335
Practical Peripherals, 335
Promise Technology Inc., 335
Que, 341
Quote.com, 350
Roll Call Online, 351
Scan Shop, 178
Seagate, 335
secured, 216
Senior.com, 351
Sequent, 335
Sharp Electronics, 335
Sony, 335
Standard Microsystems, 336
Star Wars, 351
Stroud's Consummate Winsock
    Applications, 240, 342
Sun Microsystems, 336
SuperSeek, 342
Supra, 336
Switchboard, 351
Symantec, 336, 342
TechWeb, 264
Texas Instruments, 336
Thomas: The U.S.
    Congress, 351
Toshiba, 336
TuneUp, 342
UCS Knowledge Base, 267
US-Robotics, 336
USA Today, 352
Virgin Interactive
    Entertainment, 337
VRML (Virtual World),
    exploring, 218-219
Wall Street Journal, 352
Warner Bros. Movies, 352
Western Digital, 337
Westwood Studios, 337
White House, 352
WhoWhere, 352
Windows 95.com, 342
Winsite, 240

X-Files, 353
Xircom, 337
Yahoo!, 169, 219, 342
Yahooligans, 343
ZDNet, 264, 266, 343
ZDNet HealthyPC.com Support
    Finder, 271
Ziff-Davis Publishing, 337
Zoom Technologies, 337

weight, notebooks, 293

Western Digital
    FTP site, 337
    Web site, 337

Westwood Studios
    FTP site, 337
    Web site, 337

What's Cool? button, 213

What's New? button, 213

White House Web site, 352

WhoWhere Web site, 352

wildcards, 322
    * (asterisk), 221

Windows, 322

windows
    Backup, 94, 98
    Composition, 229
    Control Panel, 279
        opening, 275
    Help, locating, 255
    Help Topics, 254
    My Computer, 25
        views, changing, 26
    New Message, 229
    Notepad, 51
    open, hiding temporarily, 43
    Print Troubleshooter, 257

Windows 95, 290
    Bitmap format, 123
    exiting, 48
    files, backing up, 94-97
    Help system, 254-256
    keyboards, special keys, 129
    locking up (troubleshooting),
        47
    logo keys, 129
    Menu key, 129
    modems, installing, 161-162
    monitors
        colors, changing numbers
            of, 119-120
        patterns, changing, 121-123
        setting up, 117-118
        wallpaper, 121-123

Platinum Edition Using Windows 95, 357
printers, installing, 151-152
Safe mode, restarting, 47-48
scanners, recognizing, 183-184
sounds
    events, playing for, 167-168
    microphone and input levels, adjusting, 173-174
    problems, troubleshooting, 174-175
    recording, 172-173
speakers
    tone, adjusting, 170-171
    volume, adjusting, 170-171
taskbar (System Tray), 44
troubleshooting, 257-259
uninstall programs, 279

Windows 95 Communications Handbook, 359

Windows 95.com Web site, 342

Windows Explorer, 85-86
files
    copying, 88
    moving, 87
folders
    copying, 88
    moving, 87
programs, starting, 51-53

Windows Explorer commands
Delete, 89
Rename, 90

Windows folder, 51

Windows key combination, 129

Windows Messaging, see Microsoft Exchange

Windows NT Server, 105-106

Windows screen (taskbar), 43

Windows Setup tab, 94, 204

WINDOWS+Break key combination, 129

WINDOWS+E key combination, 129

WINDOWS+F key combination, 129

WINDOWS+F1 key combination, 129

WINDOWS+M key combination, 129

WINDOWS+R key combination, 129

WINDOWS+Tab key combination, 129

Winsite Web site, 240

WinZip, 322

wizards
Add Hardware, 142
Add New Hardware, 162
Add Printer, starting, 151
Backup, 94
Install New Modem, 161
Program Installation, 275

word processors, 62-63, 322

World Wide Web, see WWW

worldwide online services, 201

write-protection, 323

WWW (World Wide Web), 191, 322
exploring, 211-214
FTP (File Transfer Protocol), alternatives to, 240
information, searching, 219-221
protocols
    FTP (File Transfer Protocol), 213
    Gopher, 213
    HTTP (HyperText Transfer Protocol), 213
    newsgroup, 213
search engines, 219

X-Y-Z

X-Files Web site, 353

XGA video card, 113

Xircom
FTP site, 337
Web site, 337

Yahoo! Web site, 219

Yahooligans Web site, 343

ZD*Net Software Library, 240

ZDNet HealthyPC.com Support Finder Web site, 271

ZDNet Web site, 264, 266, 343

Ziff-Davis Publishing
FTP site, 337
Web site, 337

ZiffDavis Benchmarks (video cards), 115

.ZIP, 323

ZIP disks, files, backing up, 101

Zip drives, replacing, 284

Zoom Technologies
FTP site, 337
Web site, 337

Check out Que® Books
on the World Wide Web
http://www.quecorp.com

As the biggest software release in computer history, Windows 95 continues to redefine the computer industry. Click here for the latest info on our Windows 95 books

Make computing quick and easy with these products designed exclusively for new and casual users

Examine the latest releases in word processing, spreadsheets, operating systems, and suites

Desktop Applications & Operating Systems

que®

new Users

what's new?

Que's Publishing Areas

Windows 95

Internet
And New Technologies

The Internet, The World Wide Web, CompuServe®, America Online®, Prodigy® —it's a world of ever-changing information. Don't get left behind!

Find out about new additions to our site, new bestsellers and hot topics

Calendar of Events

DEVELOPER AND EXPERT USERS

ZD ZIFF-DAVIS PRESS

Que's Top 10 Titles

Macintosh & Desktop Publishing

In-depth information on high-end topics: find the best reference books for databases, programming, networking, and client/server technologies

A recent addition to Que, Ziff-Davis Press publishes the highly-successful *How It Works* and *How to Use* series of books, as well as *PC Learning Labs Teaches* and *PC Magazine* series of book/disc packages

Stay on the cutting edge of Macintosh® technologies and visual communications

Find out which titles are making headlines

With 6 separate publishing groups, Que develops products for many specific market segments and areas of computer technology. Explore our Web Site and you'll find information on best-selling titles, newly published titles, upcoming products, authors, and much more.

- Stay informed on the latest industry trends and products available
- Visit our online bookstore for the latest information and editions
- Download software from Que's library of the best shareware and freeware

que®

Complete and Return this Card
for a *FREE* Computer Book Catalog

Thank you for purchasing this book! You have purchased a superior computer book written expressly for your needs. To continue to provide the kind of up-to-date, pertinent coverage you've come to expect from us, we need to hear from you. Please take a minute to complete and return this self-addressed, postage-paid form. In return, we'll send you a free catalog of all our computer books on topics ranging from word processing to programming and the internet.

Mr. ☐   Mrs. ☐   Ms. ☐   Dr. ☐

Name (first) ☐☐☐☐☐☐☐☐☐☐☐   (M.I.) ☐   (last) ☐☐☐☐☐☐☐☐☐☐☐☐☐☐☐☐

Address ☐☐☐☐☐☐☐☐☐☐☐☐☐☐☐☐☐☐☐☐☐☐☐☐☐☐☐☐☐

☐☐☐☐☐☐☐☐☐☐☐☐☐☐☐☐☐☐☐☐☐☐☐☐☐☐☐☐☐

City ☐☐☐☐☐☐☐☐☐☐☐☐☐   State ☐☐   Zip ☐☐☐☐☐ ☐☐☐☐

Phone ☐☐☐ ☐☐☐ ☐☐☐☐   Fax ☐☐☐ ☐☐☐ ☐☐☐☐

Company Name ☐☐☐☐☐☐☐☐☐☐☐☐☐☐☐☐☐☐☐☐☐☐☐☐☐☐☐☐

E-mail address ☐☐☐☐☐☐☐☐☐☐☐☐☐☐☐☐☐☐☐☐☐☐☐☐☐☐☐☐

1. Please check at least (3) influencing factors for purchasing this book.

Front or back cover information on book .... ☐
Special approach to the content .... ☐
Completeness of content .... ☐
Author's reputation .... ☐
Publisher's reputation .... ☐
Book cover design or layout .... ☐
Index or table of contents of book .... ☐
Price of book .... ☐
Special effects, graphics, illustrations .... ☐
Other (Please specify): _____ ☐

2. How did you first learn about this book?

Saw in Macmillan Computer Publishing catalog .... ☐
Recommended by store personnel .... ☐
Saw the book on bookshelf at store .... ☐
Recommended by a friend .... ☐
Received advertisement in the mail .... ☐
Saw an advertisement in: _____ ☐
Read book review in: _____ ☐
Other (Please specify): _____ ☐

3. How many computer books have you purchased in the last six months?

This book only .... ☐   3 to 5 books .... ☐
2 books .... ☐   More than 5 .... ☐

4. Where did you purchase this book?

Bookstore .... ☐
Computer Store .... ☐
Consumer Electronics Store .... ☐
Department Store .... ☐
Office Club .... ☐
Warehouse Club .... ☐
Mail Order .... ☐
Direct from Publisher .... ☐
Internet site .... ☐
Other (Please specify): _____ ☐

5. How long have you been using a computer?

☐ Less than 6 months   ☐ 6 months to a year
☐ 1 to 3 years   ☐ More than 3 years

6. What is your level of experience with personal computers and with the subject of this book?

	With PCs	With subject of book
New	☐	☐
Casual	☐	☐
Accomplished	☐	☐
Expert	☐	☐

Source Code ISBN: 0-0000-0000-0

7. Which of the following best describes your job title?

Administrative Assistant .... ☐
Coordinator .... ☐
Manager/Supervisor .... ☐
Director .... ☐
Vice President .... ☐
President/CEO/COO .... ☐
Lawyer/Doctor/Medical Professional .... ☐
Teacher/Educator/Trainer .... ☐
Engineer/Technician .... ☐
Consultant .... ☐
Not employed/Student/Retired .... ☐
Other (Please specify): _____ ☐

8. Which of the following best describes the area of the company your job title falls under?

Accounting .... ☐
Engineering .... ☐
Manufacturing .... ☐
Operations .... ☐
Marketing .... ☐
Sales .... ☐
Other (Please specify): _____ ☐

Comments: _____
_____
_____

9. What is your age?

Under 20 .... ☐
21-29 .... ☐
30-39 .... ☐
40-49 .... ☐
50-59 .... ☐
60-over .... ☐

10. Are you:

Male .... ☐
Female .... ☐

11. Which computer publications do you read regularly? (Please list)

_____
_____
_____
_____
_____
_____
_____
_____
_____
_____

Fold here and scotch-tape to mail.

MACMILLAN COMPUTER PUBLISHING USA

A VIACOM COMPANY

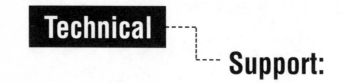

Technical ---- Support:

If you need assistance with the information in this book or with a CD/Disk accompanying the book, please access the Knowledge Base on our Web site at **http://www.superlibrary.com/general/support**. Our most Frequently Asked Questions are answered there. If you do not find the answer to your questions on our Web site, you may contact Macmillan Technical Support **(317) 581-3833** or e-mail us at **support@mcp.com**.